Street Trees in Britain

A history

by Mark Johnston

WIND *gather*
PRESS

Windgather Press is an imprint of Oxbow Books

Published in the United Kingdom in 2017 by
OXBOW BOOKS
The Old Music Hall, 106–108 Cowley Road, Oxford, OX4 1JE

and in the United States by
OXBOW BOOKS
1950 Lawrence Road, Havertown, PA 19083

© Windgather Press and Mark Johnston 2017

Paperback Edition: 978-1-91118-823-0
Digital Edition: 978-1-91118-824-7 (epub)

A CIP record for this book is available from the British Library

Printed in Malta by Melita Press

For a complete list of Windgather titles, please contact:

United Kingdom
OXBOW BOOKS
Telephone (01865) 241249
Fax (01865) 794449
Email: oxbow@oxbowbooks.com
www.oxbowbooks.com

United States of America
OXBOW BOOKS
Telephone (800) 791-9354
Fax (610) 853-9146
Email: queries@casemateacademic.com
www.casemateacademic.com/oxbow

Oxbow Books is part of the Casemate group

Cover image: The Cross Tree in the High Street of Messingham, North Lincolnshire, *c.* 1898.

Contents

List of Figures

Preface

....

Throughout my life I have always been fascinated with street trees. As a young boy I enjoyed climbing trees in my local park and the next day it always amused me to see these living monuments standing in the pavement as I walked to school. When I worked as a tree surgeon the most dangerous but most exhilarating work was taking down large dead or dangerous trees by the roadside in busy city centres – work that literally stopped traffic and captivated the passing public. Then, when I realised that I didn't want to swing around in trees for a living when I reached 40, I started gathering qualifications and became a local authority tree officer. Again, street trees were always the most interesting and challenging part of the job. Working for a suburban London borough I was responsible for endless miles of flowering cherries and other small ornamentals, many of which were dying through fireblight disease. Later, as the tree officer for an inner-London borough, I was responsible for the management of thousands of pollarded plane and lime trees that lined many of the streets. In the context of budget cuts and privatisation, that was a really challenging time and I learned a huge amount very quickly about urban forest management. When I became a consultant and worked on policies and strategies at a national and international level, I was always conscious of how a network of tree-lined streets can provide the essential framework for a green urban environment. They are capable of acting as 'green corridors', linking other greenspaces and bringing fresh air and wildlife into the heart of the 'urban jungle'.

I would like to say a few words about how this book came about. From my earlier research on the history of urban trees in Britain it was clear that there was limited material on street trees. Nevertheless, I believed that a book on this needed to be written, it was a subject that really interested me and maybe I was in a good position to do this. I soon discovered that while there was a reasonable amount of written material that was relevant to the history of street trees in major cities, garden suburbs and garden cities, there was precious little that related to the many Victorian and Edwardian suburbs or the vast expanses of suburbia in the twentieth century. That nearly threw me because I was not expecting the huge amount of original research that was now required to explore these aspects of the project. In total, the work involved in delivering this book has taken around three years to complete. This was much longer than I had anticipated and maybe if I had known that at the start I might have waited for somebody else to write the book. But now that it's done, I'm so glad that I took this on myself.

Some of my colleagues working in the arboriculture, landscape and urban forestry professions may be slightly disappointed that there is little comment in this book on some of today's controversial urban tree management issues. I would just ask them to remember that this is a history book and not a textbook on modern principles and practice in urban tree management. Nevertheless, they may well recognise that some of the issues that preoccupied our Victorian and Edwardian forebears have a familiar sound today – and some of the errors of the past are still being repeated.

A great many people have assisted me with this book and those who contributed significantly to the research aspects are listed in the Acknowledgements section. On a personal level, I want to take this opportunity to thank a few people from my family who have played a crucial role in enabling me to complete the book. Thanks to the generosity of my sister, Christine Truesdale, I was able to acquire a substantial proportion of the old photographs and postcards that have played a vital role in the research process. I hope that Christine enjoys reading the book and gets particularly pleasure from looking at the illustrations.

My deepest thanks go to my mother, Barbara Johnston, who sadly passed away in November 2016. She was always hugely supportive of my work and helped in many different ways. Furthermore, I can honestly say that both my parents provided me with a remarkable and really stimulating upbringing where social and political issues were openly and enthusiastically discussed in our family, and especially when some of my father's friends visited the house. They included university lecturers, social researchers, politicians, trade unionists, community workers and activists, all with a range of views and perspectives. As their children, my parents always encouraged us to listen and learn and to make a contribution to the discussions whenever we wanted. However, this was never about gaining knowledge just for the sake of it. My father 'John' Johnston, a very knowledgeable man but also a lifelong activist, was always keen to point out that we should use that knowledge to make the world a better place, for everyone. I have certainly been able to draw on that early education and grounding while researching and writing this book.

Finally, I want to record my sincere thanks to my dear wife, Anne. I cannot express in words just how much her encouragement and support has meant to me over the years. Without it, I might have lost my way long ago and this book would most certainly never have been written.

Mark Johnston
Belfast, February 2017

Acknowledgements

Very many people have made some contribution, however great or small, to the research for this book and without all that assistance it could never have been written. The assistance has included sourcing and supplying information, providing images, provision and assistance with technology, engaging in stimulating discussion of relevant topics, help with site visits and much more. If there is any incorrect information in the text then I accept full responsibility for this and it is not a reflection on anyone else. The following is a list of individuals who have made a particularly helpful contribution and they are listed in no particular order. I offer my sincere apologies to anyone who believes I have omitted them.

Alexandra Caccamo, Librarian, National Botanic Gardens, Dublin
Dianne Heath, photographer, Belfast
Prof Paul Elliott, University of Derby
Ann Stark and the Cockburn Association, Edinburgh
Bob Gray, Glasgow Tree Lovers Society
Sue Griffiths, Birmingham Trees for Life
Dr Dealga O'Callaghan, Dealga's Tree Consultancy, Liverpool
Dr Andrew Hirons, Myerscough College
Dr Glynn Percival, Bartlett Tree Research Laboratory, University of Reading
Jim Smith, National Urban Forestry Adviser, Forestry Commission, England
Prof Cecil Konijnendijk, University of British Columbia, Canada
Paul Wood, The Street Tree.com
Keith Sacre, Chairman, Arboricultural Association
Stephanie Jenkins, Oxford History website
Gillian Ellis, Bournville Village Trust
Mrs Alex Cockshott, Ilkley Civic Society
Prof Mike Dixon, Ilkley local historian
John Medhurst, Landscape Consultant, London
Jackie Walker, Clerk, Messingham Parish Council
Dorothy Smith, Bexhill Old Town Preservation Society
Margaret Evans, Carmarthen Town Council
Adam Winson, AWA Tree Consultants, Sheffield
Michael Beddow, Beddow Tree Specialists, Leicester
Dr Margaret Scott, Leicester Civic Society
Maureen Copping, Eastbourne Local History Society

Alan Smith, Eastbourne Local History Society

Michael Ockenden, Eastbourne Local History Society

Amal Khreisheh, Assistant Curator, Somerset County Council

Carol Ince, Aberdeen City and Aberdeenshire Archives

David Oswald, Library and Information Services, Aberdeen City Council

Deirdre Sweeney, Local History Centre, Dundee Central Library

Mary Holdsworth, Acting Parish Clerk, Ramsbury and Axford Parish Council

John Fryer, Brentwood Museum

Frank Gresham, Moseley Society

Gordon Robertson, Yattendon Parish Council

Bruce Anderson, Rusholme and Victoria Park Archive

Neville Fay, Founder, Treework Environmental Practice

Alistair Smith, Arboricultural Manager, London Borough of Camden

Dr Vicky Harding, Heath and Hampstead Society

Georgina Malcolm, Hampstead Garden Suburb Trust

Pat Baxendale, Brentham Conservation Area Advisory Panel

Alan Henderson, Brentham Society Archivist

Diane Fraser, Local Studies Library, Doncaster Central Library

Mike Byrne, Acocks Green Historical Society

Harley Jones, Rhiwbina Garden Village Residents' Association

Glenn Mellor, Oldham Garden Suburb Association

Paul Brohan and Sue Avery, Arboretum Residents Association, Worcester

Gregory Waine, Senior Arboricultural Officer, Nottingham City Council

Rupert Bentley Walls, former Senior Tree Officer, London Borough of Hackney

Barbara Nomikos, Moor Pool Heritage Trust

Tina O'Neill and Pete Tolputt, London

Pete Stringer and Andrew Long, City of Trees, Salford

David Hardy, Centre for Data Digitisation and Analysis, Queens University
   Belfast

Staff at the Local Studies Department, Cardiff Central Library

James Carless, Witton Lodge Community Association

Dr Jonathan Oates, Ealing Local History Centre

Lisa Soverall, Southwark Local History Library and Archive

Oliver Stutter, Senior Planner-Urban Forester, Southwark Council

Sandy Masterton, Rosyth Garden City Association

John McQueen, Parks, Streets and Open Spaces, Fife Council

Ben Morris, Senior Arboricultural and Woodlands Officer, London Borough
   of Sutton

Mark Acton, Society for Lincolnshire History and Archaeology

Francis Treuherz and Sue Young, British Homeopathic Association

Rob Greenland, former Arboriculturist, Brighton Borough Council

Neil Brothers, Arboriculturist Operations, Brighton and Hove City Council

Glyn Tully, Head of Urban Design, Levitt Bernstein

Matthew Bardsley, Tree Officer, Conwy County Borough Council

John Lawson-Reay, local historian and author, Llandudno
Alan Taylor, Folkestone and District Local History Society
Liz East, Society for Lincolnshire History and Archaeology
Monica Gillespie, Arboricultural Officer, High Peak Borough Council
Joyce Cummings, Cheltenham Local History Society
Chris Chavasse, Senior Trees Officer, Cheltenham Borough Council
Nick George, GIS Development Officer, Cheltenham Borough Council
Sally Self, Journal Editor, Cheltenham Local History Society
John Simpson, Pittville History Works, Cheltenham
Paul Evans, Collections Management Archivist, Gloucestershire Archives
David Ivison, Vice Chairman, The Royal Parks Guild
Rev David W. Clark, Chairman, Helensburgh Heritage Trust
Alexander Kerr, Helensburgh Heritage Trust
Donald Rodger, Arboricultural Consultant, Gullane
Steve Cox, Treecall Consulting, Poole
Jason Croden, Ashwood Tree Care, Ruislip
Paul Nolan, Director of the Mersey Forest, Warrington
Caroline Brown, Senior Associate, David Lock Associates, Milton Keynes
Brian Salter, former Chief Executive, Milton Keynes Parks Trust
Theo Chalmers, Urban Eden, Milton Keynes
Helen Innes, Living Archive, Milton Keynes Museum
Dr Gary Watson, Head of Research, The Morton Arboretum, Illinois, USA
Lim Cho Choi (Kingsley), Vice-President, ISA Hong Kong Chapter, China
Kevin Collins, Regional Inspector, Irish Forest Service, Dublin
Prof. Carl Chinn, Department of History, University of Birmingham
Dr Kathleen Wolf, University of Washington, USA
John McCrory, local historian, Burnage, Manchester

CHAPTER ONE

Introduction and Research Methods

The trees which line many streets in towns and cities throughout the world can often be regarded as part of a heritage landscape. Despite the difficult and demanding conditions of an urban environment, these trees may live for 100 years or more and represent 'living history' in the midst of our modern streetscapes. To really appreciate the importance of these trees and to understand how they should be managed, we need to recognise their historical and cultural significance. Much has been written about the history of other aspects of urban infrastructure, such as roads, railways, canals and public utilities. There has also been much historical research into aspects of 'green' infrastructure and the urban forest, such as parks, open spaces and private gardens. However, in most countries there has been little research into the origin and history of their street trees and how this major feature of the urban landscape has developed to the present time. In Britain, street trees have been planted systematically along many of the thoroughfares in our towns and cities for the past 160 years. This book presents the first detailed research to give an account of this remarkable story.

The trees in our streets are often the most noticeable in the urban forest and given the space to grow they can have a dramatic and very beneficial impact on urban life. In the summer they provide welcome shade in hot streets while their leaves soak up some of the harmful pollution generated by motor vehicles. Throughout the year the sequence of emerging leaves, flowers, fruit, autumn colour and leaf fall mark the passage of nature's seasons on our doorstep. The stature and age of the trees in some of our famous boulevards, such as The Mall and Park Lane in London, make these arboreal landmarks part of our national heritage. While admiring these trees we should always remember that their vital heritage value is not something that can just be caught on a camera by a passing pedestrian. It is bound up in the history of the trees and people need to be told about that to be able to appreciate it.

A network of tree-lined streets throughout our towns and cities can help provide the essential framework for a green and pleasant urban environment. Lines of large mature trees on the main arterial routes through the city act as 'green corridors', linking other greenspaces and bringing fresh air and wildlife into the heart of the metropolis. Some of our towns and cities are fortunate in having many large street trees, often a legacy from Victorian or Edwardian times. However, before the mid-nineteenth century, many urban areas, even the city centres, were virtually devoid of street trees. Nowadays, these are a common sight in many urban areas, from the busy downtown areas through to the commercial and industrial districts to the many residential neighbourhoods and suburbs. For those readers who have travelled to a number of British cities, one fact may have become apparent; the extent of street tree planting can vary enormously both within the same urban area and also between different towns and cities. Older readers may also recall how the number of trees in a particular street can change significantly over time, for better or worse, often in the course of a few decades.

This book tells the story of how trees came to be planted in Britain's streets, the factors that initially influenced this and the agencies that were involved. It then charts the distribution of those trees in different towns and cities, especially in relation to the social-economic class of local residents. An assessment is made of how this street treecover has changed over the years, from the early plantings to the present day. A range of urban locations are examined, such as the city centres, suburbs, spa towns, seaside resorts, gardens cities and new towns. The various threats to street trees over the years are also described. The book concludes with a look at the history of some technical aspects associated with engineering trees into the hard landscape of streets, such as tree selection, planting, maintenance and management.

The benefits of street trees

While this book is about the history of our street trees, it is important to remember their vital role in creating a liveable urban environment. In common with other urban trees they can provide a wide range of environmental, economic and social benefits (Forest Research 2010). Street trees in particular can help moderate urban temperature extremes, provide cool shade in hot summers, play a role in sustainable urban drainage systems, improve air quality by pollutant interception, contribute to carbon sequestration, promote urban regeneration and increase nearby property values (Dawe 2011, 426–431). In terms of their social and psychological benefits, street trees can contribute to our mental health and wellbeing. However, arboriculturists and urban foresters can sometimes get carried away and 'blind people with science' when talking about the benefits of urban trees. We forget to mention that trees are simply the most beautiful and majestic natural objects in an often dirty and depressing urban landscape (Schroeder 2012, 159–165).

Most people in Britain today would probably agree that having trees along our streets is a good idea, as long as they are maintained properly. Nevertheless, there will always be those who view street trees as nothing but a liability, especially the one outside their house. When working as a tree officer in London, the author remembers one local resident objecting to a tree being planted outside his house with the words, 'The proper place for trees is in the park, not in the street'.

Scope of the book

When this book was envisaged its scope was intended to be the same as the chapter entitled 'Street and Highway Trees' in the author's previous book (Johnston 2015). In researching that chapter a substantial amount of material was not used. That is how the idea for a complete book on this topic came about. However, as work on the new book progressed, it became obvious there was far more material than had been anticipated, especially with all the original research, and it was necessary to limit its scope due to lack of space. Therefore, the book does not give an account of motorways and generally does not include trunk roads, except in special circumstances. These are also excluded because trees at the side of motorways and many trunk roads do not fall within this book's definition of a street tree. Other major topics such as community involvement, which were originally separate chapters, have partly been incorporated in other chapters. A huge amount of material was gathered for the last two chapters focusing on the history of technical aspects such as planting, maintenance and management. Again, lack of space meant much of this material had to be left out, although it is possible this might be used later in a separate book.

Definition of terms used

In the course of this research the author was frequently asked by colleagues what was the correct definition of a 'street tree'. The simple answer is that there is no single 'correct' definition and those available range from the simple to the very complex. The definition given by Philip Wilson (2013, 175) in his book *A–Z of Tree Terms* is generally adequate. This describes a street tree as: 'a tree growing in a street (occasionally at the edge of a carriageway, usually in a verge or footway) maintained by a local authority or highways authority'. However, for the purpose of this book we should highlight or expand on some aspects of this.

Although street trees are usually publicly owned and come under the control of a local authority or highway authority, some exceptions are mentioned in the book. For example, in nineteenth century suburbs roads were often constructed by private developers who initially planted the street trees, and both were then later adopted by the local authority. Another more recent exception is where trees alongside roads on private industrial estates or business parks may be standing on privately owned land. Our definition of street trees also includes trees located on the central reservation of dual carriageways and on roundabouts. It does not include trees in modern pedestrianised walkways and malls, often located in city centre shopping and commercial districts, even where these were formerly roads. Neither does it include trees planted on the embankments at the side of major roads or motorways, especially where these are part of a clump of trees or woodland. Trees in the front garden of residential properties, even when they overhang the road, are 'garden trees' not street trees. One situation that is less clear is where trees are growing in small open spaces that are alongside streets. The Victorians often referred to these as 'street gardens', although the term also embraced large open spaces behind railings such as residential squares and crescents (Smith 1852, 166–167). When first constructed many were privately owned landscape features, like the squares and crescents, and located on residential estates developed by private landowners and investors. Many are now publicly owned and managed by local authorities. Where the trees on these small streetside open spaces are next to the pavement and overhang the road, we regard them as street trees.

Terms relating to roads and associated features need some clarification. A range of terms describe the hard surfaces in British towns and cities used to convey modes of transport, such as 'street', 'road' and 'highway' (Fry 2003, 1–15). Other terms make specific reference to trees along the route, such as 'avenue' and 'boulevard'. Some definitions of these can be confusing and overlapping. This book uses most of these terms and also some that are historical and no longer in common use. The hard-surfaced area along the side of the road where pedestrians normally walk is commonly called the 'pavement' in Britain and the 'sidewalk' in North America. Because of the confusion with the American definition of 'pavement', which usually means the hard surface of the road itself, and because many pavements in Britain are not actually paved, that term is not used. Instead, what is commonly called the pavement in Britain is referred to in this book as the 'footway'. This is in accordance with terms used in British highway classification and defined in Section 66 of the *Highways Act* of 1980 which states that a footway is a pavement or path running alongside a road over which the public has a right of way on foot only (Thompson Reuters 2016). It is not to be confused with a 'footpath' which is defined as a way over which the public has a right of way on foot only (frequently used in a countryside context) and which is not a footway.

With regard to technical arboricultural terms, these have been used sparingly in view of the potential readership of those with a general as well as a professional interest. Furthermore, some technical descriptions of trees are not given every time they are relevant. For example, most of the planes and limes in streets that date from Victorian and Edwardian times have been pollarded from an early stage. However, the term 'pollarded' is not stated every time because of the endless repetition this would entail. When readers are unclear of the meaning of technical terms they should consult Philip Wilson's *A–Z of Tree Terms*.

Research methods

This section of the chapter gives a description of how the research for this book was undertaken and the methods used. While this topic may not be of great interest to the general reader, it is important to establish the academic credibility of the work. As with historical research in general, the research drew on a range of primary and secondary sources (Gunn and Faire 2016).

Published and unpublished literature

The first stage of the research involved a detailed search of the published literature relevant to this subject, covering mainly the past 300 years. This included a wide range of books, not only those on tree and landscape topics but also some travel books. Then, a search was undertaken of a wide range of horticultural, arboricultural and landscape journals and magazines dating from the early 1800s. The most useful included Loudon's *Gardener's Magazine*, Robinson's *The Garden* and especially *Gardeners' Chronicle* and the later variation of this title. Additional information on some topics was provided by articles in the popular press. This was obtained from searches of relevant national and local newspapers using the internet database of The British Newspaper Archive.

A wide range of unpublished literature was used in this research. This included minutes from the meetings of local authority councils and committees, minutes and annual reports from civic societies and other voluntary organisations, and transcripts from oral history projects. Historical and more recent surveys and reports on urban trees and landscapes were also obtained. Personal communications have been a valuable source of material and this has included correspondence with individuals with specialist knowledge of particular topics, mostly local historians and local authority tree officers. These were mainly used in terms of gathering information on current situations but also for some aspects of historical knowledge where other sources were not available.

Photographs and other images

A major source of research material for this book has been a wide range of images. This includes paintings, drawings, lithographs, engravings, magic lantern slides and photographs. Of all the types of image used, photographs were generally the most useful. Fortunately, the Victorian street tree movement in Britain emerged at a time when the practice of photography was already established. As well as photographs taken by individuals and organisations for personal or corporate reasons, a huge number of photos were taken for the commercial production of postcards. The heyday of picture postcards was from 1900 to the Second World War, although they still remain quite popular to this day. Many postcards show street scenes that often depicted trees, either as part of a picturesque view or included incidentally when photographing something else. In the early days of postcard production, many depicted new roads and estates and were often sold to the new occupants to show friends and relatives where their house was located. These images were usually excellent panoramic views of the road to include as many houses as possible, thus making them very useful for this research. Postcards of this type usually featured private sector housing but in the 1920s and 1930s it was not unusual to have postcards of council housing. The picture on many postcards was of a type known as a 'real photographic' image. A real photo postcard (RPPC) is a continuous-tone photographic image printed on postcard stock. The term recognises a distinction between the real photo process and the lithographic or offset printing processes employed in the manufacture of most postcard images. RPPCs were most useful in this research because the quality of the image was generally high.

The photographs used in the research came from a variety of sources. Many were from the author's own library of photos containing over 1200 images relating to the history and development of street trees. Most of the illustrations used in this book came from that source. Access to many thousands of other images was obtained through national and local photographic libraries. At a national level these included those belonging to Historic England, The National Archives, Mary Evans Picture Library and Britain from Above. Many local photo libraries were also accessed, such as the Museum of London Picture Library, Liverpool Picturebook and Manchester Local Image Collection. Another major source of photographs was the many books that are compilations of photos taken over the years featuring particular towns and cities. These books are often part of a series of titles with collective names such as *Britain in Old Photographs*, *Images of Wales* and *The Archive Photographs Series*. Aerial photographs of urban areas often gave an especially useful perspective that could not be gained from ground level.

An invaluable tool for assessing the current nature and extent of street tree planting throughout Britain has been the geospatial technology known as Google Street View. This was launched in 2007 for several cities in the United States and now provides panoramic views from positions along most streets in Britain as well as in many other countries. It was possible to take historical photographs of streets and their tree planting and then match this with current images of the same street using Google Street View to make some assessment of the changes to both the trees and physical structure of the street that had occurred over the years. Identifying the species and especially the cultivar or variety of trees from images on Google Street View was not always easy. Where there was doubt the local authority tree officers were consulted. This work may be easier in the future as software is now being developed that will enable tree surveys that identify tree species to be conducted using satellite and street-level images, although the level of accuracy at the moment is only 80% (Wegner *et al.* 2016). In the course of this research many hundreds of miles of streets in towns and cities across Britain were scrutinised from the comfort of the author's home. Site visits were also made by the author and others to assess the current nature and extent of street tree planting in many different urban centres. These were usually high-profile locations such as the main thoroughfares of cities, and various new towns, garden cities and garden suburbs. Photographs were taken on these site visits for later examination and also for comparison with early photographs of the same scene.

In both site visits and to a lesser extent using Google Street View visual tree inspections were often made on individual trees. This inspection included a form of visual tree assessment (VTA), which is a standard arboricultural practice to identify structural defects from visible signs and the application of biomechanical criteria (Mattheck 1994). These tree inspections gave some indication of the current health, vitality and structural stability of the tree. The shape and form of a tree can reveal much about its history. This can apply equally to the examination of trees in early or modern photographs as well those inspected via site visits or Google Street View. Aspects of the tree's history can be quite obvious to the trained arboriculturist and are often revealed through the evidence of past tree maintenance work, such as crown shape and size, old pruning cuts and other tree care activities.

Maps

Valuable information about the history of street trees and urban development in general was gained from examining old maps of towns and cities. These were accessed using a well-known online historical map archive that has an extensive collection of maps covering England, Wales and Scotland. Particularly useful were the Ordnance Survey (OS) County Series and OS Town Plans (Oliver 1993). These maps were used to get an approximate date for the construction of roads, housing estates and individual houses. They could also provide some information on street trees. Those maps at 1:2500 often indicate the presence of street trees, although this information is not entirely reliable and needs to be treated with caution. For example, on roads running east to west the maps sometimes only show trees on the southern side of the road even when they are planted on both sides. Similarly, roads running north to south sometimes only show trees on one side, when it is known they were on both sides. Also, some maps do not show recently-planted street trees, only those that are large or mature.

Socio-economic status of the residents

Throughout the research it was necessary to get some indication of the socio-economic status of the residents living in a particular street at a particular time and this was often given in contemporary published and unpublished literature. With regard to various streets and districts in London, reference was made to the 1889 poverty maps of Charles Booth (LSE 2016). It was also important to establish the current socio-economic status of the residents to see how this might have changed over the years. To this end, a preliminary assessment for streets in England was made using *English Indices of Depravation 2015* (DCLG 2015). This is a government-commissioned qualitative study of relative deprivation for small areas or neighbourhoods in English local authority districts. It is based on a measure of a range of factors, including income, employment, health and disability, education and skills, barriers to public service, crime and living environment. In parts of Britain not covered by this, and also to assist further in an assessment of English streets, current house prices were used to give some indication of the socio-economic status of the residents, using popular property websites. It should be stressed that the information gained in this way was only used to establish broad socio-economic categories such as working class or middle class.

In conclusion, this research touches on the history of street trees in many different urban centres in England, Scotland and Wales but can only give an outline of the story in each location. It is the author's hope that some of the people who read this book will be encouraged to conduct a detailed history of the street trees in their own town or city.

CHAPTER TWO

Walks, Allées, Promenades and *Cours*

When viewed from an international perspective the history of street trees goes back a very long way. There is evidence of trees being cultivated in the streets of some of the earliest civilisations. The Egyptian used tree-lined avenues as an ornamental feature both inside and outside their cities. Howard Carter, the famous archaeologist, wrote about a religious complex some 4000 years old where the long causeway leading up to the main tomb was lined with an avenue of trees (Mattocks 1925, 253). The road to the gods had to be more splendid than anything used by mortals and this was reflected in spectacular features that included the magnificent avenue of trees alongside the route. An ancient Chinese book, *Jin Shu*, published 1500 years ago, mentions that poplars and pagoda trees (*Styphnolobium japonicum*) were planted along the sides of roads in cities to provide shade (Dickmann and Kuzovkina 2014, 12).

In Britain, the systematic planting of trees in urban streets took a long time to arrive. There is no evidence of street trees being planted to any extent within Roman towns. The presence of trees in their settlements was generally limited to private open space such as gardens and orchards (De la Bédoyère 1992). In the medieval era, many of Britain's towns and cities were surrounded by defensive walls constructed to repel hostile forces and maintain the authority of the monarch or local aristocrat (Morris 1994, 92–156; Keene 2000, 83). These walls restricted urban growth and this resulted in intense competition for space and little room for public open space, except in churchyards or around the market place. The streets were generally a complex pattern of irregular and organically evolved lanes that united public and private spaces. These lanes were very narrow and together with the jettied upper floors of the buildings they presented a quite dark and confined space where the provision of any trees would have constituted an obstruction and not regarded as appropriate (Figure 1).

The medieval pattern of urban development continued to dominate in many of Britain's towns and cities throughout the sixteenth century. It was not until the seventeenth century that this began to change and various landscape forms emerged in the urban realm that were the precursors of the street trees we recognise today. In a pioneering paper on the origins of the tree-lined boulevard in an international context, Henry Lawrence (1988) offers a typology of landscape forms that have had significant influence on its emergence, particularly in Europe and North America. In this chapter we explore the early influences of these landscape forms on the development of street tree planting in Britain. Lawrence's typology has been adapted to provide a framework for this.

FIGURE 1. The Shambles in York gives a good indication of the typical medieval street pattern of irregular, narrow and organically evolved lanes with overhanging timber-framed buildings. This photograph was taken *c.* 1890 but the scene is much the same today.

Garden allée

The contribution of the garden *allée* to the development of tree-lined streets and boulevards is fundamental (Lawrence 1988, 356). In Renaissance Italy in the first half of the sixteenth century, pathways lined with trees provided a framework for the spatial organisation of a new style of landscape garden embraced by the aristocracy. It was almost always enclosed by walls, a continuation of a medieval tradition in garden design. These garden features were then 'imported' to France where they were soon described using the term 'allée' which had been used for passageways in buildings in previous centuries and now came to designate a passageway in a virtual edifice, the garden (Pradines 2009, 6). The allée has come to be inextricably linked with the formal French style of gardening and is used as a general term for a walk bordered by trees or clipped hedges in a garden or park (Jellicoe *et al.* 1966, 9). True to its Italian origins, the allées in the formal French garden constitute the framework and are its most important features. André Mollet, the great seventeenth century French landscape gardener, placed much emphasis on the allée as the primary ornament of the garden and wrote extensively on its use in his classic work *Le Jardin de Plaisir*, first published towards the end of his career in 1651. Mollet was invited to London *c.* 1630 to lay out gardens for Charles I and returned again in 1642 to design gardens for Queen Henrietta Maria at Wimbledon Palace. As a result of his time in England and his published work, Mollet was particularly influential in introducing the formal French style into England (Pattacini 1998).

Exterior avenues

Another great French landscape gardener, André Le Nôtre, was largely responsible for pioneering the extension of the allée or avenue beyond the confines of the formal garden into the landscape beyond (Bouchenot-Dechin and Farhat 2013). This began when he was engaged in redesigning the gardens at the Palais des Tuileries in Paris. In 1667, Le Nôtre created the Avenue des Tuileries, which started at the Château du Louvre in Paris and opened onto the countryside, with two rows of elms framed by two rows of plane trees extending for over 1 mile (1.6 km). This central pathway through the Tuileries became the grand axis of Paris running to the Arc de Triomphe and on to La Defense. Although the Baroque tree-lined avenue was primarily associated with manor houses, castles and their surrounding areas, it also appeared at town gateways in France in the sixteenth century in the form of ornamental promenades and malls, or connecting the town with a nearby castle or château (Pradines 2009, 7).

Within a few decades the French fashion to extend tree-lined avenues or drives beyond the formal garden wall began to be copied in many other European countries, not least in Britain (Crouch 1992, 174). In Tudor England tree-lined drives were associated with ceremonial routes and some of the earliest known examples were related to royal palaces, such as the tree-lined approach shown in the Flemish painting of Nunsuch of about 1620 (Harris 1979, 24). By the end of the seventeenth century many English gardens were being laid out in the Baroque style and displayed extensive avenue layouts (Knyff and Kip 1984). One of the most magnificent Baroque avenues was at Blenheim, planted by Henry Wise for Vanbrugh (Crouch 1992, 176). This militaristic formation was laid out between 1705 and 1715 with double rows of elm, a central formation and side blocks of trees. The radiating avenues of the Baroque landscape were undoubtedly an important expression of power and authority, signifying the domination and manipulation of nature and the total control over their domain by the monarchy or aristocrat.

The species of trees most commonly used for avenue planting in Britain at that time were lime and elm, followed by horse chestnut. Beech was rarely used but sweet chestnut was quite frequent, particularly in the earlier period (Crouch 1992, 179). Many landscape designers gave specific instructions in their published works for the spacing of trees in avenues and walks, depending on the situation of the avenue and the trees it contained. Large sections of the available British texts were devoted to geometry and the accurate laying out of geometric plantings. While John Evelyn's (1664) *Sylva* referred to trees planted in avenues, a more detailed account of the topic was given by Moses Cook (1676) in *The Manner of Raising, Ordering, and Improving Forest-Trees*. This included instructions on planting and maintaining walks and avenues, along with related mathematical calculations. There was often much debate about the appropriate length and width of the avenue. Both Moses Cook and Batty Langley (1728) bemoaned the narrowness of walks. With regard to the spacing of trees in their rows, where authors differentiated between main avenues and other walks, a wide spacing was given for main avenues.

During the early part of the eighteenth century when the Hanoverians came to the British throne, the popular style of garden design for the upper class was to become far more simplified. This reflected the ascendency of the Whig party which tended to associate formal gardens, particularly in the French style, with royal tyranny and autocratic power (Everett 1994). The ostentation of the Baroque landscape was to give way to the concept of rural improvement and an idealised version of natural beauty that became embodied in the English landscape movement. While those radiating avenues and other formal elements of the Baroque landscape were being swept away, the naturalistic and more subtle vista of the English landscape garden nevertheless performed a similar function in expressing the power and authority of the landowner. In order to understand the real significance of this dramatic shift in landscape aesthetics it is necessary to understand the underlining political, economic and social factors that drove this. Particularly significant was the Whig political ideology that emphasised the market economy and power of the individual capitalist, which was in sharp contrast to the traditional Tory and more formal and aristocratic view of landscape.

From the mid-eighteenth century the straight line and therefore the avenue was rarely included in garden design, although many writers continued to give advice on planting avenues well into the latter half of the century (Crouch 1992, 193). In purely aesthetic and practical terms, contemporary writers raised various popular objections to the avenue as a landscape feature, focusing mainly on its 'sameness' and that it cut the scenery in two and obscured the view (Whately 1771, 139). Of all the leading British landscape gardeners of the time it was Capability Brown who was responsible for felling many of the fine avenues on country estates in his work of creating numerous English landscape gardens in the naturalistic style. This assault on the avenue was so widespread that William Chambers (1773, xi) was moved to comment, 'Our virtuosi have scarcely left an acre of shade, nor three trees growing in a line, from the Land's-end to the Tweed'. While the English landscape garden is often considered to be Britain's finest contribution to the annals of international landscape design, it should not be forgotten what a destructive impact this had on the many fine old gardens and landscapes that were swept away and on the lives of the dispossessed working families who stood in the way of 'improvement'.

In the early nineteenth century the tide in taste was turning once again, not only for the restoration of avenues, but also for the planting of new avenues. Landscapes were becoming more eclectic and some formal elements were finding favour again with the emergence of John Claudius Loudon's gardenesque approach. This led to a reaffirmation of the value of the avenue as a landscape feature which helped pave the way for the eventual introduction of tree-lined streets in British towns and cities later in the nineteenth century.

Tree-lined walks and promenades

A new form of British urban landscape that arose in the seventeenth century was 'the walk' or tree-lined promenade (Borsay 1986). These were essentially garden allées outside the garden which were used for exercise or promenading, although some were also used for games. In this respect they were different to the exterior avenues which functioned more as grand entrances for impressive buildings or axial avenues to frame views, essentially for the use of carriages and horse riders rather than for pedestrians.

As early as 1597 a walk or promenade was laid out by the Benchers of Gray's Inn, then as now a centre for the legal profession (MacLeod 1972, 105). The Benchers paid Francis Bacon, later Lord Chancellor and an authority on gardens, for planting the trees that comprised mainly elms. Throughout the seventeenth century these avenues of trees, clipped into shapes, acquired a reputation as a place of fashion where high society came to observe and be observed. In the summer of 1661, the first year of the Restoration, Samuel Pepys (always a man with an eye for the ladies) wrote, 'And so I and the young company to walk first to Graye's Inn Walks, where great store of gallants, but above all the ladies that I there saw, or ever did see, Mrs Frances Butler is the greatest beauty' (Pepys 1661, 125). Often called simply the 'Walkes', this remained a fashionable London promenade for over 200 years.

Another influential public walk in London was on Moorfields, a connected series of fields just beyond the old city walls that the Corporation of the City of London leased from St Paul's Cathedral (Harding 1990, 49). In the sixteenth century this undeveloped land was subject to common rights and was the nearest open space to the city centre. It was used for a variety of activities but was in danger of encroachment and abuse as a dumping ground. In 1593, the City ordered that it be inspected and subsequently kept clean and tidy. In 1605–1607, two gardeners were contracted to drain and level the ground and plant elm trees along new paths. The result was a transformation of this marshy and neglected area into what the contemporary writer Richard Johnson (1607, 3) described as: 'Those sweet and delightfull walkes of More fields as it seems a garden in this Citty, and a pleasurable place of sweet ayres for Cittizens to walke in ...'.

The main period for laying out new walks came with the Restoration, although the true rise of the provincial promenade dates from the 1680s to 1690s (Borsay 1986, 126). Most of these walks were separate from gardens, although some were in parkland. Many were isolated in the urban landscape, usually near a city wall or river, almost always with a view of the surrounding countryside. These promenades were often paved or laid with gravel, and lined with hedges or trees, such as limes, sycamores, elms and firs.

As well as somewhere to take exercise these walks and promenades were also fashionable places where people came to observe the social scene and be noticed. By the eighteenth century, many towns and cities had some provision for their citizens to delight in the 'Walking Exercise' (Longstaffe-Gowan 2001, 196). However, they were not equally accessible to everyone to stroll and socialise. In London, the walks at Moorfields, Charterhouse, Drapers' Hall, Somerset House, St James's Park, the Temple and several Inns of Court were generally open 'to every person above inferior rank'. By contrast, the fine walks of the Royal Gardens of Kensington were open 'only for persons of distinction'.

Provincial towns followed London's lead by creating their own walks. The first provincial town walks appear to be those planted by the Oxford and Cambridge colleges during the course of the seventeenth century (Borsay 1986, 126). Although these were intended mainly for the use of staff, students and their guests, 'respectable' society as a whole was permitted access to them. Preston's role as a fashionable county centre required it to include a formal promenade among its recreational attractions (Borsay 1989, 163). Already in the late 1680s polite society was frequenting an area called Avenham Gardens but the first reference to the walk of the same name comes in the following decade when a corporation committee was ordered to negotiate the permanent use of the area as a walk and to organise the planting of trees and the laying of a gravel path.

Seeing the fashionable world let loose in these places, visitors from abroad sometimes mistook them for public parks (MacLeod 1972, 106). In some respects these early seventeenth century walks marked the transition from the introspective and essentially non-public enclosed garden of medieval times to the relatively public one which was conceived as integral to later town planning.

New walks and promenades continued to be laid out in town and cities throughout the eighteenth century, although now mainly in parks, gardens or outside the municipal boundaries. In York, the centre of fashionable leisure in the north, the earliest purpose-built promenade was probably that called the

Lord Mayor's Walk, which was situated north of the Minster adjacent to the city walls (Borsay 1989, 163). It is unclear when this was initially constructed but in 1719 the Mayor was given permission to 'order such number of trees as he shall judge necessary and convenient to be planted ... as an ornament to the walk'. This walk does not seem to have provided adequate provision to meet the public demand and in the early 1730s the gap was filled with the laying out of the New Walk (or Noble Terra Walk), a tree-lined avenue of elms that ran south from the town walls for about a mile along the east bank of the Ouse River (Figure 2). Access was obtained at the city end through a handsome iron palisade. In keeping with the preference of the time for order and formality, hedges were planted to separate the gentrified walk from the surrounding natural and wilder landscape. The ground was levelled and further rows of elms were planted, providing a shaded leafy avenue with dappled, light filtering through in the summertime.

The creation of the New Walk was an important part of the attempts made by the eighteenth century City Corporation to raise York's status to that of a leading Georgian social centre. The city sought to provide attractive entertainment that the gentry and expanding middle classes of the period could enjoy. The New Walk was just one of the developments aimed at attracting such people to York, along with other important contemporary landmarks such the Assembly Rooms, the Mansion House and the Racecourse (Nuttgens 2001). During the 1830s the first houses were built alongside the New Walk in York and it became popular as a safe alternative to the main road into the city.

FIGURE 2. Prospect of the Noble Terras Walk in York. This engraving is by Nathan Drake and dated 1756.

Walks and the growth of spa towns

As the eighteenth century progressed the benefits of a strengthening economy were reflected in what has become recognised as the English Urban Renaissance (Borsay 1989). This was a period of dramatic urban improvements that transformed many urban landscapes under the influence of classical architecture and the emergent forces of planning. It also witnessed a remarkable expansion in the provision of public leisure. With the nation's growing prosperity spreading among the burgeoning urban middle class, there was a steady increase in people with the time and money to enjoy their leisure – and they often chose to do this in places planted with trees (Lawrence 2006, 61).

The growth of spa towns that had began in the late seventeenth century and blossomed in the eighteenth century was a crucial part of that leisure explosion. Their development also gave a major boost to the creation of more walks and promenades. These spa towns were specialised resort towns situated around a mineral spa where visitors came 'to take the waters' for their believed health benefits. One of the reasons that spas grew so rapidly was that they were not only centres of medicinal treatment but were also at the forefront of the development of a new culture of fashionable leisure and tourism that acquired a powerful hold on the minds of the elite and those who aspired to join them (Borsay 2012, 156). To service this new leisure market and the increase in visitor numbers spa towns provided new built facilities such as lodging houses, assembly rooms, music galleries and coffee-houses (Hembry 1990, 67).

An additional attraction of the spa towns and resorts was their access to greenspace. With the destruction of town walls, the planting of squares and the provision of public walks, greenery began to flow into the towns and the towns themselves were opened up to the countryside (Girouard 1990, 76). There is little doubt that the presence of numerous trees and extensive greenspace within their boundaries was much valued by the visitors. Daniel Defoe, the famous English author, was suitably impressed with this aspect of Epsom, a spa town in the south of England. He wrote:

> It is to be observ'd too, that for shady walks, and innumerable trees planted before the houses, Epsome differs much from itself, that is to say, as it was twenty or thirty years ago; for then those trees that were planted were generally young and not grown; and now not only the trees then young, are grown large and fair, but thousands are planted since: so that the town, at a distance, looks like a great wood full of houses, scatter'd everywhere, all over it.
>
> Defoe 1724, 162

The visitors who flocked to the spa towns and resorts were keen to be associated with the new social elite (Girouard 1990, 76). The people who emerged from the terraces to visit assembly rooms or theatres, promenade on the walks, or make excursions to the resorts, formed a recognisable class, similar to but not quite the same as the upper social strata of earlier centuries. They were regarded at the time as 'polite society', a social elite that viewed itself as superior in its behaviour, etiquette and appreciation of the arts. An essential requirement for being part of this elite involved engaging in social interaction at appropriate venues where the behaviour and appearance of those attending could be closely observed. Assembly rooms often acted as the main indoor arena for this overt personal display, while out of doors this was a role that fell to public walks and gardens (Borsay 1989, 162). While the pursuit of status involved considerable competition among the participants, some historians have also highlighted the role of promenading in helping to strengthen social ties (Borsay 1986, 131). At the time this provided a vital contribution towards maintaining social stability. The intense political and religious divisions that had torn apart the ruling class during and after the Civil War continued to threaten social cohesion in the early eighteenth century. Promenades provided a relatively neutral space in which Whigs and Tories, High Church and Low Church, could mix together and begin to heal the wounds that still festered among them.

As walks were a fundamental part of the spa town's attractions, there was competition between them to provide the most extensive and impressive facilities (Borsay 1989, 168). To provide some attractive landscaping and to give protection from the weather, the walks were normally lined with corridors of trees and often hedges. Limes, sycamores elms, and firs were commonly planted and they required regular maintenance because of aging, disease, and damage from the elements. To ensure a secure footing and to protect the promenaders from getting their footwear and clothes soiled from mud and dirt, many of these walks were laid with gravel or paved with stone and brick. In terms of location they needed to be close to the watering facilities, since walking and 'taking the waters' were associated regimes.

Quite apart from the provision of formal walks, many streets in the more salubrious parts of towns became potential walking spaces as they were lined with elegant architecture and were becoming more spacious, better cleaned and paved (Borsay 1989, 172). However, as yet, there was no systematic planting of street trees. A brief description is give below of some of the more prominent walks in spa towns and other fashionable towns.

Tunbridge Wells

Of all the embryonic spas of the early Stuart period, the town of Tunbridge Wells was the most successful. Nevertheless, despite the mark of fashionable approval that had been bestowed by a visit from Queen Henrietta Maria (wife of Charles I) little was done initially to exploit the visitor potential or improve the primitive facilities at Tunbridge Wells (Hembry 1990, 47). In 1636, however, shelter was provided for the water-drinkers when two small houses were erected, and in 1638 the first of the walks or promenades was constructed. A green bank, later paved and called the Upper Walk, was raised, levelled and planted with a double row of trees, and here the company found shelter and the opportunity for exercise and conversation, and tradesmen came to display their wares once a day. Around 1660–1664, the first fixed booths or shops were laid out on the west of the Upper Walk and the Lower Walk was marked out on the east (*ibid.*, 80), By 1700 there about 25 shops along the Upper Walk and on the Lower Walk, below the tree-lined bank where the musicians played, were about 20 more shops, a tavern, a coffee-house and a 'pissing-house' (*ibid.*, 83).

In the late seventeenth century, Tunbridge Wells enjoyed the patronage of Princess Anne (daughter of James II) who spent many seasons there (Hembry 1990, 84). In 1697 Princess Anne and her husband Prince George visited the town again along with the Lord Chamberlain and other courtiers. When her young son the Duke of Gloucester, who had water on the brain and tended to overbalance, fell down Anne entrusted £100 to a cottager to pave and level the walks. However, on a later visit she became angry when she noticed that the work was incomplete, she appointed a more reliable person and angrily drove away. In 1700 the walks were eventually paved with a form of baked tile called pantiles and thereafter they became known as the Pantiles (Amsinck 1810, 10). With Princess Anne's accession to the throne (1702), the inhabitants of Tunbridge Wells were to commemorate her acts of generosity towards the town. They did this by planting a triple row of birch trees on the part of the common where she had usually been encamped, and this became known as Queen's Grove. Even so, after the accident to her son and the delay in completing the improvements to the walks she had ordered, she had switched her favour to Bath and never returned to Tunbridge Wells.

Despite all the redevelopment that Tunbridge Wells has undergone over the centuries, the Pantiles and its avenue of trees has remained as an attractive feature of the town centre (Figure 3). The Pantiles today includes a variety of specialist shops, art galleries, cafés, restaurants and bars.

Bath and Cheltenham

Bath was the leading spa town and resort in Britain by the middle of the eighteenth century and it naturally came to possess the most impressive group of provincial walks and gardens (Borsay 1986, 129). These included the Gravel Walk and the Grove, Harrison's Walks and Gardens, the Terrace Walk, the Parades, and the Spring Gardens. All lay in a tightly knit group in the eastern corner of the city, and were lined by luxury shops, assembly rooms and superior domestic accommodation. Together they formed the most sophisticated complex of leisure facilities to be found in the provinces, and probably rivalled those in many continental resorts. Of all these walks in Bath, the Gravel Walk became the major social attraction. In 1734, the original trees along the side of the walk were felled and replaced with new trees. Gravel Walk was something of a Lover's Lane in the days of Jane Austen, the famous author, and it was the setting for a touching love scene in her novel *Persuasion*. As well as a venue for promenading, the walk was used as a route for Sedan chairs heading to and from the Royal Crescent to the town centre.

Cheltenham's famous tree-lined walks surrounding its spas were first designed by Captain Henry Skillicorne, the spa town's 'founding father'. He was assisted

FIGURE 3. The Pantiles in Tunbridge Wells as it looked in 1885. Despite all the redevelopment that Tunbridge Wells has undergone over the centuries, the Pantiles and its trees has remained an attractive feature of the town centre.

by a group of 'wealthy and travelled' friends who also understood the value of relaxing avenues of trees as the perfect complement to the beneficial water (Hembry 1990, 179–181). An extract from Skillicorne's diary reads, 'In the winter of 1739 I made the upper walk, planted elm and lime to the number of 37, and made a new orchard adjoining. To the winter of 1740 I made the lower walk, planted 96 elms at the expense of £56' (Hart 1981, 116). However, the following two summers were extremely dry and 76 of the trees on his walks died through drought, although he replaced them in 1743.

There was always a degree of rivalry between the different walks at Cheltenham. In the 1830s what was called the Long Walk was beginning to be overshadowed by new developments in the Montpellier district. It was said that in the mornings 'there were few scenes more animated and inspiring than the Montpellier Promenade'. Between the hours of eight and ten, it was frequented by 'the lovely, the titled and the fashionable, as they paraded up and down the grand walk to the sound of music'. When entertainments were being presented the promenade was for subscribers only and the rules stated that 'no servant of any description is allowed to come on the walk during the hours of the Promenade and dogs are likewise prohibited' (Hart 1981, 181). Entertainments were a regular feature of the walks at Cheltenham but occasionally these were particularly extravagant to mark a special event. A 'grand celebration' was held in 1838 to commemorate the centenary of the Old Well and the planting of the Long Walk. A public breakfast was followed by music and dancing and a procession to plant a young oak tree. When the fête began in the evening the whole scene was enchanting, most notably with the avenue of trees in the Long Walk illuminated with thousands of 'lights forming innumerable arches of gold and green, in the manner of a cathedral nave' (*ibid.*, 194–195).

Of all the walks established at Cheltenham the most celebrated has become known simply as The Promenade (Figure 4). Its origins go back to the 1790s when a row of shops, called the Colonnade, was built on the south side of the High Street, where that street now joins the Promenade (Hodson 1997). The intention was to continue the line of shops southwards, but that had to wait for another 20 years. Originally known as Sherborne, or Imperial Promenade, The Promenade was established in 1818 as a tree-lined carriage drive connecting the High Street to the new Sherborne Spa, which stood where The Queens Hotel now stands. That same year the town also acquired gas light.

The trees that were initially planted along the sides of the Promenade were horse chestnuts and for many years this magnificent avenue of trees was much admired (Biddle 1977, 2). However, as these original trees have grown to maturity and become very large they have raised various maintenance issues resulting in their progressive removal and subsequent replacement with other species considered more suitable. Nevertheless, the Promenade remains

FIGURE 4. The Promenade, Cheltenham, from a lithograph *c.* 1840 by George Rowe. Of all the walks established at Cheltenham the most celebrated has become known simply as The Promenade and its origins go back to the 1790s.

Cheltenham's most impressive tree-lined street located right in the heart of the elegant Georgian part of the town.

Before leaving the topic of spa towns it should be noted that the first public walk to be called a 'parade' was in Epsom (Girouard 1990, 147). Sometime between 1707 and 1711, a row of trimmed elms and a paved Parade were laid out on the south side of its main street, 'for visitors to exercise on after taking the waters'. A similar New Parade was formed on the opposite site of the street between 1711 and 1718. Previous to this the term 'parade' had only been applied in a topographical sense, to exercise grounds for soldiers.

Other early walks and promenades

Some other early walks and promenades not associated with spa towns should be mentioned, although limited space does not allow much detail to be given.

Avenham Walk in Preston lay on a piece of ground that projected on the south side of the town and either side of it the land dropped steeply away towards the River Ribble (Borsay 1986, 129). Although it had been used as a walking area from at least the late 1680s, improvements were made in 1698 that included a paved footpath. While Preston Corporation could not afford such elaborate developments as in York or Bath, they were still very proud of their public amenity and took care to maintain and protect their investment and ensure it was worthy of the county town of South Lancashire.

The Walks at King Lynn is the only surviving eighteenth century town walk in Norfolk (Friends of the Walks 2015). The originator of the earliest promenade, from the precinct of the Greyfriars in the west to Gannock Gate is unknown, but the Mayoral Chronicles of 1714 record that this was a 'handsome lime-planted walk put in the year before'. By 1753, the walk was raised up for drainage and gravelled, and bounded on both sides by a hawthorn hedge with trees at intervals. A description of 1773 tells us that 'The new walk or mall, from the bars of the workhouse to Gannock-gates, is about 340 yards [*c.* 311 m] long and 11 yards [*c.* 10 m] wide'. The Broad Walk Extension running east from Gannock Gate to Tennyson Road was initially proposed in the late 1790s but not finally made until 1843 when the necessary funds were donated by a local benefactor. Also raised and laid with gravel like the other Walks, it was planted on both sides with alternating lime and horse chestnut trees. The whole area covered by the Walks is now an urban park of 17 ha, managed by the local authority with the support of a Friends Group.

A particularly fine example of a walk was created in Leicester when in 1785 the Corporation resolved to form a tree-lined promenade for the recreation of the local residents. Called the New Walk, this was gravelled from one end to the other and 'ornamented most delightfully with young trees of various sorts' which had been donated by Mr Cradock of Gumley (Boynton 2002, 7). Houses were constructed initially along one side of the walk from 1824 when several building plots were sold (*ibid.*, 10). Further built development followed as the

FIGURE 5. A fine example of a tree-lined promenade was created in Leicester in 1785, called the New Walk. This photograph was taken *c.* 1910 and the New Walk still remains as a pleasant urban footway from Victoria Park down to the city centre.

area around the walk became increasingly urbanised (Figure 5). However, the New Walk still remains as a pleasant urban footway from Victoria Park down to the city centre.

Some of the early walks were associated with the first seaside resorts. A tree-lined promenade along the seafront where visitors could take in the bracing sea air was considered an important attraction for the resort and much in keeping with its image of health and vitality. Ladies Walk at Liverpool was a typical example (Borsay 2013, 56–57). In 1750, this was reported as being a very fine location, commanding views over the sea and divided into three parts by narrow strips of grass and two rows of trees. The sea view and the beauty of the natural landscape were considered an essential part of the visitor experience. At Weymouth a seaside promenade probably started developing *c.* 1772 (Girouard 1990, 151). What was initially a walk along the sands was supplemented by a surfaced walk in about 1786. The result became known as the Esplanade. Technically an esplanade was an open area to allowing a free field of fire around a fortification, and the Weymouth esplanade may have been so called from forts built along the beach in the civil war, and still in use in the 1780s. It was the ancestor of seaside esplanades all around the world.

The Mall and palemail

Some of the seventeenth century promenade plantings in London and other major cities were encouraged initially by a continental trend, although not one directly connected with trees. They were prompted by interest in playing a new popular game, *palemail*, which had been introduced from the continent (Lawrence 2006, 32). This involved hitting a ball with a mallet in a manner that was similar to modern croquet. Trees were planted simply for shade and to mark the sides of the course. When these areas were not being used for the game they functioned as shady promenades that were a popular haunt of the urban upper and middle classes.

The game was first known in Italy as *pallo a maglio* and as *palemail* in France, becoming very fashionable in Paris and then widely adopted elsewhere. In London, the game was a popular amusement in the reign of Charles II. Originally, it was played on the site of the street in London that still bears its name, Pall Mall. Rows of elms were planted on either side of the promenade but as the coach traffic and the nuisance of dust increased when games were not being played, Charles II had a new mall, now called The Mall, planted inside the northern edge of the park in the 1660s (Strutt 1810, 103). This was generally open to 'respectable' members of the public as long as they behaved themselves (Lawrence 2006, 33). The famous view of the Mall from St James's Park painted by Marco Ricci, the Italian artist of the Baroque period, does show a social mix of people (Figure 6). However, from their dress and demeanour most appear to be from the upper or middle class who are there at their leisure, although there are also a few individuals present in a working capacity.

After the game began to fall out of favour later in the seventeenth century, the long allées of trees were used predominantly as pedestrian promenades. Some also became archery grounds or bowling allées (Lawrence 1988, 360). By the eighteenth century the terms *mail* and *mall* were often used for promenades that were not covered with grass or associated with any games. The Mall itself was steadily transformed by the impact of the built development around it until it was eventually developed in the early twentieth century as a tree-lined main road and ceremonial route leading to Buckingham Palace (see Chapter 5).

From tree-lined walks and promenades to street trees

As we have seen in the examples above, there is plenty of evidence that many of these walks or promenades did effectively become very similar to streets lined with trees, even from an early stage in their development. While most tree-lined walks remained relatively open in nature, some became quite heavily developed along one or both sides, particularly with shops offering luxury goods or refreshments (Borsay 1986, 129–130). In the 1690s, Celia Fiennes (1888, 17), the English traveller and writer, found 'several little cake-houses where you have fruit sulibubs and summer liquors' on the Kings Mead walks at Bath, while one side of the Gravel Walks in the east of the city quickly emerged as a luxury shopping centre. The same pattern of development could also be found on the Pantiles at Tunbridge Wells. Shortly after the Restoration it could already be claimed that 'on one side of the walk is a long row of shops, plentifully stocked with all manner of toys, lace, gloves, stockings', while on the other side of the walk was a market selling game, vegetables, flowers and fruit. When Celia Fiennes visited in 1697 there was still a flourishing market, although the shops

were now protected by a 'piazza' (Borsay 1986, 130). There is also evidence of residential development alongside walks or promenades in spa towns such as Cheltenham. As the demand for building land increased in the early decades of the nineteenth century, the land alongside walks came to provide an ideal site for houses to accommodate seasonal visitors and wealthy residents, and thereby to increase the landowners' potential profits still further (Blake 1988, 5).

    While these tree-lined walks were still pedestrian promenades descended from the garden allée, the built development that accompanied many of them ensured these were decidedly urban in nature. Loudon (1835, 646) was later to define public walks as promenades or roads among trees. Although these linear greenspaces in the urban landscape were essentially for pedestrians and disappeared in their original form long before the arrival of modern road and motor vehicles, some did permit carriages, carts and other early modes of transport when not being used for special events. For that reason, even when the use of these walks was restricted solely to pedestrians, there can be little doubt that the planting of regularly spaced trees lining a public walk, often paved or gravelled, in combination with shops, houses and other forms of built development along the sides, effectively amounted to the first organised

FIGURE 6. A view of the Mall from St James's Park, London, dated *c.* 1710 by Marco Ricci. This fashionable promenade began as a venue for the popular game known as palemail.

establishment of street trees in Britain. Indeed, quite a number of those walks were later to become celebrated as fine examples of street tree plantings, such as The Promenade in Cheltenham.

Carriage promenades or *cours*

Closely related to the pedestrian walk or promenade was the carriage promenade or *cours*. At the beginning of the seventeenth century another new recreational pastime, originating in Italy and blossoming in France, became popular among the upper classes in many parts of Western Europe. This was the riding in carriages for pleasure by the rich and fashionable along specifically designated routes. It was another urban landscape feature inspired by garden allées that would exert some influence on the future development of street trees in Britain. In some respects the carriage promenade or *cours* was especially important because it transformed the garden allée into a place for vehicles, albeit one not yet integrated into a city's street system (Lawrence 1988, 361).

It is thought that the fashion for carriage drives or promenades was initially inspired by a rural allée that functioned as a recreational carriageway running along the Arno River outside the Cascine Gardens in Florence (Lawrence 2006, 34). Marie de Medici, queen of France's Henry IV, had been born in Florence in 1575 and enjoyed this carriage drive as a young girl. After the assassination of her husband in 1610 she became Regent and proceeded to exert a considerable influence on French political and cultural life. In 1616, nostalgic for her Florentine roots, she ordered the creation of a carriage promenade, later called the Cours la Reine, over 1 km in length along the right bank of the Seine near the Tuileries gardens. She had ornamental gates built at both ends and the planting of four rows of elm trees along its length, with a wide roadway in the middle for the carriages. Access to the Cours la Reine was restricted by invitation to only the wealthiest Parisians. It soon became a hugely popular venue for the ostentatious display of wealth and social interaction among young upper class men and women, who were able to engage in private conversation while still within public view. The essential structure of the Cours la Reine still exists, although the elms have been substituted with horse chestnuts, the roadway is now mown grass and pedestrians have replaced the carriages. It now functions as a public park for all the people of Paris.

By the middle of the seventeenth century recreational carriage promenades or *cours* were becoming popular in many European cities and London was no exception (Lawrence 2006, 34). Inspired by other European examples, Charles I created Britain's first carriage promenade in Hyde Park in the 1630s. Although the use of the Ring was reserved for the carriages of members of the royal court, the park itself was opened to the public in 1637 and the circular track soon became a fashionable place to visit, particularly on May Day. The earliest planting around the Ring would probably have comprised mainly native trees together with some of the early introduced species such as common lime and horse chestnut.

Larwood (1880) and Walford (1878) give good accounts of the history and cultural significance the Ring (sometimes called the Tour) from its origins up to late Victorian times. During the Commonwealth it became rather dilapidated but was then renovated back to its former condition under Charles II. In 1719, the Ring was described by a French traveller as two or three hundred paces in diameter with the circuit marked by a balustrade of poles placed upon stakes about three feet from the ground (Larwood 1880, 47). The carriages were able to drive slowly in either direction around the Ring. This was a daytime activity and the venue was quickly deserted once night fell. During the reign of Queen Anne, the Ring held its place as the resort of all the fashionable gentry and nobility, even in winter (Walford 1878). Guidance on the latest fashion for travelling in the carriages was available from magazines of 'good taste', such as Rudolp Ackerman's *Repository of Arts* that was very popular in late Georgian times (Ackerman 1810, 45–46). In 1730, when the Serpentine Lake was created in Hyde Park at the behest of Caroline, Queen of George II, the Ring was partly destroyed to accommodate this, although it was later reinstated (Larwood 1880, 100). In the late nineteenth century, the planting around the Ring was notable for some large elms trees which provided shade and shelter for the spectators to watch the coaches driving around (Amherst 1907, 29). As the popularity of the Ring declined other routes through and round Hyde Park became fashionable for carriage drives. These included the West Carriage Drive, created in the 1820s, to make a route through the centre of the park dividing Hyde Park from Kensington Gardens.

John Claudius Loudon, the renowned horticulturist of the first half of the nineteenth century, was one of a number of writers who viewed carriage promenades as valuable additions to large cities. He also gave advice on how they should be designed and operated:

> Extent and free air are the principal requisites, and the roads should be arranged as to produce few intersections; but at the same time so as carriages may make either the tour of the whole scene, or adopt a shorter tour at pleasure. In the course of long roads, there ought to be occasional bays or side expansions, to admit of carriages separating from the course, halting or turning. Where such promenades are very extensive, they should be furnished with places of accommodation and refreshment, both for men and horses; and this is a valuable part of their arrangement for occasional visitors from a distance, or in hired vehicles.
>
> Loudon 1835, 1206

As well as carriage promenades it appears that there were also some equestrian promenades that were primarily for horse riding. However, the use of these two terms by different writers, as with some descriptions of the Ring, suggests a possible confusion in terminology or the fact that some of the promenades may have been used for both carriages and horse riders. Nevertheless, on the evidence of some writers, such as Loudon (1835, 363), it also seems that while many continental cities had some form of equestrian promenade within their boundaries, these were much less common in Britain.

Pleasure garden promenades

As well as the promenades that appeared in many fashionable towns and resorts, similar features were included in the pleasure gardens. These were a uniquely British form of public open space that emerged in many towns and cities after the restoration of the monarchy in 1660 and endured for some 200 years (Johnston 2015, 144–150).

A 'pleasure garden' can be defined as a privately owned enclosed ornamental piece of land, open to the public as a resort or amusement area almost exclusively in the summertime and operated as a business (Conlin 2013, 5). They were usually located in the urban fringe, although with later urban expansion many were subsequently surrounded on all sides by built development. The term should not be confused with a 'pleasure ground', a feature of the English landscape garden close to the house that included a wide range of trees and shrubs. While the private pleasure ground of the eighteenth century aristocrat has been described as a 'landscape of exclusion', the pleasure garden was definitely a landscape of inclusion (Williamson 1995, 107). Anyone who could afford the price of admission and whose behaviour was unlikely to upset other customers was welcome to enter. There was much to enjoy and experience in the varied and sometimes bizarre attractions found in the magical world of the pleasure garden.

Trees were a universal feature of the pleasure gardens and had both aesthetic and functional roles. The larger pleasure gardens usually had extensive plantings of trees that were established in formal avenue plantings that functioned as promenades in much the same way as these did in other urban landscapes. They were located along the main and often crowded walkways that were set out in straight lines or gently curving to ensure plenty of visibility for those promenading. These promenades were often the principal attraction of the gardens and the centre of social interaction (Wroth 1896, 204). At the main entrance to Vauxhall Gardens, London's premier venue for most of the early part of the eighteenth century, the Grand Walk lined with elm trees led away for more than 300 yards (274 m) to a gilded statue of Aurora and the eastern perimeter of the gardens (Downing 2009, 23). At Cremorne Gardens, which in the nineteenth century succeeded Vauxhall as London's most fashionable venue, its Promenade de Versailles was a spectacular and hugely popular attraction (Nead 2000, 112). These open avenues contrasted with the dark walks of denser tree planting that led off the main thoroughfares where couples could find some seclusion and privacy. Trees along the main paths were used for the attachment of lamps that not only illuminated the way at night but also lit up the trees and highlighted their natural beauty, shape and texture in an atmospheric glow (Conlin 2013, 23).

Just like the promenades in the spa towns and resorts, the main tree-lined walkways in the larger pleasure gardens were often flanked by refreshment rooms, entertainment booths and other built facilities. This also gave them something of the appearance of tree-lined streets, particularly when the walkways were filled with a throng of promenading patrons and the facilities

along their flanks were open for business. The painting of The Grand Walk at Vauxhall Gardens by Canaletto, the great Italian artist, gives a good impression of this, although at the busiest times there would have been more people than he depicted (Figure 7). In mid-Victorian times when the debate regarding the advantages and disadvantages of planting Britain's streets with trees was beginning to be featured in the press, it is likely that the presence of promenades in many pleasure gardens had some influence on this. Certainly, the superbly attractive landscapes of the main promenades in the larger pleasure gardens, with their appearance of tree-lined streets, would likely have encouraged a positive association of streets and trees.

While it is true that the pleasure gardens were generally open to people from all classes, the degree of social interaction should not be overstated. Some control of access still existed, especially with the most prestigious gardens and the working class (Wroth 1896, 8), but this was less overt than with the promenades in the fashionable towns and resorts. There were a number of factors involved in limiting the access of working people, apart from the obvious conflict with the working day (Borsay, 2013, 65–68). While admission charges might be reasonably priced in comparison to the working man's wages, there were associated costs in visiting the pleasure gardens, such as travel (often considerable when including tolls) and the cost of leisure clothing to ensure

FIGURE 7. The Grand Walk at Vauxhall Gardens *c.* 1751 painted by the great Italian artist Canaletto. Vauxhall Gardens was London's premier pleasure garden in the early part of the eighteenth century and its Grand Walk was lined with elm trees.

your appearance was appropriate. Food and drink in the gardens could also be expensive. It is therefore understandable that in the major gardens working people would often appear to be in the minority. Nevertheless, the working class were never entirely absent from even the more exclusive and polite pleasure gardens. There were the service workers such as cooks, waiters, musicians and gardeners. There were also the servants of the rich clientele, although domestic servants in livery were banned from the walks at Vauxhall and segregated in a 'coop' outside the gardens.

We have noted above that the closely controlled environment of the promenades in the spa towns and resorts had a role in strengthening social ties and promoting social stability. However, some historians believe that the more open access of the pleasure gardens had the reverse effect. The growth of the middle class and the growing presence of working class people led to tensions in the use of these public spaces and threatened the established social hierarchies. Anyone who could now afford the right clothes could pose as a gentleman or a lady and promenade in the pleasure gardens, creating confusion in the social standing of people seen in these public places (Lawrence 2006, 61).

Place promenade

Another continental landscape form with a more tenuous influence on street trees in Britain was the *place* or square. In the early seventeenth century the Italian Renaissance had inspired examples like the Place Royale or Place des Vosges in Paris and Covent Garden in London (Borsay 1986, 363). While these were initially rigidly symmetrical and devoid of vegetation, by the eighteenth century new French *places* had become spatially complex. They were often elongated at important street intersections, with trees planted either in allées or in quincunx that functioned as public promenades.

Spatially distinct from tree-lined streets, the place promenade contributed to their development by using vegetative alignment in new ways in town and city centres (Borsay 1986, 364). Usually open to vehicles and integrated with surrounding structures, the French place often formed the centrepiece of an urban design. This was in contrast to the British towns and cities where the eighteenth century preference for urban greenspace was in the form of squares, crescents and pleasure gardens, with a distinct absence of street trees. There are, however, some examples of early British squares where the use of trees does seem to have been a precursor to the later development of street trees. The original design of St Ann's Square in Manchester shows this clearly, although there is no longer any trace of it. At the beginning of the eighteenth century, this area was a large cornfield called Acre's Field when part of it was selected as the site for St Ann's Church (Procter 1874, 258). Towards the end of the seventeenth century, streets became more numerous in the St Ann's district as the town of Manchester expanded. By 1720, it was decided to lay out St Ann's Square in imitation of the fashionable squares of London and Bath. The landscape design was notable for its use of closely pruned trees in formal lines along two sides

that resembled the appearance of street trees (Figure 8). In his book, *Memorials of Manchester Streets*, Richard Proctor describes the scene which was much the same in his day:

> On emerging into the square, we are confronted by two rows of trees, standing as Indian file, one row on each side. They profess to be young plane-trees, duly rooted in the earth, but to uncultured visions they resemble vegetable ninepins as placed in a skittle-alley, and awaiting the bowlers to topple them over.
>
> Procter 1874, 258

FIGURE 8. St Ann's Square in Manchester in 1746. The landscape design was notable for its use of closely pruned trees in formal lines along two sides that resembled the appearance of street trees.

During the Georgian era the design of squares in British cities, underwent a radical transformation (Johnston 2015, 112–117). The open spaces of the squares changed from open plazas in the seventeenth century to enclosed private parks at the end of the eighteenth century, a trend based on the social values of the aristocracy, later adopted by the middle class (Lawrence 1993, 90). Public rights of access were steadily extinguished through parliamentary enclosure acts similar to those used at the same time on rural estates. From the late 1720s onwards, squares were consistently regarded as the most fashionable urban districts and their continuing respectability largely depended on the exclusion of 'undesirables'. Railings went up around the squares and access was limited to a select group of keyholders who lived in the surrounding residential property. At the same time, any trees in the locality were also located inside the railings of the squares or in the gardens of individual houses and they remained absent from the footways of the surrounding streets.

Some landscape writers in the early and mid-nineteenth century referred to 'street gardens' and their associated trees (Smith 1852, 166–167). However, this term embraced greenspaces in squares, crescents and other street-side locations and did not include street trees.

Changing patterns in urban greenspace

Those landscape forms that the British had adapted from the Continent into our urban landscapes were largely disappearing by the mid-eighteenth century (Lawrence 1988, 373). This was especially true of the formal French styles of gardening which were replaced by naturalistic English ones. Many of the walks, promenades and other avenues of trees in our towns and cities were now being obliterated by urban expansion and replaced with English park-like landscapes in residential squares and crescents, a distinctive British contribution to international urban design.

The Regency era in the early nineteenth century was a period of major experimentation in urban design and it witnessed some important innovations in the urban landscape (Lawrence 2006, 177). This was driven by hugely significant events that had an enormous impact on the political, economic and social life of Britain. When the French and their allies had finally been defeated at the battle of Waterloo in 1815, the British economy entered a period of domestic growth. This translated immediately into a boom in house building and property speculation. In turn, this gave a major boost to the landscape and horticultural industries that led to an increase in the numbers of urban trees. A number of grand urban development schemes were undertaken during this period. The largest and most innovative was Regent's Park in London on land privately owned by the Prince Regent (MacLeod 1972, 250–255; Johnston 2015, 45–46). While the details of this remarkable scheme are beyond the scope of this book, one aspect needs to be mentioned. The entire development was connected southwards to the palaces at Westminster by an impressive new road called Regent Street. However, no trees were planted along the new route. Instead, they were reserved for Regent's Park and the private gardens of the villas. This reflected the widely-held view in British urban design in the Georgian era that trees did not belong along major thoroughfares or in streets in commercial districts, only in residential areas, and then almost exclusively in privately owned squares and crescents. As the Victorian age dawned, there were still no systematic planting of street trees in Britain.

CHAPTER THREE

Remnants from Past Landscapes

Long before there was any systematic planting of street trees in Britain, there had always been some trees located in the streets in our towns and cities. These were invariably not planted as street trees but were remnants of past landscapes, usually rural ones, that had been incorporated in the streetscape following urban expansion and built development. These 'remnant street trees' can be found either as individuals, in groups or as distinct avenues. This chapter describes some examples of remnant street trees and explores how they came to be incorporated into the urban landscape. These trees often had considerable historical and cultural significance, not just to the communities living in their vicinity but sometimes in a regional and national context as well. While some of these examples have been moderately well-documented in the popular or academic literature, much of the information in this chapter has emerged through original research. More examples of remnant street trees can be found in other chapters of this book.

Individual trees of heritage value

While some of the individual trees of heritage value featured below had already been growing for many years, mostly in gardens or rural landscapes, by the 1870s or 1880s some had become part of the streetscape of rapidly expanding towns and cities. In these circumstances it is likely they would have had some influence on public attitudes towards the whole idea of systematic street tree planting in Britain that was being debated at that time. Many of these remnant trees were adversely affected by built development and road construction and also subject to calls for their removal by people who saw the presence of mature trees in streets as liabilities. At the same time, there would have been other people who saw these trees as assets to the urban landscape, bringing a sense of history, natural beauty and living architecture to the street scene.

Research for this book uncovered many cases of this type of remnant street tree. In the examples given below we look at individual trees that have had considerable historical and cultural significance for the communities in their locality. This is one of the major reasons why these trees were retained in the streetscape over the years and the various pressures to remove them were resisted. While some of these trees have since died, some have also been 'replaced' by more recent plantings that serve as a living reminder of the original tree's symbolic importance.

The Old Oak, Carmarthen

This famous tree was once located in the centre of the town of Carmarthen, West Wales. In recent times, all that was left of the tree was a short stump, which stood by the side of the road at the junction of Priory Street and Old Oak Lane (Davies, 2012). Known to most local people as the Old Oak (*Quercus robur*), the tree has also been called Merlin's Oak or the Priory Oak. There is a local tradition that Carmarthen is the birthplace of the mythical magician Merlin, and the origin of the name Carmarthen, or Caerfyrddin comes from Myrddin, the Welsh name for Merlin (Randall 1980). As late as 1697, visitors to the town were shown the 'house of his nativity' in Priory Street. Merlin is said to have made a prophecy regarding the old oak tree:

When Merlin's Oak shall tumble down,
Then shall fall Carmarthen Town.

There is another version of the prophecy which states that when the tree falls, the town will drown or flood. Throughout the centuries generations of town councillors have done their very best to preserve this remarkable tree even though it was inconveniently placed in the roadway, perhaps calculating that it was better to be safe than sorry. The oak tree's origins are uncertain but it is said to have sprung from an acorn planted in 1659 by a master named Adams from the Queen Elizabeth Grammar School who is supposed to have been an ancestor of the American President of that name (Randall 1980). It is thought that Adams planted the acorn to celebrate the return of King Charles II of England to the throne. It can also be speculated that the tree was originally located within the grounds of the medieval Carmarthen Priory. In support of that assumption it should be noted that the planting site is only about 100 yards (91 m) north-west of the former gatehouse of the priory and this might also explain why the tree is sometimes called the Priory Oak. As the lands of the former priory were transformed under built development and new roads were constructed in the vicinity of the old tree, it effectively became a street tree in the heart of this busy market town.

By the mid-nineteenth century this revered tree was long dead. Some sources suggest it was intentionally killed around 1800 by a nearby shopkeeper who disapproved of the age-old practice of people congregating under its spreading branches 'at all hours of the day and night' (Davies 2012). While other sources concur with this version of events, the date of the eventual demise of the tree is given as 1856. No doubt conscious of the prophecy linking the fate of the tree and the town, the town councillors refused to contemplate removing the dead tree. By 1900, the withered stump had to be supported by a stone plinth and iron railings and later, as vehicle traffic volumes increased, the area surrounding the tree was made into a traffic island (Pyke 2014). Late one night in the early 1970s, it was said that local students tried to attack the stump with a chainsaw as a rag day 'prank' but the noise alerted nearby residents and the prospective vandals quickly disappeared before any damage was done. In fairness to the student population at the time, some of the town's residents were also convinced that there was never any intention to cause damage and the incident was just a practical joke designed to generate publicity and challenge some age-old beliefs.

In 1978, despite vigorous objections from many local residents, what was left of the Old Oak was removed to help the flow of traffic at a busy junction. The remaining pieces of the stump were placed on permanent display at Carmarthenshire County Museum in Abergwili and in the foyer of St Peter's Civic Hall in Nott Square. The only evidence of the tree at its former site is an interpretive board and a young evergreen oak in a containerised planter on the nearby footway. However, the legend of the Old Oak lives on in the hearts and minds of local people and it is still commemorated, not least in the song *The Old Carmarthen Oak* popularised by the Welsh Folk Group called *Ar Log*.

FIGURE 9. The Cross Tree in the High Street of Messingham, North Lincolnshire, with a group of villagers in the foreground. The photograph was taken around 1898 and shows the replacement for an earlier tree which had stood in the same location for possibly 200 years previously.

Cross Tree, Messingham

While researching through a collection of early photographs the author spotted a scene taken *c.* 1898 of the High Street in Messingham, a village in North Lincolnshire (Figure 9). Behind the group of local residents in the foreground

was a solitary young tree standing in the road, the wrought iron guard around its trunk indicating it was held in some regard. Research revealed that this tree had gone and there were now no trees at all in the High Street of the village. However, just beside where the tree once stood was a public house called the Green Tree Inn. This intriguing discovery prompted an enquiry to the local parish council which uncovered the history behind this tree.

The tree in the early photograph was a sycamore (*Acer pseudoplatanus*) planted in 1878 as a replacement for an earlier tree, also a sycamore, which had stood in the same location for possibly 200 years previously (MacKinnon 1825, 22). The tree was known as the Cross Tree because it grew on the spot where the village cross had stood in the days before the Reformation. John Wesley, the founder of Methodism, preached under the 'green tree' on 24 July, 1772 (Messingham History Group 2006). The tree became well known throughout the district and recognised as a focal point for the village. Close to the tree stood the wooden stocks, which were used as a form of punishment where the limbs of petty offenders were immobilised as they were left there to be subjected to public humiliation. The original tree died around 1870 but because of its historic and cultural significance the villagers decided to plant a replacement, marking the occasion with a community festival. This new tree stood in the High Street until it was the felled in the late 1920s, apparently by order of the local Highways Committee who deemed it to be a hazard. However, the memory of the tree lives on in the public house named after it, and in Cross Tree Road which is directly opposite the pub.

Old Walnut Tree, Bexhill-on-Sea

A remarkable old walnut tree (*Juglan regia*) once stood in the middle of the road at a major junction in the centre of Bexhill-on-Sea, a seaside town in East Sussex (Anon 1921). For many years this ancient landmark was one of the town's most popular features until its eventual demise following a violent storm in July, 1921. An investigation into the origins of this tree has revealed a fascinating story of how an uncommon species for such a location came to be recognised as the town's most famous street tree.

This walnut tree was originally located in a corner of the pleasure ground of the town's Manor House (Smith pers. comm., 2015). As the town expanded and its roads became busier these were widened to accommodate the increasing flow of pedestrians and carts, although this was before the advent of motor vehicles. As part of the road widening, the walnut tree became part of the street scene by being incorporated into a new roundabout in the middle of the road at the crossroads of the High Street, Church Street, De La Warr Road and Sea Road (formerly Sea Lane). Photographic evidence indicates this happened *c.* 1890, since an image taken in 1888 shows the tree still in the grounds of the Manor House and another dated 1891 shows the tree now located in the road (Figure 10). The roundabout consisted of a wall around the tree, about

waist height and faced with cobblestones, and on the top of this were placed wrought iron railings.

As Bexhill-on-Sea became an ever more popular seaside resort in the 1890s, so the fame of the Old Walnut Tree grew with this. Its reputation was confirmed by an article in *The Sketch* newspaper in 1894 entitled 'A Rising Watering-Place – Bexhill-on-Sea' (Anon 1894). Of four photographs of attractive scenes from the town, one specifically features this tree. However, all was not well with its health and it soon began to show sign of severe stress. In the process of constructing the roundabout the soil level around the tree was raised a few feet. Combined with the likely disturbance to the tree's roots in the construction process, this would have undoubtedly had a detrimental impact on its health and vitality. The inevitable dieback in its crown is almost certainly one of the reasons for the heavy lopping of the Old Walnut Tree that took place about a decade later, evidenced by a picture of the severely topped tree taken in 1903. The increasingly dilapidated appearance of the tree prompted regular debates in the town's Council Chamber about having it felled. On each occasion this was vigorously resisted by the townsfolk (Anon 1921).

The fate of this much-weakened and decaying tree was final sealed by the violent storm that battered the south coast of England in July, 1921 (Anon 1921). The ancient landmark was toppled in the night and in the morning

FIGURE 10. The Old Walnut Tree that once stood in the centre of Bexhill-on-Sea, East Sussex, photographed in 1891. The tree was originally located in a corner of the pleasure ground of the town's Manor House.

CREDIT: BEXHILL OLD TOWN PRESERVATION SOCIETY.

as it lay sprawled across the road there were widespread feelings of sadness among the local residents. The remains of the tree were soon cleared away and the roundabout removed. While the tree may have disappeared from the landscape of the town, it is remembered fondly by local people even though almost nobody in the town is now old enough to have actually seen it. It is amusing to note that although the tree has gone, it will always feature in the Town Council's debates as the Mayoral gavel has been made out of wood from the tree. Today's visitors to Bexhill-on-Sea can also take refreshment in the *Old Walnut Tree Tea Rooms*, located in the High Street close to the site of the tree.

The Selly Oak, Birmingham

Selly Oak is well known to many people as a district of Birmingham. However, few would probably know that the name is associated with an oak tree (*Quercus robur*) that until 1909 stood proudly beside the junction of Oak Tree Lane and Bristol Road.

Despite the obvious assumption that the district is named after the once-famous oak tree, how Selly Oak got its name is a matter of some debate (Leonard 1933, 1–2). Some believe that the name Selly is derived from variants of 'scelf-lei' or shelf-meadow, which is pasture land on a shelf or terrace of land. Others claim that it results from the Saxon word 'ley' meaning clearing in the forest, because of its position in the Forest of Arden. Whatever may be the origin and meaning of the place name, it seems likely that in more recent times the place took its additional name 'Oak' from a prominent tree within the village. Some sources claim that this refers to Sarah's oak (later Sally's oak) after a local witch who was either hanged from it or was buried under it with an oak stake through her heart, which later it was claimed grew into an oak tree. The 'Oak' part of the name is found in two canal survey maps of the 1790s although one does call it Sally Oak. What is clear is that the name Selly Oak pre-dates the famous local oak tree by some years but the name may have come from an earlier tree, such as Sarah's Oak.

The famous oak tree that stood until 1909 was planted around 1831 in the grounds of Selly Oak House by the owner John Rodway (Leonard 1933, 9). It is possible that the occasion for the planting was to celebrate the coronation of King William IV in that year. As time went by, the young oak grew into a magnificent mature tree. The tree might still be standing there, had not the rapid development of the city of Birmingham caught up with it. Following the sale of land that had been part of the house, the tree found itself exposed to the public roadway that now ran in front of it. In the early 1900s, permission was given for residential (later commercial) property to be built close to the edge of that roadway (Hyland, no date). The buildings came so near to the tree that many of its branches had to be cut off to make room for the property. As early as 1894, the Northfield Highway Board

FIGURE 11 *(opposite)*. The Selly Oak, Birmingham, being felled in 1909. The old oak had eventually become a danger to pedestrians and the growing volume of traffic and in the interests of public safety it was removed by Council workmen.

lobbied vociferously to have the tree removed but the storm of protest from local residents prevented them from carrying out the work. Sadly, the old oak eventually became a danger to pedestrians and the growing volume of traffic and in the interests of public safety it was felled by Council workmen in 1909 (Figure 11).

Although this famous tree had finally disappeared from the Birmingham landscape, there was reluctance among local people to part with it completely. The stump of the tree was placed in Selly Oak Park, where it still remains on display (Dowling *et al.* 1987, 2). A brass plaque attached to it reads: 'Butt of Old Oak Tree from which the name of Selly Oak was derived'. Over the years there have been repeated requests for a 'living' reminder of the old tree. In March 1985, a 'new' Selly Oak was planted by local councillors on the north side of the Bristol Road on the small triangle of land located between Harborne Lane and the Sainsbury's supermarket, following road improvements to the junction (Anon 1985, 5).

Martyr's Elm, Brentwood

Brentwood is a small town in Essex that can trace its origins as a settlement back to Saxon times. For almost 400 years the celebrated Martyr's Elm (possibly *Ulmus glabra*) stood on a site in the town on what is now Ingrave Road (Wreyford 2015). Although the tree has been gone for over 60 years, its story remains hugely significant in the context of England's social and religious history.

The tree marks the spot at the side of the road where the Protestant martyr William Hunter was burnt at the stake in 1555 by order of Sir Anthony Browne, a local magistrate (Wilks 1972, 84). Browne was an active persecutor of 'heretics' during the reign of Queen Mary I, the Catholic monarch who gained the nickname Bloody Mary. The teenage Hunter had been caught reading an English translation of the Bible, something that was illegal at the time. Brown interrogated Hunter but despite being fully aware of the consequence of his actions the youngster refused to recant his religious beliefs and was executed at the age of 19 on 27 March, 1555.

It is said that the elm started to grow following the death of Hunter, on the exact spot where he was put to death (Wreyford 2013). For hundreds of years the Martyr's Elm (also called Hunter's Tree) stood as a reminder of the martyrdom of Hunter and was celebrated as a vital part of the living history of the town and of Protestant England itself. As such, every effort was made to protect this hugely symbolic street tree in its exposed position by the roadside. This included placing sturdy iron railings around it and keeping a watchful eye for prospective souvenir hunters wanting to remove a sprig of foliage or others who might seek to harm the tree.

In 1558, Browne founded Brentwood School with the assistance of a grant from Queen Mary and ten years later this was housed in its first purpose-built school room (Wreyford 2013). This building is still standing and forms part of the independent school that now provides full-time education and boarding facilities for both boys and girls. This part of the school is on ground which is immediately behind the tree that was to become known as the Martyr's Elm. It has always been suggested by some that Browne established the school to ease his conscience when he reflected on the terrible deed he had done to Hunter.

By the start of the twentieth century the elm had grown to an enormous size but was in poor health. Progressive die-back of the crown had led to a stag-headed appearance and then these major branches were removed as the deadwood presented a hazard to pedestrians and road users. Photographs from 1915 show a massive stump but hardly any recent growth. By the late-1940s it was assumed that the tree was dead and after much debate the stump was finally removed for safety reasons in 1952 (Brentwood Council 2015). In 1936, an oak tree had been planted in the roadside verge close to the ailing tree, in a civic tree planting ceremony to mark the accession of King George VI. This tree is flourishing and now regarded by some as a new Martyr's Tree.

Old Elm Tree, Ramsbury

Until as recently as 1986, there was a huge and ancient elm tree (*Ulmus glabra*) situated in the middle of the road at the end of the High Street in the village of Ramsbury in Wiltshire. Like the Martyr's Elm in Brentford, this tree also had ancient religious associations, although in this case they were Pagan rather than Christian. According to local legend, the large hollow in the base of this gigantic tree had once been the home of a witch called Maud Toogood who warned that if the old elm ever fell, the village would fall with it (Davies 1993). That prophesy has echoes of the one said to have been made by Merlin with regard to the Old Oak in Carmarthen.

Regardless of whether they believed the legend, the Old Elm Tree (sometimes called the Witch Tree) was always much admired by local residents for its stature and beauty and for its symbolism and fame across the county (Davies 1993). The area around the tree was known as the Square and the centre of a major road junction that became the focal point in the village. The tree was first mentioned in a report in 1751, by which time it must have already been established for a considerable time. In its full maturity the spread of tree was said to have touched the buildings on all sides of the Square. Photographic evidence from 1906 shows the tree much reduced in crown spread due to pollarding, although the foliage was still in a healthy condition. It also shows that the tree was located directly in the roadway with no protection around it. Sadly, by the 1920s, the tree's condition had begun to deteriorate, although it continued to symbolise the heart of the village and act as a venue for meetings and festivities well into the second half of the twentieth century (Holdsworth pers. comm., 2016). However, the tree continued to decline steadily until it eventually died in 1983.

The gnarled stump remained in the Square for several years while a replacement was discussed. Many villagers wanted to keep the stump as a reminder of the famous tree in the place where it had stood for so many centuries. In an effort to resolve the matter, a referendum was held which threatened to split the village and the story was reported in the national newspapers (Greaves 1983, 7). After much discussion it was eventually agreed that the tree should be replaced and the remains of the old tree were grubbed out by local council workers (Croucher 1995, 57). Due to the ravages of Dutch elm disease that was now decimating the elm population across the English countryside, it was decided not to replant with an elm tree and instead to use a young oak (*Quercus robur*). A semi-mature tree was sourced from Epping Forest in Essex and the cost of this was sponsored by a regional building society that had used the elm as its logo (*ibid.*, 58). On an autumn day in 1986 the residents organised a tree planting ceremony that was part of a day of festivities for the whole village. When the tree had been planted it was blessed by the Bishop of Ramsbury in a short Christian service. Despite the bad weather on the day, the music and dancing kept people in good spirits and all the children dressed up for the occasion, the little girls as witches and the little boys as scarecrows. The oak tree itself is flourishing, thanks largely to its location on a traffic island in the centre of the Square that gives it some protection from the busy motor traffic that now passes through the village. All the festivities that happened around the Old Elm Tree now take place around the oak replacement (Holdsworth pers. comm., 2016). Various small pieces of the old tree are still kept as mementoes by people in the village, including some pieces in the Parish Council office.

Research into this form of remnant street tree identified numerous examples that included various species, although mostly old elms and oaks. These ancient trees stood proudly by the roadside in many towns and villages in Britain, often for hundreds of years. While many have now disappeared from the landscape, a detailed study of these trees would make a fascinating research project in its own right.

Remnant trees retained in the roadway

In the late nineteenth century and early twentieth century when many of our towns and cities were expanding rapidly, there is evidence that mature trees from past landscapes were left by newly-built roads, even when they had no special heritage or cultural value. These were not always left in the footway at the side of the road, as might be expected, but often in the roadway itself. In the latter case, this may now seem a strange decision on the part of the property developers and highway engineers. However, in those days there was little or no motorised traffic on Britain's roads and the relevant professionals in charge of the new development felt that these trees would add some natural beauty and mature appearance to the new suburb or housing estate. In this section we examine some examples of these trees.

Arden Road Oak, Acocks Green, Birmingham

The Arden Oak (*Quercus robur*) still stands in Arden Road in the Birmingham district of Acocks Green. Its endurance bears testament to the remarkable survival powers of some remnant street trees in the face of intense urban development. In late Victorian times, Arden Road was a narrow rural lane on the outskirts of Birmingham with a couple of small cottages on one side and a hedgerow and large oak tree on the other. At this time Birmingham was continuing to expand rapidly and by the start of the twentieth century was recognised as the greatest industrial city in the world. New residential suburbs were continually being built to house the burgeoning population that was sustained by its countless factories (McKenna 1990). In the early 1900s, a new middle class housing development was constructed in Acocks Green with high-quality residential properties on either side of Arden Road. The two existing cottages were incorporated into a row of houses on one side of the former rural lane that had now been transformed into a new residential street. At the same time it was decided to retain the large oak tree as it was felt this would add some natural beauty and sense of maturity to the newly built development.

Rather than arranging the pattern of new development to leave the oak tree on the footway either side of the new road, the highway engineers left it standing proudly in the middle of the road on a small traffic island (Figure 12). The reason for this was probably due to the size and spread of the tree, which was then about 100 years old. If it had been retained on the footway it was likely that nearby residents would complain that its branches overshadowed their front gardens and blocked out light to their living rooms. At that time nobody thought there would be any conflict with traffic on the road as motor vehicles were still a rarity. In common with many other high-quality suburban developments at that time, street trees were then planted at regular intervals along either side of the road. These were mostly London plane trees with a few common limes.

As with many remnant street trees suddenly engulfed by built development, the health of the Arden Road Oak started to decline after just a few years. Photographs from 1912 show the tree with its major limbs cut back by several feet but with the dieback in the crown continuing. Subsequently, the tree was regularly pollarded to keep the crown to a small size. Quite remarkably, the Arden Road Oak is still standing, although it is now overshadowed by the mature plane trees on either side of the street and there is fungal decay in its trunk.

Stafford Road, Weston-super-Mare

The trees that once stood in a line down the centre of Stafford Road in Weston-super-Mare, a seaside resort in Somerset, are a remarkable example of this remnant street tree phenomenon. Furthermore, this would not have come to light had it not been for the discovery of an old photograph that prompted further research.

While exploring early photographs of suburban developments in the 1900s, the author found a postcard image of a residential street in Weston-super-Mare that was taken *c*. 1915. In the middle of the road was a large mature tree, which clearly pre-dated the houses from the late Victorian or Edwardian period. There were no other trees in the photograph since regular street tree planting had not been undertaken. Current images of Stafford Road confirmed the assumption that the tree in the photo was no longer there. Local historians were then contacted to see if they could shed any light on this. One immediate point of interest arose when the photograph was examined more closely. Behind the tree in the centre of the road was a line of shadows running back up the street. These shadows were similar in shape to the shade cast by the tree in the foreground, although partly obscured by it. This seemed to indicate that there might have been a line of trees up the centre of Stafford Road but in the photo these would be hidden behind the only visible tree. This was finally confirmed when a similar photograph from *c*. 1915 was sourced, taken from a different angle, that clearly

FIGURE 12. The Arden Oak in Arden Road in the Birmingham district of Acocks Green, photographed in 1906 soon after the houses were built. The tree is still there, although it is now pollarded and has fungal decay.

shows the line of trees (Figure 13). All the little pieces of information that had been gathered regarding these trees and the immediate neighbourhood could then be put together to tell their story.

The trees were originally part of a line of boundary trees on the eastern side of the nearby Swiss Villa estate. The famous engineer Isambard Kingdom Brunel had lived at Swiss Villa while he supervised the construction of the Bristol and Exeter Railway, which opened in 1841. Along the side of this boundary ran a rough track. Land from the eastern side of the estate was sold in late Victorian times for a residential development that was constructed around 1892. This development comprised semi-detached houses on both sides of the rough track which was then transformed into a made-up carriageway called Stafford Road. While many trees were felled to make way for the houses and the new road, a line of boundary trees was retained along the centre of the new road, from its junction with Locking Road, from where the photos were taken, to the first bend in the road. The trees were probably retained for aesthetic reasons to add natural beauty and stature to the new residential development. Although it has not been possible identify

FIGURE 13. This photograph taken around 1915 shows the remarkable line of mature trees that stood in a line down the centre of Stafford Road in Weston-super-Mare. No record of these trees can be found after the 1920s.

FIGURE 14. These trees were remnants from a previous landscape and were incorporated as street trees in Wingrove Road, Newcastle, when the area was developed as a residential suburb in late Victorian and Edwardian times. The photograph was taken around 1905.

the species, they may have been elms, possibly Wheatley elm (*Ulmus minor* 'Sarniensis').

No record of these trees can be found after the 1920s and it is assumed that they were felled soon after that time as they became a hazard with the increasing use of motor vehicles. There are now a small number of street trees, mostly *Sorbus* and *Betula* species, along this part of Stafford Road that have been planted in the normal manner in the footway.

Wingrove Road, Newcastle

Wingrove Road is a residential street in Newcastle that runs northwards from its junction with the main Westgate Road (A186), a few miles west from the city centre. The road has undergone at least two major building phases from when the district was initially developed as a residential suburb in late Victorian and Edwardian times with a mix of both middle class and working class housing. Examination of a photograph of Wingrove Road from *c.* 1905 identified some trees located at the roadside on the southern end of the road (Figure 14). There are two groups of trees on either side of the road, mostly in the footway but some are in the roadway close to the kerb. A lone tree is located further down the street and this is also in the roadway. From the size of the trees, they appear to age between 20–50 years old. It is not possible to determine the species with accuracy but they may be a mix of sycamore (*Acer pseudoplantanus*) and other deciduous trees. From the age of the trees they probably pre-date the houses by many years.

From the evidence available it appears that the trees were formerly in a rural landscape and incorporated into the streetscape when the residential suburb was first built. This would have been when many existing roads and new roads were being systematically planted with street trees. The property developers for this new suburb were simply taking advantage of some existing trees on the site to provide some 'instant' street trees. This explains their random arrangement and location both on the footway and in the road. Apart from a solitary lime tree, there are no longer any street trees in the older southern part of Wingrove Road where the photo was taken. However, there are plenty of street trees in the more recently built northern end, now called Wingrove Road North.

Remnants from estates and pleasure grounds

Many examples of remnant street trees originate from the grounds of country estates formerly owned by the aristocracy or wealthy industrialists. In the case of native species these may have been located on what was agricultural land or woodland, while most of the exotic species would have been specimen trees in the pleasure grounds close to the mansion. There are also a few examples of complete avenues of trees that once stood majestically alongside the main drive to the former mansion and which now stand as massive street trees in residential developments.

Pine Tree Avenue, Leicester

If you travel east from the centre of Leicester, in the East Midlands of England, after a few miles you will come to Humberstones Park where you can turn off north into Pine Tree Avenue. Seeing the street sign for this you may expect to find some pine trees along this road. Instead, you will be amazed to discover an extraordinary avenue of giant sequoia trees (*Sequoiadendron giganteum*) lining this quiet residential road (Figure 15). How these majestic trees came to tower over the houses on either side of this suburban road is a fascinating story.

The land on which these residential properties now stand was once part of a landed estate, owned originally by the wealthy Paget family of Humberstones, then a village on the outskirts of Leicester. In the mid-nineteenth century, Thomas Paget built Humerstones Hall as the family home and commissioned the landscaping of the grounds, work that was continued by his son, Thomas Tertius Paget (Scott pers. comm., 2016). Part of this landscaping included the planting of an avenue of giant sequoia trees at the edges of the driveway up to Humberstones Hall. The discovery of this tree in California in the 1850s had caused a stir in Britain and the landed class were keen to plant it on their estates, often to create spectacular avenues (Mitchell 1996, 145–150). While there is no precise date for the planting of this avenue, it is estimated that the trees are now around 150 years old (Leicester City Council, 2014). Maps of the Humberstone Estate in 1885 clear show the line of trees along the driveway.

In the early 1920s, the Humberstone Estate was sold by the Paget family to a property developer as land for house building (Scott pers. comm., 2016). The Hall itself was demolished in 1923 but it was decided to retain the avenue of giant sequoia trees along the driveway and let them act as spectacular street trees either side of a newly constructed road called Pine Tree Avenue. The houses that were built along this road were high-quality detached dwellings.

Several trees have been lost over the years resulting in some large gaps in the original evenly-spaced avenue (Leicester City Council, 2014). The majority of the remaining trees are situated in the footways and are either owned by the Council or jointly owned with the adjacent property owner. A few are in front gardens and exclusively owned by the respective property owner. In 2001, the Council placed 28 individual trees under the protection of a Tree Preservation Order. As might be imagined, in recent years there has been some concern expressed by local residents regarding potential conflicts between these enormous trees and the foundations of the houses. This concern was followed by a number of insurance claims. In an effort to resolve the situation, some local people have been calling for the trees to be removed and replaced with more suitable species (Stephenson 2009). Others have highlighted the fact that the trees give tremendous character to the street and are of undoubted heritage value. They believe any problems caused by the trees can be managed without the necessity for removal.

It might be assumed that the extraordinary avenue of giant sequoia trees in Pine Tree Avenue would be unique in Britain. However, there is at least one similar example at Canons Park Drive in Edgware, North London. These giant sequoia trees originated as the ornamental drive to a large nineteenth century house that was on the magnificent Canons Estate that once belonged to the Dukes of Chandos in the eighteenth century (Elvin 1950). The avenue was later incorporated into a new housing development in a manner similar to that at Pine Tree Avenue.

Cedar at Wake Green, Birmingham

A few miles south from Birmingham city centre on Yardley Wood Road is the junction with Wake Green Road, located in the Moseley district of the city. There, standing proudly in the footway at this busy crossroads is a huge cedar

FIGURE 15. This extraordinary avenue of giant sequoia trees lining Pine Tree Avenue, a quiet residential road in Leicester, was formerly the avenue along the driveway up to Humberstones Hall.

PHOTO: MICHAEL BEDDOW.

tree (*Cedrus libani*) (Figure 16). It seems most unlikely that anybody would chose this spot to plant a cedar as a street tree, which raised the question of how it came to be located there. Research by the author and the Local History Group of the Moseley Society has revealed the history of this very unusual street tree.

The cedar was originally in the pleasure grounds of a large country estate called The Vale, located near the boundary of that property and close to Wake Green Road (Gresham pers. comm., 2016). A map from 1888 shows the Vale as a large house with associated grounds situated in the northeast quadrant of the junction where the cedar tree now stands. The Vale later became a school for girls, which was sold in 1891 and became known as Moseley College.

FIGURE 16. The majestic cedar tree was originally in the pleasure grounds of a large country estate and now stands at the junction of Yardley Wood Road and Wake Green Road, a few miles south of Birmingham city centre.

Throughout this time the cedar tree would have stood very close to the road junction, although behind a fence and on private land. Nevertheless, it can be ascertained from old maps that the tree would have been very visible to road users and pedestrians and a familiar feature in the landscape.

Moseley College closed in 1968 and the site was sold for housing. Around this time a road-widening scheme was undertaken at this junction to accommodate the increasing flow of traffic in this part of Birmingham. The proposed new width of the road took in land on which the cedar tree was standing (Gresham pers. comm., 2016). There was some debate about whether the tree should be removed as a potential obstruction or retained in the new footway as part of the road improvements. As the tree was in good health and considered by many local people to be an attractive feature in the landscape, it was eventually decided it should be spared. In 2015, the lower trunk of this cedar was damaged in a car crash and is hoped this will not lead to fungal infection and decay. It would be a shame to lose this remarkable tree that is such a refreshing and surprising sight at this busy crossroads not far from the centre of Birmingham.

The Boulevard, Wilmslow Road, Manchester

A section of Wilmslow Road in Manchester was a popular subject for photographs in the 1900s, appearing on several early postcards. Known as The Boulevard (also The Boulevards or The Avenue), it comprised a pleasant avenue of mature roadside trees that became a popular meeting place for local residents (Figure 17). How this attractive arboreal feature came to be established is another fascinating story of remnant street trees.

In the latter half of the nineteenth century, it was necessary to improve the construction of many major roads out of British towns and cities and this often involved road-widening schemes (Guldi 2012). This was particularly applicable to the Wilmslow Road, a major route out of the huge industrial city that was now Manchester. The land on either side of this road was originally part of the Platt Family Estate but since 1672 this had belonged to the Worsley family and was known as the Platt Hall Estate. Photographs from 1865 show this stretch of Wilmslow Road, originally known as Fallowfield Brow, as quite narrow and with no trees on the footway, only those behind walls and fences at the back of the footway (Anderson pers. comm., 2016). These were from a shelterbelt of trees that had been planted on the boundary of the estate lands. At some point over the next 30 years the road was widened, the walls and fences removed and the trees that lay behind these were incorporated into new footways. Photographs from 1903 show those trees, now much larger, growing in the footways of a much wider road. It is obvious from the random arrangement of these trees that they had not been deliberately planted as street trees but were remnants from a past landscape.

Another opportunity for further improvements to this stretch of the road arose with developments in tram technology. Horse-drawn omnibuses had operated along Wilmslow Road from before 1850 and in 1877 the Rusholme Board of Health gained Parliamentary approval to lay tramlines (Anderson 2015). When Rusholme was incorporated into the City of Manchester in 1885, the City Council decided to invest heavily in improving the route and this was electrified in 1902 together with the introduction of new trams. As part of this general upgrading of the road, there was some consideration given to felling the trees. Fortunately, the City Council decided to retain the trees when local residents expressed their firm opposition. It was also decided to incorporate

FIGURE 17. This section of Wilmslow Road in Manchester, known as The Boulevard, was a popular meeting place for local residents and the subject of many photographs and postcard images in the 1900s.

some landscape improvements and this included placing seating around the base of many of the roadside trees. It seems that the addition of seating to this stretch of road is what prompted its use as a popular meeting place.

The location of the Boulevard as an attractive and convenient gathering place for local residents was further increased when the land to the west of the road was purchased by the City of Manchester, along with the rest of the Worsley Estate, and converted into a public open space called Platt Fields Park. The souvenir booklet published in May 1910 when the Park was formally opened states that the

> gloomy high brick walls of the eighteenth century have been removed and light iron railings substituted. A wide promenade now adorns the Wilmslow Road frontage, where the fine old trees have been carefully preserved and surrounded with seats. A view of the park is thus opened out to the thousands of citizens who daily pass along the Wilmslow Road
>
> Anderson 2015

Photographs from the 1910s and 1920s show substantial numbers of people gathered on the Boulevard, many of them mothers or nannies, evidenced by all the prams that can be spotted.

Further widening of the footway and the road seems to have been undertaken around 1920, although most of the trees of the Boulevard were retained. By 1922, other less prominent roadside trees in the district were coming under threat of removal from road widening (Weston Wright 1922, 9). The trees in the Boulevard were eventually removed, although it has not been possible to establish a precise date for this. As no photos of this popular landmark could be found that were dated later than 1929, it seems likely this occurred not long after that time.

Tree-lined roads through commons and early parks

There are some interesting examples of remnant street trees that were formerly part of either semi-natural treecover alongside roads through common land or by roads in early public parks. In both cases these roadside trees were often supplemented or replaced by more formal plantings and amenity landscaping as the area became increasing urbanised and the roads carried more traffic.

Tree-lined roads through commons

Common lands have their origins in medieval times and were part of the estate held by the lord of the manor that was subject to various rights by commoners, such as the right to graze cattle or gather firewood (Shaw-Lefevre 1894). By the mid-nineteenth century, vast areas of common land had fallen victim to the enclosures, which were Acts of Parliament that privatised this land. However, some common lands on the fringe of towns and cities that were saved from enclosure had a role in helping to promote street tree planting. The naturally occurring trees on urban fringe commons that grew close to the road had always functioned as roadside trees. Then, in the late nineteenth century when street tree planting was becoming popular, the roadsides through many urban fringe commons were planted up with rows of trees at regular spacing, to supplement the trees that were already there. A good example of this is Southampton Common and its area known as the Avenue.

The first written record of Southampton Common occurs in 1228 when a dispute over ownership rights led to its legal designation as common land (Thompson 1979, 1). Even in those early times, there were well-used tracks through the common linking the town of Southampton, situated on the south coast of England, with other towns and villages to the north of this. One of these tracks eventually became the main A33 road that runs north out of Southampton towards London. This is the location of what became known as The Avenue.

From the mid-eighteenth century, the Town Council adopted a more proactive attitude towards the trees on the common (Thompson 1979, 19). On many sections of road through the common the treecover came right up to the roadside but in others this was very patchy and open. The development of Southampton as a spa town from 1740 led the Council to seek ways to improve the approaches to the town, especially the main road to London running through Southampton Common. In 1744, 138 trees were felled on the common and from the revenue generated two rows of elm trees were planted along this route at John a Guernsey's Cross, the site of a medieval cross at the south end of the road. In 1750 and 1753, the Mayor was required to replace any decayed trees 'in the Avenue on the Cross', and in 1763 the Council Minutes record that several trees in the Avenue were dead, the Mayor being ordered to replace them.

It has not been possible to establish when other parts of the Avenue were planted, although it seems likely that areas in the northern section were planted after 1760 when the newly-established Turnpike Trust straightened and widened this road through the common (Thompson 1979, 20). In 1844, the future of the common as a public open space became secure as it was designated as a public park for the people of Southampton (*ibid.*, 25). Thanks to careful management, the Avenue continued as a magnificent arboreal feature for visitors travelling to Southampton from the north. Photographs from the 1890s onwards shows a mixture of young and mature trees at regular spacing, often in two lines either side of the road. When the early horse-drawn trams in Southampton were replaced with electric trams from 1900 onwards, some trees along the Avenue were pruned back in order to accommodate the overhead wires. In recent times, there has been a noticeable change in the style of landscape management for the Avenue. There is no longer a distinct avenue as the earlier regularly spaced trees along the roadside have been replaced by more semi-natural treecover. Nevertheless, this remains a wonderful 'green' corridor into Southampton.

There are other good examples of where naturally occurring trees growing adjacent to roads through ancient commons have been the forerunners of more systematic roadside or street tree planting. South and west London is particularly fortunate in having large areas of former common land that is now managed as public parks. Through these commons run numerous roads that now carry high volumes of traffic. However, many of these stretches of road were planted with trees long before the days of the motor car. For instance, Gunnersbury Avenue through Ealing Common in West London was extensively planted from the 1880s with various species of roadside trees at regular spacings. This is now part of the very busy North Circular Road. In South London, The Avenue that runs along the side of Clapham Common was also planted in the 1880s with trees at regular spacings. This is now part of the equally busy South Circular Road.

Tree-lined roads though early public parks

Visitors to London are frequently impressed by the extensive areas of greenspace in the centre of the capital that are the Royal Parks. People without the time to explore these parks on foot can always travel through some of them in their private cars or on tourist buses. One particularly attractive route is the West Carriage Drive that runs through Hyde Park. This was constructed in the 1820s as an entirely new road, mostly for the popular upper class recreation of carriage driving (see Chapter 2). The route included a bridge over the Serpentine Lake and it served to formally divide Hyde Park from Kensington Gardens (Williams 1978, 97). As part of the landscaping that followed the road construction, many trees were planted along either side of the route. While this is possibly the most famous tree-lined road through an early British public park, another lesser known example is given.

Royal Victoria Park in Bath was opened as a public park in 1830, although not initially a municipal park as the Corporation only leased the land and did not own it (Conway 1991, 15). The park was designed by Edward Davis, the city architect, and the trees are believed to have been selected by John Claudius Loudon. This beautiful 57 acre (23 ha) site has always been popular with local residents and tourists being just a short walk from the city centre. From the outset one of its most attractive landscape features was its approach road, known as the Avenue, leading up to the stone entrance plinths and the main part of the park. Photographs from 1906, before the arrival of any significant motor traffic, shows the Avenue as a well-constructed road with wide footways and street lighting and plenty of mature trees lining the route. In recent years, the approach road to the park has become known as Royal Avenue and at weekends and holidays in the summer months this can carry a significant volume of traffic to and from the park. The landscape along the route remains semi-formal with plenty of treecover in addition to some formal elements such as displays of bedding plants. Royal Victoria Park's beautifully landscaped approach road remains a popular attraction for Bath's tourists and locals.

Early street trees in Oxford and London

By the start of the nineteenth century in Britain there was still no concerted effort to establish trees in streets on a systematic basis. Nevertheless, there were some examples of trees that had been planted many years ago near to country roads or lanes that with urban expansion were now effectively functioning as street trees. Because the location of these trees was not originally alongside a busy urban road we can consider them as another type of remnant street trees. We conclude this chapter by looking at an example from Oxford and two from London.

St Giles, Oxford

St Giles is a wide boulevard that runs north from the city centre in modern Oxford. Its origins go back several hundred years as it was named after the parish and church of St Giles, founded in the twelfth century in fields to the north of the medieval town (Wood 1974). After the English Civil War there was an increase in house building in the area and it became more urbanised with a ribbon development of houses either side of what was now St Giles Street. An engraving of this from 1779 shows some mature elm trees on either side of the road (Figure 18). A few years before this engraving was made, Sir John Peshall described St Giles Street as a 'rus in urbe' (having all the advantages of town and country) being planted with rows of elms on each side and having parterres of green before the respective houses (Jenkins 2015). Although there is no record to say whether these elms had been specifically planted as roadside trees, this reference suggests they were.

Despite being regarded by Peshall as an attractive feature, the elm trees were all cut down in an 'improvement scheme' towards the end of eighteenth century (Jenkins 2015). It is likely that this action was prompted by some proposals for improving St Giles put forward by Rev. E. Tatham, later the Rector of Lincoln College. He thought that since the trees were 'out of character, and break in upon the eye, they should by all means be removed'. The felling of these trees was met with considerable disapproval in some quarters and an epigram on the deed was written entitled *Ye bursar of St John's cutting down a fine Row of Trees*. This ends with the lines: 'This rogue the gallows for his fate foresees/And bears a like antipathy to trees.'

While the elm trees were undoubtedly missed by some local residents, it was many years before they were replaced and majestic trees once again lined the roadside of St Giles (Jenkins 2015). Around 1875, plane trees (*Platanus x acerifolia*) were planted at a time when street tree planting was becoming popular and the plane was the preferred choice for many urban locations. These trees have now

FIGURE 18. St Giles, Oxford, in 1779, drawn and engraved by M.A. Rooker. Compared with the same view today, it is remarkable how little has changed in the basic appearance of the street in over 200 years.

CREDIT: STEPHANIE JENKINS.

grown to a similar size to the original elms. If the 1779 engraving is compared with the same view of St Giles today, it is remarkable how little has changed in the basic appearance of the street in over 200 years. St Giles and its trees make an attractive venue for the famous St Giles Fair, which dates back to medieval times. The street is closed off to regular traffic for the two days of the fair.

Cheyne Walk, Chelsea and Church Row, Hampstead

At Cheyne Walk in Chelsea, on the north bank of the River Thames, a number of trees were planted in the early 1800s along the length of rough roadway running parallel to the river. They may have been planted to provide the residents of Cheyne Walk with some protection from the wind and rain that could blow across river. As the nineteenth century progressed, more expensive houses and shops were established along Cheyne Walk and the route became a made-up road. A print from 1860 shows that the trees were retained and these were now mature specimens (Walford 1878, 60). It can also be established that the trees were elms from an article in *The Garden* (1874, 524) that records their demise. This states that recent improvements made to the Embankment had resulted in the death of several fine elm trees along the river at Cheyne Walk. It was thought this was due to grade changes around the base of the trees. This section of the riverfront is now called the Chelsea Embankment and is lined with magnificent plane trees.

Hampstead has long been one of London's desirable residential districts. Located in the north of the city it has some very expensive areas, particularly next to the beautiful Hampstead Heath. In the eighteenth century Hampstead was not part of London but a separate village in the countryside north of the capital (Richardson 1999). From the early seventeenth century, many grand houses were built in Hampstead and in 1747 the newly rebuilt church of St John-at-Hampstead was dedicated by the Bishop of Llanduff. The street that ran across the front of the church was known as Church Row and the buildings on the south side date from 1720. An engraving from 1750 shows some mature trees on the other side of the street opposite smart Georgian terraced houses (Figure 19). From the shape of the trees and records of similarly aged trees in the vicinity it is likely that these were elms (Smith pers. comm., 2016). No records were found giving the origin of these trees but they may have been remnants from a past landscape or planted specifically as street trees to adorn the new residential development. Whatever the case, trees have always been present at this location in Church Row. As Hampstead became more urbanised it was incorporated into the London metropolis in 1889. Despite all the built development around those original trees, when they finally declined or died they were replaced with new plantings. Photographs from 1890 show a line of six lime trees probably 30 years old, standing directly in the carriageway at the same location and without any physical protection (Figure 20). These may be the first replacements for the trees shown in the 1750 print or later replacements. The trees are still growing at this location, although the line is now on a traffic island. The lime tree at the end furthest from the Church is the only original tree from the 1890 photograph, the others having been replaced with different species after the 1970s (Smith pers. comm., 2016). Sadly, this remaining lime has suffered damage to its base from vehicle strikes in its exposed position and may have to be removed within a few years. Nevertheless, it was pleasing to note that the London Borough of Camden maintains this historic landscape feature with careful management and replacement trees when necessary.

FIGURE 19. A view of Church Row, Hampstead, in 1750 that shows some mature trees on the other side of the street opposite smart Georgian terraced houses. The church of St John-at-Hampstead is in the background.

FIGURE 20. This photograph of Church Row, Hampstead, was taken around 1890 and shows a similar view to the one above. There is now a line of six lime trees standing directly in the carriageway at the same location as the trees in the 1750 image.

CHAPTER FOUR

Early Influences from Overseas

The overseas influences on the early development of street tree planting in Britain were many and varied. In terms of the landscape forms that were precursors to street trees, many originated in continental Europe, especially France (see Chapter 2). In this chapter we explore how early examples of actual street tree planting in overseas countries, especially in continental Europe, encouraged British efforts to green the streets of our towns and cities. These early practical examples ranged from the street planting in seventeenth century Amsterdam to the first Parisian boulevards in the 1830s. While Georgian Britain did not respond to those early continental examples of street tree planting, it did pioneer some important street improvements that helped pave the way for tree planting later. When some British cities eventually began to systematically plant their streets with trees from the 1860s onwards, other high-profile overseas examples from cities such as Paris, Vienna, Berlin and Washington were crucial in helping to maintain the momentum of the developing Victorian street tree movement. Also examined in this chapter are some instances of the resistance to this idea from those who did not view streets as a suitable location for trees.

Moses Cook, John Evelyn and the seventeenth century

Although the early walks, promenades and cours in British towns and cities were a welcome addition to the urban scene in the eighteenth century, there was no real attempt to plant trees in streets. Any existing street trees that were remnants from past landscapes would often have been regarded as obstructions and subject to pressures to have them removed, even when they had strong historical or cultural significance. Most streets in urban centres were quite narrow and meandering lanes. They were not viewed as appropriate locations for tree planting, even where there might have been space to establish one or two trees.

Despite these generally negative attitudes towards street trees, some highly-regarded British horticulturists who had travelled on the Continent were able to witness for themselves that streets and trees were not necessarily mutually exclusive. Both Moses Cook and John Evelyn were full of admiration for the street tree planting in some cities in Holland, particularly Amsterdam. Cook (1676) remarked, 'And a wise man's opinion was that the [street] plantings of lime-trees in the Cities in Holland adde much to the Health of the Inhabitants; and it is my belief.' Evelyn was even more enthusiastic when he visited

Amsterdam and saw plenty of lime trees along many streets in the Dutch capital (Figure 21). Writing in his diary in 1641, he stated:

> ... and yet their streets even, straight, and well paved, the houses so uniform and planted with lime trees, as nothing can be more beautiful ... The Kaiser's or Emperor's Graft, which is an ample and long street, appearing like a city in a forest; the lime trees planted just before each house.
>
> Evelyn 1901, 22–23

John Evelyn is famous as the author of *Sylva or a Discourse of Forest Trees*, first published in 1664 and regarded by some authorities as one of the world's greatest books on trees in any language (Campbell-Culver 2006, 46). Despite Evelyn's obvious love of trees and his admiration for the trees in the streets of Amsterdam, there is no mention of street trees in his *Sylva* (Evelyn 1664). In some respects this is not surprising since the writers of that time on horticultural and landscape subjects did not have any significant urban focus. Public parks of the sort we enjoy today where but a distant dream and the idea of lining our streets with trees would have seemed to many a ridiculous proposition. Even when Thomas Fairchild (1722) wrote his influential book *The City Gardener*, the first British text on urban horticulture, there was no mention of street trees. This is despite the book having a specific urban focus that included information about the trees, shrubs and other plants which thrived best in the smoke-filled air of London. There was also plenty of discussion of trees in residential squares and even some mention of growing fruit trees in roof gardens (*ibid.*, 57) – but the thought of trees growing along the streets of London did not occur to him.

It is sometimes remarked that the tragedy of the Great Fire of London in 1666 also offered a unique opportunity to redesign London. After the Great Fire, in which Covent Garden and its pioneering Italianate piazza survived, John Evelyn proposed a scheme for a garden city that included a greenbelt of gardens and plantations to make London the envy of the world (Evelyn 1938). Christopher Wren and Robert Hooke also proposed equally ambitious and visionary plans. The rebuilding of London was an opportunity to implement new ideas in town planning on a scale that was previously inconceivable. Many of those ideas were emanating from the Continent and this was a chance to pioneer some of those imaginative urban landscapes in Britain. Although not specifically identified by any of the designers, the remodelling of the capital's streets into broad and straight thoroughfares would have created plenty of opportunities for street tree planting at a later date. Unfortunately, this huge but nonetheless exciting challenge was not taken up by Charles II. Instead of seizing the moment with an imaginative redesigning of his capital, he succumbed to pressure from vested interests. Everything was put back as it was, apart from some major new buildings and the broadening of a few streets. This historic lack of vision in seventeenth century London can be contrasted with the assertive approach of Napoleon III and Baron von Haussmann in rebuilding Paris in the nineteenth century, now an internationally admired model of urban planning (Kirkland 2013).

Improvements in Georgian London and continental cities

Despite the virtual absence of trees from British streets in the seventeenth and eighteenth centuries, by the eighteenth century they were a more common sight in some other European cities (Lawrence 2006, 43). Some leading European authorities on urban landscaping were now actively promoting formal street plantings where they were not already established. Johann Peter Willebrand, a Danish architect working in Germany, was one of these. In his influential work *Grundriß einer schönen Stadt* (plan of a beautiful city), Willebrand (1775, section 93) highlights the prestige value of trees in front of houses. At the same time he warns against them being planted too close to houses where they could offer a hiding place for thieves or trap moisture that could damage the building fabric. Willebrand also gave recommendations for species of tree suitable for this purpose and this mainly featured large forest-type trees such as lime, horse chestnut, spruce and fir.

While Britain was not following the growing continental fashion of planting street trees, it was about to lead the way in other urban improvements related to streets. As with many aspects of urban life, both good and bad, eighteenth century London led the way for the rest of the country. A real turning-point in the urban improvement of the capital was the first *Westminster Paving Act* of 1762 (Rudé 1971, 136). This was quickly followed by Acts applied to other parts of the metropolis and also to towns and cities throughout Britain. Prior to these Acts, all measures relating to paving had depended on the civic duty of the householder to keep the street in front of their own door in good repair. Without the cooperation of the householder, little would happen as the old methods of enforcement were cumbersome, slow and uncertain. Now paving commissioners were appointed with paid staff at their disposal, and infringement of the Acts brought summary punishment by the magistrates. Gutters were now built on either side of the road, and in the main streets flat Purbeck stone replaced the old rounded pebbles. The Acts also provided for basic maintenance and cleaning as well as the removal of obstructions. Other road improvements included convex carriageways and underground drains. Among other provisions of the 1762 Act was a requirement that the major streets in Westminster should be provided with separate footways (Lawrence 2006, 86). This was accomplished mostly by erecting posts of wood or stone to separate the pedestrian zone on each side from the space reserved for horses and vehicles in the centre. While these were not uncommon by then, this was the first law requiring them to be widely used in a city. The addition of footways transformed street use for pedestrians who could now stroll along them undisturbed by vehicles and animals. While this improvement had no immediate impact on the planting of trees, it would provide a suitable place in the urban streetscape for trees in the nineteenth century. The essential conditions for tree survival in streets had been created with the footway space providing a planting site with improved drainage and some protection from

soil compaction and injury. Further advances were made in London with the *Metropolitan Paving Act* of 1817 that permitted the various paving authorities to extend their boundaries to fill in the gaps that lay between them (Hart 1959, 65). It also gave them, as local authorities, the power to acquire land for street widening and extension (Edwards 1898, 11).

As a consequence of these various Acts, London and other British cities took on a far more attractive appearance. Twenty-five years after the first Paving Acts were passed, a commentator based in London proudly described the whole enterprise as 'an undertaking which has introduced a degree of elegance and symmetry into the streets of the metropolis that is the admiration of all Europe and far exceeds anything of the kind in the modern world' (Rudé 1971, 137).

With more suitable conditions for street trees created by the Paving Acts, and with the tree-lined streets in some continental cities now admired by many relevant professionals, it seemed possible that this form of urban improvement might be encouraged in Britain. However, there still appeared to be little interest in this prospect among the wider urban population and some outright opposition from some supposedly enlightened minds. For example, the author John Stewart defined the city in opposition to the country and insisted that

FIGURE 21. View of Westerkerk, Amsterdam, painted around 1660 by Jan van der Heyden. In the mid-seventeenth century both Moses Cook and John Evelyn were full of admiration for the street tree planting in some Dutch cities, particularly Amsterdam.

its identity should not be compromised by such ineffectual and anomalous rural reminders as street trees (Longstaffe-Gowan 2001, 208). He was not supportive of the concept of *rus in urbe* (the countryside in the city) that was preoccupying the minds of many other Enlightenment intellectuals. In his influential book *Critical Observations on the Buildings and Improvements of London*, Stewart states:

> The rus in urbe is a preposterous idea at best; a garden in a street is not less absurd than a street in a garden; and he that wishes to have a row of trees before his door in town, betrays almost as false a taste as he that would build a row of houses for an avenue to his seat in the country.
>
> Stewart 1771, 14

By the end of the eighteenth century there was increasing interest and international uniformity in the design of city streets. Many new features had been developed and popularised in Britain, such as macadam road surfaces, storm drains and sewers, piped water, footways, house numbering and post boxes (Elmes 1828). While these did not apply universally to all urban areas and were initially in the more wealthy districts of the larger cities, they did signal that Britain was one of the leading European countries in these aspects of urban improvement and civil engineering. It is interesting to note that the British examples in road construction and street amenities were widely admired and later adopted in other parts of Europe (Lawrence 1988, 370). For example, before 1800 few cities in continental Europe had footways. By 1822 only 267 m of footways existed in all of Paris, but by 1848 the total had risen to 260 km. Nevertheless, as the Victorian era approached trees were not an element of British street design and it would be some time before they embraced this continental fashion. Instead, the British continued their preference for locating urban trees mainly in residential squares, crescents and pleasure gardens.

Continental travels of Loudon and others

The continental influences on British landscape during the seventeenth and eighteenth centuries had resulted largely from the observations and experiences of upper class young men from Britain who had travelled through Europe on their Grand Tour as part of an educational rite of passage (Hibbert 1987). During the Napoleonic Wars (1803–1815) this practice virtually ceased as much of the Continent and many of the usual destinations became caught up in violent conflict. After Waterloo and the defeat of the French and their allies, travel to Continental Europe resumed and British citizens once again became confident they could journey in safety. Embarking on the Grand Tour was now a cheaper and easier proposition, thanks in part to the introduction of steam-powered transportation. This made it more accessible to educated men and women of privilege rather than just for the ruling elite. While visiting the great cities of Europe they could see for themselves the exciting developments being made in urban design, landscape and town planning.

Some of those new British travellers to the Continent in the 1820s and 30s were inspired by the recent urban improvements in some of the cities they visited and were keen to pass on those ideas to their contemporaries at home. Leading the way was John Claudius Loudon, the most eminent horticulturist. Loudon undertook a number of European tours during this time and reported on these in his own publication, the *Gardener's Magazine*. This was Britain's first periodical devoted solely to horticulture and was published from 1826 until its last issue in January 1844, just a month after Loudon's death. Loudon and some of his other correspondents inevitably made comparisons between what they had witnessed on the Continent and the shortcomings of the current situation in Britain.

There is an amusing account of Loudon's own practical efforts to introduce Londoners to the continental idea of street tree planting. In the early 1820s, when Loudon built his house in Porchester Terrace, Bayswater, he decided to plant a sumach (*Rhus typhina*) at the edge of the footway, opposite his residence (Humphreys 1873, 130). Unfortunately, this unusual action was met with firm opposition from both the authorities and his neighbours. The district surveyor complained that this would shade the pathway and keep it damp, and the neighbours declared that it would be very unpleasant to pass under the drip of its leaves in wet weather. So, the beautiful young sumach had to be rooted out and the footway reinstated.

Like many of his contemporaries, Loudon admired some of the well-planned cities on the Continent and he noted that much of this was achieved through efficient and effective systems of governance. Returning from his third journey abroad, in January 1829, he was excited by the integrated approach to all manner of civil engineering projects he had observed in the southeast of Germany. The Bavarian government had formed a standing commission made up of councillors, engineers, architects, and the landscape gardener Charles Sekell, Director General of the Court Gardens (Simo 1988, 221). This commission was empowered to improve the management of canals, bridges, public buildings and gardens, national forests, and public roads. Loudon had much to say on the subject of roads when comparing the German and British situation. On the topic of the governance of roads, Loudon was unequivocal in his belief that Britain should adopt the German approach and envisioned the whole country laid out with roads 'as fine as in a gentleman's park', where all roads would be subject to one general law relating to every aspect of road design and construction, including the planting and management of roadside trees (Loudon 1831a, 522). However, Loudon was enough of a realist to foresee the difficulties in trying to impose national standards for roads in Britain, a country where the independence of local government was highly prized. These are astute observations by Loudon on the importance of governance with regard to roads. As will be seen in Chapter 5, it was the reforms in local government in Britain in the mid-nineteenth century that helped pave the way for the systematic planting of street trees.

When it came to Belgium and especially its capital city, Loudon's interest was focused directly on urban trees. In 1827, he published an account of the boulevards of Brussels written by a regular but anonymous reader of *Gardener's Magazine* who lived in the city (*Gardener's Magazine* 1827, 87). The reader noted that among the most recent improvements in Brussels, the boulevards were particularly notable. In 1818, after the Napoleonic Wars when political stability had returned, the city authorities organised a contest for plans to demolish the city's ramparts and replace them with boulevards. The proposal of Jean-Baptiste Vifquain was ultimately chosen. His design comprised lines of elm or lime trees, enclosing three distinct and parallel roads for foot passengers, carriages and horses. The boulevards were located on the site of the city's old ramparts, which had now been removed and levelled. To allow continued taxation of commercial goods entering the city, a barrier with a ditch running its length was installed and some of the gateways retained. Uninterrupted views of the beautiful surrounding countryside were afforded on one side of the boulevards, while the side next to the city was faced with handsome new houses or gardens. In 1827, the improvement was ongoing, having been completed on the east, south, and south-west sides of the city. This now offered the city's residents and visitors a delightful walk, ride or carriage drive under the shade of beautiful trees which ran for two or three miles along the line of the former city walls (Figure 22). Work was still in progress on the north side.

FIGURE 22. Boulevard et Porte de Laeken in Brussels, Belgium, from an engraving drawn by Fussell Delt in 1838. When John Claudius Loudon visited Brussels in the late 1820s he was able to see for himself the city's magnificent new boulevards.

When Loudon visited Brussels he was able to see for himself the city's new boulevards (Loudon 1827, 461). Apart from the beautiful spectacle of these lengthy avenues of trees, what struck him most was the arboricultural competence of Belgians. In his view, the careful preparation of the tree-pit, the attention to post-planting maintenance and standards of tree pruning were in advance of the usual standards of practice in Britain.

Of all the early nineteenth century continental developments concerning street trees, Loudon and his contemporaries were most impressed with those in the French capital, Paris. On returning from his tour of France and Germany in the autumn of 1828, Loudon wrote enthusiastically about the Parisian *Grands Boulevards*, which along with its public parks, acted like 'breathing zones' and were a source of great enjoyment for everyone (Loudon 1830, 644). These boulevards were pedestrian promenades and, like those in Brussels, built on the remnants of the old city walls. The trees on the boulevards consisted almost entirely of the small-leaved elm, although by the time Loudon wrote the account of his visit, many had been cut down during the disturbances of the July Revolution in 1830. While Loudon was confident that these would be replaced very soon, he did have some concerns about the choice of replacement species. He felt that instead of 'monotonous lines of elms they may be a representative system of all the vigorous-growing timber trees which would flourish in the open air in the latitude of Paris'. Always keen to promote his own ideas and connections, Loudon suggests that these boulevards should use his own designs and that suitable trees could be obtained from his friends at Loddiges Nursery in Hackney, London.

It should be noted that when Loudon visited Paris in 1828 the Champs Elysées was not the busy urban thoroughfare we know today (Figure 23). Instead, Loudon describes it as 'rather a wood, than either gardens or fields, as its name might seem to import; and it partakes of the mingled characteristics of our Hyde Park and Kensington Gardens' (Loudon 1830, 646). It was still functioning as a public promenade, although this was to change when it became the property of the city of Paris in 1828, the same year as Loudon's visit. From 1830 onwards, some time before Haussmann's renovation of Paris, the prefect Rambuteau created the Champs-Élysées avenue in Paris, lined with British-style footways and planted with trees (Pradines 2009, 8). By contrast, when Loudon visited the Bois de Boulogne, it was much as we know it today, a great wooded area with tree-lined roads running through it. Unfortunately, the trees had suffered much damage when the wood was occupied by the Cossacks and other foreign troops after the defeat of Napoleon's forces at the battle of Paris in 1814 (Loudon 1831b, 7). While many of the trees that had lined its roads were cut down by the troops, Loudon was delighted to see that these had been replanted in considerable numbers by the French authorities and were being maintained to a high standard.

Despite the growing number of favourable reports of street tree planting in some continental cities, there were still voices that cautioned against this in Britain. While some were in outright opposition to any street tree planting,

FIGURE 23. View of the Champs Elysées in Paris from an engraving dated 1789. At that time it not the busy urban thoroughfare we know today or even a tree-lined boulevard but functioned more as a public promenade.

others would only consider this prospect if it involved the sparing use of small ornamental trees. Justification for this was made on the basis of comparing the supposedly spacious conditions of streets in many continental cities with those of the narrow and meandering streets of London. One such voice was Thomas Rutger, a frequent contributor to *Gardener's Magazine*, who resided in Portland Place, London. While Rutger (1835, 513) admired the wide continental boulevards and their large mature trees, he believed the use of the same forest-type trees in the confined and crowded London streets would be 'a great error'.

Boulevards of Paris, Vienna, Berlin and elsewhere

By the 1860s, the systematic planting of trees in streets had finally begun in London and some other British cities and soon developed into a street tree movement across the whole country (see Chapter 5). Throughout the latter part of the nineteenth century, more and more urban centres would begin their own programmes of street tree planting as the idea became increasingly acceptable and popular. While this street tree movement was gaining momentum from its own successes here in Britain, it continued to be encouraged and inspired by continental models, such as the spectacular boulevards of Paris, Brussels, Vienna and Berlin. In numerous articles in British gardening magazines, journals and books the call rang out: if this can be done in those other European cities, why not here? The continental boulevards were also much admired for their generally high standards of maintenance and management, although there were also some British critics of this.

While a detailed account of these continental examples is beyond the scope of this book, it is necessary to give a brief description in order to record their impact on attitudes in Britain. These successful continental efforts to establish trees along busy urban thoroughfares were a major factor in helping to maintain the momentum of Britain's emerging street tree movement in the latter part of the Victorian era.

The boulevards of Paris

By the mid-nineteenth century, Paris led the way with the development of street trees along some of its major routes as other European cities tried to emulate its example (Lawrence 1988, 355). The terms *avenue* and *boulevard* became widely adopted to refer to these wide tree-lined streets that formed a prominent and distinctive element of the street system in Paris. As noted in Chapter 2, the avenue originated as a French Baroque landscape feature involving a straight route lined with trees which prolonged the garden *allée* out into the private park and even beyond. The French word *boulevard* had originally referred to the flat part of a rampart or fortification. The early Parisian *Grands Boulevards* had actually been built on top of the remnants of the old city walls and the more recent outer ring that was pieced together in the 1830s and 1840s (Lawrence 2006, 238). The word *boulevard* acquired its modern meaning when applied to the new streets of central Paris created in the mid-nineteenth century (Jacobs *et al.* 2003, 76–81).

The creation of the Parisian boulevards in the 1850s and '60s was part of a wider renovation of the French capital commissioned by Emperor Napoleon III and directed by his prefect of the Seine, Georges-Eugène Haussmann (Kirkland 2013). This was preceded by the demolition of crowded and unhealthy medieval neighbourhoods that enabled the construction of these new tree-lined streets. It also included the building of parks and squares, the construction of new sewers, fountains and aqueducts and the annexation of suburbs around Paris. Not only were many new boulevards created but the existing old Parisian boulevards were 'Haussmannised' by being broadened and with the addition of more trees, strips of parkland and often bridle-paths (Girouard 1985, 327). This vast urban planning initiative was motivated by a range of factors that were not just about creating a more pleasant, attractive and healthier urban environment. In terms of the new streets, which were often driven through the revolutionary working class districts of the city, there was also an underlying political agenda (Hunt 2004, 230). It is ironic that the magnificent lines of large mature trees that now adorn the Paris boulevards were the result of an urban planning initiative that had highlighted the need for wide avenues to assist the movement of troops, to facilitate artillery fire and discourage the formation of barricades (Jacobs *et al.* 2003, 78).

It should be noted that Haussmann's ability to forge ahead with the new streets, despite widespread opposition from those in his way, was due largely to changes in property rights following the French Revolution (Sala 1864, 337). While Paris was still like London in having many narrow, filthy lanes and old houses, the Revolution had put an end to the property rights of the aristocracy and their resistance to such change, which would undoubtedly have been encountered in London, was no longer an issue. As a result, Napoleon III and Haussmann were able to transform Paris into the cleanest and most handsome city in the world.

It was not long before these wide new Parisian boulevards had an impact on some prominent visitors from Britain. In 1867, the young Irish horticulturist William Robinson travelled to France to cover the Paris *Exposition universelle de 1867*, an international exhibition to showcase French art and industry (Bisgrove 2008, 43). Robinson had been based in London and was engaged by *The Times, Gardeners' Chronicle* and *The Field* to report on this event for their readers. While staying in Paris he was hugely impressed not only by the new parks that had been created but also by the magnificent tree-lined boulevards, unlike anything that was to be found in London (Figure 24). On his return to

FIGURE 24. This engraving shows the Boulevard du Temple in the 1860s and is taken from William Robinson's book *The Parks, Promenades and Gardens of Paris.* When Robinson visited Paris in 1867 he was hugely impressed with the magnificent tree-lined boulevards that had recently been created by Baron von Haussmann for Napoleon III. On his return he argued that British cities should adopt a similarly bold approach to street tree planting.

London he published *The Parks, Promenades and Gardens of Paris*, in which he not only described and evaluated these but also considered them 'in relation to the wants of our own cities', especially the role of smaller parks and boulevards (Robinson 1869). Robinson praises the creation of the Parisian boulevards and bemoans the fact that London has nothing of their equal. While admiring the extensive use of semi-mature tree transplanting in Paris, he was also quite critical of some aspects of practical tree maintenance.

Following William Robinson's visit to Paris his career blossomed to the point where he not only became a leading figure in British gardening but also a major influence on ideas regarding the management of the urban landscape (Bisgrove 2008). He was never short of opinions on horticultural and arboricultural topics and having learnt from the Parisian experience he had much to say about urban greening. For example, he was critical of the substantial amounts of money spent on highly ornamental features such as expensive bedding plants in public parks and felt that some of this money would be better spent on street trees. Robinson was one of the first to highlight the success of the new Parisian boulevards and champion the need for systematic street tree planting in Britain. However, he was quickly followed by other prominent voices from British horticulture and landscape calling for a more continental approach to improving the urban landscape that included the provision of street trees. Of course, there were a few dissenting voices but these tended to focus more on the French approach to the practical management of their street trees (Tillery 1861, 906).

One fascinating piece of information about the Paris boulevards that generated interest among British professionals appeared in *The Garden* in 1874 and this gave details of the costs involved in the planting (*The Garden* 1874a, 205). The information had been reproduced from a recent issue of the French magazine *La Municipalité* and applied to 3- or 4-year old planes (*Platanus x acerifolia*) or horse chestnuts (*Aesculus hippocastanum*). All the operations and materials were costed individually so that British professionals could make the comparisons with these costs in Britain. At the end of the article the total cost for each tree planted was given and when converted to pounds sterling this was £8 1s 7½d. It is interesting to note that almost 85% of the costs were for the removal and replacement of the soil and the cast-iron grating around the base of the tree. In reproducing this article the editors of *The Garden* seemed to be saying to its readers that if the French could afford these costs to produce beautiful tree-lined boulevards, then so should the British.

As time went by, an increasing number of articles appeared in British gardening magazines that lavished praise on the Parisian boulevards. By the end of the Victorian era it was clear to many British professionals that the achievements of the Parisian authorities were far in advance of anything that had happened in London. In 1896 an editorial of the *Gardeners' Chronicle* exclaimed,

The Parisians had the start of us in embellishing their streets, and they carry it out even now on a scale beyond anything we attempt. They have accumulated experience as to what trees to plant in particular localities, how to plant them, in fact, how best to put the trees into such a position as best to adapt themselves to the 'environment' surrounding them.

Gardeners' Chronicle 1896, 400

The following year the same magazine issued another editorial extolling the virtues of the Parisian boulevards. This time it highlighted how much progress had been made by the French capital over recent decades and emphasises the essential role of the municipal authority in achieving this:

> Hardly more than sixty years has passed since the Champs Elysées were truthfully described as impassable by day on account of the bad state of the roads, and by night by reason of the host of vagrants that frequented them. For many years past, thanks largely to improved sanitation and the planting of street trees as a science and an every-day practice, Paris has become assuredly one of the fairest, safest, pleasantest cities in the world. We are often told in this country that land is too valuable to be spared for the growth of trees in our great cities and towns. But 'where there is a will, there is a way'. ...By planting such grand avenues [various famous ones are named], and scores of others almost equally long and spacious, tree-planting has been firmly established as one of the most important functions of the municipality of Paris, and is prosecuted with a skill and energy almost unknown to us in this country.

Gardeners' Chronicle 1897, 165

One of the most eloquent endorsements of the Parisian boulevards was written by an anonymous correspondent to *Woods and Forests* magazine who simply called themselves 'A Traveller'. Although the writer goes on to recognise the constraints of Victorian London's air pollution, they are more concerned with the government's lack of imagination and political will:

> The first thing that strikes an English visitor to Paris is the height and bright aspect of the houses and the abundance of trees, the verdure of which, especially at this season, imparts an air of freshness and beauty on all sides. The English traveller, on issuing from the Gare du Nord, that is to say the station of the French 'Great Northern', and driving to one of those favourite quarters on New Paris which have sprung up around the Arc de l'Etoile, will pass along a series of streets, avenues and boulevards all rendered charmingly fresh and attractive by rows of well-selected trees – first, perhaps an avenue of Horse-Chestnuts; next, a long line of Paulownias ... In other places Limes are substituted, and I notice that an avenue of Ailanthus glandulosa, with its tropical looking pinnate foliage, produced a charming and luxuriant effect; while in other places the Oriental Plane plays a distinguished part. The comparatively smokeless atmosphere of Paris is, it must be admitted, far more favourable to tree growth than that of London; but we might do very much more than has been yet attempted, and if the use of smoke-consuming fire-grates were enforced, there is no reason why London should not rival Paris in the attractive feature of street trees. Many of the new boulevards and avenues of New Paris, in addition to ample trees, are bordered on either side by broad spaces of turf ornamentally planted with flowering shrubs and flower-beds. ...At the west end of London something similar might be effected in many situations ready to hand, if only the taste of those who rule such matters in England could be just a little educated.

Woods and Forests 1884, 499

Boulevards of Vienna, Brussels and Berlin

While the boulevards of Paris were the focus of most British interest, some individuals considered those in Vienna, the Austrian capital, to be superior. The main attraction was the Ringstrasse (Ring Boulevard), the construction of which had been ordered by Emperor Franz Joseph I on Christmas Day in 1857 (Nierhaus 2014). Following a design competition in 1858 civil engineering works continued for several years until it was officially inaugurated in 1865. This magnificent road extends for 2½ miles (4 km) encircling the city centre and was constructed on the space formerly occupied by the city walls, extensive glacis and military fortifications that had protected the heart of Vienna. Within the Ringstrasse a wide belt of parks and tree-lined boulevards was laid out as a suitably grand setting for elegant new government buildings, cultural institutions and apartments, all designed to showcase the grandeur of the Hapsburg Empire (Figure 25). While the Ringstrasse was inspired by the magnificence of the Paris boulevards, the emperor and his advisors were also aware of how these significantly wider streets had demonstrated that the erection of revolutionary barricades was made more difficult.

It was the sheer spaciousness of the Ringstrasse and boulevards of Vienna that attracted most of the favourable comment from British visitors. In many

FIGURE 25. An albumen print dated *c.* 1880 showing of part of the Ringstrasse, Vienna. This wide belt of parks and tree-lined boulevards was laid out as a suitably grand setting for elegant new government buildings, cultural institutions and apartments, all designed to showcase the grandeur of the Hapsburg Empire. It was the sheer spaciousness of the Ringstrasse and boulevards of Vienna that attracted most of the favourable comment from British visitors.

of the boulevards the main carriageway was noticeably wider than those of Paris and the wide paved footways, parallel gravelled roads for equestrians and associated landscaping gave them scale and splendour that some thought was unequalled in Europe:

> The boulevards of Vienna are more spacious than those of Paris. In the more important parts they are about 160 feet [48.8 m] wide, and thus divided – the paved footpaths on each side are about 18 feet [5.5m] wide; adjoining them, on each side, are paved roadways for heavy traffic 20 feet [6.1 m]wide; next come, on each side, loose gravel roads, bordered with trees, for equestrians. The trees are, in some places, Oriental plane and *Ailanthus glandulosa*, alternately. In other places they are horse chestnut and *Robinia pseudoacacia*, all of which, from the favourable nature of the soil, are doing well.
>
> *The Garden* 1874b, 402

Elsewhere in Europe, other major cities were making advances in urban planning that involved new or improved boulevards. By the 1860s, the old style boulevards of Brussels that Loudon had admired in the late 1820s had been subject to further improvements though 'Haussmannisation' (Girouard 1985, 327). Also in the 1860s, the Mayor of Brussels, Jules Anspach, oversaw a programme of new boulevards, including a major *percée* (opening) through the heart of the city now bearing his name (Lawrence 2006, 239). These attracted a new generation of admirers among the British visitors to the Belgian capital. As well as creating and upgrading boulevards, Anspach was responsible for initiating many other renovations in the city that mirrored what Haussmann had achieved in Paris.

In Berlin, Unter den Linden is a famous boulevard in the Mitte district, named for its linden (*Tilia*) or lime trees that line the grassed pedestrian walkway between two carriageways. It was originally a bridle-path in the sixteenth century but that was replaced in 1647 by the 'Great Elector' Frederick William with a boulevard of lime trees that extended from the city palace to the gates of the city (Lawrence 2006, 74). By the nineteenth century Unter den Linden had become the best known and grandest street in Berlin, a major attraction for visitors and famous throughout Europe. In 1851 the celebrated equestrian statue of King Frederick II of Prussia was erected on the centre strip of the boulevard. At the end of the Franco-Prussian War in 1871, when the Kingdom of Prussia and its allies defeated the forces of the Second French Empire, Unter den Linden was used as a ceremonial route for the parade of victorious troops. During the Victorian era this impressive boulevard was much admired in Britain and it had a major influence, along with the Champs Elysées in Paris, on the redesign of The Mall in London as a ceremonial route following the death of Queen Victoria in 1901 (see Chapter 5).

With the growing internationalisation of the horticulture, landscape and planning professions in the late nineteenth century, influences beyond Europe also had an impact on maintaining the momentum of the British street tree movement. One fertile source of ideas and practical examples was the United

States of America. Of all the towns and cities that were developing their street tree programmes, it was the capital Washington that seems to have generated most interest in Britain. As well as the fine trees on its impressive avenues and boulevards, this interest was also due to the way these were integrated into the urban fabric as part of a wider urban plan. Washington had been designed as a grand city from the outset with the publication of the city plan by Pierre Charles L'Enfant in 1791 that included many wide and tree-lined streets (Lawrence 2006, 168). In 1803, Thomas Jefferson planted poplars along Pennsylvania Avenue, the city's main route linking the White House with the Capitol. An article about Washington in the *Gardeners' Chronicle* in 1878 chose to highlight the scale and diversity of its street tree planting. It noted that 40,000 trees had been planted in the avenues and boulevards of the city, with some 30 different species and cultivars being used (*Gardeners' Chronicle* 1878, 501). Most of the trees were various forms of maple (*Acer* spp.), along with plenty of planes (*Platanus occidentalis*), tulip tree (*Liriodendron tilipifera*) and honey locust (*Gleditschia triacanthos*). The article concluded by stating that much more could be done in Britain to increase the diversity of tree planting in streets since many of the species used in Washington should be suitable for the British climate. This would also help our municipal authorities to move away from their overreliance on the London plane.

By the late Victorian era the power and influence of the British Empire stretched around the world embracing numerous countries and territories (Hobsbawm 1987). What was happening in London and other British cities was often closely observed by British administrators serving overseas in the Empire who were frequently keen to try and imitate in their own sphere of influence some of the many technical and cultural innovations from back home. This included championing the trend towards street tree planting that was now thriving in many British towns and cities. Reports began to appear in the British gardening magazines of street tree planting programmes in some major cities of the Empire, for example, in Calcutta in India (Clarke 1883) and Dublin in Ireland (M'Nab 1874). These reports would also have had the effect of helping to maintain the momentum of Britain's own street tree movement. Not only was extensive street tree planting by municipal authorities now a much admired enterprise in cities throughout Europe and the United States, it was also happening around the British Empire.

Relevant overseas literature

All those practical examples of successful street tree planting in overseas cities were also supported by a significant amount of literature describing these achievements and detailing the technical work involved. While much of this was not initially published in English, reviews and summaries of the more important publications often appeared in the British gardening press.

Alphonse Du Breuil was appointed professor of agriculture in 1848 at the School of Agriculture and Rural Economy in the Department of the

Lower Seine. He soon established an excellent reputation for his knowledge of viticulture and fruit production. In 1853, he was appointed professor of arboriculture at the Conservatoire National for Arts and Crafts in Paris where he continued his focus on fruit growing. He then developed an interest in urban trees that brought him to the attention of relevant professionals throughout Europe. Much of that attention was prompted by the publication in 1865 of a book entitled *Manuel D'arboriculture Des Ingénieurs* (Du Breuil 1865). This contained plenty of material that was relevant to street trees, particularly the sections on planting and pruning. In 1867, when the School of Theoretical and Practical Arboriculture was founded in Paris, Du Breuil and Jean Darcel were appointed as the first directors. Darcel had been the Chief Engineer in the Department of Bridges and Roads for the City of Paris.

By the late 1860s, Alphonse Du Breuil was regarded as one of the foremost authorities on arboriculture and urban trees, not just in France but also throughout Europe. He continued to lecture frequently on these subjects to great acclaim. In Britain in 1873, *The Garden* magazine promoted a series of public lectures by Du Breuil that were due to take place at his School of Arboriculture at the Bois de Vincennes in Paris. The magazine commented, 'These lectures are free to all who chose to attend them [and] we regret to reflect, it is not open to [the] brethren in our own metropolis' (*The Garden* 1873, 330).

The impact of Du Breuil's books and lectures on those involved with Britain's emerging street tree movement is difficult to gauge. Occasional mention of his work in the pages of British gardening magazines and journals of the late Victorian era suggests that his name was fairly well known. The extent to which his theoretical and practical ideas on urban arboriculture, and especially the contents of his *Manuel D'arboriculture Des Ingénieurs*, were understood in Britain is another matter. It seems likely that his greatest impact was indirect, in that he had considerable influence on the planting and management of the boulevards of Paris and elsewhere, and the results of this where much admired and respected in Britain.

Perhaps the best known nineteenth century French exponent of landscape and garden design is Jean-Charles Adolphe Alphand, who had also worked as an engineer in the Department of Bridges and Roads for the City of Paris. Between 1852–1870, Alphand played a major role in the renovation of Paris, working under the direction of Baron Haussmann to realise the vision of Napoleon III. Much of this was achieved by working closely with another engineer Eugène Belgrand and the landscape architect Jean-Pierre Barillet-Deschamps. His accomplishments include many of the notable public parks and gardens of Paris, such as the Bois de Vincennes, Parc Monceau, Bios du Boulogne and the Square des Batignolles. He was also responsible for landscaping some of Hausmann's wide tree-lined boulevards, such as the Boulevard Richard-Lenoir, running from the Bastille to the Avenue de la République.

Between 1867 and 1873, Adolphe Alphand published his seminal work *Les Promenades de Paris*, issued in two volumes (Alphand 1867). The book set out in great detail the theoretical and practical basis of his work on parks and gardens and although it is essentially a technical book, it does include substantial sections on the artistic aspects of the work. Much of the technical content does have considerable relevance to street trees but there is only a limited amount that refers directly to this form of urban landscaping. In this respect it is difficult to appraise how much impact Alphand's text had on the emerging street tree movement in Britain. While the book had almost a thousand subscribers worldwide, it has not been ascertained how many of these were based in Britain. What is more certain is the enormous impact of Alphand's work 'on the ground' in helping to create those Parisian boulevards that were so admired by British visitors.

As well as reading their own country's journals and periodicals on gardening and landscape, British readers were also encouraged through these publications to take a look at some overseas magazine and journals. Some of these would occasionally carry articles of relevance to street and roadside trees, which would help stimulate interest in this subject in Britain. The Belgian *Bulletins d'Arboriculture*, launched in 1865 by the Cercle Professoral pour le Progrès de L'arboriculture en Belgique, advertised regularly in the *Gardeners' Chronicle*, particularly in the 1870s. As well carrying articles on tree planting and care, aspects of landscape management were also included, occasionally mentioning the much acclaimed boulevards of Brussels. However, as the magazine's subtitle suggests, *de culture portagère et de floriculture* (vegetable gardening and floriculture), it embraced a very broad definition of arboriculture.

One relevant American periodical of the late Victorian era not only had a huge impact in the United States but its pioneering promotion of landscape architecture and urban planning was also influential in Britain where it had a small number of regular readers. This weekly magazine called *Garden and Forest* was subtitled as *A Journal of Horticulture, Landscape Art, and Forestry* and although it existed for only nine years (1888–1897), it benefited from an extraordinarily talented group of editors and contributors (Hou 2013). In its advocacy of the principles of urban planning and landscape design, its scope was far beyond that of any of the contemporary British gardening magazines. Its report on the advanced street tree programmes of cities such as Washington and Boston, and how these were integrated into an overall urban plan, showed just how far British efforts still had to go. In its promotion of the value of urban trees, the magazine focused as much on their health benefits (both physical and psychological) as on their aesthetic contribution. In these respects some of the content of *Garden and Forest* magazine, which was occasionally reproduced in British magazines, helped to support the theoretical basis for the British street tree movement. Later in the Edwardian era there would be some major American texts that were directly relevant to street trees, such as William Solotaroff's (1910) *Shade-Trees in Towns and Cities*.

A major French contribution to the literature on street trees came at the very end of the Victorian era and its impact in Britain continued into the early twentieth century. This text was Adolphe Chargueraud's classic work *Les Arbres de la Ville de Paris*, published in 1896, just 2 years before he died. Chargueraud held the post of professor of arboriculture for the City of Paris and at the same time he was also having considerable influence on the management of urban trees across the city. This is a truly remarkable and comprehensive account of what would now be called arboriculture and urban forestry. The detail and depth of understanding in the book is far beyond any British or American texts of that time and a considerable amount of it relates directly to street and roadside trees, known to the French as *les arbres d'alignement*. Even for readers without a good grasp of the French language the many diagrams and illustrations are quite revealing in themselves. The book was in three parts with the first dealing with avenues and street planting, giving simple details of the method of planting, the species of trees to be selected, their management, and the diseases and injuries to which they are subjected. The second part was devoted to planting along the roads in country districts with the third looking at suitable equipment and the costs associated with different practical operations.

Soon after Chargueraud's book was published it was given a very favourable review by *Gardeners' Chronicle* (1896, 400). The magazine strongly recommended the book to its readers and considered the work to be of the same stature as those by Adolphe Alphand and the landscape architect Jean-Pierre Barillet-Deschamps, but more compact and accessible. The magazine noted that it had been published under the auspices of the Prefect of the Seine, and it believed that the London County Council would do a useful service if it arranged for the book to be translated into English. Unfortunately, it never was.

Further recognition for Chargueraud's book in Britain also came in the 1920s and '30s, largely due to the connection made between Denis Le Sueur, the eminent British arboriculturist, and the Department of Bridges and Roads for the City of Paris. Le Sueur, who was originally from Jersey, was working as an arboricultural and forestry consultant in London in the 1920s and was employed frequently by the Corporation of the City of London (Boulton 1969; Johnston 2015, 22). In an effort to broaden his knowledge Le Sueur contacted the Parisian authorities and following a visit to Paris they presented him with a copy of Chargueraud's book. He was clearly very impressed with the book and also the standards of tree management for the boulevards and parks of Paris. This undoubtedly had a major impact on his own approach to urban trees, which he expressed in his consultancy work and teaching in Britain. In 1934, when he published his classic book *The Care and Repair of Ornamental Trees*, he included Chargueraud's work among several titles in the bibliography, even though there was no English translation (Le Sueur 1934, 249). Chargueraud's pioneering work continues to have an impact on French arboriculture and urban forestry and is still mentioned in quite recent textbooks (Mollie 2007, 92).

Much of the overseas and mainly continental literature in the nineteenth century that had a significant influence on promoting street tree planting in Britain came from the world of horticulture and landscape. At the same time there was also some support for these ideas from continental voices among the emerging profession of urban planning. It is difficult to gauge how much these continental contributions influenced the British professionals with a primary interest in horticulture and landscape as their access to planning profession literature, especially in a foreign language, would probably have been quite limited. What seems more certain is the influence this had on individuals in the emerging British urban planning profession and their attitudes towards planting trees in streets.

While there was now widespread acceptance in the British planning profession that trees had an important role in urban landscapes, there was still plenty of debate about how that could be accomplished. A powerful voice among designers and planners of the age was that of Joseph Stübben, an influential planner from Cologne who was frequently consulted by other cities. In a public lecture in 1885 entitled 'Practical and Aesthetic Principles for the Laying Out of Cities', Stübben (1885) set out many of his recommendations for urban planning and this included plenty of detailed specifications on street tree plantings, such as the distances between trees and distances from various elements of urban development and infrastructure. He strongly advocated the planting of trees in rows, not just at the sides of the road but also, where possible, in the central reservation of dual carriageways. As well as being an internationally recognised consultant in the field of planning, Stübben also wrote some major texts. His classic work entitled *Der Städtebau* was published in 1890 and became the most widely used manual on urban planning and was reprinted many times (Stübben 1890).

Not all urban planners in Europe were in agreement regarding the value of street trees. By the end of the nineteenth century, the aesthetic of tree-lined streets laid out in geometric order was being criticised by some European professionals as being soulless and too regimented (Lawrence 2006, 258). The most vocal opponent of the Haussmann-Stübben tradition was Camillo Sitte, an Austrian architect who is now regarded as a pioneer in urban planning. His major work entitled *City Planning according to Artistic Principles*, published in 1889, raised issues that are still regarded as contentious in urban planning. Sitte (1889, 176) stated, 'All tree-lined streets are tedious but no city can do completely without them …' He had particularly disdain for the boulevards of Paris, saying that the trees would have been better planted in a few parks instead. He believed that rigid adherence to symmetry in the tree planting gave no consideration to the healthy growth of the trees, to the light or to the surrounding cityscape. While some British planning professionals found sympathy with Sitte's views, others were adamantly opposed, especially those who were later associated with the garden city movement led by Ebenezer Howard (see Chapter 8).

A continental twist from Southport

The theme of this chapter has been the overseas influences on early British street tree planting, with much of that resulting from the magnificent boulevards of Paris created by order of Napoleon III. In an interesting twist to this we conclude by investigating a claim that much of the Emperor's inspiration for this came originally from Britain.

In April 2000, *The Times* newspaper reported that Quentin Hughes, a former professor of architecture, had stated that Napoleon III was inspired to create the new boulevards of Paris as a result of his stay in Southport, a seaside town in Lancashire (Jenkins 2000). The young Prince Louis Napoleon, as he was then, had taken a flat off Lord Street for a season in 1846 during his stay in Britain before he returned to France to eventually take power as Emperor in the *coup d'etat* of 1851. Hughes believed that the future Emperor was so taken with the sweeping panorama of Lord Street, Southport's tree-lined boulevard, that he wanted to recreate it in Paris. When this claim appeared in *The Times* it generated a lot of interest and the story has been repeated periodically (Nevin 2004). As this claim could have significant implications for the theme of this chapter it was important to see if there was any supporting evidence. As there was little published information the author decided to contact local historians and also undertook his own research. A considerable amount of material, both written and visual, was examined and only a summary of the main conclusions are given here. As Quentin Hughes died in 2004, no additional information could be gathered from him.

It has been stated that Lord Street was laid out in the 1820s during a period of significant investment in Southport (Hardy 2000, 15) and the street is mentioned in historical material at least as early as 1821 (Bland 1903, 95). In a history of Southport by Frank Robinson (1848, 31) he states that considerable improvements were made to Lord Street in the 1840s, which included a gravel walk or invalids' carriage drive on the south-eastern side and ensuring that the street was a uniform width. There is a detailed description of this very broad and lengthy road and the impressive architecture of its buildings. Robinson asserts that 'Lord Street is acknowledged by all who have seen it to be one of the most splendid thoroughfares in the kingdom' (*ibid.*, 38). However, there is no mention of any street trees. It can be ascertained from the *Annals of Southport and District* by Mr E. Bland (1903, 129) that these improvements to Lord Street were part of a range of measures included in the first *Southport Improvement Act*, which received royal assent in 1846, and those involving Lord Street were undertaken in the following years at the cost of £2000. The timing of these major improvements to the town coincided with the arrival of the railways. In 1864, a 'Boulevard Committee' was appointed by the town's Improvement Commissioners and it is stated that the credit for promoting the boulevards must be given to Mr Charles Barrow, a dentist then practicing in the town (*ibid.*, 171).

If Lord Street was renowned for its trees and landscaping before the 1860s, it seems likely that this would have been mentioned by one of the horticultural writers of the time. However, an exploration of relevant British gardening literature, especially the works of the well-travelled John Claudius Loudon, could find no reference to Lord Street in relation to landscaping or street trees.

There is no doubt that in the late Victorian era Lord Street did establish a reputation for being an attractive tree-lined boulevard (Anon 1901). However, in terms of its impact on Louis Napoleon during the 1840s and subsequent influence on the creation of the tree-lined boulevards of Paris by Baron Haussmann, no evidence could be found for this. In the historical material examined there was no mention of planting street trees along Lord Street from when it was initially laid out in the 1820s, the later improvements in 1847 and up to the establishment of Southport's Boulevard Committee in 1864. On this basis it seems reasonable to conclude that if Louis Napoleon was impressed by Lord Street during his stay in 1846, it was probably due to the width of the street and its architecture and not by any street trees.

CHAPTER FIVE

The Victorian Street Tree Movement

Throughout the 1830s and 1840s there was a growing call among public figures and prominent horticulturists for the systematic planting of street trees in our towns and cities. As noted in the previous chapter this was influenced by their admiration of the tree-lined boulevards that now graced some major cities in continental Europe. If trees could adorn major thoroughfares in Paris, Brussels and Berlin, this could also happen in London, Edinburgh and Cardiff. Nevertheless, despite the compelling arguments in favour of extensive street tree planting, this had to wait until the right conditions to facilitate this were in place.

This chapter explores the initial development of the Victorian street tree movement in the mid-nineteenth century and focuses on a number of major cities, some of which were pioneers in this respect. It then charts the development of this movement through the late Victorian and Edwardian eras and how its momentum was sustained across Britain. Much of the focus of this chapter is on the central areas of cities with the suburbs considered in the following chapter. Before considering individual street tree programmes it is necessary to give a brief account of some relevant developments in British society at both a national and local level. These were fundamental in creating the conditions that led to the widespread introduction of public green space into the urban realm in Britain, firstly in the form of public parks and later with the establishment of street tree programmes (Johnston 2014, 50–54).

Local authorities and the growth of democracy

From the 1830s significant advances were made in the development of local government in Britain and some of the initial impetus for this began as a movement towards greater democracy at a national level (Morton 1938, 371–446). At the beginning of the 1830s, the essential character of Parliament, the landed class that dominated it, the methods by which elections were carried out, and the very limited and unrepresentative electorate, had remained virtually unchanged from that which prevailed in the eighteenth century. However, the dramatic changes in society spawned by the Industrial Revolution ensured that the agitation of the working class for fundamental reform and democratic representation was now more widespread and more 'dangerous' than ever before. Although the passing of the *Reform Act* of 1832 by the Whig government was finally meant to address this issue, it was really only a small step towards democracy. While it abolished the Rotten Boroughs and opened up the franchise to more property-owners, this succeeded in placing power more firmly in the hands of the industrialists and their middle class followers.

After the *Reform Act* of 1832, the Whig government's first task was to extend these gains into the sphere of local government (Morton 1938, 384). The *Burgh Act* 1833 in Scotland and the *Municipal Corporations Act* 1835 for England and Wales swept away a number of existing bodies and replaced them by elected corporations, which ensured the Whig middle class had control of most of the cities and larger towns. After the 1832 *Reform Act* the threat of 'revolution' posed by the rise of the Chartist movement and its demand for far-reaching electoral reform was employed by the middle class to bring their own influence to bear on achieving some change. Meanwhile, ordinary people remained essentially powerless and it was a century later that the working class entered national and municipal politics as an independent force. In 1833, the Parliamentary Select Committee on Public Walks issued its report urging the development of urban public parks, partly motivated by a health agenda but also mindful of the potential role of these parks in pacifying the working class and heading off civil unrest (Conway 1991, 35–36). While some of the early parks with public access were the initiative of wealthy benefactors, the main thrust of the public parks movement had to wait for some significant developments in local government.

The *Municipal Corporations Act* 1835 was notable for recognising the weakness of existing local government and marking the beginning of a formal structure for it (Conway 1991, 17). The four different types of institution responsible for local government in the 1830s were the Municipal Corporation, the Improvement Commission, which existed in most large towns, the Manorial Court and the Surveyors of Highways. The latter were to be found in every parish or town in the country, but the existence of the other three depended on the local historical background. The Act gave a more liberal constitution to those boroughs where it applied, although major towns such as Manchester and Birmingham that lay outside its scope did not achieve municipal incorporation until 1838. The City of London was also excluded and it was 20 years later before it achieved a major breakthrough in local government (Chadwick 1966, 135). The new Act did not automatically make the new corporations more effective as the divided responsibility between the Corporations and Improvement Commissions continued. Nevertheless, the Act was an important measure that meant much to the social life of cities as the basis on which was to arise, during the next hundred years, the great structure of municipal social service for the benefit of all classes of the community, particularly the poor (Trevelyan 1952, 63–64). It was also notable in giving the local franchise to all ratepayers, ensuring the working class had a say at least in local elections and some 'official' influence over local government services.

As Britain became a predominantly urban society by the mid-nineteenth century, the poor sanitation and overcrowding in its major cities began to attract the attention of Parliament and fuel demands for a remedy (Trevelyan 1952, 65). The *Public Health Act* of 1848 was prompted by the recent cholera epidemic that had devastated the population of many urban slums. Although a step forward, the main principle of the Act was permission rather than compulsion to take action and it was not properly enacted by the municipalities for another twenty years. In the 1860s, much of the local improvement activity for housing and sanitation was an indirect result of the *Local Government Act* of 1858 which was a crucial step forward in formalising central and institutional control of buildings (Burnett 1986, 158–159). In 1871, the *Public Parks Act* allowed land to be donated for use as a public park. The *Public Health Act* of 1875 gave local authorities powers to control housing conditions in their district, which also included the specifications for new streets and street improvements, thus raising the possibility of establishing street trees in the future. The Act also enabled local authorities to raise loans through government and to levy their own rate to create and manage parks (Lasdun 1991, 165).

As the nineteenth century advanced, local government was gradually made to attend to its duties, by being subjected to local elections and to central control from Whitehall (Trevelyan 1952, 116–117). A major advance was the establishment of the Local Government Board in 1871, the government's supervisory body to oversee and enforce local government in England and Wales. The idea of urban self-government that had started with the *Municipal Reform Act* of 1835 was now made general throughout England and Wales by the *Local Government Act* of 1888. The Act established County Councils and County Boroughs and although the sections of the legislation relating to the creation of District Councils were withdrawn, these were eventually brought into existence by the *Local Government Act* 1894.

The public health agenda

The public parks movement from the mid-Victorian era onwards was motivated largely by a public heath agenda, although there was also a keen awareness of the potential role of parks in deflecting the working class away from civil unrest. This recognition of the value of public greenspace in promoting public health was initially confined to the creation of public parks and it was not until later that similar arguments were to be used to promote the establishment of street trees. It is worth giving a brief account of the context and progress of this public health debate in relation to urban greenspace.

By the 1830s and '40s, the Industrial Revolution that had begun in the 1780s was in full force across much of Britain (Hobsbawm 1975). While the process of industrialisation is inevitably painful and must involve the erosion of traditional patterns of life, it was carried through with exceptional violence in Britain (Thompson 1963, 486). Although it had brought unimaginable wealth to a very small number of people, the bulk of the population at the bottom of the social scale had suffered severe reductions in their living standards. The novels of Charles Dickens graphically record the unrelenting poverty, sickness and exploitation. For working class families the urban environment in which they had to live and work was far from healthy (Gauldie 1974). Disease and malnutrition was rife in Britain's slums and responsible for the disability and death of vast numbers of men, women and children. In London alone between 1838 and 1844 over 100,000 people died by causes peculiar to the insanitary conditions of their environment (Hunt 2004, 26).

In 1842, when Sir Edwin Chadwick's *Report on the Sanitary Conditions of the Labouring Populations of Great Britain* was presented to Parliament, this was a major 'wake-up call' for the nation (Hunt 2004, 26–27). The report was widely-read, outselling every previous government publication. Even though the science in parts of Chadwick's report was erroneous, this was not known at the time and did not lessen the impact. Chadwick and his contemporaries believed that disease was spread through the 'miasmas', a form of noxious gas or 'bad' air emitted by refuse in sewers. Cholera was a particularly deadly disease and the spread of a series of devastating outbreaks in London and other cities was explained through miasmas theory. At this time many streets were unpaved and without drains or sewers. In 1854, the English physician Dr John Snow demonstrated that contaminated water was the main agent spreading cholera, although he did not identify the contaminant. It would take many years for this message to be believed and acted upon and it was only in 1884 that it was finally accepted that the cholera bacterium could be water-borne. In the meantime, those advocating the provision of public parks and street trees were able to use miasmas theory to their advantage. While arguments in favour of street trees had mainly emphasised their aesthetic value and role in urban improvement, these now focused increasingly on their health benefits. As well as providing much needed shade from the summer sunshine, street trees were also thought to purify the air by removing harmful elements from the miasmas (Lawrence 1988, 371). One of the more prominent voices was Dr John Samuel Phené who set out his views in a paper *On the Sanitary Results of Planting Trees in Towns*, published by the National Association for the Promotion of Social Science (Phené 1880). As well as advocating urban trees in general in the belief they helped to purify the air and prevent epidemics, Phené was especially eager to promote street trees which he viewed as having a distinct role in terms of light and colour:

> So in streets, to the occupants of houses having a northern aspect, the glare of the reflected light is injurious; but the effect would be much modified by the coolness to the eye produced by the green of trees. In ancient surgery persons having weak or declining sight were advised to look at the emerald. It was shown that in the old style of building, the streets, being narrow, were both cooler from the sun not being able to penetrate them with direct rays, and less subject to noxious exhalations from the scouring and purifying effects of the searching air to which narrow streets were subject; so that, while there was no space for trees, there was also less necessity. Wide streets, on the contrary, are hotter, and require the shade of trees to cool them, and, as in the case of London, which has so far done to a great extent without trees in its streets, not only are modern streets compulsorily wide, but the enormous increase in metropolitan buildings renders every sanitary question one of importance; and the chemical properties of trees, as shown by experiment, give them an important standing on that ground, irrespective of ornament or the pleasure they produce.
>
> Phené 1880, 615

Phené was soon joined by other authoritative voices in support of the health benefits of street trees. In 1883, the comments of the highly-respected Swiss scientist Charles Soret of Geneva University were reported in British newspapers such as *The Times* and *Daily Telegraph* and influential journals including *The Builder* and *The Lancet* (Elliott 2016, 313). According to Soret, 'trees in streets temper the heat and serve as a protection from dust', while evaporation from their leaves keeps the surrounding air cool and moist. Tree roots also drew up stagnant water and served as 'disinfectants' by absorbing organic matter and 'filth' which was a frequent cause of fevers and infection.

The abject poverty and poor health of much of the Victorian working class was detailed by Friedrich Engels, the German social scientist and businessman, in his classic work *The Condition of the Working Class in England in 1844*. Engels also described how the bourgeoisie rarely had to come face to face with the horrors of proletarian existence (Engels 1892, 28–29). The prosperous middle class had now abandoned the dirty, unhealthy and crime-ridden inner city areas in favour of making their homes in the new affluent suburbs (see Chapter 6). When travelling to and from the city centre to supervise their workers or conduct other business they made their way along routes that avoided them having to see the grimy misery that lurked behind the relatively neat facades. In Manchester, the thoroughfares leading from the Exchange were lined with an almost unbroken series of shops run by the lower middle class determined from commercial necessity to keep up appearances. Engels believed he had never seen 'so systematic a shutting out of the working class from the thoroughfares, so tender a concealment of everything which might affront the eye and nerves of the bourgeoisie'.

Despite a widespread reluctance on the part of the upper and middle classes to see directly for themselves the appalling conditions for many working class families, many were becoming increasingly aware of this, if only in an intellectual way. The popular media was recording the grim facts in the newspapers of the day, while the novels of some popular authors also described the gruesome details. All this inevitably had an impact of those wealthy individuals with a social conscious and those in political life who feared the consequences of ignoring the urgent need for widespread political and social reform. There was now a growing body of political opinion that was contrasting the poor state of British cities with many of those on the Continent that had been transformed by extensive new building and infrastructure projects (Hunt 2004, 170). As a result, from the 1850s onwards there was a marked increase in what would now be termed 'prestige developments', symbolic, ostentatious new structures and civil engineering projects designed both to beautify and celebrate the achievements of the industrial cities. As will be noted later in this chapter, some of the civil engineering projects were to have an impact on facilitating street tree planting.

While central government was urging local government to tackle the poverty, disease and dilapidation afflicting many urban areas, responsibility for sanitary reform in the Victorian city was not a clear-cut issue (Hunt 2004, 217). A range of competing boards, authorities and surveyors exercised control over different aspects of the urban infrastructure. With regard to streets, the infrastructure associated with these had become progressively more complex since the first *Westminster Paving Act* of 1762, which was followed by similar legislation for other urban areas (Rudé 1971, 136). This had led to the introduction of a range of improvements, predominantly in the more affluent districts, that included macadam road surfaces, paved footways, gas lighting, storm drains and sewers, piped water and post boxes. The responsibility for all this lay with various paving boards, lighting boards, vesties, highway surveyors, magistrates and others. They rarely coordinated their action with one another and always jealously guarded their own administrative patch. The inevitable result was that city authorities found it incredibly difficult to organise a coherent response to the challenges or opportunities concerning streets or any aspect of urban infrastructure.

Those municipal corporations faced with pressing public health concerns were able to promote sanitary reform by submitting Improvement Bills to Parliament. These applied only to the sponsoring city and gave local authorities the right to levy rates for certain purposes or even borrow money if necessary. It was often the case that the middle class owners of small businesses were not keen on any improvements that were likely to increase the rates. They were not wealthy enough to move out to the suburbs but liable as the owners of small property interests within the city. They were often represented in considerable numbers on the Council and used their political clout to fight hard against measures that would result in an increase in the rates. By the 1860s, there was mounting impatience with the usual Victorian way of getting things done through voluntarism, civic association and just muddling along (Hunt 2004, 231). Since 1833 in Scotland and 1835 for England and Wales, municipal corporations had been placed in nominal charge of their towns and cities yet very little seemed to have been achieved by them. In some cases, local authorities were actually going backwards. For example, in Birmingham in the 1850s, a group of tradesmen, victuallers, shopkeepers and small manufacturers took control of the Council (*ibid.*, 239). In one of their first actions they slashed spending on the roads and dismissed the Borough Engineer, replacing him with his assistant on half the salary.

Instead of progressive local government, in many towns and cities it was the churches, business leaders and friendly societies which ran the districts. Furthermore, the distribution of public goods and services as a result of the individual preferences and priorities of private citizens was often far from equitable. The socialist and reformer Sidney Webb was one of the leading critics of the nineteenth century's tradition of 'local patriotism' which he believed was almost entirely confined to the fortunate minority of prosperous businessmen (Hunt 2004, 275). In his view, while they had enriched their cities with fine public buildings and parks, in the slums of Liverpool, Manchester and Birmingham anything like municipal patriotism and civic pride remained almost unknown.

Housing developments and powers to plant street trees

As many British cities grew in population during the eighteenth and nineteenth century, they also grew in size (Burnett 1986, 4–7). This new mainly residential development was outside the existing urban core and became known as the suburbs. While the growth of the suburbs is covered in Chapter 6, brief reference to its impact on the layout of street and housing should be made here to help place the early street plantings in some context.

These suburban areas were generally less densely settled than the older sections of towns and cities. This was due largely to the presence of more greenspace in the wealthier middle class residential suburbs, mainly in the form of individual gardens. There was also more treecover than the old neighbourhoods due to trees in the private gardens and occasionally along some of the new roads. Furthermore, as suburbia expanded into what was previously countryside, some tree-lined country roads subsequently became tree-lined suburban streets (see Chapter 3). For the vast majority of working class families in the old established parts of the city, they lived in a virtually treeless environment. As their homes had no gardens, garden trees were out of the question (Roger 2000, 236–244) and their streets of tenements or terraced houses were inevitably treeless.

Despite the continuing problems of poor housing for working class families in the older urban districts, conditions did improve for some from the 1870s with the construction of new, healthier housing (Burnett 1986, 158–159). The *Public Health Act* of 1875 required local authorities to implement building regulations, or bye-laws, which insisted that each house should be self-contained, with its own sanitation and water. This change in the design of housing complemented the public investment in sewers and water supply. Section 157 of the Act allowed for bye-laws governing the layout, width and construction of new streets. Two years later in 1877, the Local Government Board issued a set of model bye-laws for the guidance of local authorities. These recommended that new streets over 100 ft (30.5 m) in length were to be at least 36 ft wide (11 m) and open at one end throughout their full width and height. Although the powers in the 1875 Act were extensive, the adoption of the bye-laws was permissive, not mandatory. Nevertheless, they did enable local authorities to establish their own specifications for new streets and street improvements, thus raising the possibility of establishing street trees in the future. In the last quarter of the nineteenth century, huge numbers of new bye-law houses were built in British cities, along with the construction of thousands of miles of grid-pattern bye-law streets (see Chapter 6).

Despite urban authorities now having some control over their streets, this did not immediately lead to the widespread and systematic planting of street trees. Indeed, it was not until the latter part of the nineteenth century that urban local authorities formally acquired powers to plant trees in highways with the *Public Health Acts Amendment Act* 1890 (Mynors 2002, 180). Under Section 43 of this Act, which only related to highways maintainable at public expense, authorities could plant trees, shrubs and other plants and lay out, alter or remove grass verges. This legislation was particularly welcome as many authorities were confused about their legal position on this matter. Although the growing momentum of the Victorian street tree movement was pressuring local authorities to act, many had become quite cautious since Lewes Corporation had been convicted at Sussex Assizes in 1886 for causing a nuisance by planting trees on a public highway (Pettigrew 1937, 182). The move towards giving local authorities powers to plant street trees had been facilitated in part by the 1888 *Local Government Act* that passed responsibility for main roads to County and County Borough Councils.

Early systematic plantings in London, Cardiff and Edinburgh

As noted in Chapter 3, there were always some isolated examples of trees in streets at various locations in and around London, often as remnants from past landscapes that had been incorporated into newly constructed streets following urban expansion. However, the systematic planting of trees in streets, conducted as part of an organised programme, had to wait until the development of local government and the appropriate political, economic and social conditions to facilitate this. Although we have given a brief account above of those conditions at the national level, many of the larger urban centres had their own individual set of circumstances. While the bulk of this chapter focuses on the practical achievements of street tree planting in some of our major cities, this is sometimes prefaced by a brief account of relevant developments in local government, where appropriate.

London

In some respects local government was slow to arrive in London. The City of London was not included in the *Municipal Corporations Act* 1835 and it was twenty years later when a major breakthrough in local government occurred there (Chadwick 1966, 135). In 1855, the *Metropolis Management Act* set up the Metropolitan Board of Works, the first comprehensive body to be constituted for the government of London. The Board, which was appointed rather than elected, was responsible for the London-wide construction of infrastructure. This meant that the government could absolve itself completely of such irritations as the provision of new public parks and street improvements for London, and transfer them to the new body.

Nineteenth century London's street pattern was often not conducive to the planting of street trees, unlike the wide boulevards of some major continental cites. Writing in *Temple Bar* magazine an anonymous visitor admitted, 'Most of the streets are narrow, crooked and running in every possible direction' (Anon 1862). After walking through a maze of streets for half an hour they had found themselves quite lost. This was contrasted with the models of urban planning that had transformed the centres of Paris and Vienna. In 1838, a Select Committee had been appointed to consider plans for the improvement of the metropolis and it reported that there were districts of London through which no great thoroughfares passed (Edwards 1998, 9–10). The committee's report stated that:

> These [districts] were wholly occupied by a dense population composed of the lower classes of persons who being entirely excluded from observation and influence of better educated neighbours, exhibited a state of moral degradation deeply to be deplored. This lamentable state of affairs would be remedied whenever the great streams of public intercourse could be made to pass through the districts in question. The moral condition of these poorer occupants would necessarily be improved by communication with more respectable inhabitants, and that the introduction at the same time of improved habits and a freer circulation of air would tend materially to extirpate those prevalent diseases which not only ravaged the poorer districts in question, but were also dangerous to the adjacent localities.
>
> Edwards 1998, 10

The Select Committee's position has echoes of the underlying political and social agenda for Haussmann's street improvements in Paris. As a result of further Select Committees from 1832–1851 many large-scale improvements were brought before Parliament, the work to be undertaken by the Commissioners of Woods and Forests, subject to the immediate control of the Treasury (Edwards 1898, 10–11). Very few schemes, however, were actually undertaken and it was not until 1855 and the establishment of the Metropolitan Board of Works (MBW) as the principal instrument of London-wide government that significant progress was made. Street improvements were an immediate priority for the MBW and through its Streets Committee it undertook a large number of projects for new streets and street widening, mostly in central London. As a result of the MBW's work the total length of new streets constructed and of the thoroughfares widened was nearly 16 miles (25.7 km), while the average width was about 60 ft (18.3 m). The *Local Government (England and Wales) Act* 1888 abolished the MBW and transferred its powers, duties and liabilities to the new London County Council (LCC) (Edwards 1898, 161). One of the earliest acts of the LCC was to appoint various committees to carry on its work that included control of working class housing, parks and open spaces, building regulations and tramways. Its Improvements Committee was specifically responsible for ongoing and new street improvements.

The transformation of central London in the second part of the nineteenth century with its new roads, railways, underground tunnels, buildings and monuments, created the modern capital of which its upper and middle class residents could at last be proud. Unfortunately, all this construction work proved disastrous for the tenement dwellers and casual workers of central London and vast numbers of working class families were forced to flee from this chaotic landscape (Hunt 2004, 293). Between 1840 and 1900 an estimated

120,000 of the 'labouring classes' were evicted from their homes in the city. The construction of major arterial roads such as Victoria Street, New Oxford Street, Commercial Street and Shaftesbury Avenue undoubtedly assisted the flow of traffic and benefited commerce. Many of these developments were also regarded as purposefully ideological, being designed like Haussmann's boulevards to expose the 'dangerous rookeries' of a potentially revolutionary proletariat. For the displaced, a move to the suburbs was not an option. Apart from being too expensive, most were invariably tied to their place of work in the urban core. For them it was either homelessness or a move to another overcrowded neighbourhood nearby.

Despite the compelling arguments for trees to be included in some of London's new street improvements, many members of the public remained quite resistant to this. Back in 1824 William Trench MP had planned to include tree-lined promenades in his proposal for a major new built development along the Thames in London (Barker and Hyde 1982, 65). This was vigorously opposed by riparian property owners and shopkeepers, which was sufficient to prevent the project and it was not until the 1860s that the Thames was embanked.

When tree-lined boulevards finally arrived in London, it was fitting that one of the first projects should have been conceived by Dr John Samuel Phené, that dedicated advocate of street tree planting. Phené was a scholar and antiquarian who lived and worked in Chelsea, then on the western fringe of the city. In 1850 he developed a nearby tract of vacant land as a new suburban residential development that is now Margaretta Terrace (named after his first wife), Oakley Street and Phene Street. In 1851, in accordance with his belief in the value of urban greenspace, he planted plane trees along both sides of the streets. The OS Town Plan of 1868 clearly marks the location of the individual trees. These leafy and affluent suburban streets with their charming houses of classical architecture soon attracted much praise. Prince Albert thought the addition of trees along the footway an excellent idea and it motivated him to support further street tree planting in London. Sadly, all Phené's original trees seem to have long since gone and only a few more recent trees are now in these streets.

The first major street tree scheme to be undertaken in central London came as a result of two closely related icons of Victorian engineering, the London Main Drainage System and the Thames Embankment. Following the Great Stink of 1858, caused by a combination of hot weather and raw sewage on the banks of the Thames, Parliament resolved to finally tackle the problem of London's lack of an adequate main drainage system (Hunt 2004, 194). The scheme was the brainchild of the Benthamite public health advocate Edwin Chadwick and was intended to permanently clean up the polluted River Thames and remove what many regarded as a primary source of disease (Porter 1998, 6). Joseph Bazalgette, the Chief Engineer of the MBW, was given responsibility for the construction work which comprised five main brick-lined interceptor sewers measuring 82 miles (132 km); three north of the river and two to the south (*ibid.*, 72). These connected with existing sewers and pumping stations were built at strategic locations to keep the sewage flowing. The Thames Embankment was authorised by Parliament in 1862 and was an integral part of the scheme as its construction was designed to enclose the lowest-level intercepting sewer, protecting the river from further degradation. When the entire project was finished in 1874 Bazalgette was duly knighted.

The Thames Embankment was a remarkable achievement of Victorian engineering that turned London's dirty and dilapidated riverfront from an embarrassment to many Victorians into an internationally admired feature of urban design and construction. Some authorities consider the Thames Embankment as comprising three sections: the Victoria Embankment and the Chelsea Embankment on the north side of the river, and the Albert Embankment on the south side. Others only consider the Victoria and Chelsea embankments as part of the Thames Embankment. Nevertheless, it is only the Victoria and Chelsea sections that are considered here in relation to street trees.

One early decision in the design of the Victoria and Chelsea Embankments was crucial in facilitating these as a location for street tree planting. This was the choice of roadways rather than railways as the transportation mode for the Embankment (Porter 1998, 118). Roads were cheaper to build and easier for the public MBW to control as the railways were all private ventures. The construction of new roadways would improve access to riverside properties as well as relieving local traffic congestion as they could be linked easily to the Strand and other existing streets. Finally, to people of 'taste and discernment', roads were good and railways were bad.

The Victoria Embankment was the 'star' in this embankment project and the most complex of the sections (Porter 1998, 32). It began at the foot of Westminster Bridge (itself a brand-new structure in 1860) as a 70 ft (21.3 m) roadway with a wide pedestrian walkway on the riverside and ended at Blackfriars Bridge. The work commenced in 1864 and when it was completed in 1870 it was formally opened by the Prince and Princess of Wales (*ibid.*, 264–265). Also constructed in 1874 was the Victoria Embankment Gardens on an area of reclaimed land on the inward side of the new embankment roadway. The Chelsea section of the Embankment was also on the north side of the river but to the west of the Victoria Embankment. At its western end it included a stretch of Cheyne Walk and at its eastern end what is now Grosvenor Road and Millbank. The major part of the work commenced in 1868 and was completed and opened in 1874. Unlike the more famous Victoria section of the Embankment, the Chelsea wall contained few tunnels, arches or utility lines.

The first trees to appear alongside the roadway of the new Embankment were planted in 1869 in the Victoria Embankment section. These were established on the edge of the footway next to the riverside before the roadway itself had been completed. The footway was then opened as a pedestrian promenade while the

remaining construction work continued (Harley 2005, 19) (Figure 26). When the whole of this section of the Embankment was finally completed, London planes (*Platanus x acerifolia*) had been planted in the footway on both sides of the roadway. This majestic forest-type tree was considered ideal for the site, especially as it was tolerant of the smoky atmosphere of the metropolis. The only other species used was the closely related oriental plane (*Platanus orientalis*) with a number of these planted on the landward side of the road at the junction with Horse Guards Avenue (*ibid.*, 20). Along with the trees and some ironwork benches, the only other ornamentation was decorative gas lampposts with a distinctive double-dolphin design (see Figure 97). After the official opening of the Victoria Embankment the MBW provoked an outcry when it asked for legislation to give it control of the Embankment roadway (Porter 1998, 210). Most London streets, once completed by the MBW, were turned over to the local vestry or district ownership. The MBW argued that the embankment was a 'national' work belonging to the general public, not to some particular locality, and the *Thames Embankment (North) Act* of 1872 confirmed this.

The broad Victoria Embankment boulevard was quite different from the cramped confines of Fleet Street and the congestion of the Strand. To some

FIGURE 26. The first trees to appear alongside the roadway of the new Thames Embankment in London were planted in 1869 in the Victoria Embankment section. As can be seen in this contemporary engraving, the trees were established on the edge of the footway next to the riverside before the roadway itself had been completed.

observers, it evoked memories of the Regency. To others, it suggested Haussmann's Paris. When the MBW opened the Chelsea Embankment a few years later, it called attention to the trees and ornamental gardens 'in imitation of the Boulevards of Paris, a feature somewhat novel in this country' (Porter 1998, 211). Why not then introduce roadside cafés and a few restaurants? London newspapers were horrified at the thought, insisting that English men and women preferred home and family to the decadent street life of the Parisians. Nevertheless, the MBW and everyone associated with the project were proud that their pioneering work was typical of Paris and some other continental cities and much appreciated by the public. As Percy Edwards, Clerk of the LCC Improvement Committee, later noted:

> In designing the Embankments an endeavour had been made to render them not only useful, but agreeable, by giving some architectural embellishments to the wall and its accessories, laying out the surplus ground as ornamental gardens and planting trees on either side of the road, in imitation of the Boulevards of Paris, a feature somewhat novel in this country. When the whole length of the road is completed from Blackfriars to Battersea, and fringed with building worthy of the site, it is probable that it will scarcely be surpassed as an agreeable promenade for both foot and carriage traffic. The ample width of the road with its continuous avenue of trees, flanked on one side by the river and on the other by ornamental grounds and handsome buildings, will form a thoroughfare not unworthy of the great capital. The crowds which throng the existing embankment on fine summer Sundays afford proof that its advantages are fully appreciated by the public.
>
> Edwards 1898, 129

Reaction in the Victorian horticultural world to the tree planting on the Thames Embankment was a mixture of relief and pride. When the announcement was made that the Embankment project was going ahead the gardening magazines issued repeated calls for trees to be planted along the side of the new roadway. In the face of some vocal opposition and in the absence of any official confirmation, there was increasing frustration among many horticulturists and their allies that this might not happen (Humphreys 1873, 130). In March 1863, the *Gardeners' Chronicle* (1863, 219) published a strongly worded editorial about its fears that 'this glorious opportunity' to create a magnificent tree-lined boulevard in the centre of London would be abandoned. These concerns were raised with the Committee on Arboriculture that had recently been appointed by the Royal Horticultural Society, and its advice was also sought on the choice of suitable species. The editorial ended with a sarcastic reference to the Parisian boulevards by adding, 'We have at all events the satisfaction of knowing that *our* trees, whatever they may be, will not have to be cut down every 20 or 30 years to form barricades'. When the trees were eventually planted, the gardening press was generally delighted with the results. Noel Humphreys (1871, 47), the well-respected horticulturist, declared, 'The most notable of the recent additions to the splendour of our British Babylon is, undoubtedly, the Thames Embankment'. In later years, the maintenance and management of the trees on the Thames Embankment would become a hotly debated topic and this is explored in Chapter 12.

The planting of trees along the Embankment was widely regarded as a novelty by the public and to some extent it was allowed to go ahead on that basis, despite opposition from some influential figures (Humphreys 1873, 130). The fact that the trees survived and generally flourished, and were seen to enhance the new roadway, helped to promote the case for tree planting along more of London's main thoroughfares. It was suggested that if the Embankment had remained unplanted for twenty years, the opposition to the planting may have eventually triumphed and this would have been a major blow to the Victorian street tree movement almost before it had started. Fortunately, the success of this innovation, especially at such a high-profile location, helped pave the way for more street tree planting throughout Britain.

When the Victoria Embankment was opened in 1870 it provided a wide and convenient thoroughfare from the west of the metropolis to the heart of the City. However, as its road linkages with the old thoroughfares of the Strand and Fleet Street were few and inconvenient, the Embankment was not utilised to the extent that had been anticipated (Edwards 1898, 57). A large amount of traffic from the west and north of the capital centred at Charing Cross but from this point there was no good approach to the Embankment. Although the MBW had long wanted to form a direct approach to the Embankment from Charing Cross, the only effective route was through the old mansion of the Duke of Northumberland, and the Duke objected to its demolition. Parliamentary approval was eventually obtained in 1873, work commenced in 1874 and the route opened in 1876. To preserve the historical associations of the site, the road was named Northumberland Avenue.

The creation of this major new thoroughfare in the centre of London provided another opportunity for street tree planting on a grand scale. The dimensions of the road were ideal being 1000 ft (309 m) in length and 90 ft (27.4 m) wide (Edwards 1898, 58). As with the Thames Embankment, London plane trees were selected as the most suitable for the location. A tremendous amount of care was taken in the design and specification of the tree-pits to ensure the survival of trees. It involved an early example of a suspended pavement, described in Chapter 11. The spacing of the trees on Northumberland Avenue was significantly greater than those on the Thames Embankment, although there is no record of the reason for this (Figure 27). This remains one of London's finest tree-lined thoroughfares, especially in summer when the majestic plane trees form an almost complete green canopy.

In the early 1870s, street tree planting in London was still in its infancy and although articles were now appearing in the gardening magazines with suggestions for suitable streets to be lined with trees, little was happening on the ground (Newton 1870, 1087–1088). Some streets in central London, such as Oxford Terrace, Cambridge Terrace and Westbourne Terrace, were considered ideal candidates. Advantage could be taken of the unusually wide distances between opposite houses, especially if the footway could be extended by removing the iron railings and shrubberies in front of the houses. Other streets near the north bank of the Thames were proposed for street tree planting

FIGURE 27.
Northumberland Avenue in London and the Constitutional Club, photographed in 1896, ten years after this major new thoroughfare was opened. The spacing of the London plane trees was significantly greater than those on the Thames Embankment.

in order that 'gracefully planted connections might easily be formed with the Thames Embankment on which young planes are already planted' (*ibid.*, 1087). This proposal indicates that even at this early stage in the Victorian street tree movement there was an awareness of the potential to create 'green networks' through street tree planting. Some very grandiose schemes were also suggested, such as planting along the length of the Edgware Road from Marble Arch to Maida Hill (Humphreys 1873, 130). Portland Place was another location considered suitable for a grand avenue by several leading horticulturists (Humphreys 1874, 277). In the event, none of these proposed planting schemes went ahead at that time.

Towards the end of the 1870s, there seems to have been a modest increase in the number of new street tree planting schemes as the movement gained some momentum. Some of these schemes were south of the river. In 1878, the local authority in Southwark placed a contract with Messrs Goff and Sons, nurserymen based on Old Kent Road, to plant plane trees along St George's Road, from the Elephant and Castle to the Westminster Bridge Road (*The Garden* 1878a, 500). The company was also engaged to complete the planting of the Blackfriars Road up to the approach to Blackfriars Bridge. Around the same time, plane trees were planted in Tooley Street, Bermondsey, a major road running east from London Bridge (*Gardeners' Chronicle* 1882, 306). A few years later this was declared a great success when out of 84 trees planted only 12 had died, and of these some were killed by 'over-kindness' at the hands of local residents.

Although the street tree movement was now gaining momentum and the number of trees in London's streets was rising, there were many people, from major public figures to ordinary citizens, who did not welcome this innovation. In 1878, it was reported in *The Garden* (1878b, 239) that the Hounslow Local Board had recently debated the desirability of planting trees in some of the broadest thoroughfares in the district. There were a number of objections and the motion in favour was narrowly defeated. One speaker objected on the grounds that the trees would grow up and shade the fruit trees in the market gardens; another stated that the roots would get into the drains and choke them, and that the leaves falling in autumn would be a nuisance; and a third remarked that the trees would injure the roads by keeping off the sun and the wind. In another part of London the opposition to street trees had a financial aspect. At the auditing of the accounts of the Tottenham Local Board one parishioner objected to an item of £117 10s, the cost of the trees planted at the sides of the High Road; and also to an item of £258 15s, the cost of the tree guards for these trees (*The Garden* 1882, 74). Other objections were that the tree roots would choke the culverts and prevent the storm waters from being carried away. In the discussion that followed, a case tried at Essex Assizes in 1852 was cited in which a nurseryman, who planted some street trees on behalf of the Chelmsford Local Board of Health, was indicted for creating a nuisance. He was found guilty and all the newly-planted trees had to be removed. Before proceeding with any further street tree planting in Tottenham, the auditor decided to take legal advice on the matter.

Those objecting to their streets being planted with trees sometimes resorted to direct action. In 1879, the Westminster Vestry resolved to plant trees on a small patch of vacant land adjacent to a road in Knightsbridge, known as Knightsbridge Green. This met with unexpected opposition from local tradesmen who considered the presence of the trees would injure their business, presumably by obscuring the shop fronts. Local cab-drivers also objected, believing the proposed work was an invasion of their rights. At a local community meeting a resolution was passed condemning the tree planting, following which a group of cabmen and others proceeded to the Green, where, according to one eye-witness, 'they gave emphasis to their resolution by seizing the shovels of the workmen and filling up the holes which had been dug to receive the trees' (*Gardeners' Chronicle* 1879a, 375).

While some people claimed not to have any fundamental objection to street tree planting, they argued that it was useless to attempt this because the trees would not grow. This was not on account of the polluted atmosphere of Britain's major cities, as the success of the London plane tree had largely countered that argument, but an entirely new difficulty related to water

(Humphreys 1873, 130). It was claimed that the recently completed main drainage and sewerage works in London had greatly exhausted the water-bearing strata of the city and caused the gradual drying up of many of its ancient and celebrated wells. It was said that this was now having a most injurious effect upon all kinds of vegetation and would be a very great problem for any newly planted street trees. Because there was no firm evidence to support this assertion, it was generally dismissed as fanciful by those with sound horticultural knowledge.

In their efforts to counter some of the negativity towards street tree planting, those promoting this were often not helped by the poor standard of some of the planting schemes. Although understandable in what was a novel activity, specifications for street tree planting and the standard of work to implement this varied enormously both between and within local authority districts (see Chapter 11). It was common for trees to fail through poor quality nursery stock, poor planting or lack of aftercare and then have to be replaced. Perhaps these negative attitudes and critical reports of planting schemes were eventually starting to unnerve those who were trying to promote this. In 1880, in a surprisingly pessimistic item in the *Gardeners' Chronicle* (1880, 18), the editors urged caution regarding street tree planting. This repeated some of the familiar arguments against this, such as the narrowness of most of London's streets, the obstruction of light to nearby houses, not allowing the road surface to dry out quickly, and the insignificant value of any shade in a typically cloudy British summer. In an effort to mitigate some of these problems the editors recommended that 'groups of trees and single specimens would, under the circumstances be found more effective than a row or rows of trees on each side of the street'. Fortunately, the magazine soon returned to its more positive approach, although continuing to present a range of views from its correspondents.

Many of the early street tree plantings in London and elsewhere in Britain were funded by private individuals. In 1878, it was reported in the *Sanitary Record* and the *Gardeners' Chronicle* (1878a, 50) that an anonymous gentleman with an interest in tree planting in London was willing to give £1000, to be divided equally between ten parishes. This was to facilitate the planting of plane trees in streets and other locations 'where the need for shade was greatest'. That same year, at a meeting of the Hornsey Local Board of Health the clerk stated that a gentleman, who had previously resided in the locality, had expressed his willingness to give £100 to the Board for the purpose of planting plane trees along the roads around Highgate (*Gardeners' Chronicle* 1878b, 534). A motion was passed that the offer be accepted with thanks, and that it be referred to the General Purposes Committee to carry out the proposal. One committee member opposed the motion on the grounds that the planting of trees was injurious to the roads and entailed a considerable amount of unnecessary expense. In 1879, it was proposed to plant trees along a new street called Fitzjohn's Avenue, which connected Hampstead with Swiss

Cottage. This was prompted by a donation from Sir Spencer Wilson of £100, which was half the cost of the scheme (*Gardeners' Chronicle* 1879b, 656). Local people had said it was a misnomer to call the new road the 'Avenue' unless it had trees and as its width was between 50 ft and 60 ft (15.2–18.3 m), they believed there was sufficient room to accommodate this. The trees selected were horse chestnuts, alternately white and pink (*Aesculus hippocastanum* and *Aesculus x carnea*).

A significant source of private funding for street tree planting in London was the Metropolitan Public Gardens Association (MPGA). Founded in London in 1882 under the Chairmanship of Lord Brabazon (later the Earl of Meath), it continues to operate today (Malchow 1988, 109). Its main aim was the protection, preservation and acquiring of open space in London for public use. An additional aim was to promote and support the planting of street trees. In 1885, the MPGA offered a contribution of £100 towards the expense of planting trees in the thoroughfares of Lambeth (*Woods and Forests* 1885, 70). The subject was referred to the committee of the local vestry but it recommended declining the offer. Despite this, the vestry itself had a different opinion to its own committee. Canon Pelham, the rector, made a strong speech in favour of planting street trees in Lambeth and he was supported by several members of the vestry. It was not uncommon for the MPGA's offers of funding for street trees to meet with opposition. In 1890, the Vestry of St Marylebone received an MPGA offer to contribute £100 towards the expense of planting trees in the thoroughfares of the parish (*Gardeners' Chronicle* 1890, 597). This offer had been made previously and once again, Mr Harris, Chairman of the Works Committee, recommended it be declined. The trees, he said, would cost between £4 and £5 each, and how many, he asked, would they get for £100? While he agreed that Portland Place would make a splendid boulevard if planted with trees, he thought the MPGA should do the work themselves, particularly as objections had been raised regarding the planting. Despite these difficulties the MPGA still had significant success in many parts of London. Its annual reports throughout the late 1880s and 1890s consistently record is practical or financial support for a wide range of street tree planting schemes. For example, in 1897 the MPGA contributed to schemes along the Great Western Road and Great Russell Street as well as Pender Street in Deptford (MPGA 1898, 16).

Throughout the 1880s, the MBW continued its construction of major thoroughfares to improve traffic flow through the centre of London. This included the building of Charing Cross Road and Shaftesbury Avenue, both planted with trees as soon as they were completed (*Gardeners' Chronicle* 1887, 462). Many of the main thoroughfares leading to the suburbs had also been planted. Almost everywhere, the species chosen was the London plane, although the horse chestnut, lime and elm featured occasionally. When the old elm trees in Brompton Road were finally cut down, these decayed remnants of a past landscape were replaced with plane trees. With the winding-up of the MBW and the establishment of the LCC in 1888, the rate of street tree plantings seems to have increased (Edwards 1898, 163). As well as the important role of new roads and road widening schemes in assisting traffic flow, attention was also given to their health benefits by emphasising how these routes could provide a breathing space for the neighbourhood when planted with street trees. Two of the last major roads constructed around this time by the LCC's Improvements Committee were Aldwych and Kingsway, completed in the early 1900s (*Gardeners' Chronicle* 1905, 313). Both were eventually planted when the Improvements Committee authorised the expenditure, with 240 trees planted at a cost of £825.

In the summer of 1892, the popular *Daily News* newspaper published a survey it had conducted on street tree planting in London and the article was reproduced in the *Gardeners' Chronicle* (1892, 530). This gave a fascinating insight into the scale of progress made so far by the Victorian street tree movement in London. From enquiries made in seventeen London districts, it had been found that only three were now absolutely treeless, while in the other fourteen the total number of street trees was 14,700. Out of these, 5158 had been planted by the boards and vestries and a further 5323 planted by builders and property owners. When the article appeared in the *Gardeners' Chronicle* it was followed immediately by an item on the scale of street tree planting in Paris, reproduced from the current issue of *Revue de l'Horticulture Belge*. This stated that there were now about 100,000 trees planted in the streets and roads of Paris, a figure that put the London achievement in perspective.

At the end of the Victorian era, London and the nation finally got its ceremonial tree-lined boulevard to compare with those created in European cities such as the Champs Elysées in Paris and Unter den Linden in Berlin. These were used for staging important national occasions, for example, victory parades, state funerals and royal weddings. When Queen Victoria died in 1901, it was decided to redesign The Mall as a ceremonial route in her memory by making this a major tree-lined thoroughfare running from Trafalgar Square to Buckingham Palace. As noted in Chapter 2, Charles II had initially created the Mall in the 1660s as a replacement venue for the playing of *pailmail* and when the game fell out of favour in the seventeenth century, it was used as a pedestrian promenade. By the mid-nineteenth century, many of the elm trees that lined the promenade were diseased and dying and what had been an attractive landscape feature was now attracting adverse comment. William Robinson, the eminent horticulturists, remarked:

> I can imagine nothing more calculated to bring town-gardening into disrepute than such a specimen of planting as that in The Mall in St James's Park. Had the Plane been planted it would have made a noble avenue – the Elm now forms a miserable one.
>
> Robinson 1869, 166

When the Mall was redesigned in the 1900s into a broad thoroughfare, a double avenue of plane trees was planted on either side (Figure 28). Perhaps those involved had listened to Robinson or maybe they were just following the

FIGURE 28. When the Mall was redesigned in the 1900s as a ceremonial route in memory of Queen Victoria, a double avenue of London plane trees was planted on either side. This photograph was taken around 1925 when the trees were becoming well established and careful formative pruning had been undertaken.

general trend of favouring this species for street tree planting. The Mall has since become world-famous as an historic and spectacular avenue.

Cardiff

As the capital of Wales, Cardiff has always been at the forefront of Welsh efforts to introduce street trees to their urban centres. A small town until the early nineteenth century, it then expanded rapidly with its development as a major port for the transport of coal following the arrival of heavy industry in the region. In 1835, the administration of Cardiff came under a Corporation with an elected Council. It later became an independent County Borough in 1889 and achieved city status in 1905. This account of its early street trees programme draws heavily on *The Public Parks and Recreation Grounds of Cardiff*, an unpublished work by Andrew Alexander Pettigrew (1926), the city's Chief Officer of Parks and Open Spaces from 1915 until his death in 1936. Various members of the Pettigrew family were central to park design and tree planting in late Victorian and Edwardian Cardiff (Elliott 2016, 237).

In 1871, Cardiff Corporation decided to adopt a policy of introducing trees along some of its streets (Pettigrew 1926, 70). It had been aware of recent plantings in London and elsewhere and was generally in favour of street trees where the streets could accommodate this. However, the original planting of streets with trees, where this was done, was the responsibility of the owners of the land being developed, not of the Corporation. While the Corporation stipulated that trees should not be planted without its consent, this implied no discouragement but merely the enforcement of some sort of system. Once the trees were established, the Corporation accepted responsibility for their protection and maintenance, and for the replacement of any trees that died. A report entitled *Public Improvements*, prepared by the Borough Engineer and dated March 1881, gives an indication of the streets already planted by that date. New trees were established in St Andrew's Place in Tredegarville, Newport Road (western half), Partridge Road and Wordsworth Street, to replace trees that had died or been destroyed. Other streets planted by this date, at the expense of the residents, included Cathedral Road (Figure 29), Clive Road, Church Road, Fitzalan Road and Richmond Terrace (now Museum place). It seems that most of the trees planted were common lime (*Tilia x europeae*). Planting had also taken place in Cathays Park in the winter of 1879–1880 with a double avenue of elms that was later utilised in a new built development to flank the road which became known as King Edward VII Avenue (*ibid.*, 72). It is interesting to note that this avenue of trees in due course dictated the layout of what became Cardiff Civic Centre, a complex of civic and national buildings in the Edwardian Baroque style that were connected by tree-lined boulevards (Elliott 2016, 244).

A second stage in the development of the city's street tree planting programme was reached in January 1884 after various Council meetings (Pettigrew 1926, 70). In response to the question of planting trees in Richmond Road it was resolved that the Council would undertake the planting of the proposed trees, on condition the owner guaranteed payment by the residents within one month of completion. The owner agreed and both sides of Richmond Road were planted later in the winter of 1883–1884. Unfortunately, due to an administrative error, not everything went to plan. While the residents along the southern half of the road received and paid their bills, those living along the northern half never received theirs. When this was realised two years later, those who had paid protested and demanded the return of their money. Nearly a year later the Council agreed to reimburse them. As a result, Richmond Road became the first street in Cardiff to be planted throughout its length by the Corporation and at its expense, although this had not been intended. In the intervening period, the Corporation had already planted trees along both sides of Senghenydd Road at its own expense, without any suggestion of the owners paying or sharing the cost. While Richmond Road had been planted by contract, Senghenydd Road and all others after were planted by direct labour. The planting of Newport Road, from Pengam bridge to Rumney bridge, was authorised by the Council in 1887, again at its own expense.

In the cases of Richmond Road, Senghenyyd Road and Newport Road, these were not regarded as setting a precedent that the Council would fund all future street tree plantings (Pettigrew 1926, 71). This is evidenced from Council minutes that give details of the discussion of requests from residents for permission to plant particular roads with trees. Different proposals and amendments were made with various votes for and against and sometimes the requests were allowed if the planting was at the residents' expense. A general proposal was also made that all streets with a width of at least 50 ft (15.2 m) be planted with trees. Because the rates at that time were considered exceedingly high, it was suggested it would be impolitic that public money be spent on

planting the trees. Another proposal requested the Borough Engineer to furnish a report showing what roads and streets within the Borough were available for planting with trees so that an estimate of the overall cost could be obtained. This motion was eventually carried.

In 1889, a motion was put before Council to approve a request by the residents of Oakfield Street to plant that road with trees, at their own expense. While such a proposal was not unusual, the general discussion that it provoked on street tree planting in the city proved something of a watershed moment for Cardiff's entire policy on this matter. While the Council's official minutes give no indication of some of the strongly held views that were expressed, this came out later in reports that appeared in the local newspapers. The following is a collection of quotes from newspapers given in Pettigrew's unpublished report (Pettigrew 1926, 71). In a comment on the Council's general policy, Councillor Milton is reported to have 'protested strongly against trees and shrubs being paid for out of the rates to beautify places were aristocrats lived'. Councillor Sanders enquired 'where the line was drawn in selecting streets for planting. The trees did not find their way into the smaller streets'. He begged the Council 'not to let it be said that certain places were planted because certain people lived in them'. Councillor T. Rees responded by saying 'if trees were planted in narrow streets they would shut out the light and sunshine from the cottages'. Councillor Sir Morgan Morgan then said he 'would plant every poor street in

FIGURE 29. The common lime trees in Cathedral Road, Cardiff, were some of the first street trees to be planted in that city. The work had been undertaken at the expense of the residents, as were many of the earliest street plantings in Cardiff. This photograph was taken in 1904 when the trees were around 25 years old.

Cardiff if there was room; it was narrow-minded and illiberal to oppose such a thing'. In response to that, Councillor F.J. Bevan believed:

> It was a positive fact that no poor man's street was planted. There was a desire to make a selection, a very strong desire. At any rate that was his conviction, and in his judgement it was improper to fix on the poor people of the town the expense necessary to beautify and adorn the aristocratic quarters. The people living in these streets had plenty of money and could well afford to pay for their trees. They would not, however. They would take from the poor every penny they had.
>
> Pettigrew 1926, 71 (quoting Councillor Bevan)

All these quotes show just how much street tree planting in Cardiff was a hot political issue and something that highlighted significant class divisions. Although the motion to allow the residents of Oakfield Street to finance their plantings was eventually passed, this was the last street tree plantings to be paid for by the residents. Following this debacle the Corporation assumed control of street tree planting and maintenance in the city.

Around this time, a report on street tree planting that had been requested by the Council in 1889 was submitted by the Borough Engineer. The matter was then referred to the Public Works Committee which resolved 'that the sum of £100 a year be spent on the planting of [street] trees, and that the Borough Engineer submit a report to this Committee at an early date, showing what planting he would recommend to be done this season in accordance with this resolution' (Pettigrew 1926, 72). This was then adopted as Cardiff Corporation's policy on street tree planting for some years to come. Sometime later, the responsibility for the planting and management of street trees passed from the Public Works Committee to the Parks Committee.

Edinburgh

By the start of the nineteenth century, Edinburgh had become Scotland's political, commercial and cultural centre. In contrast to Glasgow, which in 1821 overtook it as Scotland's largest city, Edinburgh had experienced comparatively little industrialisation. The city had also undergone a transformation from the late 1760s when the professional and business classes gradually deserted what was known as the Old Town in favour of the more desirable and expensive residential properties of the neo-classical New Town (Carley *et al.* 2015). In the meantime, the Old Town continued to decay into an increasingly dilapidated, overcrowded slum with high mortality rates that was segregated practically and socially from the rest of the city (Hogg 1973). The city had always enjoyed a degree of autonomy and its urban self-government was confirmed under the *Local Government Act (Scotland)* of 1889 when it was one of four cities that were made counties in their own right.

The residents of Edinburgh's New Town always had access to a good number of private residential squares and some had private gardens to the rear of their property (Johnston 215, 116). For many of these fortunate and influential citizens the planting of trees in the city's streets was probably not a priority and this may be partly responsible for Edinburgh having a slow and sometimes difficult start to its street tree programme. When trees finally began to appear in the streets of Edinburgh this owed much to the work of the Cockburn Association, a local civic society, and its close working relationship with the city authorities. When the Association was founded in 1875, it was said that 'the planting of trees on the broad thoroughfares of the city was scarcely dreamed of' (Robinson 1901, 128). In recognition of this sad situation, the new Association included 'the preservation and planting of ornamental trees in and around the city' as one of its aims to improve the built environment of Edinburgh (Cockburn Association 1897, 4–6).

In the early years of the Association some major improvements were made to the landscape in the vicinity of Princes Street, the main thoroughfare through the city centre (Cockburn Association 1897, 8). This mainly involved the formerly private Princes Street Gardens, which the Town Council acquired in 1876 for a public park despite much opposition from local residents. As part of a later agreement, the Council undertook to widen Princes Street and as a result some of the few trees that stood by the roadside were felled. Lord Moncreiff, the Lord Chief Justice of the time and also President of the Cockburn Association, came across this work on his way to court one morning. By remonstrating with the workmen he was able to save some of the trees. Then, using his undoubted influence he was also able to secure an assurance from the Council that when the road improvements in Princes Street had been completed, more ornamental trees would be planted in the place of those that had been lost. After a few years, the trees had not been planted and a deputation from the Association met with the Parks Committee of the Council to get confirmation of this assurance (Cockburn Association 1879, 3–4). The Association cited the fine example that had been set by London with the young trees on the Thames Embankment and it urged the Council to do something similar for Edinburgh. The subsequent annual reports of the Association refer again and again to this understanding regarding Princes Street, but the work was never effectively carried out. The Association's ongoing frustration with the lack of action in Princes Street was undoubtedly channelled into its efforts to promote street trees in other parts of the city (Masson 1926, 45–49). Today, there are only a small number of trees adjacent to Princes Street, those growing in the Gardens behind railings or those in the grounds of St John's Episcopal Church at its western end.

One of the earliest successes of the Cockburn Association was to secure some tree planting in Lothian Road. This was initially recommended in its annual report of 1879, with the suggestion that the planting take place on the east side of Lothian Road between Castle Terrace and Bread Street, 'where the breadth of the street would easily admit this' (Cockburn Association 1879, 5). Although it did not happen immediately, it was undertaken before 1884 as the Association was then able to cite this as a successful example of street tree planting (Cockburn Association 1884, 5). It is interesting to note that Lothian Road no longer has any trees located in the footway. By 1888, a stretch of Regent Road near the Dugald Stewart Monument had also been planted (Cockburn Association 1888, 5). The Association was always keen to ensure that all new street trees received adequate post-planting maintenance to make certain they survived and flourished. In the summer after the trees in Lothian Road and Regent Road were planted the Association contacted the Council as it was concerned for the survival of these trees in the very dry weather and stressed the need for watering (Cockburn Association 1888, 5). The following year it was requesting that some judicious pruning be given to the young trees in Regent Road (Cockburn Association 1889, 7). This prompting of the Council by the Association was not indicative of any lack of confidence in its ability to plant and care of trees at that time. In one of its early annual reports it makes reference to Mr MacLeod, 'the able City Gardener', who was responsible for these matters as Superintendent of Parks and Gardens (Cockburn Association 1897, 10).

The success of the planting in Lothian Road, Regents Road and a few other locations was used by the Association to put pressure on the Council to approve and undertake more street tree plantings (Cockburn Association 1897, 11). Nevertheless, progress continued to be painfully slow. In an editorial in the *Gardeners' Chronicle* in 1897 there was praise for Edinburgh Council's work with the Princes Street Gardens (*Gardeners' Chronicle* 1897, 165). In contrast to this, it pointed out that the majority of the streets and main thoroughfares of the city remained treeless, or nearly so. Furthermore, it was said that the very massiveness and coldness of the city's stone architecture made matters worse. The Association was in full agreement with this view. In an account of its achievements so far, published in 1897, it pleaded,

> The Reports of the Association are full of recommendations as to the planting of trees in [Edinburgh's] streets. Some of these have been already referred to, but with the exception of the few trees in the Lothian and Regents Roads and Castle Terrace, little has yet been accomplished in that direction. Few improvements would do so much for the City at so little cost.
>
> Cockburn Association 1897, 22

For the Association, the lack of action on the part of the Edinburgh Council was inexplicable. In the same published account of its achievements it stated:

> Indeed, there are few of our leading thoroughfares which do not contain ample space for trees, and they would add greatly to the amenities of the City, protecting passengers from wind and dust, and adding (with the window flower-boxes which are now being cultivated by most persons of taste) the elements of freshness and colour to the monotony and dullness of our grey streets.
>
> Cockburn Association 1897, 12

A few years later, R.C. Munro Ferguson, the Member of Parliament and amateur arboriculturist, expressed his own frustration with the lack of progress by observing:

> That some shade is needed in our streets and public places is shown by the fact that though the heat of Edinburgh is less appreciable than that of London, the glare of Princes Street or of Leith Walk is as depressing as that of any other of the world's thoroughfares.
>
> Munro Ferguson 1901, 388

As well as doing its utmost to encourage Edinburgh Council to plant more streets with trees, the Association was keen to promote the protection of existing trees throughout the city, including those threatened by new built development. One particular threat that not only affected existing trees but also undermined the prospect of new trees being planted was the Scottish system of feuing that relates to the transfer of land (Cockburn Association 1882, 2). This imposed terms and conditions on the land transfer that could involve the design of any new building, including the distance the property is setback from the street or road. In its annual reports and other publications the Association frequently appealed 'to property owners and feuars, when laying out ground for feuing, to spare existing trees, and avail themselves of suitable assistance for the immediate planting of all gardens and streets suitable for the purpose' (Cockburn Association 1897, 13).

When encouraging Edinburgh Council to undertake more street tree plantings the Cockburn Association was always keen to the highlight progress made in other towns and cities. While it occasionally made reference to London, it frequently pointed to achievements much closer to home in Aberdeen and St Andrews. The street tree planting in Aberdeen was often cited by the Association as a model of good practice:

> The City of Aberdeen ... has set us a splendid example in the planting of [street] trees. Being exposed nearly as much as Edinburgh to cold winds from the north and east, which render shelter, if not shade, almost a necessity of existence, Aberdeen can now boast of having no less than twenty-five miles of trees in and around the City.
>
> Cockburn Association 1897, 22

In Aberdeen much of the success of its street tree programme was due to the efforts of Robert Walker, Keeper of Victoria Park in the city. While his career is described later, its impact on the situation in Edinburgh should be mentioned here. By the 1890s and with little progress in the city's street tree programme, the Cockburn Association was beginning to ask questions about the level and type of expertise that the Council was employing. It noted:

> In other large cities trees are more extensively planted, more skilfully tended, and greater care is taken to replace the failures than is the case in Edinburgh. Here, also, little skill is shown in the mode of planting trees, and in their management. These

defects may be observed more or less in public and private gardens, and in many of the streets throughout the town.

Cockburn Association 1899, 9

While still praising the general work of Mr McLeod, Edinburgh's Superintendent of Parks and Gardens, doubts were raised within the Cockburn Association about his level of expertise, as a horticulturist, in the tasks of street tree planting and management. Aberdeen employed Robert Walker, a forester, and the city had been very successful in planting many thousands of street trees. Perhaps it did not occur to the Association that the real secret to Aberdeen's success with street trees might rest with its progressive Council. Nevertheless, the Association decided to recommended to Edinburgh's Council 'that a forester of experience should either be retained by the city, or should be requested to report annually upon the state of the trees in the gardens, parks, and streets, and to advise what should be done in regard to them' (Cockburn Association 1899, 9).

As the nineteenth century drew to a close, the Cockburn Association was starting to feel more optimistic that a determined effort would now be made by Edinburgh Council with regard to street trees The relationship between the Town Council and the Association had become even closer when the current Lord Provost of the City became President of the Association after the death of Lord Moncreiff (Cockburn Association 1897, 21). In its annual report for 1902 the Association welcomed enthusiastically the news that George Street would at last be planted with trees (Cockburn Association 1902, 10). However, by 1904 nothing had happened and it was reported that because some difficulties had arisen it was now doubtful whether this proposal would ever be realised (*The Garden* 1904, 70). While there were some technical challenges due to poor quality soil, the main problem was opposition to the street tree project from local businessmen. Meanwhile, other high-profile streets in the city were still waiting for trees. For example, photographs of the famous Grassmarket taken in 1908 show this devoid of trees. This was eventually planted in 1935 and the Association was happy to report, 'The Grassmarket has been much improved by the groups of trees, as anyone who recalls the wide stretch of bare granite paving will agree' (Cockburn Association 1935, 7). This is now one of Edinburgh's most celebrated public spaces with some fine mature trees.

There can be little doubt that without the constant lobbying of the Cockburn Association Edinburgh Council's street tree programme at the end of the nineteenth century would have been even less developed than it was. Throughout the twentieth century the Association had the benefit of a more proactive and forward looking City Council and was able to continue to play a vital role in promoting and protecting street trees in Edinburgh.

Early plantings in other cities

An example in the improved provision of public services to address urban problems was set by Birmingham in the 1870s under the leadership of Joseph

Chamberlain. This was then emulated by the LCC twenty years later and widely followed elsewhere (Trevelyan 1952, 118). The circumstances that helped facilitate what has been described as 'municipal socialism' came with a change in composition of the elected Council in Birmingham (Hunt 2004, 248–250). Between 1862 and 1882, the balance of power shifted decisively away from the shopkeepers and tradesmen towards those with more substantial business interests. In 1873, the Liberal Party swept to victory in the municipal elections and Joseph Chamberlain was elected Mayor of Birmingham. His solution to overcoming the fear of rate increases became known as 'Gas and Water' socialism. The municipal ownership of the utilities could bypass the council's limited tax base by using the profits which would have gone to shareholders to fund instead various civic improvements, or even reduce the rates. In turn, a sustained programme of investment in improving sanitation and civic infrastructure could alleviate the most expensive forms of urban degeneration and, in a virtuous circle, reduce the burden on the ratepayers.

Under the *Artisans' and Labourers' Dwellings Improvement Act* 1875 corporations were given powers to acquire, demolish and redevelop slum areas (Chinn 1999, 7). Birmingham Corporation was the first to use this law when it decided to make the dilapidated St Mary's Ward the subject of an improvement scheme. In 1876, the *Birmingham Improvement Act* received the Royal Assent and major construction work started 2 years later when it bought property worth £1.3 million for levelling and redevelopment, in the process expelling some 9000 residents without any thought to their rehousing needs (Hunt 2004, 260). This massive redevelopment scheme focused on building grandiose civic buildings and the widening of key thoroughfares. It also included the construction of a major new road, aptly called Corporation Street, planned as a Parisian-style boulevard to reflect Birmingham's position as the metropolis of the Midlands. Meanwhile, various street improvements had already commenced and these included tree planting along some of the main streets in the city. In September 1876, the *Gardeners' Chronicle* declared:

> Birmingham has been one of the first of our large towns to try the experiment of planting trees in the public streets, and, so far, with considerable success. In Broad Street, which is one of the principal thoroughfares leading from the heart of the town to Edgbaston, Harborne, Hagley, and other outskirts of Birmingham, and is a street with good shops and pavements the entire distance, now presents an appearance which thoroughly astonishes even the oldest inhabitant, for at intervals of about 20 yards [18.3 m] on either side of the street, and arising out of the pavement, 99 fine plane trees were planted in the spring of this year.
>
> *Gardeners' Chronicle* 1876, 354

The trees planted in Broad Street (Figure 30) in the winter of 1875–1876 had been supplied and planted for the Corporation of Birmingham by Mr R.H. Vertegans, of the Chad Valley Nurseries (*Gardeners' Chronicle* 1876, 355). The Corporation was pleased with the work as only two of the trees had died and with two or three exceptions all the others were in good heath and had made satisfactory growth in their first year. This was quite surprising to many people who expected the poor atmospheric conditions and the gas-polluted soil to have decimated the young trees. More planting was undertaken in Stephenson Place and Stephenson Street, the principal thoroughfares to New Street Station, where 24 plane trees were established. With the exception of two trees, all were doing well after their first year. It was said that some of the trees were in such good health they might have been growing in the pleasure grounds of a stately house rather than in the centre of a notoriously polluted manufacturing city.

Also in the winter of 1875–1876, the Corporation had engaged Mr Vertegens to plant nearly 100 lime trees in Bristol Street and the city end of Bristol Road. With the exception of four of the trees that were located close to gas pipes, all these had survived, although it was noticeable that they had dropped their foliage much earlier than the plane trees. The success of all the new planting was due largely to the post-planting maintenance the trees had received. Mr Till, the Borough Surveyor, had taken great interest in the planting of the streets, and had ordered that the trees be liberally watered during the dry, hot weather. Between the late 1870s and 1890s, Birmingham Corporation expanded its street tree programme to include other major thoroughfares in the city centre.

Coventry was another city in the Midlands to embark on planting at an early stage in the Victorian street tree movement. It was reported by *The Garden* in 1872 that the local authority had formed a committee some years earlier with the specific aim of planting trees in the streets and roads around Coventry (*The Garden* 1872, 76). The committee was composed of some 'influential gentlemen of the town' and the planting was being carried out by Mr Dawson, the manager of the Coventry cemetery. Each scheme was paid for by subscription from local residents and landowners, and as no scheme could go ahead unless there were funds to cover this, no debts were incurred. The editors of *The Garden* recommended 'the excellent example thus set by Coventry to many others of our towns, in which the hideousness of acres of brick is not relieved by a single tree'.

Further north in Manchester another street tree planting initiative began a few years later. In 1878, a meeting was organised by the Council of the Royal Botanical and Horticultural Society in the city and invitations were issued to all those interested in the topic of street trees (*Gardeners' Chronicle* 1878c, 560). The Chairman for the meeting, Alderman Heywood, said it had been called as a result of correspondence in the local newspapers during the last two or three months that had raised the topic of planting trees in the city's streets. As he was Chairman of the Highways Committee and this was a matter that came within the committee's responsibility, it was right for him to take the initiative. Heywood added that his committee had done their utmost to preserve those trees which they found growing in the streets, where these were threatened with paving work or the installation of sewers. Nevertheless, there was clearly a desire by residents to have many new trees planted into streets in and around the city. To help promote this, the meeting was addressed by Mr Bruce Finlay, regarded as an expert on the topic. As well as speaking about the constraints on urban trees, Finlay highlighted the opportunities for street tree planting and

FIGURE 30. Birmingham was one of the first major cities to begin systematically planting trees in some of its major thoroughfares. In the winter of 1875–1876, 99 plane trees were planted in Broad Street and only a few trees had to be replaced in this very successful planting scheme. This photograph was taken *c.* 1893.

gave examples of trees that might be suitable for planting in these locations. While this meeting seems to have acted as a catalyst for some initial action in Manchester, the early plantings did not always meet with the approval of the local horticultural establishment. In 1890, when Finlay addressed a meeting of Manchester Horticultural Improvement Society, his critical remarks about some shrubs planted in tubs in Albert Square prompted a much wider debate about the poor state of some of the street tree plantings in the city (*The Garden* 1890, 570). Critical articles appeared in the local newspapers and a war of words broke out between two local horticulturists writing in *The Garden* magazine. It was said that some of the leading horticulturists in Manchester had been invited to join the Town Gardening Committee to give their advice but had declined to do so, stating that the committee did not require their services and also that they did not want to interfere in the matter. In view of that, their subsequent criticism of the city's street tree planting did not go down well in some quarters. One individual complained that:

> ... after the Town Gardening Committee had worked so hard and done its best to try at least to make the streets more pleasant in the way indicated, without the assistance of those who refuse their help, [these people] now come forward and find fault, and suggest that the trees be 'carted away to the rubbish heap', and much more to the same effect.
>
> *The Garden* 1891, 18

It was clear that Manchester's early attempts to plant street trees in the city did not meet with universal approval or prompt a coordinated effort on the part of those supportive of this idea. Nevertheless, it seems that those difficulties raised in the early 1890s were resolved fairly quickly and the city subsequently developed a more extensive and more appreciated street tree programme.

In Liverpool there had been some major urban improvement schemes undertaken even before those in Birmingham (Briggs 1968, 236). This included significant street improvements as early as 1846 when Princes Road was laid out as a boulevard extending from the northern tip of Princes Park to Upper Parliament Street. Running parallel along most of its length was Princes Avenue with its row of elegant merchant's houses. Between the two thoroughfares was a central reservation of public open space some 50 ft (15 m) wide that was used as a promenade. Other schemes followed and in the 1860s the improvement of streets and boulevards was described by one Liverpool councillor as a subject 'seriously affecting the welfare of the burgesses at large' and of direct concern to 'our well-conducted and industrious working classes'. Although the improvement work was often extensive, it did not generally include the addition of street trees until much later. In the case of the impressive Princes Road and Princes Avenue 'boulevard', the trees were planted in the central reservation in the 1890s as two regularly spaced rows of London planes standing in the hard surfaced footway along with seating and some pavilion-like shelters (Figure 31). This continues to be a well-treed thoroughfare with a mix of mature trees on the central reservation, which itself is now mainly grass with narrow paths.

Although street tree planting in Cardiff had progressed at a steady pace from 1871, this developed more slowly in Swansea, the second largest city in Wales. Some of the first plantings date from the early 1880s with regularly spaced trees established on both sides of Walter Road. This continues to be a well-treed thoroughfare close to the city centre. There were also more scattered plantings in Bryn Road from the late 1880s, although this road no longer has any street trees.

In Scotland, St Andrews and Aberdeen were the pioneers in street tree planting. In the ancient town of St Andrews around the late 1870s, Alexander Milne, who had been Dean of Guild in Aberdeen, managed to overcome the

FIGURE 31. Trees were planted in the central reservation of Liverpool's Princes Avenue 'boulevard' in the 1890s. They comprised two regularly spaced rows of London planes standing in the hard surfaced footway along with seating and some pavilion-like shelters. This photograph was taken in 1904.

prejudice of a number of his municipal colleagues and had common lime trees planted on each side of the wide South Street, extending from the Cathedral grounds and Pends to the West Port (Anon 1905a, 4). To the surprise of many, the trees flourished and soon formed an attractive landscape feature. A few years after they had been planted the trees were admired by Robert Walker, the superintendent of the Victoria Park in Aberdeen. Some street tree planting had already taken place in Aberdeen in the time of Sir Alexander Anderson, First Lord Provost of Aberdeen from 1859–1865 (Anon 1905b, 4). Service trees (*Sorbus x thuringiaca*) were planted in Fountainhall Road and ash, beech and plane planted in Beechgrove Terrace. Anderson also had similar trees planted as far up what is now King's Gate as his residence at Hillhead, near Summerfield. Inspired by the success of the St Andrew plantings and the earlier plantings in Aberdeen, Walker resolved to undertake more extensive planting in the city where he was employed.

Robert Walker was the son of a Perthshire gardener and had come to Aberdeen as a nurseryman (Anon 1930, 6). In 1873, he was chosen out of 450 applicants to be Aberdeen's first public park keeper, being appointed keeper to Victoria Park, which he then transformed from a waste ground into a beautiful landscape. Recognising Walker's skill, the Corporation extended his 'sphere of usefulness' and he went on to lay out Westburn Park, Stewart Park, Union Terrace Gardens and the Promenade. His success with public parks encouraged the Corporation to extend his remit still further into developing a major programme of street tree planting, beginning in the residential district of the West End. These included the planting of service trees in Hamilton Place and hawthorns (*Crataegus monogyna*) in Whitehall Road and Blenheim Place (Anon 1905b, 4). The Rosemount area was particularly well supplied with trees, with avenues of trees in the streets that led to Rosemount Place towards Victoria Park. This included plane trees (*Platanus spp.*) in Belvidere Street, poplars in Thomson Street and Loanhead Terrace, and ash (*Fraxinus excelsior*), plane and other trees in Richmond Terrace. One of Walker's most ambitious schemes that he commenced around 1900 was the planting up of Anderson Drive, a major route that was intended to encircle the city and which now forms part of the main A90 dual carriageway to the west of the city. This was envisioned as a lengthy boulevard that would compare favourably with those in many continental cities. Purple plane trees (most likely *Acer pseudoplatanus* 'Purpureum') were planted in a double row on either side, initially on the section extending from Great Western Road to Queen's Road and beyond Rubislaw Den to the Stocket. It was hoped that this would 'become a picturesque source of pleasure to pedestrians as well as to 'carriage folk', with delightful shady walks on either side'.

As Walker's street tree plantings flourished and grew into mature trees, they were increasingly admired by the city's many visitors, and his reputation grew with the trees. He was frequently invited to give talks to interested parties around Scotland and also to host groups of horticulturists and municipal delegations visiting Aberdeen. In 1890, he wrote a booklet entitled *On the*

Planting of Trees in Towns that set out his approach to the topic and his views on suitable species for planting (Walker 1890). The content of this was based on a lecture he had delivered before the North of Scotland Horticultural Association (Cockburn Association 1902, 10). It was printed by Aberdeen University Press and 'issued' by the two Aberdeen members of John Ruskin's Guild of St George, a charitable education trust he founded in the 1870s. The booklet was widely read and among the many who acknowledged Walker's expertise was William Gladstone, the British Prime Minister, who spread the word on the benefits of urban trees among his social and political contacts (Anon 1930, 6).

Not surprisingly, Walker's booklet begins by comparing the 'verdant avenues' of the boulevards of some continental cities with the virtually treeless streets of Britain. He then gives a concise summary of the benefits of street tree planting:

> Planting of trees in streets, in a sanitary point of view, cannot be over-estimated. Besides exerting a beneficial influence in promoting improved habits, it awakens new thoughts and suggests fresh subjects for the mental exercise of the thousands who might otherwise be employed in the study of less desirable objects than those which nature provides and art cultivates. Trees not only afford shade and shelter, but adorn the landscape and purify the air. They improve the heart as well as the taste; they refresh the body and enlighten the spirit. And the more refined the taste is, the more exquisite is the gratification that may be enjoyed from every leaf-bearing tree.
>
> Walker 1890, 2–3

In 1905, Aberdeen's local paper *The Press and Journal* ran two articles that gave an overview of Walker's achievements in planting trees in many of the city's streets, mostly in residential districts (Anon 1905a, 4; 1905b, 4). Later in 1914, a few years before Walker's retirement, the same local paper gave another review of his achievements. This article is notable for making two points that highlight aspects of his management approach (Anon 1914, 5). First, it praises his systematic approach to planting by stating, 'When seen at the present time, Hamilton Place demonstrates the wisdom of having a systematic scheme for planting particular streets of the city. The trees have thrived remarkably well and now, in certain parts, almost form a canopy across the street'. Secondly, it praised Walker's use of remnant trees in new street improvements by stating, 'King's Gate, Beechgrove Terrace and several of the side streets in this district of the west end owe much of their charm to the way in which old trees have been retained to form part of the street ornamentation'.

While Robert Walker is not a name familiar to most of today's professionals, his contribution to promoting the systematic planting of trees in British streets is considerable. His success in Aberdeen had a direct impact on the development of similar programmes in Edinburgh and elsewhere in Scotland, even though many of those programmes took some years to get going. Dundee was one of the first Scottish cities to follow in the footsteps of Aberdeen (Anon 1905a, 4). This began in 1879 when a committee of Dundee Council approved the planting of 40 trees on the eastern end of the Esplanade that ran along the banks of the River Tay (Anon 1879a). The trees were planted in an avenue either side of the roadway and comprised mainly horse chestnuts, limes and sycamore (Anon 1879b). The trees were supplied by the local nursery of Messrs John Stewart and Son, and the work was supervised by Mr McKelvie, the Council's Superintendent of Cemeteries. This limited planting was regarded as an experiment to see if the trees could survive the exposed position and salt water spray. Although many of the trees did not thrive, it was still considered sufficiently successful to complete the planting a few years later with an additional 300 trees (Anon 1882) (Figure 32). It was only after completion of tree planting along the Esplanade (now called Riverside Drive) that serious consideration was then given to more planting schemes in the main thoroughfares and other streets in the city.

In Glasgow, Scotland's largest city, there was an early emphasis on urban improvement to combat the many environmental and social problems in the city. Even more than Birmingham, Glasgow's Town Council elders championed a belief in public services and the virtue of the municipality, as well as acting on this some years before Birmingham (Hunt 2004, 266–270). In 1866, the *City of Glasgow Improvement Act* launched the most comprehensive plan of civic improvement in Britain in the nineteenth century. During the latter part of the century, Glasgow's industrial and commercial might helped fund the construction of many of the city's greatest architectural masterpieces and most ambitious civil engineering projects. In terms of public green space, this embraced the creation of public parks on a scale that was the envy of many other towns and cities (McLellan 1894; Maver 1998). New public squares were constructed and attractively landscaped with trees and shrubs (Maver 1998, 335). Street improvements were another major feature of Glasgow's

FIGURE 32. Tree planting along the Esplanade (now called Riverside Drive) in Dundee began in 1879 as an experiment and although many of those trees did not thrive, it was considered sufficiently successful to plant a further 300 a few years later. This photograph shows the main planting scheme and was taken *c.* 1900.

urban renewal and this aimed to improve traffic flow, assist ventilation and promote sanitary reform. Having cleared the congested slums that stood in the way, the city embarked on the construction of 39 new streets as well as reshaping and widening a further 12, many of these located in the central district (Hunt 2004, 256).

It is surprising that with all this urban improvement in Glasgow, much of it street improvements, it did not include a concerted programme of street tree planting. This is despite a delegation from the city visiting Paris in 1866 to learn from the urban improvements being achieved under Baron Haussman's direction, which would have included the laying out of new tree-lined boulevards (Edwards 1993, 88). Instead, the introduction of street trees into Glasgow seems to have happened in a way similar to Edinburgh, in a rather slow and painstaking manner. This assessment is based on the fact that there is virtually no mention of any street tree planting in the contemporary press, little indication of street trees on OS maps and early photographs of the city's streets show these as virtually treeless. While the city's coat of arms features an oak tree at its centre, Glasgow Town Council's interest in amenity trees in the late nineteenth century was focused firmly on its public parks and squares (McLellean 1894, 125). Even when many of its major thoroughfares were widened and new ones constructed, these were generally not planted with trees, despite an attempt to model the width of their carriageways on the boulevards of Paris (Maver 1998, 335). Despite this, there is photographic evidence of at least some street trees in Glasgow in the late nineteenth century. There appears to have been some planting in Sauchiehall Street from about 1880, although on a limited scale. A photograph from 1907 shows a common lime about 30 years old (Figure 33). A slightly later image with a more extensive view of another part of the street has no trees at all.

In the residential districts of Glasgow in late Victorian times, as in many other cities, a considerable number of the streets were privately owned and here the responsibility for the planting and care of any street trees rested with the owners and proprietors whose properties fronted these. In 1896, 'the custody and care of all trees' was transferred to the parks committee of the new Corporation of the City of Glasgow, which formed a new sub-committee to consider how best street and footpath trees could be protected, and which department should bear the cost (Elliott 2016, 205–207). While many new trees were planted, these efforts continued to focus on open spaces adjacent to streets rather than planting in the footway itself. Some requests for street trees came from the public, such as a call to plant them along Great Western Road and Crow Road in 1901, but these were declined.

By 1910, there were still difficulties in getting trees planted in Glasgow's streets, particularly in and around the city centre. The *Gardeners' Chronicle* reported on a Corporation initiative with the aim of 'improving the appearance of some of the broader Glasgow thoroughfares, such as the Great Western Road, by the planting of trees' (*Gardeners' Chronicle* 1910, 490). This was the

FIGURE 33. Glasgow Town Council's interest in amenity trees in the late nineteenth century was focused firmly on its public parks and squares rather than street tree planting. Nevertheless, there appears to have been some planting in Sauchiehall Street from about 1880, although on a limited scale. This photograph that was taken in 1907 shows part of the street with a common lime about 30 years old.

same road where a public call for trees had been declined a decade before. The Corporation now requested the Superintendent of Parks, James Whitton, and the Master of Works to report on the subject. Unfortunately, their report advised against the work. It was estimated that 867 trees would be required and the cost of these, about £1300, was too great an expense. Furthermore, the gas and electricity mains were generally laid in the lines in which the trees would be planted, and moving these would involve even greater expense. In view of the report the Statute Labour Committee came to the conclusion that it was not expedient to precede with the suggested improvements. It was only later after the First World War that Glasgow would develop a substantial street tree planting programme.

While this chapter has focused on the Victorian street tree movement in some of our major cities, it should be mentioned that some of the smaller towns were not slow to emulate these efforts and were sometimes ahead of their larger neighbours. Kettering in Northamptonshire was one of these and had begun planting some of its streets from the 1880s (Figure 34). The gardening magazines of the late Victorian era frequently contained reports on the achievements of some of the smaller towns, where the early planting in many of the streets was often paid for by public subscription. Examples where residents paid for some of their street trees include Shrewsbury, Grantham and Romford (*Gardeners' Chronicle* 1881, 374). Even without the influence of residents who could afford their own trees, it is interesting to note that the pattern of early street tree planting in many towns and cities

FIGURE 34. Kettering in Northamptonshire was one of the smaller towns that was quick to embrace the Victorian street tree movement and it had begun planting some of its streets from the 1880s. This photograph of The Headlands was taken around 1910 and shows rapidly maturing trees that are already contributing much to the attractiveness of the streetscape.

often favoured those districts where the wealthier people lived. Although the power to influence the public urban landscape was now under the control of elected politicians and their officials, this did not mean a more democratic landscape. As the acrimonious debate among the Cardiff councillors forcefully demonstrated, decisions about where street trees were planted often reflected the wishes of the upper and middle classes than those of the working class. This pattern in the provision of street trees and the urban forest in general is one that largely continues today.

As street tree planting became an increasingly common sight in late Victorian towns and cities, some people were unnerved by these dramatic visual changes to once familiar streets. One correspondent in *The Garden* expressed the fears of many when they wrote, 'Street tree planting, like most other new fashions, appears likely to be overdone, as already we find them being planted where before there was barely space for the traffic' (Gosport 1886, 121). However, these dissenting voices were increasingly outnumbered by those who were generally supportive of the idea of greening our streets. Any concerns regarding street tree planting were now mostly about how this was being done, with the focus on poor tree selection, planting and maintenance (see Chapters 11 and 12).

CHAPTER SIX

Victorian and Edwardian Suburbs

The establishment of trees along thoroughfares in the centre of cities such as London, Birmingham, Cardiff and Aberdeen generated much public interest and promoted the Victorian street tree movement nationally in the second half of the nineteenth century. Meanwhile, the planting of street trees was also beginning in the suburbs that were developing rapidly on the periphery of many towns and cities across Britain. This chapter begins by exploring the major factors behind the spread of suburbia in Britain during the late Victorian and Edwardian eras. It then focuses on major cities, including London, Birmingham, Manchester, Cardiff and Glasgow, and charts the development of a number of their suburbs. The introduction of trees into many individual streets is recorded and an assessment made of how the treescapes have developed to the present day. A similar treatment is then given to three individual suburbs in Nottingham, Kingston upon Hull and Worcester. While there is sometimes a reasonable amount of historical literature relating to tree planting in the main thoroughfares of cities, sourcing information about early street tree planting in the suburbs has mainly involved a considerable amount of original research. The chapter concludes with an account of street trees in the Garden Suburbs from the earliest examples of this town planning phenomenon up to the outbreak of the First World War in 1914. Some early suburbs in spa towns and seaside resorts are covered in Chapter 8.

The early suburbs and some relevant legislation

For the Victorian upper class the city was decreasingly regarded as an arena to be celebrated but instead as a mode of existence best rejected altogether (Hunt 2004, 287). The deepening gulf between the rich and poor was generating increasing alarm among the ruling class and their allies and increasing anger and resentment among the working class (*ibid.*, 290–291). This was especially apparent in London with its stark contrast between the affluent West End and the desolate East End and when fears of an insurrection were heightened after revolutionary events on the Continent such as the 1871 Paris Commune. Previously, the rich and poor had lived in the same districts with the rich in the main streets and the poor hidden away in the service streets behind. Their narrow streets and labyrinthine courtyards seemed forbidding and unwelcoming and their poor housing was increasingly linked to poor morals and behaviour as well as poor health. The impetus for suburbanisation has always contained a large element of class fear and the desire to isolate one's family from the

turbulent lower orders of the urban core (Fishman 1987, 82). As the wealthy
Victorians moved out of town centres to the new suburbs, much of the housing
for the poor was demolished for commercial spaces, or to make way for the
railway stations and lines that appeared from the 1840s. While the property
owners received compensation, those who rented the properties did not. In
urban improvement schemes it was always cheaper to compensate the owners
of a few tenements than the houses of many middle-class owners. Thus the
homes of the poor were always the first to be destroyed.

What made much of this suburban living practical was the gradual
improvement in public transport and the transport network (Barratt 2012, 105).
It began with the introduction of the horse-drawn omnibus, followed by the
railways, trams and motor buses. Once established in their new suburbs, the
upper and middle classes were keen to insulate their salubrious neighbourhoods
from the potentially 'troublesome' working class by severely restricting any
access (Atkins 1993). The urban enclosure movement and privatisation of the
urban landscape that had preceded these suburban developments had become
widespread by the beginning of the nineteenth century and now also affected
many streets. Throughout the first half of the nineteenth century numerous
streets in London and other major cities had barriers to prevent non-residents,
'undesirables' and through traffic from entering. It was not until the late
nineteenth century that concerted public efforts led to municipal acts to remove
them and free all public streets to true public access.

The suburban building boom that began in earnest in the 1840s was entirely
the result of private enterprise (Barson 1999, 65). The land on which the houses
were built came mainly from large country estates. The landowner would first
secure an Act of Parliament to abolish manorial rights on the land. Building
leases on small parcels of land were then offered to builders who erected homes
for rent. The housing pattern frequently followed the rural field pattern that
had existed previously. The units of purchase by builders were fields, and the
houses and streets had to be fitted into them (Briggs 1968, 29). To maximise
income they fitted as many dwellings as possible onto a given plot, which is
why most developments of this type featured some type of terraced housing.
On the outskirts of every city undeveloped land was now being turned into
suburbia. But who was moving into these new suburbs? The Victorians tended
to lump all the suburbs together and disapprove of them equally (Barratt 2012,
197). Some worried that the 'higher class suburbs' were being brought down
to the levels of the poorer districts. Those who made some distinction tended
to differentiate between the 'polite' suburbs (often described in London as the
homes of 'city men'), the dreary, cramped ones (home to a class known vaguely
as 'clerks') and the impoverished ones (home to the 'working or labouring
classes'). This latter category, comprising vast expanses of monotonous and
tightly packed terraced housing covering much of new suburbia in the larger
cities, was roundly condemned as vulgar, cheap and depressing.

The greatest wave of Victorian suburbanisation took place in the last few
decades of the nineteenth century when it catered for the fast expanding

middle class and 'superior' working class (Ravetz 2001, 9–10). In order to meet the requirements of the *Public Health Act* 1875, a national code of bye-laws for building regulations was issued by the Local Government Board which governed aspects such as the distance between buildings and street width (see Chapter 5). While the regulations were not restricted to any particular house type or social class, what are usually referred to as 'bye-law' houses were the smaller and working class varieties. Although widely criticised for their grimly utilitarian nature, this bye-law housing represented a significant improvement from the usual working class housing of back-to-backs, courts, closes and tenements (Burnett 1986, 161). Environmentally, it produced wider, connected streets in place of enclosed courts and back alleys which led nowhere. Bye-law housing was especially appropriate for the development of new areas where the rectilinear layout of streets and terraces could be imposed over open land. It therefore fitted ideally, both spatially and chronologically, into the pattern of suburban development which most large towns were experiencing in this period, and especially from the 1870s onwards. In some cities developers also built blocks of middle class flats of up to five storeys. These were often given the title of 'mansions', such as the Prince of Wales Mansions in Battersea, to give them prestige and encourage more acceptability.

Various Acts of Parliament in the Victorian era helped to facilitate the clearance of slum housing and the building of the new suburbs. Under the *Artisans' and Labourers' Dwellings Improvement Act* 1875 corporations were given powers to acquire, demolish and redevelop slum areas (Chinn 1999, 7). However, only limited progress was made in addressing the housing problem until the *Housing of the Working Classes Act* of 1890 (Barson 1999, 78). This empowered local authorities to buy as much land as might be necessary for the long-term planning of improvement schemes, to rehouse people displaced through slum clearance, and to build houses themselves. While this eventually heralded in the age of council housing estates, it took time for many local authorities to start to use these new powers.

London's early suburbs and street tree planting

London has been called the birthplace of suburbia (Fishman 1987, 18). The creation of the Eyre Estate in St John's Wood in North London was arguably one of the first consciously suburban developments, artfully mixing the benefits of urban proximity with the villa aesthetic. There quickly followed the less elegant Kentish Town, Gospel Oak, Primrose Hill and other London neighbourhoods which started to submerge the old outlying villages into one larger, unitary metropolis. Nevertheless, in the first half of the nineteenth century middle class London families leaving the urban core did not always go all the way to suburbia. The upper class had remained loyal to the fashionable squares of the West End, and substantial portions of the bourgeoisie imitated them by settling in the large townhouses of South Kensington and Bayswater. The early Victorian suburbs in Clapham, Camberwell, Hackney, Newington and

Islington were primarily middle class residential suburbs from which the wage-earning male could travel daily into the city or the West End (Barson 1999, 65). This commuting was facilitated by the development of various forms of public transport. Expansion south of the River Thames was initially slow due to the lack of bridges but by the 1830s, Brixton, Stockwell and Kennington were all becoming suburban villages, their desirability enhanced by the new Vauxhall Bridge completed in 1816 (Barratt 2012, 176). Nevertheless, it was not until the 1870s that middle class London shifted decisively to the peripheral suburb as the model of middle class residence (Fishman 1987, 74) and from the 1880s there was a 'great flood' of people to the suburbs (Hunt 2004, 302–303).

By 1900, London sprawled over a hundred square miles and its population had reached 6.5 million people, mostly in the outer suburbs (Barratt 2012, 212–215). To many contemporaries, these suburbs were unwelcome intrusions that all looked the same but in reality they were often quite different and also changing over time. Maida Vale and Warwick Avenue were intended for the more well-to-do from the start and stayed that way. Others, like Notting Hill Gate or Ladbroke Grove, began life as relatively grand developments and then suffered a period of decline before climbing back up the social ladder.

As the outer suburbs expanded, this took some pressure off the creaking inner suburbs (Barratt 2012, 238–242). Charities and individual philanthropists were involved in providing some housing for the poor, who were often displaced by urban improvements schemes such as new roads. The Peabody Trust was the largest and the first to build housing specifically for the working class by providing high-density blocks in inner-city areas (Barson 1999, 77). Although the local pattern was complex, some generalisations can be made about the inner suburbs. As a rule, the West End was generally home to wealthier white-collar workers (Barratt 2012, 248). By contrast, Stepney, Whitechapel, Limehouse and Wapping in the East End, and Bermondsey and Southwark across the river, were among London's poorest inner suburbs.

Chiswick

Chiswick is a district now mostly in the London Borough of Hounslow, with other parts in the London Borough of Ealing. In the nineteenth century its population grew from 3250 in 1801 to 29,809 in 1901 as it experienced rapid suburban expansion (*Vision of Britain* 2016). The district rapidly became a desirable location for the more wealthy, such as the aristocracy, prominent artists, poets and horticulturists (Williams 1975, 170–179). While Chiswick's earliest suburban developments where not planted with street trees, once the Victorian street tree movement had gathered momentum by the 1880s it was one of the first London suburbs to embrace this on a considerable scale. Part of the reason for this may lie in the developers' and residents' appreciation of the many fine ornamental trees inherited from the old landed estates. There may also have been a heightened interest in horticulture encouraged by the presence of the Royal Horticultural Society's Chiswick Garden and its annual shows.

One early and spectacular example of street trees in Chiswick was Duke's Avenue, a remnant from a past landscape. A map of 1866 shows this as an entrance avenue of common lime (*Tilia x europeae*) through the fields leading to Chiswick House, home of the Dukes of Devonshire. In the 1890s this land was developed for housing, mostly with fine semi-detached villas. Rather than fell the magnificent limes, these were skilfully retained as street trees along both sides of the new road (Figure 35). Although the original trees seem to have gone, extensive replanting over the years has ensured this is still a magnificent avenue in a very expensive residential road. Another early planting was in Sutton Court Road, a long road running from Turnham Green at the north end to Burlington Lane at the south (Hammond 1994). In the 1870s this was planted along both sides with robinia (*Robinia pseudoacacia*), then a more unusual species for street planting. The trees initially flourished and grew so fast that hard pruning was applied every two years (*Gardeners' Chronicle* 1890, 700). By 1890, when the footways have been asphalted and the road covered with granite, the trees suffered from lack of moisture and began to decline. Today, the robinias have long since gone, the road has been extensively redeveloped and the street tree planting is a mix of ages and species. Although there are substantial gaps in the planting this is compensated by the trees in front gardens.

One of the district's major thoroughfares is Chiswick High Road that runs east/west. While this has been redeveloped massively over the years, it has always

FIGURE 35. One early and spectacular example of street trees in Chiswick was Duke's Avenue, a remnant from a past landscape. In the 1890s when the land was developed for housing, mostly with fine semi-detached villas, these magnificent limes were skilfully retained as street trees along both sides of the new road. This photograph dates from around 1900.

been a busy retail area since the first shops were established 150 years ago to service the large houses and the expanding suburb. London planes (*Platanus x acerifolia*) were planted along both sides of the High Road at 30 ft (9.1 m) spacing, with some sections established as early as the 1870s. Today, this is still a leafy road even though many of the original trees have been lost and those remaining are often at 3–4 times their original spacing, with some even wider gaps in places. Fortunately, there has been some replanting over the years.

By the outbreak of the First World War Chiswick had many residential streets that were attractive avenues of trees (Hammond 1994). Some of the best included Hartington Road, Burlington Lane, Beverley Road, Paxton Road and Silver Crescent. The trees were invariably plane or lime, although horse chestnut was also used, as in Bolton Road. While many of those roads still have some original trees, these are generally severely depleted and replacement planting, often using small or medium-sized ornamentals, has frequently been quite limited. Nevertheless, as a residential district Chiswick remains a mostly leafy and desirable location, something that is reflected in its high property values.

Ealing

Ealing, like Chiswick, was another early west London suburb and now the administrative centre of the London Borough of Ealing. From the start of the nineteenth century wealthy Londoners viewed Ealing as a place to escape from the smoke and somewhere still conveniently close to the centre of London. However, its rise as a suburb can be charted from the start of its train service in 1838 (Oates and Hounsell 2014, 39–45). In 1861, Ealing's population was 5,064 but this had risen to 33,031 in 1901, which was accommodated by a large quantity of new housing (*ibid.*, 47). Some of this occurred on small parcels of land acquired by builders, while other housing schemes were developed by Land Societies. The majority of these housing schemes were described as high-class developments, although there were some small cottages in Stevens Town for poor working class families.

The rapid urbanisation of Ealing in the late nineteenth century was recorded by the architect Charles Jones in his book *Ealing from Village to Corporate Town*. In the preface he wrote,

> The once comparatively unknown village [of Ealing] is recognised as the Queen of Suburbs with a name that stands out, far and near, for its advance in sanitary works, and its retention to the fullest extent of its floriculture and sylvan beauty.
>
> Jones 1902

Although the phrase 'Queen of Suburbs' was already being used for Richmond and Surbiton, it became permanently associated with Ealing and was used over the following decades to promote the district (Oates and Hounsell 2014, 64–65). Its sylvan beauty alluded to its many tree-lined streets with beautiful avenues as well as its numerous parks and open spaces. One notable example of its early street tree planting is The Avenue, a road comprising mostly high-quality

Victorian detached and semi-detached houses. As the name implies, this was planted along both sides in the late 1880s with plane trees at approximately 25 ft (7.6 m) spacing. The trees in the shopping centre part of the road were located directly in the footway, while those in the remaining residential sections were planted in grass verges. Today, this is still a fine avenue of mature planes and although many original trees have gone as well as the grass verges, there is a very impressive treescape all along this affluent residential road.

The modern centre of Ealing and its main thoroughfare is the stretch of the London-Uxbridge road known successively as The Mall, The Broadway and New Broadway. This area has been extensively redeveloped over the years and it is not always easy to compare historical photographs with the current scene. The Mall appears to have been planted around 1880 with plane trees, mostly on the northern side of the road. The trees outside the shops were planted at very close spacing and then regularly crown-lifted so as not to obscure the shop-fronts. Now, the eastern section of the Mall is sparsely treed with some original planes and a few replacements of other species, while parts of the western section by the shops have more original plane trees. Photos of Ealing Broadway from 1887 show this to be devoid of trees along a considerable length of the road. By 1910 some plane trees were planted, although the vast majority of these have been lost over the years with few replacements. However, the section that runs up to the station benefits from the trees around Haven Green. Photos of the New Broadway from 1905 show some large mature trees at least 70 years old interspersed with some more recent plantings that are approximately 10–20 years old. It is likely that the mature trees were remnants from the previous rural landscape, possible hedgerow elms or limes, which were retained when the area was first developed. Today, there are just a handful of plane trees from the original plantings and none of the remnants remain. However, due to a reasonable level of replanting over the years this part of Ealing's main thoroughfare still looks fairly green.

Muswell Hill

Muswell Hill is a district of north London that is now mostly in the London Borough of Haringey, with a small portion in the north lying in the London Borough of Barnet. In 1896, the area came to the attention of a major developer, James Edmondson (Gay 1999, 53–56). He began the development of Muswell Hill as a modern suburb by purchasing the estate occupied by The Limes and Fortis House, two fine mansions. As Edmondson transformed the land into a middle class suburb this convinced the owners of the surrounding estates to sell their land to him. This enabled him to expand the area of his proposed suburb and he was assisted in this by the purchase of more land by other private developers. Plans were finally agreed with Hornsey Urban District Council in October 1896, which included 19 houses and shops along Muswell Hill Road, to be called Queens Parade, and 55 houses in Queens Avenue, the major residential road of his new suburb.

There is much evidence to show that Edmondson recognised the value of street trees for his new suburb (Gay 1999, 57). Queens Avenue was made 65 ft (19.8 m) wide as his fine central residential thoroughfare, designed to attract the best middle class residents. Photos from 1905 show recently planted plane trees in the footway on both sides of the street at 25 ft (7.6 m) spacing with wrought-iron guards. Today, this is still a fine avenue of planes, especially along the eastern section, although with the loss of many trees and few replacements there are now some large gaps. Princes Avenue, just south of Queens Avenue, was regarded by some residents as the most exclusive street in the new suburb (Schwitzer and Gay 1995, 107). Here, Edmondson not only planted new street trees but also retained some existing trees in the development. A photograph from 1910 shows two mature trees, probably limes, in the footway together with recently planted trees with wrought-iron guards along both sides of the street (Figure 36). Nowadays, there are still a good number of the original trees ensuring this remains a leafy and attractive residential location (Figure 37). A fine cedar tree that had been growing in the grounds of Fortis House was retained by Edmondson on the corner of Princes Avenue and Fortis Green Road in response to public demand. The cedar tree has long since gone but the little public garden where it stood does remain. Once Queens Avenue and Princes Avenue were completed various other Parades and Avenues were then added.

As Edmondson was building the core of his new suburb, other developers were planning to extend this outwards (Gay 1999, 62–65). One of these was

FIGURE 36. Muswell Hill was developed as a fine new suburb in north London from 1896 by James Edmondson. Princes Avenue was regarded by some residents as the most exclusive street in the suburb. Here, Edmondson not only planted new street trees but was also keen to retain some existing trees. This photograph from 1910 shows two large mature trees, probably limes, together with recently planted trees.

FIGURE 37. This photograph from 2016 shows the same view of Princes Avenue, Muswell Hill, as the image opposite. The large mature trees have gone and the plane trees that were recently planted in 1910 have now grown into substantial trees that are being regularly pollarded.

PHOTO: PAUL WOOD.

William Jefferies Collins who submitted building plans in 1898 that gained approval in 1899. This first phase of his development included 32 houses in Grand Avenue, which was to be the main residential road. The choice of this name is interesting as it is the same name that Ebenezer Howard used for his proposed main thoroughfare in his 1898 book on the garden city. Running north from Collins' Grand Avenue were five smaller residential roads, all planted with regularly spaced plane trees complete with wrought-iron guards. Today, Grand Avenue still has many of its original trees and remains an exceedingly leafy residential road. The treescape in the adjacent roads is similar, which makes this a very attractive and green neighbourhood.

Edmondson's desire to create a leafy and affluent suburb in Muswell Hill was undoubtedly realised. From the outset many of the new roads were planted with trees, often with expensive wrought-iron guards and sometimes also with metal grilles around their base (see Figure 88). Plenty of the original plane and lime trees remain, although now subject to regular pruning to maintain their shape and size. Even where street tree planting was not initially undertaken in the suburb, such as in Muswell Avenue and Hillfield Park, the residential properties had small front gardens where the presence of shrubs and small trees gave the road a leafy appearance. Some of these initially treeless roads have now been planted with small or medium-sized ornamental trees, although there are often wide gaps between them.

Wandsworth

Wandsworth is a district of south-west London in what is now the London Borough of Wandsworth. While this modern borough covers an extensive area, we are only concerned here with the original Wandsworth suburbs and two distinct Victorian suburban estates, one in Tooting and the other in Battersea.

In the Wandsworth area during the late Victorian era many thousands of houses were built, transforming this into part of the London metropolis (Loobey 1994). Many types of homes were built, from large detached houses surrounded by gardens to one-storey terraced cottages for railway workers. By 1896, OS maps show the area considerably urbanised, especially around Wandsworth Common although less so around Tooting Bec Common. Most of the houses catered for the middle class and those aspiring to this.

The pattern of early street tree plantings in Wandsworth was quite varied. The main thoroughfares of East Hill and West Hill showed a clear disparity in the extent of this. Photographs of East Hill in the 1900s show a virtually treeless road of mixed retail, institutional and residential properties. By contrast, West Hill, the main route to Kingston, was always a leafy thoroughfare. It was lined with large mansions with carriage entrances and plenty of mature trees in their front gardens. In the early 1900s the road was extensively planted with plane trees, the majority on the southern side. Today, West Hill remains a green road with plenty of large trees on private land but also a good number of original planes as street trees. East Hill continues to be virtually treeless, apart from some trees near the junction where it separates from the A3. Wandsworth High Street, which connects East Hill and West Hill, has always been devoid of street trees and remains that way.

Away from the centre of Wandsworth, the early street tree planting appears to have focused more on the quiet residential suburban streets rather than the main roads connecting these. For example, in Nightingale Lane the treecover relied on the front gardens of some of the larger residential properties. Along Garratt Lane, a major road running south, there was a similar lack of early street tree planting. In the case of Bolingbroke Grove, the lack of planting was compensated by the treecover on Wandsworth Common that runs along its western side. In contrast to these major roads, many of the smaller residential streets benefited from a substantial amount of early planting. Just south of Southfields underground station, the extensive grid pattern of suburban residential streets was generously planted with a mix of planes and limes. In many of these streets a large number of the original trees have now gone, usually replaced at a considerably reduced density by small and medium-sized ornamentals. In contrast to this early planting, some networks of streets were left unplanted. For example, just north of Wandsworth High Street is a group of five streets running parallel to each other and bounded at their north end by Oakhill Road. There is no evidence of early planting in any of these streets. While many new suburban streets in Wandsworth were left unplanted, many benefited from the ornamental trees and shrubs that residents planted in the small front gardens.

There are several Wandsworth streets that still retain a good number of their original trees. One of the best is Jessica Road, planted with planes in the early 1900s. Nearby, Crieff Road is similar but also has some limes. In both these streets there is evidence of some replanting over the years. Swanage Road, planted around the same time, still has many original planes and limes on its southern section, although much less on the rest of the road. With most of the Victorian and Edwardian street tree planting in Wandsworth, there seems to be little use of wrought-iron tree guards. This was similar to most of the residential streets in other early London suburbs, except Muswell Hill where their use was more common.

This account of Wandsworth concludes with two distinct suburban estates in what is now the wider area of the London Borough of Wandsworth. While much of the suburban development around Wandsworth was planned to cater for the middle class, these estates were designed specifically for working class families. The first is the Shaftesbury Park Estate in Battersea, commonly called just the Shaftesbury Estate, located just south of Battersea Park. The estate was laid out by the Artisans, Labourers and General Dwelling Company from 1872 to 1877, the first stone being laid by the Earl of Shaftesbury (Stern *et al.* 2013, 40–42). The company was dedicated to providing decent accommodation for the working class at a time when many poor families were living in appalling conditions. This large scheme comprised about 1200 units, mostly two-storey small terraced houses. Taverns and beer houses were excluded as the developers believed alcohol to be the 'curse of the working man' (Loobey 2000, 89). Although the houses had small gardens, front and back, there was only one public open space and this was built over when the developers hit financial problems (Stern *et al.* 2013, 40). The street plan was a grid layout with streets of varying lengths but always straight, except for Eversleigh Road which was aligned with the railway embankment. In contrast to much Victorian working class housing, this development had trees planted along every street, exclusively planes and limes. The quality of the housing and the attractive streets ensured that this estate was much appreciated by its early residents. The Peabody Trust, a major housing association, now owns most of the Shaftesbury Estate, although many homes are already privately owned as the Trust gradually releases units for sale. Plenty of original street trees remain, although the losses in some streets have been considerable. Since the Second World War, replanting has focused on smaller ornamental species, although this has been at the expense of the original intention to create a continuous and uniform avenue effect (Wandsworth Council 2009, 18). Furthermore, the extent of the replanting does vary considerably between streets. The estate was designated a conservation area in 1976.

Totterdown Fields Estate, near Tooting Common, was constructed from 1903 to 1911 as the London County Council's (LCC) first cottage estate, authorised under the *Housing of the Working Classes Act* 1890 (Stilwell 2015, 3–5). The building was in three phases giving a total of 1229 cottages designed to accommodate a maximum of 8788 persons, plus four shops. Owen Fleming, a notable Arts and Crafts architect, was responsible for the layout and design of the estate. While the gridded street pattern did not reflect any current ideas regarding garden suburb layout, the design of the small houses, grouped in rows of 12 units, was applauded for its elegant Arts and Crafts detail that gave the residents some sense of the country house idea (Stern *et al.* 2013, 382). Fleming also tried to retain as many existing trees as possible, mostly in the back gardens (Wandsworth Council 2010, 10). The roads were wide and the intention may have been to plant most of these with trees. However, the 1913 LCC map of the completed estate shows just Lessingham Avenue and two shorter stretches of road in Franciscan Road and Blakenham Road as planted or planned to be planted with trees (Stilwell 2015, 3–5). The street treecover now existing on the estate tends to confirm only a limited amount of early planting with some original lime trees remaining on Lessingham Avenue and Franciscan Road but not elsewhere. On the other streets there is now a scattering of small and medium-sized ornamental trees, often with wide gaps between them. However, considering the original lack of street tree planting on this estate, it seems likely this is greater now than at any time previously. The estate was designated a conservation area in 1978.

Birmingham's early suburbs and street tree planting

In the latter part of the nineteenth century Birmingham expanded enormously with the building of new suburbs. Since the 1860s, speculative builders had erected houses in outlying districts for the better-paid of the working class. By the 1880s, areas like Sparkbrook, Saltley and Winson Green were mostly covered with six-bedroom tunnel-back dwellings, each with its own back garden (Chinn 1999, 20). Increasingly, the central wards of Birmingham were left to the poor.

The *Housing of the Working Classes Act* 1890 had allowed Birmingham to prepare improvement schemes outside the Corporation Street area. However, in 1900 a proposal to build council houses on 17 acres (6.9 ha) of land in Bordesley Green was opposed by those councillors who did not want any municipal involvement in house-building (Chinn 1999, 15). Intent on finding imaginative solutions to the city's housing problems, a deputation from Birmingham's Housing Committee visited Berlin in 1905 (*ibid.*, 24–26). One important lesson learnt from this forward-thinking European city was the significance of town planning. The deputation recommended the council seek more powers to control the building of new areas, aimed at a better distribution of housing and the building of wide arterial roads for through traffic. Also, it advised the council to buy and lay out land in the suburbs, mark out open spaces and encourage the building of houses at a rental affordable to working class people. The approval of these proposals is regarded by some as signalling the beginning of the Town Planning Movement in Britain. John Sutton Nettlefold, Chair of the Housing Committee, and Dr John Robertson, Birmingham's Medical Officer for Health, were leading proponents of the concept of town planning and wanted to spread the word about its benefits to other towns and cities. Following a conference in Manchester, the idea was taken up nationally and in 1909 the *Housing and Town Planning Act* was passed, which aimed to transform the dismal industrial towns into pleasant garden cities, based on the model of Bournville (see Chapter 9).

Edwardian Birmingham was now a very congested city and there was a need for expansion outside its existing boundaries (Chinn 1999, 27–28). This became possible in 1911 when Birmingham extended its boundaries and gained swathes of farmland in Erdington, Kings Norton, Northfield and Yardley. With the inclusion also of Aston and Handsworth, Birmingham's size increased dramatically. This would allow the council to tackle the housing question with vigour once it had accepted the need for municipal housing. In the meantime, most councillors still believed that private enterprise would provide the solution to the city's housing needs.

Back in the 1870s, Birmingham had been praised for being one of the first British cities to introduce tree-line boulevards in its city centre (*Gardeners' Chronicle* 1876, 354). From the 1880s onwards the local authority was keen to encourage street tree planting beyond its centre and into the many private residential developments in its rapidly growing suburbs. Research suggests that in many of these suburbs the developers were keen to retain existing trees, many lining country lanes, and incorporate them into the footway of roads in these new residential developments, where appropriate. This seems more apparent in Birmingham than in any other of the cities studied. At the same time, Birmingham maintained its reputation for a very successful street tree planting programme. Throughout the late Victorian and Edwardian eras, many thousands of street trees were established in Birmingham's rapidly expanding suburbs. The planting and initial maintenance of these trees was the responsibility of the developers until the new roads were adopted by the local authority. As with other British cities, the pattern of street tree planting varied considerably from district to district, and between the poorer working class areas and the more affluent suburbs. To explore this further a considerable amount of original research was undertaken focusing on several districts of Birmingham. A sample of that is given below.

Bordesley Green

Bordesley Green in now an inner-city area of Birmingham located two miles east of the city centre. This close proximity to the heart of the city ensured that it was one of the first outlying districts to become suburbanised (Bick 2012). From as early as 1834 there was scattered ribbon development along the road called Bordesley Green from the junction of Cattell Road and Garrison Lane as far east as Blake Lane (Dargue 2016a). By 1888 the area was completely built up from Birmingham between Bordesley Green and the Coventry Road as far as Charles Road, while to the east of that remained countryside. By 1906 urban development had spread eastwards as far as Blakesland Street and Mansell Road.

From 1905, on land to the west of Blakesland Street a series of parallel streets was developed with uniform and basic terraced housing, including Third, Fourth and Fifth Avenues. None of these streets were initially planted with trees and they remained treeless until recent times when a few small ornamentals trees were planted, with varying degrees of success, mainly on kerb extensions. These roads are connected at their northern end by the lengthy main road called Bordesley Green (the B4128). This seems to have been only patchily planted on its western section and while both sides of the road have been redeveloped massively over the years, this remains virtually treeless. By contrast, the eastern section was always well-planted, almost exclusively with common lime trees. While many of those trees on the southern side of this section of the road have now gone and not been replaced, there remains good treecover on the northern side. Part of this section of Bordesley Green connects a group of several parallel streets to the north that all have names with Boer War (1899–1902) associations. These include Pretoria Road, Botha Road, Colonial Road and Churchill Road, all built around 1910. Some of these streets were planted with lime and others with plane. Photographs of Colonial Street in 1910 show the trees planted even before the road had been properly surfaced and all the house building completed (Figure 38). Today, the extent of treecover along these roads is significantly reduced. Most of the original trees have gone and there has been

FIGURE 38. This photograph of Colonial Road in Bordesley Green, Birmingham, was taken around 1910. It shows that the street trees were planted even before the road had been properly surfaced and all the house building towards the end of the road was completed.

little replanting. Colonial Road, which probably has the most original trees remaining, still has less than 25% of these. Furthermore, while 50 years ago many of the front gardens had small trees and shrubs, these have also been lost as numerous gardens are now hard surfaced for car parking (see Chapter 10). To the east of these Boer War roads lies Fordrough Lane which was developed about the same time. This was planted with lime trees around 1920 and there are still quite a number of original trees remaining.

From 1910, to the south of the Bordesley Green (road) and to the east of Blakesland Street, a new housing development aimed to provide a higher quality residential environment than the nearby Victorian and Edwardian Terraces. This was a venture of the Ideal Benefit Society, founded by Francis Daniels in 1893 as a sickness benefit society, which had decided to move into housing provision. Called the Ideal Village, this was designed for artisan workers, with shops, a park and a school and a much lower density of housing than the usual terraces. The first houses and shops to be built were in Drummond Road and lime trees were planted along both sides at 30 ft (9.1 m) spacing. Over the years the majority of these original trees have been lost and there are now some very large gaps in the treecover but little evidence of replanting. Running off Drummond Road is Finnemore Road that was also planted with limes. This still has a good number of its original trees, particularly in the western section, and there is evidence of recent replanting. The Ideal Village is often referred as a separate area of Bordesley Green and there is no doubt that its better quality housing and many street trees make an obvious contrast with the rest of the district. These were significant factors in its designation as a conservation area in 1990.

Edgbaston

The affluent and very leafy district of Edgbaston is now regarded as one of the most exclusive suburbs of any provincial city and sometimes called the 'Belgravia of Birmingham' (Slater 2002). From its origins in the eighteenth century this was always how it was planned. The aristocratic Gough-Calthorpe family, which had steadily acquired all the land in Edgbaston since its initial purchase of a large estate in 1717, saw the potential of the land for building development (Cannadine 1980, 81–93). Their first foray into this was in 1786 with the granting of a number of leases for building plots in the triangle of land between the Hagley and Harborne Roads at Five Ways (Slater 2002, 25). These leases were for a period of 99 years, stipulating a minimum value for the houses to be built and that the plans be vetted by the estate's agent. These conditions ensured that only people of an appropriate social class would be able to build at Edgbaston which was, in almost all respects, the ideal location for middle class suburban residential development. It was located to the south-west of the city, so prevailing winds would blow away smoke and polluted air, it stood on high and well-drained land with views out across the surrounding countryside, and the existing landscape park and farmland ensured there was already many mature trees to enhance the new properties. In addition, the single landowner ensured that nobody was able to disrupt the social homogeneity by building working class housing or industrial buildings.

Building plans began to develop after the depression years of the Napoleonic Wars (1803–1815) when George, the 3rd Lord Calthorpe, acceded to the title (Slater 2002, 25). Calthorpe saw there were now many wealthy entrepreneurs in Birmingham who would welcome the chance to buy a house of quality in semi-rural surroundings among people of their own class (Dargue 2016b). Although progress was initially slow, by 1881 the population of Edgbaston had grown to 22,700. The fact that only high quality mansions and villas could be erected ensured that the suburbs did indeed attract the wealthiest entrepreneurs, merchants and professional men.

Since its foundation as a suburb Edgbaston has always been an attractive and well-treed environment. When the first occupants of the mansions and villas developed their extensive gardens they planted large numbers of trees (Slater 2002, 33). The few residents that were not particularly interested in doing this soon realised they were bound by covenants that required the planting of trees in their private gardens (Birmingham CC 2006, 18). Some of these trees were planted on the embanked soil inside boundary walls so that they overhung the roads. It is these privately owned garden trees, rather than any local authority street tree planting, that continues to give Edgbaston its leafy streetscapes.

The major roads in the Calthorpe Estate, such as a Hagley Road and Harborne Road, show the contribution of these privately owned trees to the streetscape particularly well. Photographs of Hagley Road in the early 1900s show the boundary walls of the large residential properties behind which are growing many tall mature trees giving dense treecover along the side of the road, without a single street tree in the footway. While the road has now been extensively redeveloped, especially in the eastern section near the city centre, there continues to be many mature trees on privately owned land bordering the road, although mostly in the western section which still has plenty of its original properties. Hagley Road West is also now a dual carriageway and in recent times there has been plenty of municipal tree planting on the central reservation. Photos of Harborne Road *c.* 1910 show a similar pattern of residential properties and dense treecover in front gardens. From Five Ways near the city centre to what is now the Green Man public house, the treecover of this road, especially in its western section, has changed surprisingly little in the past century. However, part of Harborne Road, near the junction with Westfield Road, now has some large mature street trees in grass verges by the southern side of the road. These are probably remnants from privately owned front gardens that were incorporated when the road was widened and then supplemented with some recent municipal tree planting.

Through the south-east portion of the Calthorpe Estate runs the Bristol Road (A38), one of the main thoroughfares out of the city heading west. In common with the main roads described above, this also did not benefit from any early municipal street tree planting. However, this changed in 1952 when the trams stopped running along the road. Soon after its junction with Priory Road, the central tramway was turned into a central reservation, which was then covered with grass and planted with both deciduous and coniferous trees. At the same time, street trees were planted in the footway on either side of this dual carriageway and also along the single carriageway section nearer the city centre. All these trees along the Bristol Road now make an attractive landscape setting for this busy traffic route.

Along the quiet residential roads within the Calthorpe Estate the same historical pattern of treecover applies. Photos of some roads in Edwardian times show the usual large houses with extensive treecover in their front garden, but with no municipal tree planting in the footways. This is supported by an OS map dated 1904 covering the Calthorpe Estate. The enormous contribution that privately owned trees can make to greening the streetscapes of a suburb is greater in the Calthorpe Estate than in any other Victorian or Edwardian suburb examined in this research. As a result, Edgbaston continues to have a reputation as the most desirable and affluent residential district of Birmingham and the place 'where the trees begin'. In 1978, the Edgbaston Conservation Area was designated and this has since been extended significantly to include more than half of the total area of the Calthorpe Estate. This is now believed to be the largest single conservation area in Britain and larger than all of the other conservation areas in Birmingham put together.

Handsworth

The inner city area of Handsworth lies just to the west of the Birmingham city centre. In 1700 this was an area of scattered farmsteads with small concentrations of cottages, barely big enough to be called hamlets (Drake 1998, 7). Towards the end of the eighteenth century some large villas were built on Handsworth Heath and further building was stimulated with the enclosure of the heath in 1793 (Dargue 2016c). By 1840 the southern part of Handsworth parish had developed into an upper-middle class suburb with aspirations to rival Edgbaston, though without the leasehold arrangements that were to preserve the latter's social standing. Building development northwards was encouraged following the opening of railway links in 1837 and 1854. By the end of the nineteenth century the suburban area had reached northwards into Handsworth Wood, houses there being large and few to the acre. South of the Holyhead/Soho Road a much greater density of working-class housing was beginning to be developed. However, in spite of its association with the early factories of Matthew Boulton and James Watt, Handsworth never became highly industrialised and developed into a pleasant residential suburb with few back-to-back houses and many streets of good quality terraced housing (Twist 2004, 7). With an increasing population Handsworth Urban Sanitary Authority was set up in 1874. The district became an Urban District under the *Local Government Act* in 1888 which was amalgamated with the City of Birmingham in 1911.

In late Victorian times Handsworth was an attractive new suburb with its mix of terraced and more expensive housing. Its greatest public amenity was the beautiful Handsworth Park, laid out in 1888 and added to subsequently (Twist 2004, 7). Many the new roads of the suburb were also planted extensively with street trees. As with other suburbs around Birmingham, the property speculators and builders seem to have had a good understanding of the value that existing mature trees could bring their developments. An example was in Church Lane (A4040) near the junction with what are now the Hinstock and Selbourne Roads. A photograph from 1905 shows several remnant limes, perhaps 70 years old, protruding several feet into the road along the northern side, even though there is a footway on both sides of the road. These were probably hedgerow trees that were left standing in the roadway when this was widened. The trees had disappeared by 1917 before the area became more urbanised. Another example of remnant street trees was identified from a photograph *c.* 1900 of Friary Road, to the north of Church Lane in the area called Handsworth Wood. In this case the trees were in the footway rather than the road. The land around Friary Road has since become urbanised and there is now a wide grass-covered reservation running along the northern side. This has many large and mature trees of various species and a few could be the original remnants.

As well as having plenty of remnant street trees, the new suburban streets of Handsworth benefited from some extensive planting. A good example was the streets around Handsworth Park. A photo *c.* 1909 of Wye Cliff Road, to the west of the public park, shows recently built middle class housing with lime trees around ten years old along both sides (Figure 39). However, one tree is larger than the others, maybe 20–25 years old, and probably a remnant. Wye Cliff Road is still a middle class street with a number of original trees remaining and some recent replanting to fill gaps. Douglas Road, to the east of the park, has Edwardian working class terraced housing that was mostly completed by 1890, although this was not planted with lime trees until about 1910. There are now very few original trees and no replanting. Linwood Road, which connects with Douglas Road and runs south to Soho Road (A41), has mostly working class terraced housing that was also largely completed by 1890. Its lime trees were also not planted until about 1910. Many of the original limes are now gone but treecover is still quite good in comparison to other working class streets in this district. Stafford Road is yet another residential street near Handsworth Park, this time to the south of it, and is a mix of two and three-storey Victorian terraced houses, probably designed more for middle class families. Again, the houses were completed by 1890 but the planting had to wait until about 1910. This time, as well as the usual lime trees for this area, there were also some planes that were planted with wrought-iron tree guards. Today, the vast majority of the original trees have gone and there is little evidence of any replanting. Similar in many respects to Stafford Road is Thornhill Road, although the original planting around 1910 is notable for not only having wrought-iron tree guards but also ridiculously tall and robust tree stakes (see Figure 87). Today,

FIGURE 39. As well as having remnant street trees, some of the new Victorian and Edwardian streets of Handsworth, Birmingham, were also extensively planted. This photo *c.* 1910 of Wye Cliff Road shows recently built middle class housing with lime trees around ten years old along both sides. However, one tree is larger than the others, maybe 20–25 years old, and probably a remnant. The workmen in the background are surfacing the road.

there is just a scattering of original limes in the north and south sections but still a substantial number of original planes in the larger middle section. There is little evidence of any recent replacements.

Having described a sample of the shorter residential streets in Handsworth, we now explore two of its longer and busier roads. Grove Lane runs north–south along the west side of Handsworth Park. A photograph from 1914 show a section of this with a tramway and central reservation containing a line of mature trees that extends for at least 500 yards. The photo is taken from a postcard that calls this the 'Boulevard'. Unfortunately, it has not been possible to identify where precisely on the road the photo was taken. Now, the northern section is dual carriageway with a central reservation that has a number of mature forest-type trees and some recent planting. The middle section alongside Handsworth Park has virtually no street trees but benefits from treecover in the park. The southern section just south of the park has a scattering of mature planes but the rest of this section down to the Soho Road is treeless. Heathfield Road is another long road running west off the Birchfield Road (A34). By 1890, this was quite heavily developed with houses along both sides, although some sections were still interspersed with a few rural fields until at least 1905. By 1910, various sections of the road were planted with lime trees, which were supplemented by trees and shrubs growing in many of the front gardens. Nowadays, there is a scattering of original lime trees along the most eastern section of this road but the rest is devoid of trees. There are a few mature trees adjacent to the road on privately owned land and in the grounds of Mayfield School.

Sparkbrook and Sparkhill

Sparkbrook is now an inner-city area in south-east Birmingham. In 1834 the area was still completely rural but by 1888 building had spread from Birmingham into parts of this (Dargue 2016d). By 1906 Sparkbrook was enclosed by urban Greet and Sparkhill and much of it was middle class housing, while on the Balsall Heath side the housing was of poorer quality.

The extent of street tree planting in the Victorian and Edwardian suburbs of Sparkbrook varied considerably with many streets left unplanted. Among those with trees, Grantham Road has Victorian terraced housing and was planted up with limes soon after this was built. In the southern section of the road, built slightly later, the trees were provided with wrought-iron guards. This whole road has since been extensively redeveloped and while a number of lime trees remain there also are some very wide gaps and no recent planting. Sampson Road is an extension of Grantham Road running north until it meets Bordesley Middleway (A4540). Although built up with Victorian terraced housing since at least 1889, this has never had many street trees. Now, the northern section of this road (called Sampson Road North) is a light industrial area and devoid of street trees. The southern part has the benefit of running alongside Farm Park for much of its length but still has hardly any street trees. Gladstone Road runs parallel to Grantham Road and had similar Victorian residential properties. While this may have had some planting soon after the housing was built, this is now almost devoid of trees apart from a few mature planes located on kerb extensions.

The extent of early planting on some of the longer roads in Sparkbrook also varied considerably. Osborn Road runs north from the Warwick Road and was built later than the roads described above, probably in the early 1900s. When the Edwardian terraced housing had been completed, this road was planted up mainly with plane trees along both sides at about 30 ft (9.1 m) spacing. There are some original planes remaining but with many substantial gaps between them and no evidence of any recent replacements. Another lengthy but much busier thoroughfare is Walford Road (the A4126), which runs east off Stratford Road and crosses over Osborn Road before ending at Golden Hillock Road. Probably built just before 1900, this had mainly three-storey middle class Victorian terraced housing. This was planted with plane trees soon after it was completed. Like Osborn Road this still has a scattering of original planes but many substantial gaps and no evidence of recent replanting.

Sparkhill is another inner-city area of Birmingham situated just south of Sparkbrook. In 1834 there was a hamlet identifiable as Sparkhill on the Stratford Road (Dargue 2016e). By 1888 there was new built development on the Stratford Road, although Sparkhill was still beyond the Birmingham urban area and surrounded by countryside. By 1906 it was almost entirely built up west of the River Cole with some development at Wake Green to the south and suburban Moseley to the west.

The OS County Series map of 1916 shows the whole of Sparkhill as densely developed, mostly with long straight rows of terraced housing. While a few roads are marked as having street trees, the vast majority are not. Although the map evidence is not conclusive, this is supported by contemporary photographs. The only roads shown to be planted on the 1916 map are Ivor Road, Esme Road and Doris Road and this is confirmed by photographs taken *c*. 1910. All the trees were planted at about 25 ft (7.6 m) spacing. Ivor Road was planted with planes but now has few trees left. Esme Road was also planted with planes and now has a similarly sparse treecover (Figure 40). Although early photos of Doris Road could not be found, this was also planted with plane trees and very few remain. Current images show no evidence of any replanting in these roads. While some greenery in the small front gardens used to make a contribution in the past this is now almost completely absent with many hard-surfaced for car parking.

One longer road in Sparkhill that did have good treecover from the early days of the suburb was Showell Green Lane. This affluent road was completely built up by 1916 and included many large three-storey houses. Plenty of street trees were planted and there were plenty of large remnants, some on the footway and some in front gardens. Showell Green Lane has now been heavily redeveloped and is not looking quite so affluent. Nor is it particularly green, especially in its northern section, where there are just a few street trees, mainly small ornamentals. The southern section is a little greener as the small numbers of street trees are supplemented by more trees on private property.

FIGURE 40. By 1916 the whole of the new suburb of Sparkhill, Birmingham, was densely developed, mostly with long straight rows of terraced housing. One of the few roads in the district that was planted by that time was Esme Road, shown here in a photograph that was taken around 1910.

On the available evidence from maps and photographs it appears that the extent of early street tree planting in Sparkbrook and Sparkhill, especially the latter, was significantly less than many other Birmingham suburbs. This seems particularly true for the many roads of working class terraced housing. Generally, where street trees were planted, these roads now have poor treecover with a distinct lack of replanting.

Manchester's early suburbs and street tree planting

There was a huge growth in Manchester's suburbs between 1835 and 1845 (Fishman 1987, 74–75). In that single decade it achieved a higher degree of suburbanisation than London did in the whole century from 1770 to 1870. Even before the commuter railway Manchester established the pattern of middle class suburbanisation in the industrial city. It brought to almost total completion that tendency towards class segregation and the separation of bourgeois work and residence which had first been seen in eighteenth century London. In 1844, when Friedrich Engels wrote *The Condition of the Working Class in England* he depicted Manchester as a modern industrial city that had already achieved its classic form: a central business district now almost devoid of residents; a factory zone surrounding the core densely packed with industry and worker's housing; and a peripheral suburban zone for the villas of the upper and middle class.

Wherever industry grew, it repelled middle class housing. By the early nineteenth century East Manchester was already blighted by it and this part of the city has remained predominantly working class (Rogers 1962, 5). The city's western outskirts had fewer factories and here were built a number of districts of pleasant villas and terraces. However, it has always been to the north and south that the suburban expansion of Manchester has been most rapid. Within those suburbs a twofold division in types of housing began to emerge. Some consisted entirely of imposing terraces and large villas set in gardens of park-like dimensions and occupied by the city's most successful entrepreneurs. Meanwhile, over the majority of the suburbs the solid terraced housing of more modest size units predominated.

After 1850, there were two solutions to preserving the integrity and character of the middle class suburbs against the working class housing (Rogers 1962, 8). The first was to surround middle class suburbs by a ring fence with toll-bars, thus protecting them against the tide of more modest housing. Victoria Park was established in 1837 by a group of Manchester's business and political leaders who were the pioneers in this. They formed the Victoria Park Company to purchase 140 acres (57 ha) located 2 miles (3.2 km) south of the Royal Exchange less than ½ mile (0.8 km) from Little Ireland, one of the worst slums in the district (Fishman 1987, 92–94). The designation 'Park' referred unmistakably to the country estates of the aristocracy. In case the point was missed, the whole development was surrounded by walls similar to those which ringed a country estate and could be entered only through a gatehouse, where a watchman refused entrance to all but residents and their guests. Victoria Park's success then encouraged other similar ventures around Manchester and more than 20 had appeared before the First World War.

The second trend in the suburban expansion of Manchester in the late nineteenth century was the establishment of outlying dormitories, made possible by the establishment of new railway links (Rogers 1962, 9). While existing separately for a while these were eventually absorbed into the overall conurbation as this spread outwards. By the 1900s, vast swathes of an expanded Manchester were covered with new suburbs with rows of terraced housing or the affluent villa communities, all with a network of new roads between and within them. As much of Britain was now witnessing the relatively novel sight of trees being planted in streets, this was a popular topic of discussion everywhere. With regard to its city centre, the Victorian street tree movement in Manchester had experienced a rather hesitant start compared with some other British cities. Would this also be the case in its suburbs? To assess the extent of early street tree planting in the late Victorian and Edwardian suburbs of Manchester several districts were examined. An account is given here of two of these, Longsight and Levenshulme.

Longsight

Longsight is now an inner-city area about 3 miles (4.8 km) south of Manchester city centre. It was incorporated into the City of Manchester in 1890 and by 2001 had a population of over 16,500 (Cooper 2002, 104). In the mid-nineteenth century, Longsight was attracting some wealthy new residents from Manchester's growing class of entrepreneurs and merchants who built attractive villas with substantial gardens (Cronin and Rhodes 2010, 5). By the 1870s, it was attracting working class families out from the city centre and these were accommodated in tightly-packed rows of terraced housing. Much of the housing stock of Longsight now comprises these red-brick Victorian terraced houses. The larger Victorian properties are predominantly clustered around the leafy western parts of Longsight. Many grand Victorian villas can also be found overlooking Crowcroft Park in the most southern part of Longsight.

Northmore Road runs north from Stovell Avenue and its southern section runs alongside Crowcroft Park, a public open space. The housing in this long residential road was mostly completed around 1910 and much of it was then planted along both sides. Although it has not been possible to determine the original species, they were planted quite closely and protected with wrought-iron guards on the southern end of the road. Over the years this road has been extensively redeveloped. None of the original street trees have survived and there are now just a handful of medium-sized ornamentals opposite the park. Stovell Avenue itself runs north from Matthews Lane and around 1900 basic terraced housing was built along both sides. This was never planted with trees and today it remains treeless. Matthews Lane runs east to west and leading off this, both north and south, are a series of streets with the same basic terraced housing. These were never initially planted with trees and most remain treeless.

However, the situation is now starting to change. In Matthews Lane, to the west of the junction with Randolph Street, Chinese birch trees (*Betula albosinensis* 'Fascination') have recently been planted. Furthermore, in a few of the side streets, such as Longden Road and Hannah Street, other small ornamentals (varieties of *Prunus* and *Crataegus*) have also been planted. For those who argue that narrow terraced streets are unsuitable for any tree planting, what is occurring here should encourage them to reconsider (Figure 41).

To the east of Stockport Road and to the north of East Road there is a similar network of terraced housing to that in the vicinity of Stovell Avenue and Matthews Lane. This network of streets was also never planted and most remain virtually treeless. However, in a few streets some small ornamentals have been planted recently as part of street redesign and traffic calming measures. Some sections of East Road itself were planted at an early date. Now, the western end has a mix of street trees but at quite wide spacing, while the eastern section is almost treeless. Yet another network of terraced streets can be found off either side of Hamilton Road, located on the east side of Stockport Road. The terraces to the east of Hamilton Road were built by 1908, while those to the west were mostly completed after that. Once again, these narrow terraced streets were never planted with trees and most remain treeless. However, there is also evidence of a few recent plantings, for example, in St Agnes Road and Duncan Road. Hamilton Road itself did benefit from early street tree

FIGURE 41. This is Longden Road in Longsight, Manchester, with recently planted small ornamental trees, mainly varieties of *Prunus* and *Crataegus*. For those who argue that narrow terraced streets are unsuitable for any tree planting, what is occurring here should encourage them to reconsider.

PHOTO: DAVE BURROWS.

planting, mainly with limes, and there is still quite good treecover on sections of this.

Early street tree planting did take place on some of the main and more affluent residential roads in Longsight, although the extent varied. Plymouth Grove runs west off the main A6 Stockport Road and was always a busy and fashionable road that was once a tram route. A number of expensive residential properties were built along this road and sections photographed *c.* 1910 show it planted with trees, probably limes, with wrought-iron guards. From the mid-twentieth century the road has undergone extensive redevelopment and many of the original large properties have gone. There is now just a scattering of mature forest-type trees, a few of which may be originals. Dickinson Road is another busy route that also runs west from Stockport Road and is located south of Plymouth Grove. In many respects this was always similar to Plymouth Grove in its fashionable housing and tramway. While this was not initially planted with street trees, it did benefit from plenty of mature trees and shrubs in the front gardens of the larger properties. Dickinson Road has also undergone much redevelopment and while it still lacks street trees and large parts of it are very 'grey', other sections still benefit from trees on private land.

Levenshulme

Another Victorian suburb of Manchester is Levenshulme, now 4 miles (6.4 km) from the city centre and immediately south of Longsight. It was incorporated with Manchester in 1909 and by 2001 had a population of just over 13,000 (Cooper 2002, 101). The typical housing of Levenshulme consists of terraced houses, the majority built between 1880 and 1890, with most streets laid out in a grid pattern (Sussex *et al.* 1987).

Errwood Road is a major thoroughfare that begins in Levenshulme near the Stockport Road at Alma Park and runs south to Burnage. While the most northern part of this to Clare Road was built by 1907, the remainder was only completed after the First World War. Photographs of this Edwardian section taken *c.* 1910 shows newly planted trees on both sides of the road in front of elegant semi-detached houses with quite spacious front gardens. This continues to be a leafy section of road with large mature planes that are possibly the original trees. At that time there was no built development south from the junction with Clare Road, although in the 1920s Errwood Road would be extended and become a magnificent avenue of trees (see Chapter 7).

Levenshulme has many residential streets dating from late Victorian and Edwardian times and while most were not initially planted with street trees, many of the houses had trees or shrubs in their front gardens. An example was Albert Road, running west from Stockport Road by Levenshulme Station. Although there was no early street planting, photos from 1910 show the many elegant semi-detached houses had medium-sized gardens with plenty of small trees and shrubs. Nowadays, there are still no street trees and the road continues to rely on some vegetation in front gardens, although in the eastern section of the road this is quite sparse. Marshall Road, running between Errwood Road and Albert Road, is another example, although with smaller houses than Albert Road. There are still no street trees and the road now has a 'grey' look with just a few small trees in front gardens. Cromwell Grove, which runs east from Stockport Road near Levenshulme Station, is yet another example with a similar history of treecover. Many of the streets described above have now become relatively deprived working class neighbourhoods, even though much of the housing was originally occupied by middle class families.

In concluding this look at Levenshulme we focus on one neighbourhood that was always affluent and well-treed and which remains that way today. Grange Avenue is located just east of the junction of Kingsway and Birchfields Road and forms three sides of a square joining Slade Lane. This housing development started as early as 1890 when it was then located on the suburban fringe of the rapidly expanding Levenshulme suburbs. From the outset, it was intended as a more exclusive middle class residential development with detached houses, distinct from both the nearby working class terraced housing and middle class semi-detached properties. Over the years, more properties were added including some semi-detached. Photos of Grange Avenue taken in the 1920s show a very attractive avenue of fine mature trees on both sides of the road, probably planted when this was first constructed. Today, Grange Avenue remains a very leafy and attractive neighbourhood. While a number of the mature street trees have been lost and not replaced, extensive planting in front gardens partially compensates for that.

Cardiff and Glasgow suburbs

Having investigated suburbs in London, Birmingham and Manchester, we look briefly at Cardiff and Glasgow. Although several districts in these cities were explored, only a few streets in each are described, which does give some indication of the contrasts that were found.

In 1801 only 1,870 people lived in the borough of Cardiff but a century later in 1901 the population was nearly 165,000 (Morgan 2003, 9). The development of the Docks had made Cardiff a major port by the 1830s and this was bringing vast numbers of people into the city (Tilney 1985, 50). To cope with this flood of newcomers there was a desperate need for room to expand. Initially, ramshackle tenements and hovels were built in seedy courts and alleys, which became breeding grounds for disease. In Thomas Rammell's *Public Health Report* of 1850 he described the town's overcrowding as 'fearful beyond anything of the kind I have ever known of' (James 1984, 158). From the 1850s, after the course of the River Taff was altered, land became available which was reclaimed for working class accommodation which mainly comprised numerous rows of terraced housing. During Cardiff's period of most rapid expansion in the late Victorian era some 20,000 houses were built between 1881 and 1902 (Tilney 1985, 51). When the popular contemporary writer H.V. Morton called Cardiff 'the only beautiful city that has grown out of the Industrial Revolution', this referred to the ethereal beauty of Cardiff's towers and not to the drabness of her back streets (*ibid.*, 1).

Roath is a district of Cardiff that lies just north-east of the city centre. Its Emerald Street was typical of Cardiff's late nineteenth century building boom with two-storey small working class terraced housing with no front gardens. It was one of about 15 similar streets in the district, all named after precious metals and stones. None of the streets had trees planted and they remain treeless today. However, not every street in Roath was devoid of trees from the start and this was especially the case in some of its middle class neighbourhoods. Albany Road (now the A469) is a main thoroughfare that is less than a mile north of the Emerald Street neighbourhood. Around 1900, lime trees were planted along both sides of this long road, although predominantly in the residential eastern section rather than the more commercial western part. Today, the eastern section of the road still has much of its middle class housing and there are many fine street trees. While only a few of these may be original plantings, there has been some good replacement planting over the years.

Roath Park is a district of Cardiff that includes a network of streets running between Ninian Road and Pen-Y-Wain Road, just south of Cardiff's first public park called Roath Park. These were built in Edwardian times and many were initially planted with street trees. Ninian Road had plane trees along its south side in front of its large semi-detached houses and some of the originals remain as fine mature trees. Photographs from *c.* 1912 of Hendy Street, one of the side roads leading off from Ninian Road, show this just planted with trees protected with wrought-iron guards. It was not possible to identify the species but none of the originals have survived and there are now just a few small ornamentals as replacements. This pattern of treecover is similar in the other streets of the neighbourhood, although a few like Morlais and Boverton Street have more trees.

Glasgow's suburbs have quite early origins. During the eighteenth century the new merchant elite and many professionals moved out of the old town into Merchant City and new residential developments to the south, before leaving for suburbia from the middle of the nineteenth century (MacKenzie 1999, 217–218). The West End of Glasgow was originally developed as a suburb from the 1820s onwards by James Gibson, the Laird of Hillhead, who enclosed and developed the Kelvinside family estates into a fashionable suburb centred upon Kelvingrove Park (Reed 1993, 57–83). In the 1840s, as Glasgow embarked on a period of great urban expansion, the thrust of the growing city was already towards the west (*ibid.*, 57–58). Those who could afford it were looking for a different style of living, one that was both healthier and more securely distanced from the older and declining part of the city.

Whiteinch is a residential area to the west of the city centre that was in the separate burgh of Partick until assimilated into Glasgow in 1912. Part of Whiteinch to the south of Victoria Park and away from the riverside formed a middle class enclave where street trees were planted from as early as 1890. In 1894, the *Glasgow Herald* described these streets as 'liberally treated' by the developer, James Gordon Oswald, who planted them with 'avenues of suitable shade trees' (Elliott 2016, 208). The species were common lime, although in Victoria Park Street a photograph from 1905 shows what might be a line of poplars on one side, possibly remnants from the rural landscape. While Lime Street and Elm Street still have some original lime trees there has been no replanting. Victoria Park Street is now treeless. In Victoria Park Drive South, along the southern boundary of Victoria Park, a photograph from 1910 shows elegant Victorian houses and two large remnant trees located in the pavement (Durie 2001, 100).

The owners of the middle class residential properties in Whiteinch were protective of their street trees. From the 1890s, the Partick burgh parks committee faced opposition from residents when they tried to remove old, probably remnant, trees and plant new ones in Balshagray Avenue to the east of Victoria Park (Elliott 2016, 208). The situation was complicated by a claim that the trees still belonged to the feuars of the Scotstoun estate who needed to grant permission for their removal. The plans became entangled with street widening and extension schemes and were deferred by the committee until the burgh was incorporated into Glasgow. Meanwhile, before the issue of tree removal was finally resolved, other sections of Balshagray Avenue had new trees planted. Photos from 1910 and 1911 show a long section of this road with four-storey tenements and newly planted trees on both sides protected by wrought-iron guards.

While Victorian Glasgow had a wide range of housing stock, it became famous throughout the world for a distinctive type of residential property: the tenement (Ravetz 2001, 33). These were effectively blocks of flats, sometimes several storeys high, occupied by multiple households and with no gardens. Photographic evidence from the 1900s indicates that many of Glasgow's streets where tenements were located were devoid of trees.

Individual suburbs in Nottingham, Hull and Worcester

The Park Estate in Nottingham, located to the west of the city centre, is a nineteenth century suburb that is notable for its street trees. However, even before this development Nottingham had a reputation for trees in some of its streets. William Howie Wylie (1855, 45–46), the Scottish journalist, noted that in Nottingham around 1750 'trees were a common feature of the street scenery of the town'. This situation seems to have changed by the mid-nineteenth century. The local historian Robert Mellors (1926, 120–121) recalled a rather treeless Nottingham in the 1850s. He stated that the tree-lined walks of Elm Avenue, Queen's Walk and Victorian Embankment did not yet exist and there were 'no recreation grounds, nor boulevards, nor were any trees planted in the streets'.

The Park Estate began as a major development in the 1820s, under the 4th Duke of Newcastle-under-Lyme, despite much opposition from local people who regarded the area as public land (Brand 1990, 12). The architect Peter Frederick Robinson was engaged to produce a plan with a grid pattern of terraces and ornamental squares, based on the London squares of John Nash. Early construction according to Robinson's plan was completed on the north-east escarpment. Development continued under the 5th Duke who appointed the architect Thomas Chambers Hine to design many of the subsequent houses and make additions to the layout. Until then building in the park had been largely confined to its edges (Whitton Associates 2007, 9). Hine preferred a geometric design of concentric crescents and parallel roads around a pair of circuses to fit with the existing development, which would make the most of the existing topography and give views of Nottingham Castle. The curves contrasted strongly with Robinson's earlier rectilinear plan. Hine also proposed detached houses or pairs of semis instead of Robinson's terraces. In the 1840s, the park was open to the public and was used as a promenade by all classes of society.

While there is little archival information on the history of the street trees of the Park, some conclusions can be drawn from the available evidence (Whitton Associates 2007). It seems that the original street trees were planted to Hine's designs as formal avenues from the 1850s to the 1880s, contrasting with the earlier, narrower streets designed by Robinson that were treeless. Hines' tree-lined boulevards gave a distinct look to the estate which was important in setting the tone of the suburb and attracting buyers for its properties. It is difficult to ascertain the original tree species used. Avenues of Siberian elm (*Ulmus pumila*) appear to have been planted on some of the later, southernmost streets. This is said to be the first known planting of the Siberian elm in Britain, which was introduced in 1860. At that time it was said to form an elegant, nearly evergreen tree with a relatively light canopy (*ibid.*, 13). However, its limitations as a street tree some became apparent. While drought resistant and little affected by Dutch elm disease, it was short-lived in street situations, with brittle wood and poor crown shape. Elsewhere in the Park Estate's streets plenty of common limes, planes and horse chestnuts were planted. There are probably surviving original trees of these species, now mixed with later plantings of other species. In general, the appearance of the Park's treescape has changed over the years as the original trees have been lost and replaced with small, fastigiate or flowering trees, giving a less uniform effect. Total tree numbers have fallen by around a half from the original population.

Following the example of the Park Estate, trees were planted in other streets in Victorian Nottingham, including the creation of the Boulevards that sweep through the west of the city centre. In the 1880s, negotiations between Nottingham Corporation and the Gregory Estate resulted in the formation of Gregory Boulevard (1880–1883) followed by Vernon Road, Castle and Lenton Boulevards (1884) and Radford Boulevard (1887), all designed to produce attractive streetscapes that would also improve the health of the inhabitants (Elliott 2016, 158).

In Kingston upon Hull, in north-east England, the suburb known as The Avenues is an area of high status Victorian housing located in the north-west of the city (Ketchell, 1989). It was developed from 1875 on a green field site called Newland Tofts Lane, a part of which would be later known as Princes Avenue in the suburb. When the suburb was formally opened in 1875 by the developer David Parkinson Garbutt, the main thoroughfare of Princes Avenue had been completed and this gave access for the construction of more streets in advance of the houses being built. The suburb then grew in a segmented, piecemeal fashion for over half a century until its completion around 1929. The major part of the suburb is formed by its four main tree-lined straight avenues running west off Princes Avenue: Victoria, Park, Westbourne and Marlborough Avenues. Two cross-streets, called Salisbury Street and Richmond Street, intersect these avenues at right-angles. In 1900 electric trams began to travel on Princes Avenue on a route that linked it to the city centre by Spring Bank. As a residential location with a variety of house styles the Avenues was always intended for the middle class and was laid out on a generous scale to attract their interest. The widest street, Westbourne Avenue, was almost 80 ft (24.3 m) wide and Park Avenue was 60 ft (18.3 m) wide. The area to the south of the Avenues and north of Hull General Cemetery was developed around 1900 with terraced houses without gardens built on east-west rows of streets named after ducal seats. As a consequence the area became known as the 'Dukeries'.

Trees have always been a major feature of the Avenues area (Purkis 1989, 28). Garbutt designed the original planting of street trees to give the effect of Parisian boulevards, to enhance the beauty and character of the area. Having first lined the access road, Princes Avenue, with trees planted directly in the footway, he then planted the Avenues with the trees at 35 ft (10.6 m) spacing and located in wide grass verges. The species planted were predominantly plane, sycamore, lime and horse chestnut (Hull CC 1998). The local authority now recognises that street trees in the Avenues remain the area's strongest character. However, a replacement programme was initiated in the late 1990s which had a policy of substituting smaller species that were considered 'appropriate' to the scale of the streets, such as silver birch, field maple, red horse chestnut and wild cherry. The Avenues remain a middle class and attractive suburb.

The Arboretum is a suburb in Worcester, a city in the West Midlands of England. In the 1700s, the area was part of an open expanse known as Sansome Fields (Covins 1989, 7). An elegant villa was built there and the land laid out as a park, including a promenade with shady elms and graveled walks. In 1811, the whole estate was sold in nine lots and after years of legal argument the Worcester Public Pleasure Grounds Company bought 25 acres (10.1 ha) to retain as a public space. It then commissioned William Barron, the celebrated landscape gardener, to lay out the pleasure grounds (Elliott 2016, 22). Walks, gardens and a crystal pavilion were constructed and there was a cricket ground, bowling green and archery butts (Covins 1989, 22). The Pleasure Grounds opened in 1859 but after some financial bad luck and mismanagement the company went into liquidation. In 1866, the land was sold for building with the intention of developing a new residential suburb. In November of that same year, it was announced that there would be a clearance sale of ornamental trees and shrubs from the pleasure grounds. This coincided with another announcement that road construction in the suburb would begin, with some new streets following the line of hedgerows or tracks through the old pleasure grounds (*ibid.*, 39). Along the suburb's streets neat rows of small Victorian working class terraced houses were built, most without front gardens and just a small yard or garden at the back.

It is interesting that despite the name 'Arboretum' this suburb never really had any street trees and there are almost none now. The 1886 OS Town Plan shows street trees at regular spacing along both sides of Sansome Walk, which marks the western boundary of the suburb, but there are no trees in any of the streets in the main body of the suburb. Today, most of the original lime trees in Sansome Walk have been lost and all that remains are several widely spaced and heavily pollarded trees. Recently, when the traffic arrangements in the Arboretum were reorganised, a few trees were planted on three kerb extensions and one of these survives on East Street (Brohan pers. comm., 2015).

All three suburbs described above have names associated with trees: park, avenues and arboretum. The choice of name for the suburbs in Nottingham and Hull was undoubtedly influenced by a desire to encourage prospective middle class buyers to purchase property in these attractive and leafy environments. In the case of the Arboretum area of Hull, it seems that the origin of the name was essentially a reflection of the site as former pleasure grounds rather than a marketing strategy for this working class housing.

The first garden suburbs

The planned garden suburb can be defined as a village or enclave located within the catchment of a town or city, and sometimes embedded in the urban area itself, where there is an emphasis on the provision of greenspace and attractive landscaping (Stern *et al.* 2013, 17). These handsome and often exclusive suburbs were largely inspired by the garden city movement (see Chapter 9), although there are earlier examples. While 'garden suburbs' and 'garden cities' are often grouped together and discussed under the term 'garden communities' (Miller 2010, 109), there are some fundamental differences between the two. The concept of garden cities is to produce self-governing and relatively economically independent cities with short commute times and the preservation of the countryside. Garden suburbs arguably do the opposite. They are primarily residential neighbourhoods built on the outskirts of large cities with little or no industry and are therefore dependent on reliable transport allowing workers to commute into the city (Stern *et al.* 2013, 17). Lewis Mumford, one of Ebenezer Howard's disciples, explained the difference as 'The Garden City, as Howard defined it, is not a suburb but the antithesis of a suburb: not a rural retreat, but a more integrated foundation for an effective urban life' (Hall and Ward 1998, 41). As the twentieth century unfolded, garden suburbs and villages became more prevalent than garden cities because they were easier to establish at a smaller scale and were more commercially viable for developers (Rutherford 2014, 49).

For middle class families moving into these verdant suburbs, this often marked an exciting new chapter in their lives (Figure 42). Many garden suburbs have subsequently become conservation areas and they largely remain as a leafy and expensive refuge from the turbulent city.

It can be difficult to classify Victorian and Edwardian suburbs according to those that were 'garden suburbs' and those that are not. As we have seen earlier in this chapter, many leafy and attractive middle class suburbs were created that were not given this distinction. The addition of the word 'garden' to the title of many suburbs was probably part of their marketing strategy and was not always reflected in their landscape. Nevertheless, we largely follow the classification given in the literature (especially Stern *et al.* 2013). This section of the chapter explores the establishment of a number of garden suburbs and highlights the important role that street trees played in their early development.

FIGURE 42. For middle class Edwardian families moving into the new garden suburbs, this often marked an exciting new chapter in their lives. In this photograph of Maytree Avenue in Hull Garden Village, taken around 1910, a family group pose proudly in their newly planted street.

Eyre Estate, St John's Wood

Contrary to widespread belief, the earliest development of the garden suburb did not take place at the beginning of the twentieth century but a century earlier. This was the creation of the Eyre brothers' villa estate in St John's Wood at the beginning of the nineteenth century when this was a rural district just north of London (Girouard 1985, 277; Galinou 2010, 13). A plan for this was initially produced in 1794 but not implemented. Nevertheless, this was the earliest conception of an attractively landscaped 'planned suburb' of detached and semi-detached houses close to a town or city. Further plans followed and from 1804 to 1815 the first houses were constructed, known as the Alpha Cottages. By 1821, the Eyre Estate contained several hundred houses, its own chapel, assembly rooms, pleasure garden and cricket ground. It became a popular residential location for the middle class with plenty of writers, artists, professionals and rich men's mistresses.

One important feature of the 1794 master plan that was realised was the Avenue of Trees (Galinou 2010, 82). This was a line of trees along both sides of a section of road known as Lisson Grove and it became one of the estate's early landmarks. The trees are marked on Thomas Milne's 1800 land use map of London and environs. In 1810, the estate owner Walpole Eyre II was appalled by the actions of a tenant who had lopped all the trees in the Avenue. As this was done without authorisation, compensation was sought for the damage. The Avenue of Trees is depicted on an 1853 map of St John's Wood but by 1865 there was no trace of it. While Margaretta Terrace in Chelsea is sometimes regarded as the earliest street tree planting in Britain, the trees in Lisson Grove predate this by some 50 years. However, they may have been remnants rather than specifically planted for the development.

Nowadays, St John's Wood is a very affluent neighbourhood that is also very 'green' with plenty of trees in its many private gardens. Although trees continue to thrive along its roads, these are generally located within the residents' front gardens rather than in the footway as local authority planting (Galinou 2010, 372). Lisson Grove, site of the Avenue of Trees, is now a busy thoroughfare running south from Lords Cricket Ground and this does have plenty of local authority street trees.

Bedford Park

Bedford Park in Chiswick, West London, is often considered the world's first garden suburb, despite the claims for the Eyre Estate. In 1875, Jonathan T. Carr acquired 24 acres (9.7 ha) of land in Chiswick adjoining an old Georgian mansion called Bedford House (Creese 1966, 87–90). The owner had been Dr John Lindley, Curator of the RHS Gardens at Chiswick, and the plan was to create an attractive residential estate that would also save Lindley's extensive tree collection, something that a less imaginative development by speculative builders would destroy. Many of Lindley's mature trees were retained in the new gardens and streets, which created an immediate and mature landscape over much of the newly built estate.

The visual impact of the Bedford Park setting and its dissimilarity with the more conventional suburbs of the time was immediately obvious (Creese 1966, 88–90). This was an estate of 'pretty houses dotted among trees', where the streets were not on a typical block or grid pattern but followed the natural features of the tree collection and landscape. However, in the view of the architectural historian Walter Creese, what makes Bedford Park important is not the suburb's plan but the relationship between the placement of the houses, the quality of their design and their connection with each other (Greeves 1975). Taken together, they transformed the character of the street itself, which represented a cultural break with the dense and stiff pattern of the English town. What harmonised the disparate elements of Bedford Park was the new and revolutionary consciousness of space brought alive by light filtering through the trees. There was a quality of luminosity that suggested a watercolour sketch or the work of the French impressionist painters. This artistic image of the Park was reinforced by its many liberal-minded residents, such as the Irish poet W.B. Yeats and the French artist Camille Pissaro, who helped shape its public image as Arts and Crafts or Pre-Raphaelite 'aesthetic colony' (Creese, 1966, 100).

In the early years of the suburb, some of Lindley's retained trees did cause problems when they blew over following likely root disturbance in the course of built development (Figure 43). However, these had been supplemented along the roads with many newly planted trees such as lime, plane, horse chestnut, poplar and willow. Photos *c.* 1900 of Woodstock Road illustrate this mix of a few mature trees, some at least 70 years old, interspersed between new plantings. The Avenue was the main spine road through Bedford Park

FIGURE 43. Bedford Park in Chiswick, West London, was developed from the late 1870s as an attractive new residential estate that would also save some of Dr John Lindley's extensive tree collection, which stood on much of the site. Many of Lindley's mature trees were retained in the new gardens and streets but some did cause problems in the early years when they blew over following likely root disturbance in the course of built development. This photograph was taken around 1900.

and this was planted with common limes soon after construction. These trees were subjected to regular pollarding once they had reached about 20 years old, which was standard practice with many of the forest-type street trees. Bedford Park remains an exclusive and very leafy suburb, conveniently close to the heart of London. Some streets still retain a scattering of original street trees while in other streets there is evidence of extensive replanting over the years. This has involved an assortment of ornamental trees, including some more unusual species such as ginkgo (*Ginkgo biloba*).

Brentham Garden Suburb

Brentham Garden Suburb in Ealing, West London, was the first to be built on co-partnership principles (Rutherford 2014, 53–57). Founded in 1901 by the great promoter of the co-partnership movement, Henry Vivian, these management schemes gave residents greater equality and influence in the running of their suburb. Tenants were made joint owners of the houses they occupied, along with outside financiers or developers, with the estate managed by an elected committee of shareholders. The relatively small suburb began with housing on a conventional pattern in a tight layout. In 1907, Ealing Tenants Limited, the progressive cooperative representing the tenants, appointed architect and planner Raymond Unwin to take forward the development of their suburb. This second stage had the typical Unwin spacious garden suburb plan, incorporated culs-de-sac and informal curving roads that followed the lie of the land, with the retention of mature trees and plenty of roadside tree planting. To give the streets visual interest, he arranged the houses in small blocks of four and six, each one different. By the First World War, 620 houses had been completed, most designed in typical Arts And Crafts style (Stern *et al.* 2013, 349). As with many of the privately financed garden suburb developments, the new roads at Brentham were adopted by the local authority soon after they had been planted (Baxendale pers. comm., 2016).

One of the defining characteristics of the Brentham landscape was its street trees, which formed a foil to its garden hedges (Reid 2000, 213). Common lime formed a major proportion of the species planted in the early days of the suburb (Baxendale pers. comm., 2016). Brentham Way was originally planned as a formal lime avenue with the trees regularly pollarded and although this has been irregular in recent years the original scheme has survived with a few losses. Ludlow Road was originally planted with common lime and silver birch, with the birch trees chosen because they were considered particularly sympathetic to the architecture. Nowadays, little of this survives due to substantial losses in the Hurricane of October 1987. Meadvale Road, a long connecting road running along the south side of Pitshanger Park, was originally planted with planes and limes. The trees were located in a narrow grass verge behind the kerb that was reserved for planting, once a feature of most of Brentham's footways. Almost all the original trees have now gone, along with the grass verge, although there has been extensive replanting with a mix of small and medium-sized ornamentals.

In recent decades there has been much agonised debate about tree selection and management in Brentham. In the 1970s, concerns about the aesthetic impact of 'unnatural' pollarding and fears about structural damage to properties prompted the removal of a number of lime trees (Reid 2000, 213). To minimise the chances of trees being lost, the Brentham Society worked with Ealing Council to identify trees for pruning, and to suggest replacements when trees died. In 1981, the local authority and the Society undertook a survey of all street trees, which resulted in a schedule of tree works for the whole suburb, and a list of acceptable replacement varieties that included many small ornamentals (Baxendale pers. comm., 2016). While the Society accepted the need for trees of a manageable size, its members were not entirely happy with some of the smaller flowering trees, such as the cherries, which they considered particularly unsuitable for Brentham. It was felt they made an overly pretty frame to the architecture that was more in character with the 'country cottage' aesthetic of the 1930s chocolate box than the earlier, more consciously graphic, architectural forms favoured by Arts and Crafts landscape designers. There were also concerns about some of these trees with problems of unsightly suckering and damage to paving. After further discussions between Ealing Council and the Society, a list of suitable replacements was agreed that included a number of more traditional forest-type trees. Unfortunately, the steady improvement in tree selection and management that followed was severely disrupted when the suburb's trees suffered major damage in the Hurricane of 1987 (Reid 2000, 222). Nearly 70 trees were destroyed or damaged beyond saving. The Brentham Society immediately set up a fund to replace the lost trees and more than £1200 was raised in just one month. For this amount Ealing Council generously agreed to replace all of the lost street trees.

Hampstead Garden Suburb

The most notable example of this British town planning phenomenon is Hampstead Garden Suburb, founded in North London in 1907 (Creese 1966, 220–222). It started as an effort to save part of the fast disappearing landscape around London. By the end of the nineteenth century, the capital's rapidly advancing sprawl had made its way around to the northern side of Hampstead Heath, which was now under threat from speculative development. Henrietta Barnett, already a respected social reformer, proposed to counter that by building a garden suburb. In 1906, Barnett set up the Hampstead Garden Suburb Trust Ltd, which purchased 243 acres (98 ha) of land from Eton College and appointed Raymond Unwin as its architect. The basic aim of the new suburb was to furnish a home for the working man for a 2*d* fare from London on the tube (*ibid.*, 226). What was 'common to all', natural beauty, would then be made 'enjoyable to all' through open spaces, green gardens, and tree-lined streets. Barnett wanted to reform the suburb as it then existed by integrating all classes within it. There would be large houses for the better-off in the south of the suburb and homes for artisans in the north (Barratt 2012, 232).

It has been said that the planning arrangements for Hampstead were in some places overly organised (Creese 1966, 242–244). Unwin went to some lengths to avoid any regular, predictable layout for the roads and neighbourhoods. He had a strong dislike of the monotony of the English 'bye-law' street and his offsets, focal points, curves and angles produced in the Hampstead streets were deliberately designed to avoid that and also to discourage traffic (Unwin 1909). However, one of the early difficulties facing Barnett and Unwin was that their ideas on town planning frequently ran counter to established practice (HGS Residents Association 2016). To overcome the restrictions imposed by the bye-laws, the Trust promoted a Private Bill through Parliament to give them the necessary powers. It passed into law as the *Hampstead Garden Suburb Act* 1906. An important provision stated, 'On every road in the Garden Suburb (whatever the width of the said road) there shall be between any two houses standing on opposite sides of the road a space not less than 50 ft free of any buildings except walls, fences or gates'. Crucially, the Act added,

> Any road not exceeding 500 ft in length constructed primarily for the purpose of giving access to a group of houses in the Garden Suburb and not designed for the purposes of through traffic (known as an accommodation road), may with the consent of the local authority be exempted from any operation of any bye-laws of the local authority relating to the width of new streets and footways.
>
> *Hampstead Garden Suburb Act* 1906

Extensive new landscaping and tree planting was planned to be undertaken throughout the development with every road lined with trees. The first complete road of houses built was Asmuns Place and as soon as they were finished Barnett and a party of dignitaries planted the first street trees, which were common limes (Malcolm pers. comm., 2016). The very first tree still survives and is now marked with a commemorative plaque. The original plantings at Hampstead Garden Suburb were notable for being a wide mix of forest and small-growing ornamental trees, unlike many other street tree plantings at the time where lime and plane predominated (Marks 1913, 11). Nevertheless, this mix did not extend to individual roads which were generally limited to one or two species or varieties of this. In another departure from normal practice, instead of lining the road from one end to the other with trees at regular spacing, a method of grouping one variety was adopted leaving wide spaces between each group. While many trees were planted into grass verges, a substantial number were planted directly into the footways (Miller 1995). The planting and aftercare of the trees was supervised by Mr J. Marks, Estate Head Gardener for the Trust from 1908 to 1941 (Malcolm pers. comm., 2016).

A survey conducted by the Trust in 1997 indentified the early street tree plantings, dating from 1907 through to later plantings in the 1930s. This was based partly on Mark's records and partly on the observations of experienced tree surveyors. The survey found that a significant number of original street trees planted before 1914 still remained and these were, understandably, mainly from the longer-lived species (Malcolm pers. comm., 2016). A considerable number of the small ornamental species also remained from plantings in the 1920s and 1930s. For many years the planting and management of the suburb's street trees has been the responsibility of the London Borough of Barnet. This has seen a number of species used for replanting that were not part of the original planting schemes. In recent years, as a result of an agreement between the Residents Association and the local authority tree officers, there has been a replanting policy of returning to the original species, where this is possible (LB Barnet 1999).

While Barnett's intention was for Hampstead Garden Suburb to have residents of all classes, with particular emphasis on working class families, this has not transpired. The initial cost of the homes effectively excluded the working class from the start (Barratt 2012, 232). Today, the suburb is one of the most exclusive and expensive places to live in Britain and its attractive and its well-treed streetscapes undoubtedly contribute to this.

Other garden suburbs

Hampstead unleashed a 'golden age' of British garden suburb design (Stern *et al.* 2013, 360). It inspired developers, enlightened capitalists, aristocratic landowners and public agencies to propose garden suburbs intended to cater for the needs of both the middle and working classes.

The proposal to establish the Moor Pool Estate at Harborne in Birmingham was first mooted at a meeting in 1907 at the Harborne Institute and this led to the formation of the Harborne Tenants Association the following year (Birmingham CC 2012, 8–9). The project was championed by its Chairman, wealthy industrialist John Sutton Nettlefold, who was also Chairman of the Birmingham Housing Committee. As a leading member of the Garden City Movement he planned to construct the estate in a manner that adhered to the 'green principles' of the garden suburb. Like Hampstead, the roads were narrower in the Moor Pool Estate than the bye-laws stipulated but this was regarded as sufficient for the neighbourhood traffic while allowing for front gardens, grass verges and street trees essential for the character of the suburb (Rutherford 2014, 57). Existing mature trees were kept where possible. Once the roads were constructed, the 5 ft (1.5 m) wide grass verges were lined with trees, selected on the advice of Thomas Humphries, the curator of the Birmingham Botanical Gardens (Birmingham CC 2012, 10). Nettlefold (1908, 112) was a passionate advocate of the benefits of street trees and believed these should be available to people of all classes.

The 1918 OS map shows most of the Moor Pool's roads planted with trees. Common lime and silver birch seem to have been particularly widely planted but these were supplemented by other species that included London plane, horse chestnut, whitebeam, rowan and various cherries (Birmingham CC 2012). Over the years, some areas of the estate suffered from the loss of a significant number of original trees (*ibid.*, 36). High Brow and The Circle are now lacking in trees initially shown on the 1918 OS map. There is evidence of some replanting over the last few decades, for example, on Moor Pool Avenue. Other areas such as Carless Avenue are congested with self-sown trees to large front plots that can interfere with the streetscape. Overall, the streets of the Moor Pool Estate remain remarkable well-treed and a major asset to this attractive middle class suburb. To promote this, the Moor Pool Heritage Trust recently produced a leaflet entitled *Street Tree Walk* giving a self-guide tour of some of the more interesting trees (Nomikos pers. comm., 2016).

Oldham Garden Suburb, formerly part of Lancashire, owes its existence to two philanthropists, Mary Higgs and Sarah Lee, both early members of the Garden Cities Association (Stern *et al.* 2013, 362). In 1902, they established the Beautiful Oldham Society, focused on the deprived areas of the town. Five years later they formed the Oldham Tenants Society for the purpose of developing a garden suburb on a co-partnership basis. Less than one-third of the site was built according to the original plans, with just 156 houses completed by 1914. In typical garden suburb fashion the roads were lined with trees located in grass verges. Photographs from the 1920s show roads such as Green Lane, Brae Side, Rising Lane and South Way with mostly small and medium-sized ornamental trees. There are some trees in groups with shrubs but most of the remainder are planted at quite wide spacing. Nowadays, while the group plantings have gone from the grass verges, there are still many small and medium-sized ornamental trees due to plenty of replanting over the years.

Burnage Garden Village, 5 miles (8 km) south from the centre of Manchester, is a small enclave of 136 houses, mostly semi-detached (Stern *et al.* 2013, 374). It dates from 1906 with the formation of Manchester Tenants Limited, a co-partnership housing society (Harrison 1976, 258). At that time Burnage was a pretty village that had almost entirely avoided the development of terraced houses then engulfing the countryside around Manchester. The original stimulus of the new housing scheme was probably an address by Ebenezer Howard on Garden Cities to a group of Manchester clerks. Planned by J. Horner Hargreaves, in consultation with others including Raymond Unwin, building started in 1910 on an 11 acre (4.5 ha) site on Burnage Lane. There were several fine trees already on the site and these were incorporated into the scheme. The housing and roads were constructed in a circle around a large open space with two tennis courts, bowling green and small clubhouse. Of the roads, Main Avenue ran westward from Burnage Lane and connected this main highway with North, South, East and West Avenues and West Place (*ibid.*, 262). Although the roads should have been constructed according to the usual bye-laws, those on the estate only had an 18 ft (5.5 m) strip of macadam down the centre, bordered on each side by grass verges with trees and flagged footways. Despite some opposition from

Manchester Corporation, the tenants were never forced to change their pleasant avenues and were able to make savings on construction costs. Nettlefold (1906, 2) had put the case for this when he stated, 'The effect of reducing the cost of street-making is to reduce the rents of the houses considerably'.

It has been difficult to get information on trees initially planted along the roads of Burnage Garden Village. However, from early photographs of North, South and West Avenues these appear to have been a variety of small ornamentals, including cherries and silver birch. Today, the street tree composition continues to focus on small ornamentals, with plenty of birch, rowan and cherries. There are also several purple-leaved plums (*Prunus cerasifera* 'Nigra') whose dark colour seems a little discordant with the soft green hues around them. Trees originally stood on two small roundabouts on North Avenue and South Avenue at their junction with East Avenue but the roundabouts and their trees have long since been removed for traffic safety reasons. This rather pretty estate continues to be a desirable place to live, conveniently close to the centre of Manchester.

Chorltonville is another garden suburb in the Manchester area, located south of the city centre and to the west of Burnage (Stern *et al.* 2013, 375). This estate was conceived by two local businessmen, James Herbert Dawson and William John Vowles, and built between 1910 and 1911. When completed Chorltonville covered 36 acres (14.6 ha) and comprised 262 houses in 12 roads, centred on a 'village green' called The Meade. This enclave of winding streets and many Tudorbethan style semi-detached houses offers an even 'prettier' effect than Burnage. The wide looping roads are flanked by wide tree-lined grass verges and the developers were keen to encourage the early residents and visitors not to damage the street trees or grass verges. A photograph from 1914 taken near the entrance to the estate shows a substantial sign that states, 'You are invited to assist in the protection of the trees and grass'. Another early photograph of South Drive in the main body of the estate shows little metal plaques located at regular intervals in the grass verges that read, 'Please do not walk on the grass'.

While the garden suburbs mentioned above are all located in England, examples can be found throughout Britain. Perhaps the most outstanding example in Wales is Rhiwbina Garden Village, founded in 1912 a few miles north-west of Cardiff (Stern *et al.* 2013, 391). The suburb was planned by Raymond Unwin in 1913 and intended for both middle and working class families. By 1913, during its first phase of development, 34 houses had been built and a decade later a further 300 houses were added. The design of the roads at Rhiwbina varied considerably and they all have Welsh names.

From the available information it has not been possible to determine much about the original species composition of the street trees but this seems to have been quite varied (Graham and Taverner 2004). From the age of the current tree population there are probably very few original trees remaining, except perhaps for a few large beech in Lon Isa, which may be remnants. Some roads have grass verges while other do not. Of those that do, the width can vary along the length of the road. In Lon-Y-Dail the verge width is a constant 20 ft (6.1 m) which could accommodate an impressive avenue of forest-type species.

However, the opportunity has not been taken and there is an assortment of trees at irregular spacing. Throughout the rest of the suburb, where street trees are present, this is mainly a mix of small or medium-sized ornamentals planted at various spacings. In some roads, especially Pen-Y-Dre, the appearance of the treescape is similar to that at Burnage. In 1976, the designation of the Rhiwbina Garden Village Conservation Area gave formal recognition to its historic and architectural importance.

Glasgow (now Westerton) Garden Suburb is sometime regarded as the first and only true example in Scotland. Its development was led by Sir John Stirling Maxwell, a philanthropist and Member of Parliament, and a housing society called the Glasgow Garden Suburb Tenants Ltd, formally registered in 1912 (Stern *et al.* 2013, 397–399). Its prospectus noted that the suburb 'will be for all classes, but particularly the working classes'. The group chose its 200 acre (81 ha) site in the Westerton section of Bearsden, 6 miles (9.7 km) north-west of central Glasgow. Raymond Unwin was commissioned to prepare the plan which would accommodate the anticipated 300 houses. The first 45 houses to be built were in Stirling Avenue and Maxwell Avenue (named after Sir John). By 1915, a total of 84 houses had been built with the suburb now consisting of three streets after the addition of North View. By this time, the First World War made further expansion impossible and the suburb was completed at two thirds of its intended size.

As with other garden suburbs, trees were an important feature at Glasgow Garden Suburb (Whitelaw 1992). Photographs of the suburb being built show some large deciduous trees being retained in the development for later inclusion in the footway. Many trees and shrubs were donated by Maxwell with a considerable number planted along the roadside in Maxwell Avenue, around which the housing development is centred. Photographs from the first two decades of the suburb show plenty of trees flourishing along some of its roads. By the 1930s, however, some residents were complaining that the forest-type trees, probably limes, were cutting out the daylight to their homes and at night were obscuring the street lights (*ibid.*, 91). When pruning did not alleviate the problem it was proposed to remove a number of the trees and although other residents objected strongly, the work went ahead. Other trees were removed on Maxwell Avenue when the footways were widened and some small ornamentals were planted as replacements. Today, the extent of street trees in the suburb is quite patchy and it seems likely this was always the case. Some roads are well-treed, such as North View, which has lots of small ornamental trees in its grass verges. The first part of Sterling Avenue still has street trees but they are absent along the rest of it. While many roads lack street trees, the suburb still has a reasonably green appearance due to the many hedges and shrubs in front gardens.

Some concluding thoughts

If the garden suburbs had little effect on the housing problems of the poor, they did play an important role as models for future estate developers (Harrison 1976, 266). The *Housing and Town Planning Act* of 1909 marked a shift away from the high-density, Victorian civic planning by making the garden suburb the template for future town planning (Hunt 2004, 330). However, any major impact from that had to wait until after the First World War and this is explored in the next chapter.

As the twentieth century dawned, the planting of trees along many of Britain's streets had become routine. This had initially attracted attention in the centre of major cities but was now increasingly common in the rapidly expanding suburbs. There was also general agreement that this trend in urban landscaping was beneficial to the health of the community and enhanced the visual amenity of streets. The social divide in the early provision of street trees that was highlighted in the previous chapter now continued to a large extent in the late Victorian and Edwardian suburbs. This has been noted in some local history studies. According to Harold Dyos in his study of the Victorian suburb of Camberwell, the species of trees planted along the streets could vary with the social class of a neighbourhood's residents. He noted the following pattern in Camberwell in the last decades of the nineteenth century:

> The choice of trees, too, had its social overtones: planes and horse chestnuts for the wide avenues and lofty mansions of the well-to-do; limes, laburnums and acacias for the middle incomes; unadorned macadam for the wage-earners.
>
> Dyos 1961, 188

The social divide in the provision of publicly-owned trees that can be witnessed today in Britain's urban forests began in earnest with the street tree plantings in the new Victorian suburbs. The wealthier middle class neighbourhoods with their broader streets tended to have more street trees, while poor working class neighbourhoods often had no street trees at all. There were a number of factors that influenced this. Many of the early plantings were financed privately, either by the developers in an effort to attract middle class families or by the new residents themselves to improve the landscape of their neighbourhood. The developers of the endless rows of working class terraced housing probably saw little point in planting street trees to attract buyers and the new residents themselves had many other more important spending priorities. When roads were adopted by local authorities it is also likely that much of the public pressure to plant street trees came from middle class residents. The generally more extensive street tree planting in middle class suburbs can be seen most vividly in the garden suburbs. These have also remained largely as they were planned: leafy and expensive middle class havens from the aggressive and unpredictable city. Even in Victorian and Edwardian middle class suburbs where street tree planting did not take place, the houses often had front gardens with sufficient space for at least some tree and shrub planting by residents, giving the street a leafy and attractive appearance (Figure 44).

In this research into Victorian and Edwardian suburbs it was noticeable how their fortunes have often changed dramatically over the years. For example, some originally middle class or 'superior' working class suburbs in Manchester

FIGURE 44. Even in Victorian and Edwardian middle class suburbs where street tree planting did not take place, the houses often had front gardens with sufficient space for at least some tree and shrub planting by residents, giving the street a leafy and attractive appearance. This is St John's Grove in Holloway, north London, photographed in 1905 and despite a continued absence of local authority street trees the scene looks quite similar today.

and Birmingham have become quite deprived neighbourhoods in what are now regarded as inner-city districts. The treecover of many streets in these neighbourhoods has also changed dramatically from when they were initially lined with trees to a situation now where there are very few original trees left and little evidence of replanting. Another noticeable change in recent decades has been with the cultural background of the residents as many of these areas now have large ethnic populations (Pryor 2010, 611). Whether this has any relevance to the current extent of street trees in these neighbourhoods would be an interesting topic for research. By contrast, many of those Victorian and Edwardian suburbs examined in London have changed little over the years, and in some cases have become even more expensive and desirable places to live. They have also generally managed to retain a high level of treecover in their streets with plenty of evidence of replanting. In all this research it is hard to escape the conclusion that whatever the time or place, in residential districts street trees and the more wealthy residents tend to go together.

CHAPTER SEVEN

Suburbia in the Twentieth Century

The growth of suburbia that continued into the twentieth century entered a massive phase of expansion between the First and Second World Wars. This was necessary to accommodate Britain's growing urban population and to rehouse countless families displaced through slum clearances (Burnett 1986). Following the cessation of hostilities in 1945 there was a further period of suburban expansion as Britain sought to replace the vast numbers of houses destroyed and severely damaged by bombing and also to clear away the sprawling slums that still scarred our major cities. This chapter explores that period which spans most of the twentieth century and focuses on suburban expansion in several major cities. There is much emphasis on the contribution of public sector housing and the provision of street trees within newly built council estates and alongside major thoroughfares that were constructed in association with some estates. There is also an account of the remarkable programme of street tree planting that took place in Bermondsey, London, during the 1920s and 1930s. The chapter concludes by focusing on council housing estates after the Second World War and the provision of street trees in these developments.

Suburbia and government housing policy in the 1920s and 1930s

Before the First World War private builders had supplied virtually all new housing in towns and cities, although building came to a virtual standstill during the war. When hostilities ended in 1918 it was clear that the country faced an acute shortage of housing. Building costs were inflated and this, combined with a scarcity of materials and labour, made it impossible for private developers to provide houses with rents within reach of the average working class family. The end of the war also brought a new social attitude that focused the Government's attention on a national responsibility to provide homes, giving rise to Lloyd George's famous promise of 'homes fit for heroes' referring to the many soldiers returning from the war (Swenerton 1981). The need for action was also prompted by concerns about disgruntled ex-soldiers and workers fermenting civil unrest. As many working class families were unable to afford to rent from the private sector or buy their own home, these would be provided by rented council houses, so-called because of the role of district and borough councils in managing the housing. To provide guidance on this the government set up a committee under the chairmanship of Sir John Tudor Walters and the *Tudor Walters Report* was produced in November 1918. The *Housing and Town Planning Act* of 1919, also called the *Addison Act*, intended to implement the report and fulfil Lloyd George's promise, is seen as a watershed in the provision of council housing. Local authorities were thrust to the forefront as the providers and they began to plan their post-war housing programmes with financial assistance from central government. This resulted in an enormous increase in local authority house building throughout Britain and huge further expansion of the suburbs. In England, over 4 million new suburban homes were built between 1919 and 1939, making what had been the most urbanised country in the world at the end of the First World War the most suburbanised by the beginning of Second World War (Hollow 2011, 203). Local authorities built over 1 million of all suburban homes in this period and council housing became a significant part of twentieth century working class history.

Up until 1919, although local authorities did have the power to build houses, most had little involvement. Some council housing was provided, mainly in London, Liverpool and Glasgow, often to rehouse some families displaced as the result of street improvement schemes. The London County Council (LCC) finally got to grips with the problem in the early twentieth century. Having previously focused exclusively on building high-density inner-city flats for the working class it began to meet their needs with a series of garden-style suburbs (Stern *et al.* 2013, 382). The Totterdown Fields Estate (1902–1911) in Wandsworth was the first (see Chapter 6), followed by the White Hart Lane Estate (1903–1920s) in Tottenham. By 1914 the LCC had housed 25,000 people in a variety of estates (Barson 1999, 81).

One of the members of the Tudor Walters Committee was Raymond Unwin, a leading figure in the Garden Cities Movement. The ideas of Unwin and his mentor Ebenezer Howard had a considerable influence on the new council housing, although the report eventually proposed that the new developments should be peripheral 'satellites' rather than fully-fledged garden cities (Ravetz 2001, 41). Among the recommendations of the *Tudor Walters Report* was that building should be encouraged at no more than 12 houses per acre (0.4 ha) in towns and a minimum of 70 ft (21 m) should separate opposing houses (Chinn 1999, 35). Expressed through the report, Unwin saw low-density suburban estates as 'the best and natural way of housing the urban working class … firmly rooted in a vernacular, rural idiom which pictured groups of buildings of traditional appearance dotted about a landscape of winding lanes, trees and gardens' (Burnett 1986, 225). The concept of the 'estate' as the basic unit of settlement became an indispensable element of the new council housing (Ravetz 2001, 98). Nevertheless, the report stated, 'It is generally agreed that to cover large areas with homes, all of one size, and likely to be occupied by one class of tenant, unrelieved by any other types of dwellings occupied by different classes of society, is most undesirable, even where the depressing effect of monotonous unbroken rows in avoided'. It was anticipated that the new housing schemes would eventually contain playing fields, allotments, open spaces, shops, business premises, schools, churches, clubs and institutions, as well as larger and higher class houses. The 'civilising elements' of a tennis court and a bowling green also became a regular feature of these council estates.

While the garden suburbs had emphasised the importance of high quality amenity landscape and incorporated many trees into their street networks, it remained to be seen whether this would also be a feature of the new council estates. There was plenty of initial optimism given the recommendations of the *Tudor Walters Report* and the ongoing influence of Raymond Unwin with his well known commitment to ensuring improvements in working class housing and its landscape. That optimism, however, was short-lived as the economic reality of the times and the huge scale of the task ahead began to be realised. Soaring building costs and the desperate need to get houses up as quickly as possible meant that the ideal Tudor Walters designs were in use for barely a year (Ravetz 2001, 92). Such economies proved to the satisfaction of some that the government was no longer 'led astray by visionaries' but was prepared to house the maximum numbers at minimum cost. Although the immediate impact of these economies was an overall reduction in the size and specification of council houses, it would probably have some effect on the extent of landscaping and street tree planting on the estates.

The spiralling cost of building council houses reached a climax in 1921. The *Addison Act* then fell victim to the 'Geddes Axe', the Conservative government's drive for economies in the public sector (Chinn 1999, 42). This ambitious Act had failed to produce the hoped-for 500,000 houses, although 170,000 were built by 1921 (Home 1997, 12). The government's retrenchment drive stopped most new approvals for council-led building programmes and there was a national resurgence in support for private house-building (Chinn 1999, 45–46). This promoted the introduction of the *Housing Act* of 1923, championed by Neville Chamberlain, which reduced the housing subsidy to local authorities and aimed to stimulate private sector housing development. While the Act certainly resulted in a substantial growth in private sector housing, with 438,000 new houses built by 1929, house buying remained unobtainable for the vast majority of working class families. By the mid-1920s, the shortage of affordable housing in Britain was greater than in 1919 (*ibid.*, 50). In 1924, the first Labour government tilted the balance back in favour of council house building. It introduced the *Housing (Financial Provisions) Act 1924*, known as the *Wheatley Act* after John Wheatley the minister who had introduced it. This once again gave subsidies to local authorities to build houses and was the catalyst for a huge expansion in council house building (Ravetz 2001, 87). By 1933, it had resulted in 500,000 council houses being built across Britain, mostly on new estates located in the expanding suburbs. These new suburbs adopted a new pattern of building as Victorian terraced houses were replaced in middle class districts by the semi-detached (Barratt 2012, 366). Straight Victorian roads were out of fashion and in their place came culs-de-sac, avenues and closes.

Although the economic depression of the 1930s led to a slowing down of council house building across Britain, the inter-war years still saw huge numbers of new houses constructed. Between 1919 and 1940 4 million houses were built in England and Wales, a quarter of them by local authorities with some form of central government subsidy (Home 1997, 12). Of that million council houses, three-quarters were in the form of cottage estates. These were composed mainly of two-storey cottages, built in groups of four or six, with medium or low-pitched roofs and little exterior decoration, set among gardens, trees, privet hedges and grass verges, and laid out in culs-de-sac or around greens (Swenarton 1981, 1). The new pattern of council housing layout could provide plenty of opportunities for street tree planting. Indeed, the open space that was often left in the front of many of the blocks of council housing would provide far more opportunity for roadside planting than the narrow streets of Victorian and Edwardian terraced housing. It remained to be seen if these opportunities would be taken.

London's Metro-land and the Becontree Estate

In the 1920s, London undertook some major programmes of slum clearances, especially in Hackney and the East End, and south in Battersea, Lambeth and Southwark (Barratt 2012, 357). Around this time and extending into the 1930s was a major phase of suburban expansion, the most characteristic of which was the establishment of 'Metro-land', that swathe of suburbia on previously untouched land north-west of London and served by the Metropolitan Railway (the Met) (*ibid.*, 363). The Railway was in a privileged position allowing it to retain surplus land. From 1919 this was developed for housing by the nominally independent Metropolitan Railway Country Estates Limited. The term Metroland was coined by the Met's marketing department in 1915 when the *Guide to the Extension Line* became the *Metro-land guide*. It was published annually from 1915 until 1932 and featured evocative descriptions and photographs of historic villages and rural vistas of the area to the north-west of London served by the Met railway. Not only was it a guidebook designed to promote the area for leisure excursion travel from London but it was full of facts for the commuter about the cost of season tickets and journey times (Green 1987). It was also packed with numerous adverts for all the new housing developments springing up during the 1920s that promoted a dream of a modern home in beautiful countryside with a fast railway service to central London.

Many of the new housing estates springing up in Metro-land were built by private developers. In the more sensitive developments mature trees were retained and some were incorporated into new roads as street trees. Immediately after the First World War there were already some very good examples of this across the London region. One of the best was at Beeches Avenue in Carshalton, a suburb south of the capital, in a housing development that began around 1906. Mature beech trees were retained on mounded verges either side of the previously rural road. Photographs from 1928 show the trees in excellent condition and testament to the care and protection given when the houses and new road were constructed (Figure 45). The scene is similar today and a good example by the London Borough of Sutton of the sustainable management of a heritage arboricultural feature. The local residents are very protective of this and

FIGURE 45. In the more sensitive private housing developments in the 1920s mature trees were retained as far as possible and some were incorporated into new roads as street trees. A good example was Beeches Avenue in Carshalton, a suburb south of London, were mature beech trees were retained on mounded verges either side of the previously rural road. This photograph was taken in 1928 but thanks to good tree management the scene looks quite similar today.

when unsafe trees have to be felled they get involved in planting replacement beech trees (Morris pers. comm., 2016).

In the inter-war years the LCC was responsible for building some of the largest housing estates in Europe, and these were designed along cottage estate lines. The biggest was the Becontree Estate, now in the London Borough of Barking and Dagenham, completed in 1938 with some 27,000 houses for 120,000 people (Barratt 2012, 358). Because of the sheer scale of this public housing venture it has subsequently been the subject of various social science studies (e.g. Olechnowicz 1997). This was a massive undertaking that the LCC claimed was 'the largest municipal housing estate in the world' (Home 1997, 47). The estate was designed by the LCC's Chief Architect, George Topham Forrest (*ibid.*, 22–23). There were few natural features which could have enhanced the beauty of the district. This prompted various attempts to achieve 'variety consistent with economy' that included the alternate use of brick, and white and coloured concrete. Interestingly, no mention could be found in the literature on Becontree regarding the use of landscape features or street trees to help achieve this. The road layout was planned to incorporate the existing country lanes, and relied upon a structure of wide arterial roads. The LCC, against the opposition of Romford Council, insisted on widths of 120 ft (37 m) for these (including a 32 ft (9.7 m) reservation for a future tramway). The wide roads were not designed in anticipation of future traffic growth as nobody at the time foresaw the massive growth in car ownership which followed the Second World War. Instead, it was to provide a spacious environment with plentiful fresh air and to facilitate surveillance by the LCC's small army of estate maintenance staff.

The LCC also paid for widening over 13 miles (21 km) of local roads to 100 ft (30.5 m) at a cost of £1.3 million and in the process a number of existing trees were retained. These wide roads still had a depressing effect and a commentator at the time called Valence Avenue the 'most dismal road on earth'.

The Becontree planners, influenced by the garden city movement, wanted to avoid the 'rectilinear' street layouts created by the housing bye-laws, in favour of the 'curvilinear', organised around crescents and circuses (Home 1997, 23). The design principle of keeping the alignment of the old country roads and lanes assisted this aim. The cul-de-sac was used not only to deter through traffic but also to allow extensive frontages in relation to construction costs and avoid the cost of intersections. The economic advantages of the cul-de-sac had been presented in the *Tudor Walters Report* where it was claimed that it provided frontages for as many houses as the through road but saved more than 50% in road construction costs. The Becontree planners also deployed various types of greenspace, for example, houses along three sides (the court principle), and fenced rectangular or triangular greens on corner sites (*ibid.*, 24). There were innumerable little rectangular patches of green situated at the corner of roads, and strips between the footways and inset blocks of houses (Young 1934, 98). Although intended to break up the monotony of the flat site, they arguably did not succeed and had a high maintenance cost.

Virtually every house on the estate had a garden, front and back, with little front hedges planted and maintained by the LCC (Home 1997, 31). The *Becontree Tenants' Handbook*, issued to all new occupants, urged them to 'keep front gardens in a neat and cultivated condition' and reminded them that 'neglect of the garden spoils the appearance of any house'. To reinforce this message the proper upkeep of the garden was one of 20 conditions of tenancy. In a more positive spirit the LCC awarded prizes for the best kept gardens. A social survey conducted in the early 1930s showed that most Becontree residents were generally happy with their new home and their estate (Young 1934). These were in contrast to where they had lived previously and this was despite some well-recognised shortcomings of the estate. Some of the houses had been built and occupied in advance of even the roads and basic services (Ravetz 2001, 100).

The extent of early street tree planting on the Becontree estate has been difficult to assess due to its extensive area and the limited information available. Nevertheless, some general conclusions can be made. The wide arterial roads such as Valence Avenue and Becontree Avenue were initially planted up along both sides with forest-type trees. In the case of Valence Avenue this included a lot of plane and lime. With Becontree Avenue, which was more sparsely planted, plenty of horse chestnut was also used. Many of the original trees remain, although for Valence Avenue the gaps through losses and different pruning regimes have had a negative impact on the uniform avenue effect that once existed. On the central reservations of both roads, which were intended as future tramways, there are now trees of a range of species and ages, although with substantial gaps between some of the planting.

In the minor roads in the main body of the Becontree estate it appears that there was never any intention to systematically plant these with trees in the footways and they remain largely treeless. However, from the early days there was a reasonable amount of tree planting on the greens and other patches of open space adjacent to roads, often with forest-type trees such as lime or horse chestnut although more recently with medium and small-sized species. The result now is that where there are plenty of these greens and tree planting, the neighbourhood does not look too bleak. However, in a large numbers of roads where this is not the case, the look is very grey indeed, especially as a substantial number of the front gardens are devoid of greenery having been hard-surfaced for car parking.

It is possible that the planners and early managers of the Becontree estate thought that the tree planting on the greens, often by junctions at the end of roads, would be supplemented along the rest of the road by the neat and cultivated front gardens and the LCC's own care of the garden hedges. Together this would give quite a green look to the road and might compensate for the absence of street tree planting. If that was the case, then this has not generally happened as intended.

Birmingham's suburbs

Birmingham, like London, also underwent a period of huge suburban expansion in the inter-war years. Immediately after the First World War the city was faced with a severe housing crisis (Chinn 1999, 39). Its population had increased, new building had ceased, and there were around 40,000 back-to-backs needing to be cleared and their tenants rehoused. Alleviating the problem required a massive and sustained programme of house-building and Birmingham Corporation was determined to spearhead this, with council housing playing a major role. By 1922, agricultural land was widely falling under swathes of urbanisation and new residential areas had been formed by the council in Birchfield, Bordesley Green, Bournville, California, Erdington, Gospel Oak, Kings Heath, Little Bromwich, Quinton, Short Heath, Stechford, Stirchley and Warstock (*ibid.*, 40).

Birmingham's 40,000th council house built since 1919 was constructed at Hopstone Road, Weoley Castle. Neville Chamberlain, the government minister responsible for housing policy and the MP for Birmingham Ladysmith, hailed the accomplishment and declared that Birmingham had achieved something 'which has no parallel in this or any other country'. Photographs of some of the recently completed streets of houses in Weoley Castle show these planted with trees at a close spacing of about 20 ft (6.1 m).

As well as constructing council housing for rent, Birmingham Corporation was also involved in a scheme to enable council tenants to buy their properties, with the help of subsidies (Chinn 1999, 47). Corporation dwellings built specifically for purchase became available in several districts. By 1929, when the subsidy was discontinued, more than £1 million had been loaned by the

Birmingham Municipal Bank to buyers of 3314 council houses. Despite the assistance it had still been difficult for many working families to purchase and this frustrated the underlying aim of the policy. The Conservative council had believed that building small villas for sale would undoubtedly help the working class through a 'filtering up' process (*ibid.*, 49). Home buyers would vacate their rented accommodation which would then be occupied by the better-paid working class, and their former homes would then be rented by the poor, leaving the back-to-backs of the city empty. However, this took no account of the poor's inability to pay the rent or their need to live near available work.

For 50 years Birmingham Corporation had believed that private enterprise would provide the answer to the city's dreadful housing problems (Chinn 1999, 51). This was eventually to be proven wrong. By 1933, when the *Wheatley Act* ceased operation, 33,612 council homes had been erected by Birmingham under its provision, compared to only 3433 under Chamberlain's *Housing Act* of 1923. Birmingham had built more council houses than any other local authority in Britain. This success was due to a remarkable partnership between a Labour government and a Conservative led council supported in its housing policy by Labour representatives. Overall, between 1919 and 1939, Birmingham Corporation built 51,681 houses. This compared to 59,744 privately-built dwellings. The two sectors together allowed the rehousing of 200,000 people, amounting to one fifth of Birmingham's population.

Acocks Green

In response to Birmingham's desperate housing shortage in the mid-1920s, council housing was built on around half of Acocks Green, which had been just a small Victorian suburb to the south of the city centre (Byrne 1997, 8). For the long-established middle class residents of the original suburb the new and substantial influx of people was unwelcome. Many moved away but the unfriendly attitude of those remaining ensured Acocks Green acquired the nickname Snob's Green. For the working class families moving into the area, their low-density council housing represented a welcome improvement from the conditions they had experienced in the dilapidated and slum housing nearer the city centre.

One major council housing scheme constructed in Acocks Green in the inter-war years was the Fox Hollies Estate. Fox Hollies is an area on the edge of the district and takes its name from a country property once owned by the Walker family. In the 1920s, this showpiece council estate was built around the Fox Hollies Road, north-west of Fox Hollies Park (AGHS 2016). The city had great ambitions for the Fox Hollies estate and its design was based around the usual garden suburb elements of curving roads, circles, and culs-de-sac. Some 2500 houses were eventually built between 1926 and 1931. The original provision for street trees in the main body of this estate seems to have been quite variable. While some roads were planted, often with common lime, others were not.

Some roads had grass verges to accommodate the trees, while in others they were planted directly into the footway. Hatfield Crescent, Fox Green Crescent and Hollyhock Road still have a good number of original trees. Generally, there is little evidence of any recent replanting and where this has occurred it has usually been with small ornamental species.

In 1928, a report by Birmingham Corporation commended the overall design of the Fox Hollies Estate and singled out the proposal for the new Greenwood Avenue for particular praise. It stated:

> The lay-out of the Fox Hollies Estate, however, really represents the high-water mark of achievement…by the City Surveyor's department. An outstanding feature of the estate plan is the fine Greenwood Avenue, which is to be 140 feet wide from house fence to house fence, with an additional 20 feet of front garden on either side, to the building line. This thoroughfare, with twin concrete roads with a broad centre space separating them, will be tree lined and will give a long and beautiful vista, with a block of school buildings at the far end. This splendid avenue, with its ring-centre, forms the axis of the lay-out, with a splendid radiation of gracefully-curving roads.
>
> AGHS 2016

The old Greenwood Road later became part of an entirely new route called Olton Boulevard East, constructed as a main thoroughfare for the estate and partly as dual carriageway (Byrne pers. comm., 2016). Some of the rear gardens in the old road were used to create part of the boulevard and some of the existing trees were incorporated alongside the new road. As a result, the original trees along the boulevard were a mixture of remnant trees and new municipal planting (Byrne 1997, 48). This is now a very leafy road and worthy of the name 'boulevard'. Even in the single carriageway section there are plenty of trees in the grass verges and many more in some large open spaces running alongside part of the road. The dual carriageway section not only has plenty of mature trees in its central reservation but these were also in verges alongside the road. Greenwood Avenue, the new road to the south of Olton Boulevard, now has extensive treecover along its sides and central reservation, with plenty of mature forest-type trees. The main Fox Hollies Road running north-south through the area also has many fine mature trees, not only on its central reservation but also in sections of grass verges and open spaces along both sides. As with the smaller roads in the core of the estate, lime was the favoured species for the original planting on these main roads.

The Yarnfield Estate is another inter-war council housing scheme in Acocks Green and is located to the north of the Fox Hollies Estate. Like that estate, many of the roads of the Yarnfield estate were also planted with trees soon after the houses were built (Byrne 1997, 46). These were mainly forest-type trees, including limes and ash. There is, however, quite a contrast between the existing numbers of street trees on these two estates. Although at Yarnfield there is still some mature trees that could have been part of the original planting, many sections of road on the estate are almost entirely treeless. There are also no grass verges and only a limited amount of greenery in the front gardens as many have been hard-surfaced for car parking.

Perry Common

Perry Common is an area of north Birmingham which was extensively developed for council housing during the 1920s, creating what is known as the Perry Common Estate (Carless pers. comm., 2016). In 1924, over 1000 working class families moved into the newly-constructed homes that were in the typical cottage estate style and built mostly in groups of four or six. Many of the new houses, especially in the central part of the estate were built from concrete in a style pioneered by Henry Boot Limited and popularly known as 'Boot Houses'. The circular Whitton Lodge Road at the heart of the estate, which had a number of small shops, enclosed a large open space generously planted with trees. Photographs of the estate taken *c.* 1925 soon after the tenants moved in show footways of up to 20 ft (6.1 m) in width and not a single street tree in sight (Figure 46). Some trees were planted a few years later, although not equally along all roads. From the evidence of the oldest street trees still surviving on the estate, many were London planes with some limes added slightly later.

By the 1980s, the Perry Common estate was facing serious structural problems. Many of the Boot houses were in a poor state of repair due to significant deterioration of the concrete through carbonatation, when it chemically reacts with carbon dioxide in the air. Cracks in the walls and rising damp were just some of the many problems plaguing the now unpopular

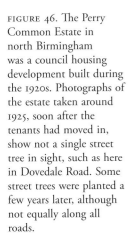

FIGURE 46. The Perry Common Estate in north Birmingham was a council housing development built during the 1920s. Photographs of the estate taken around 1925, soon after the tenants had moved in, show not a single street tree in sight, such as here in Dovedale Road. Some street trees were planted a few years later, although not equally along all roads.

homes. During the 1990s, Birmingham City Council earmarked 908 of these homes in the area for demolition. Fortunately, those houses on the outskirts of the estate were made of brick and did not require demolition. As part of the reconstruction of large parts of the estate, the layout of the streets and houses were also redesigned. This undoubtedly involved the removal of some mature street trees. However, opportunities were also taken to save a few of the mature trees located in previous gardens and incorporate these as street trees in the new road layout (Carless pers. comm., 2016).

Over the years the street tree population of the Perry Common Estate has undergone significant change, not least in recent years due to the massive redevelopment across the estate. Dovedale Road, which runs around the eastern edge of the estate, has undergone major redevelopment with many new houses. Just a few mature street trees have been retained and by the summer of 2014 there was no evidence of any new planting apart from at the far northern end of this road. However, new houses are still being built on the southern section so more planting may follow. Witton Lodge Road runs east–west through the heart of the estate and still retains its wide footways. It has a scattering of original planes trees, more on the western section near the inner circle, and evidence of some replanting, especially on the eastern section. Hastings Road, towards the centre of the estate, has also undergone significant redevelopment with many original houses demolished and new ones built. The footways are now narrower but several of the original plane trees have been retained, although there is no evidence of replanting. Generally, where there has been replanting on the estate this has focused on a range of small and medium-sized ornamentals and does not include more plane trees.

Hall Green

With regard to private housing developments and street trees, it is interesting to explore the Hall Green district of Birmingham, although only a summary of this can be given here. In this originally Victorian suburb, its extensive urbanisation southwards occurred after the First World War and was rather different from the rest of the city (Birmingham CC 2016). There was a high proportion of private housing constructed, which tended to be built without the grand and sweeping planning characteristic of inter-war council estates, and many green spaces were left enclosed behind the new roads. Much of the housing was middle class semi-detached with a reasonable amount of garden space, both front and back. The Residents Association, formed in 1925 and said to be the first in the country, sought to minimise the loss of mature trees during the urbanisation process. It continues to address this and other conservation issues vigorously.

When many of the streets and their semi-detached houses were built, these were not immediately planted even though there were grass verges that could easily accommodate this. This is supported by evidence from early photographs and OS maps of the area. However, there were some notable exceptions to this with streets such as Smirrells Road, Delrene Road and Stroud Road, the last two completed just before the start of the Second World War, where common limes were planted along both sides. These streets now have fine avenues of trees that make an outstanding landscape feature. With many of the other roads in this part of Hall Green, street tree planting seems to have come later but was then carried out very thoroughly. Now, this whole area of Hall Green has plenty of street trees, although comprising mainly small and medium-sized ornamentals. Some of the main routes within this district, such as Highfield Road and Robin Hood Lane, were planted with trees as soon as the area was developed (Byrne 1996). While large sections of these roads have subsequently been made into dual carriageways with wide grassed central reservations, they have retained their extensive treecover and added to this with plenty more trees on the central reservations. Overall, Hall Green is still one of the leafiest districts in Birmingham and much of that is due to its numerous street trees.

Manchester's suburbs

In the inter-war years Manchester's traditional cotton industry suffered badly through competition from countries such as India, China and Japan where production costs were lower (Cooper 2002, 11). In response, the city's economy diversified into the engineering, chemical and electrical industries and it managed to maintain its position as the great industrial powerhouse of the northwest of England. These employment opportunities meant that workers and their families continued to flock to the city and by 1931 its population reached 766,311. To accommodate the growing workforce its suburbs continued to expand through both private housing developments and a major programme of council house building.

Kingsway Estate, Burnage

Burnage is a district of Manchester about 4 miles (6.4 km) south of the city centre. Just after the First World War the furthest suburb south in this district was Burnage Garden Village, described in the previous chapter. The mid-1920s saw the construction of Kingsway, a major thoroughfare running south from the Manchester suburb of Levenshulme and now the main A34 road. Around the same time, Errwood Road, also running south from Levenshulme, was extended into a major '50 ft town-planning road' to a point where it joined Burnage Lane (Anon 1923, 14). In 1923, as this was being constructed, it was announced that a council housing estate would be built in Burnage, partly facilitated by the new route. When the road was completed it was planted up with trees on either side. Now, Errwood Road is a magnificent double avenue of tall mature trees, limes on one side and planes on the other, all located in wide grass verges with open spaces on both sides behind that (Figure 47).

Construction of what was initially known as the Burnage Estate, but later regarded as part of the Kingsway Estate, was undertaken around 1927 and mostly located between Burnage Lane and newly extended Errwood Road. The focal points in the estate design were two circles of housing, Western Circle to the west of Errwood Road and Eastern Circle to the east of this. Photographs of these Circles taken a few years after construction show the houses have small front gardens with plenty of hedges but there are no street trees. Nowadays, the scene looks much the same as there are still no street trees. The aptly named Arbor Drive, which is an access road into the estate off Burnage Lane, was planted with plane trees in grass verges along both sides. While quite a few trees have been lost, this remains an impressive avenue. Unfortunately, there has been no replanting over the years and when the existing trees die that could be the end of this beautiful landscape feature. In contrast to Arbor Drive, Arbor Avenue is devoid of street trees and probably always was.

In 1926, it was announced that the bulk of the new Kingsway Estate would be built following the compulsory purchase of two landed properties (Anon 1926, 9). This would be bounded on the north by Mauldeth Road, the east by Burnage Lane, the south by Fog Lane (later Lane End Road) and the west by the railway line. As with the initial development of the Kingsway Estate, a few

FIGURE 47. In the mid-1920s, Errwood Road, running south from Levenshulme in Manchester, was extended into a major '50 ft town-planning road' to a point where it joined Burnage Lane. When the road was completed it was planted up with trees on either side. Today, Errwood Road is a magnificent double avenue of tall mature trees, limes on one side and planes on the other.

PHOTO: JOHN McCRORY.

roads were planted with trees when this phase of construction was completed. Green End Road was planted with horse chestnuts in wide grass verges in front of the houses on both sides and planes were planted around a circular open space halfway along this road that was fringed with more housing. While a few trees have been lost, this is still a magnificent arboreal feature on the estate. A similar planting scheme, also using horse chestnuts, was undertaken on part of Barcicroft Road, located to the south of Green End Lane. This is now another fine avenue of mature trees, although rather shorter.

While the roads described above are now fine landscape features on the Kingsway Estate, many of its other roads are entirely treeless, despite some having names associated with trees. In the majority of roads street trees were never planted and as a result they make a stark contrast today to those with fine treescapes. It is possible that planting never occurred because the local authority considered many of the footways were too narrow. Although that may have been the case for large forest-type trees, there was often sufficient space to accommodate small and medium-sized ornamental trees. Nevertheless, efforts were made in the estate's initial construction to retain existing trees in some front and back gardens. Some trees have also been planted on patches of open space dotted about the estate.

Anson Estate, Longsight

Longsight is a district of Manchester about 3 miles (4.8 km) south of the city centre, which featured in the previous chapter. Its Anson Estate is a large council housing scheme built in the inter-war years and located between Birchfields Road and Beresford Road. Construction of the estate began in the 1920s on previous open land, part of which had been a golf course. Many of the houses were semi-detached with small front gardens and there were also plenty of short terraced groups of houses. A number of the wider roads had grass verges. Photographic evidence indicates that most of the roads in this estate were never planted with trees (Figure 48). Most of these remain virtually treeless, although there are some exceptions that should be mentioned. While Brynton Road had grass verges but no street trees around 1930, there are now a few small ornamentals on the northern section but the verges have gone. The previously treeless Meldron Road now has a few ornamental thorns (*Crataegus* spp.) as street trees located directly into the footway at its eastern end. Despite its lack of street trees, this road still has quite a 'green' look due to the presence of several large plane trees in front gardens. From the age of these trees they may predate the housing estate and be remnants from the earlier golf course.

In recent years the Anson Estate has often been in the news because of its high levels of crime and social deprivation. This has prompted some attempts at urban regeneration with a range of environmental improvement projects. As yet this does not seem to have featured any significant amount of street tree planting, even though there is plenty of space to do so. Sadly, the roads around the Anson Estate remain depressingly 'grey' and mostly treeless.

Estates in Liverpool and Cardiff

Norris Green is a large council housing estate a few miles north-east of Liverpool city centre which was built by Liverpool Corporation as its most important suburban development project in the inter-war years (Parrott 1996, 7–8). It was located mainly on agricultural land and when construction commenced in 1926 its planned population was 30,000. Most of the homes were built by private contractors in blocks of 2, 4, 6 or 8 without any ornamentation or architectural detail. Homes on the periphery of the estate and on the main routes through the area are largely brick and well-built, with those on minor routes and residential roads made of concrete in the 'Boot house' style. To avoid monotonous rows of identical streets, houses were grouped together in crescents, closes, squares and concentric circles, an arrangement which many tenants found confusing.

Due to financial pressures landscaping was reduced to a minimum on the Norris Green Estate (Parrott 1996, 8). Some street tree planting was undertaken on some of the major roads in the area such as Uttering Avenue, Lorenzo Drive and Strawberry Road. A few of the minor roads also got trees, such as the Inner Forum, Outer Forum and Beversbrook Road where common limes were planted. However, the majority of minor roads remained unplanted.

FIGURE 48. The Anson Estate in Longsight, Manchester, is a large council housing scheme built in the inter-war years. While a number of its wider roads had grass verges, photographic evidence indicates that most of the roads in this estate were never planted with trees. This is Brynton Road photographed in the 1920s.

Today, some of the major roads have some mature and majestic trees. There is a fine avenue of planes along the northern end of Parthenon Drive, a single line further south and then it briefly becomes an avenue again. This continues into Lorenzo Drive with more planes in wide verges. There is an excellent lime avenue along Uttering Avenue East with fine mature trees on both sides and on the central reservation. Further east the trees are only on the central reservation and the verges are empty. By contrast, Uttering Avenue (a continuation of Uttering Avenue East and to the west of this) could have had the same fine treescape but is virtually treeless. While Strawberry Road once had trees planted all the way along on both sides, its wide grass verges are now treeless. Overall, what really stands out now in terms of street trees on the Norris Green Estate is the stark contrast between the fine treecover on some of its main roads and the treeless, or almost treeless, roads of much of the rest of the estate. Driving around some of these minor roads you can still spot the occasional mature lime or plane tree that still remains from those streets that had benefited from the original but limited planting on the estate.

The Ely Estate in Cardiff is located a couple of miles from the city centre and is an example of a major inter-war council housing scheme in the capital of Wales. In 1922, Ely formally became a suburb of Cardiff and much of its agricultural land was immediately earmarked for housing development (Morgan 2003, 57). Within two years nearly 3500 council houses were built as part of Lloyd George's promise of 'homes fit for heroes' and with the specific intention of rehousing working class families from Cardiff's inner-city slums. The estate was built to the north of Cowbridge Road and was completed before the outbreak of the Second World War with its typical cottage estate mix of semi-detached houses and terraced groups of four and six houses. It is said to have won approval as an example of garden suburb design with 'its gabled cottages, low housing densities and the baroque pattern of the road layouts'. However, looking at the estate today it is hard to imagine any direct connection with the garden suburbs. There are virtually no trees throughout the whole estate and together with the lack of trees on any open space and in front gardens this makes for some grey and depressing streetscapes. It has been difficult to source much photographic material of the early days of this estate but from the evidence on the ground today it seems likely this was always rather treeless. The few street trees existing are probably not sufficiently old to be from any original plantings.

As part of the development of this estate, a new main thoroughfare was constructed along its southern edge. This is called Grand Avenue and it runs west from what is now Cowbridge Road West (A48) for nearly 1.4 miles (2.2 km) until it ends at Green Farm Road (Morgan 2003, 56). The road, much of it dual carriageway, was built to provide access points to the new estate and act as a link between this and Cowbridge Road West. Photos of Grand Avenue taken in the 1930s show there was some roadside planting with forest-type species such as common lime. There was also some planting in small groups on parts of the central reservation. Nowadays, while there is reasonable treecover on some sections of this road, it is very patchy on other parts. Furthermore, the trees are an assortment of species and ages without any apparent design considerations. There remains a wonderful opportunity to create a spectacular avenue of trees, especially on the central reservation, that would be worthy of the name 'Grand Avenue'.

With some council housing estates in the inter-war years, the relevant local authority undertook impressive avenue plantings on some of the approach roads, access roads or main roads through the estates. This certainly gave the impression of a leafy estate to those approaching this or just passing through, even if many streets in the heart of the estate were treeless. Norris Green has some examples of impressive avenue planting in this respect that is in sharp contrast to the planting on Grand Avenue in the Ely Estate. Whether this sort of planting was undertaken or not seems to have been a question of commitment rather than cost. In terms of the overall cost of building thousands of new homes and constructing miles of new road, the expense of planting a few impressive avenues would have been minimal.

Strategic roads and suburban expansion

In this section of the chapter we continue the link between the construction of major new thoroughfares and the expanding inter-war suburbs that was highlighted in some of the examples featured above. Here, the focus is on these major thoroughfares and their roadside trees rather than the extent of street tree planting in their associated suburbs.

Just as the railways played a crucial role in the expansion of the suburbs from the middle of the nineteenth century, so the construction of new strategic roads in the vicinity of major cities helped to speed the spread of suburbia in the early twentieth century. While the construction of the three roads described below occurred before the First World War, they are considered in this chapter because their impact was particularly noticeable in the inter-war years. What marks out these three roads is the extent of roadside tree planting following their construction.

Queen's Drive in Liverpool has been described as Britain's first ring-road. It connects many of Liverpool's huge north-eastern suburbs with the city centre and indeed enabled them to be built (Lewis 2003, 113). The idea of a road ringing the city had been discussed since the 1800s and it gained momentum as the city expanded rapidly through the first part of the nineteenth century. In 1853, a 'circular boulevard' plan was proposed which would also have provided public parks, but it did not materialise. Construction began eventually in the early 1900s and although three concentric rings were envisaged, only the middle road known as Queens Drive was built. Designed by John Alexander Brodie, the City Engineer, it incorporated many existing roads which were straightened and widened to fit the plan, while the gaps were filled by new roads. What is interesting from an arboricultural perspective is that extensive sections of Queens Drive were planted with trees, regularly spaced and of uniform appearance, during or immediately after construction and long before there was any of the planned built development in the vicinity. Early images of the road show rows of neatly-planted amenity trees alongside lengthy sections of newly-built carriageway that for the time being still pass through open countryside (Lewis 2003, 114 and 118; Parrott 1996, 41). In due course the housing estates and factories appeared as the new road opened up enormous areas of Liverpool's hinterland to development opportunities. The road was particularly significant in the 1920s and '30s when the city needed vast areas of new housing to ease overcrowding and to resettle the people being relocated from the city-centre slums. Today, Queen's Drive is a very busy arterial road that is mostly dual carriageway and the land adjacent to it has undergone much redevelopment over the years. Nevertheless, it still has some extensive and mature treecover along many of its sections.

Town Moor Avenue in Doncaster, Yorkshire, is another important strategic road with impressive avenue planting (Figure 49). It extends for approximately two-thirds of a mile (1 km) north-west from Doncaster Racecourse and cuts across what is called the Town Field, which until the late 1890s was open countryside. At the beginning of the twentieth century Doncaster was growing rapidly (Briam 1982). Practically all the available building sites in the town

FIGURE 49. Town Moor Avenue in Doncaster, Yorkshire, is another important strategic road with impressive avenue planting. Built in the 1900s, the road extends for approximately two-thirds of a mile northwest from Doncaster Racecourse. This photograph from around 1920 shows the lime trees at the western end.

had been developed, the Nether Hall Park had been built over and many new streets were being laid out at Wheatley. At the same time, the town's lack of a proper park was becoming obvious. After much negotiation an agreement was reached regarding the future of Town Field between Doncaster Corporation and Major Browne, who owned the land. It was agreed that the greater part of Town Field would be preserved as a permanent open space, for the benefit of the townspeople. At the same time, a major new road call Town Moor Avenue would be constructed from the Grandstand on the Racecourse to Thorne Road in Wheatley, which had already been developed as a residential suburb. While the land to the south-west of the road would remain open space, the land to the northeast would accommodate a new housing development.

The OS County Series Map 1903–6 shows the new Town Moor Avenue as having been built but not yet with any new housing on the north-east side. However, the young lime trees that would later form a spectacular avenue had already been planted, as indicated on the map. Photographs from *c.* 1913 show that each tree had a wrought-iron guard which must have involved a considerable expense for this lengthy road (Figure 49). By the 1930s the planned suburban expansion had taken place with a network of new roads and a mix of semi-detached and terraced houses and with larger semi-detached and detached houses fronting Town Moor Avenue. Today, this road remains a magnificent avenue of tall, mature lime trees and it is hoped that future management will keep it this way. As trees have been lost there are now some large gaps appearing but there is no evidence of recent replanting.

Sheffield has long been famous for its extensive urban forest. One of the jewels in the city's arboreal crown is the avenue of limes along Rivelin Valley Road (Winson 2015). At 3½ miles long (5.6 km), it is said to form the second longest lime avenue in the country. This spectacular natural monument is rooted in Sheffield's history. Unlike most historic tree avenues, planted to embellish the landscape of some aristocrat or wealthy industrialist, what brought about Rivelin's avenue over a century ago was a combination of high unemployment and the foresight of Sheffield Corporation's Water Committee. The committee was formed in 1830 to provide water provision for its growing population and industry. Large tracts of land were acquired in the catchment areas and a series of reservoirs built to the west of the city (Davey 1984, 16). The River Rivelin starts up on the moors near north-west Sheffield and flows through the Rivelin Valley. The river proved ideal for powering the 20 mills that developed along its course. The committee's work included an agreement that they must supply compensation water into the River Rivelin, for the benefit of the mill owners and other users further downstream.

At the start of the 1900s, there was no proper through road in the valley, although it had often been suggested (Davey 1984, 16). In 1905, the Water Committee suggested that building a 'good road' along the valley would be a solution to the high rates of unemployment that existed within the city. It purchased the required land and work on the road began in November 1905, with an average of 172 men being employed on the scheme. To create the tree-lined road, the committee purchased 700 lime trees from Messrs Dixons of

Chester, at a cost of £147 (*ibid.*, 19). Most trees were planted with wrought-iron guards and these were in place for the first 30 years, ensuring the trees were not damaged by traffic or vandals.

When the new road was being constructed there were several places where existing mature trees stood in its path (Davey 1984, 19). Those in the middle of the road were removed, but there were several that stood on what became the footway and others that only just encroached onto the road. The road builders were reluctant to fell any mature trees unnecessarily and many were allowed to stay and incorporated into the road design. The council simply painted the trunks of trees that encroached on the road with whitewash each year, so that traffic would avoid them. This solution worked well for many years, yet over the following decades, as traffic increased along the road, there were a number of accidents where the old trees were located, and eventually the decision was taken to remove them.

Following the construction of Rivelin Valley Road suburban development increased at its north-western end in the region of Walkley Bank and generally the new route made a significant contribution to the city's progress in the twentieth century. Today, the people of Sheffield and visitors reap the benefits of the Water Committee's actions over a century ago (Winson 2015). In an attempt to generate work for the city's unemployed they created a majestic green corridor that connects the urban and rural, from the built up north-western Sheffield suburbs, out to the wooded reservoirs of the Peak District (Figure 50). In recent years a number of the trees have been felled as part of highway maintenance

FIGURE 50. In an attempt to generate work for Sheffield's unemployed, work began in 1905 to construct Rivelin Valley Road and create a majestic green corridor that connects the urban and rural, from the built up north-western Sheffield suburbs, out to the wooded reservoirs of the Peak District. It is said that it now forms the second longest lime avenue in the country. This photograph was taken around 1913.

works, although it is good to see that the trees are being replaced with more lime species. It is hoped that future management will protect and sustain this spectacular natural monument rooted in Sheffield's history.

Bermondsey and the Salters

This account of the inter-war period concludes with the remarkable programme of street tree planting that took place in the London Metropolitan Borough of Bermondsey, now part of the London Borough of Southwark (Lebas 1999, 219). Bermondsey is located just south of the River Thames and in the Victorian era was one of the poorest inner London suburbs. By the 1920s, nearly one-third of the borough consisted of the Surrey Docks and bonded wharfs and warehouses. As a substantial proportion of the remaining land was devoted to economic activity there was very little left over for residential use and most of that was dilapidated Victorian housing. Although this had a declining population this was still very high density and living conditions remained very poor.

With the rise of the British labour movement after the First World War, Bermondsey became a stronghold of the Independent Labour Party with Dr Alfred Salter as its Member of Parliament from 1922–39 (Lebas 1999, 220). From the late 1920s, the borough had a pioneering policy of socialist reform and social welfare, a major part of which was its Beautification Campaign to create a healthier environment. The driving force behind this campaign was Ada Salter, wife of the MP, who was the first female councillor in London when she was elected in 1909 (Brockway 1949, 85) (Figure 51). In 1919, she became the first female Labour Mayor in Britain when she was elected to that post in Bermondsey. In 1920, she launched her Beautification Campaign led by the council's newly-formed Beautification Committee. The aim was to plant trees in every street and flowers on every square yard of unbuilt land. Around the same time she established a housing campaign, to demolish those slums that could be cleared and beautify those that could not.

To provide a workforce for the landscaping and tree planting schemes, Bermondsey Council recruited well-qualified and experienced horticultural staff who were among the highest paid of any borough in London (Lebas 1999, 229). All belonged to the National Union of Horticultural Workers. At the lower end were casual labourers, usually ex-servicemen engaged for tree

FIGURE 51. The driving force behind Bermondsey's Beautification Campaign and remarkable street tree programme in the 1920s and 1930s was Ada Salter. She was the first female councillor in London when elected in 1909. In 1919, she became the first female Labour Mayor in Britain when she was elected to that post in Bermondsey.

planting. At the top of the hierarchy was the Superintendent of Gardens. In 1923, the Kew-trained Mr W.H. Johns succeeded Mr Aggett, who had served the council for 29 years without any formal qualifications. He soon established a tree nursery where long rows of saplings of elm, poplar, plane, acacia and other species grew before they were transplanted to the streets of Bermondsey (Brockway 1949, 87–88). Alfred Salter, who had been a doctor in general practice before becoming the local MP, declared, 'The trees not only add to the beauty of the neighbourhood. All through the spring, summer and autumn the green colouring matter of the leaves is purifying the atmosphere and helping to make Bermondsey healthier'.

Before the First World War, the Metropolitan Public Gardens Association (MPGA) had carried out some street tree planting schemes elsewhere in London, although none had been undertaken in Bermondsey (Lebas 1999, 230). Minutes of the MPGA record in 1914 the council's intent to plant 831 street trees, but this project had been suspended with the First World War (MPGA 1914, 24). After the war, the Beautification Committee invoked the *LCC (General Powers) Act* 1914, which empowered a local authority to plant trees once it was confirmed that no more than two-thirds of the occupants of a highway objected to the scheme (Lebas 1999, 230). At its first meeting the committee accepted estimates for 831 planes and 831 poplars. In 1919 the borough had responsibility for only 376 street trees but by 1927 when the tree planting campaign was reaching its end, this had increased dramatically to 6156. By April 1924, 397 trees had been removed and 730 had been replanted and staked along 87 streets in an attempt to achieve some uniformity in the treescape of individual streets. In November 1925, the pace of planting slowed down due to the poor quality of nursery stock. Supplies of saplings were in great shortage after the war, although Messrs W. Cutbush and Sons (suppliers to the MPGA), Messrs Amos Perry and Sons, and Messrs W. Walters and Company managed to provide some trees, but by 1924 these had dwindled to a few larches. Mr Johns was forced to turn to new and more expensive suppliers, including some in Continental Europe. Exchanges with other local authority horticulture departments appeared to be the only viable solution until early in 1926 when on a 'botanical expedition' in Hartley Wood, near Fairby Grange, Mr Johns came across hundreds of seedlings of mainly hornbeam, dogwood, spindle and birch. These were acquired from the local farmer and established in a new nursery at Fairby Grange. After 1926, Fairby Grange became the main supplier and Bermondsey became entirely self-sufficient in nursery stock. Between 1931 and 1939 this supplied 4489 saplings.

The most used species for street trees in Bermondsey was Lombardy poplar (*Populus nigra* 'Italica') and London plane. By November 1927, out of 6156 street trees planted, 3122 were Lombardy poplar and 1861 were plane (Bermondsey Council 1927a, 258–260). While this poplar may seem a poor choice today, at the time it met the requirements of a reliable, compact and fast growing tree that could cope with the very smoky atmosphere and establish itself successfully within the political cycle of this pioneering Labour administration (Stutter pers. comm., 2016). Other trees frequently used were common lime, *Robinia pseudoacacia* and tree of heaven (*Ailanthus altissima*), which was a favourite tree of the Salters. As the planting programme progressed from the wider thoroughfares to more narrow streets, smaller and more decorative species such as cherry, birch and rowan were used. In terms of tree survival, some species did better than others. There were more social rather than arboricultural uncertainties, and these included vandalism and lack of planting skills by ex-servicemen. One factor resulting in very high losses was due to damage by motor vehicles mounting the footway (*Gardeners' Chronicle* 1931, 27). Objections from residents were few, either against planting or cutting trees down, and the council mostly ignored these by offering the unassailable explanation that it received a 60% subsidy from the Unemployment Grants Committee and this provided an alternative to the dole. One significant factor in reducing any objections to tree planting was that residents were notified in advance of this so that the trees did not just suddenly appear on their streets without warning. This seems to have been a legal requirement since relevant committee minutes state that before planting, 'In compliance with the London County Council (General Powers) Act 1904, notices of the Council's resolution be served on the occupiers of the premises in those thoroughfares' (Bermondsey Council 1927b, 230).

After several years of the Beautification Campaign, Bermondsey had trees in nearly every street and had become known as 'the borough with the most trees' (Figure 52). The campaign was now attracting national and even international attention. Nevertheless, Alfred and Ada Salter had one great disappointment in their plans for Bermondsey and that was the failure to rebuild it along garden city lines (Brockway 1949, 163). This was largely the result of high land costs and nowhere for the crowded population to go after any major low-density development. However, many new council flats were built and Wilson Grove Garden Village was created by rebuilding an old estate. This beautiful 'utopian' council housing estate naturally included plenty of street trees and stands today as a much admired example of a municipal housing scheme. In Bermondsey, the street tree had a symbolic and political value that embodied urban improvement, self-sufficiency and beauty. Today, some of Bermondsey's largest and oldest street trees remain as a living legacy of the remarkable achievements of the Beautification Campaign, even though the numbers are now becoming rapidly depleted. An even longer-lasting legacy is this inspiring example of social welfare and inclusion delivered through a pioneering programme of local authority street tree management.

Suburbs immediately after the Second World War

When the Second World War ended in 1945 it was widely accepted that London and the rest of the country needed to embark on a huge programme of urban renewal (Barratt 2012, 389). The greatest need was for housing, not only to replace some 200,000 homes in England alone that had been destroyed by bombing but also to clear away the slums that still scarred our major cities

FIGURE 52. After several years of the Beautification Campaign, Bermondsey had trees in nearly every street and had become known as 'the borough with the most trees'. Some of the early plantings were now looking quite impressive, such as these trees in Storks Road photographed in 1935.

CREDIT: SOUTHWARK LOCAL HISTORY LIBRARY AND ARCHIVE.

(Harwood 2000, 102). In 1945, it was estimated that 750,000 new homes were required in England and Wales to provide all families with accommodation. With the election of a Labour government there began a national drive to demolish sub-standard housing and embark on extensive programmes of house building (Chinn 1999, 85). However, as with the situation in 1919, economic reality meant these plans had to be tempered as a wide range of national initiatives competed for scarce resources. Nevertheless, in the late 1940s and throughout the 1950s, suburban expansion gathered pace again, although more regulated by the establishment of greenbelts. In larger cities such as London, these suburbs now include formerly separate towns and villages that had gradually been absorbed due to the city's growth and expansion. Some new council housing estates that had begun to be built just before the war were now prioritised for completion.

Typical of those incomplete housing projects was the Speke Estate on the outskirts of Liverpool. Work on constructing this estate had begun in 1937 with a layout that had much in common with the typical inter-war cottage estate (Ravetz 2001, 101). This meant that many of the roads on the estate had wide grass verges on either side in front of the blocks of two-storey houses. There were also plenty of small open spaces at the corner of road junctions and as strips of grass in front of other blocks. At the heart of the estate were the shops, community centre, church and playing fields. Running through the centre of the estate was the main axis road, named Central Avenue on its western section and Central Way on its eastern section. On the estate's western border was Western Avenue, a major dual carriageway road, and on its northern border was the main A561 road, later called Speke Boulevard, that leads into the city centre. The extent of street tree planting on this estate was always patchy from the start. While some roads, even those with wide grass verges, remained virtually treeless, other roads had an assortment of trees planted along them. Central Avenue now has quite a few mature horse chestnuts, although in places there are wide gaps between trees. The current pattern of treecover on Central Way is fairly similar. Apart from some forest-type trees such as horse chestnut and plane, it is noticeable that there has been a preference for small and medium-sized ornamentals even when there was sufficient space for larger-growing trees. On the estate today, with its vast expanses of empty grass verges and strips of open space, there is much potential for extensive street tree planting. An excellent example of bold and imaginative planting on a grand scale has been undertaken recently on the nearby Speke Boulevard (Figure 53). From 1997 to 1999 this involved the planting of around 800 semi-mature *Tilia cordata* 'Greenspire', sourced from a Dutch nursery (Tully pers. comm., 2016). This magnificent arboreal feature was created as part of the Mersey Forest initiative and is now a living 'gateway' into the city that is already doing much to transform the image of the area.

In the immediate post-war period the private housing sector also experienced a period of major expansion. While there is insufficient space here to go into much detail an assessment of a number of larger-scale schemes has shown considerable variation across a range of factors. Nevertheless, there tended to be a preference to continue with the type of scheme that had become popular in the 1930s in the Metro-land of London and suburban fringes of other major cities. The extent of public greenspace and street tree planting were factors

FIGURE 53. Speke Boulevard in Liverpool photographed in 2003. This magnificent arboreal feature was created as part of the Mersey Forest initiative and is now a living 'gateway' into the city that is already doing much to transform the image of the area.

that varied greatly between projects. Some private developers, such as Span Developments Ltd, were careful not only to retain existing trees where possible but also to create sufficient open space and roadside grass verges where new trees could be planted (Harwood 1999, 148–152; 2000, 102). This careful approach was in stark contrast to some other developers' schemes where only the hard landscape elements and most robust trees survived.

While the high-quality private sector developers were continuing to make a virtue of low-density and low-rise housing, attitudes were changing with regard to council housing schemes. Politicians and planners, influenced by visits to some of the grander continental public housing schemes, were coming to the conclusion that more cottage estates, such as the one at Becontree, would not suffice to house those who would be displaced by planned slum clearances. Bolder and more imaginative solutions were sought.

Radburn planning and the high-rise fiasco

In the post-war period various developments in the design of council housing and the layout of estates were to have a major impact on the presence of street trees in these essentially working class neighbourhoods. In 1948, the government's Central Housing Advisory Committee issued a report from one of its sub-committee's entitled *The Appearance of Housing Estates* and this included a number of proposals in relation to trees. One of these recommended that in choosing trees for street planting preference should be given to 'varieties whose natural growth is such as to reduce to a minimum the need for cutting back' (Ministry of Health 1948, 5). This was generally taken to mean a move away from forest-type trees. The report also stated, 'We recommend, as an alternative to planting roadside trees on the pavement, an extension of the practice of planting trees in front gardens where the latter are of suitable size'. As the report had earlier highlighted some of the problems associated with street and roadside trees, this signalled a preference to reduce their numbers on new housing estates. While this government-sponsored report undoubtedly led to a reduction in the use of street trees on new local authority estates, two fundamental trends in post-war housing estate design probably had an even greater impact. The first was the Radburn model for estate design and the second was the move towards high-rise housing.

The model for estate design called Radburn planning was acknowledged in the government's *Dudley Report on Housing* in 1944, it was also recommended in a 1949 *Housing Manual* and then promoted from the 1950s onwards (Ravetz 2001, 102–103). Named after the small American settlement of Radburn, New Jersey, it could be seen as the 'garden city plus motor car'. It had dual and quite separate circulation systems for cars and pedestrians. Houses were put in 'superblocks' that cars could penetrate only by means of culs-de-sac leading to the back entrance to houses. Their other side, the main living areas, turned inwards to face, first their own private gardens, then a public green space where a network of footpaths gave safe access to all the necessary urban amenities.

This layout, in a misunderstood and corrupted form, was adopted in Britain where it was applied to council housing and new towns from the early 1950s onwards. The British version of Radburn made two changes that were crucial to its operation: houses were built in short rows or terraces rather than in pairs or detached, and garages were grouped in courts some distance from, and often out of sight of, the houses. 'Radburn type' planning, rather than authentic Radburn, then became the hallmark of the 1960s and 1970s. As used, it became a merely mechanical repetition of 'superblocks' stamped, as it were, over landscapes without reference to land form or local atmosphere (Ravetz 2001, 103). This style of layout was hoped to facilitate social encounters, although the extent to which it was successful was a matter for debate. The same style of planning was also applied to the deck-access estate, where a maze of footpaths was replaced by a limited number of 'decks' giving access to scores of apartments above and below as well as on deck level. Large numbers of housing units or 'villages' were often grouped around a large green open space, as with the 1200-home deck access Hunslet Grange estate in Leeds.

The ultimate episode of utopianism in British council housing was the brief boom in high-rise housing from 1958 to 1968 (Ravetz 2001, 104). The occasion was the resumption of slum clearance announced by Prime Minister Macmillan in 1954. Over the next 20 years some 1.2 million pre-1914 dwellings were demolished in England and Wales. The demolished areas had been the neighbourhoods of working class people for upwards of 70 years, and in many places for over a century. Considering the eventual fate of much of the high-rise housing, and the recent and successful renovation of some of the old Victorian terraced housing in some cities, this policy was, in retrospect, a huge mistake on a number of levels.

During the late 1950s and 1960s, most of the new council estates were typically 'mixed-rise' as recommended by the government but in this period there was an overwhelming proportion of high-rise flats, much of it in the form of 'tower blocks'. The high-rise housing boom peaked in the mid-1960s when blocks over nine storeys accounted for up to a quarter of all council housing approvals in some years. Towards the end of the 1960s, many of Britain's cities had 'forests' of tower blocks that housed many tens of thousands of tenants in a single estate. Virtually the whole of the Hulme district in central Manchester had been cleared and redeveloped with high-rise in the 1960s, and in some of the London boroughs it formed half or more of the councils' housing stock (Ravetz 2001, 105). In Birmingham, which had resisted high-rise flats before 1939, 463 tower blocks were built, many of them in suburban locations, giving the largest concentration of high-rise flats of any city in Europe. Population densities on these estates increased to around 200 people per acre, and in exceptional cases went up to 350.

The policy of high-rise housing was fatally undermined by the Ronan Point disaster in 1968. A gas explosion near the top of this recently completed tower block caused a partial collapse of the building, killing four people. The scale of the collapse was exacerbated greatly by fundamental weaknesses in the design of the flats and a lack of quality control when they were being built (Anon 1969). The disaster caused the government and local authorities to completely rethink their housing policy and turn away from high-rise flats. Thereafter, when tower blocks became dilapidated, as many did after only a few years, they were demolished and not replaced.

Part of the rationale for high-rise housing related to the benefit to tenants from the creation of communal open space around the tower blocks, thinking that this would compensate for the lack of private gardens. Unfortunately, the theory was found to be flawed in practice. In many cases the landscaping of communal open spaces was at best a poorly executed after-thought and at worst it effectively failed to happen. On many tower block estates all that existed between the blocks were extensive swathes of mown grass, often with hardly a tree or shrub in sight. Secondly, mothers were reluctant to let their children play unsupervised on the open space many floors below where they could not keep an eye on them. Even when the mothers had time to accompany their children, the barren grassland was less than inviting and sometimes 'taken over' by 'undesirables' and rather intimidating youths from the estate. Glasgow's Gorbals Estate was typical of these unfriendly and remote places. By 1971, it had 208 towers comprising nearly 21,000 homes and a reputation for high levels of social depravation and anti-social behaviour (Ravetz 2001, 105). The communal open spaces between the blocks were just grass and there were virtually no trees lining the many roads that wove their way around this vast estate.

In both the Radburn and predominantly high-rise estates, the concept of street trees seemed largely irrelevant to many planners and landscape architects. The whole idea of the design of these modern estates was to move away from rows of houses facing directly onto roads, whether these were the straight roads of the bye-law streets with neat rows of terraced houses, or the less grid-like roads of the cottage estates and their blocks of houses. In both types of modern council estate layout the function of the roads for the tenants was largely a method of access to the car parking or to the main entrance of the tower block. There no longer seemed much point in lining these roads with regularly spaced street trees. Besides, the original idea was to have plenty of trees in nicely landscaped communal open spaces where the trees would be planted in informal groups along with shrubs and among winding paths.

The planners of these Radburn and high-rise estates hoped they would soon evolve into distinct 'places' with their own identity and community relations, but also connected as an integral part of the wider city. However, they were largely disappointed. While these council estates added vast new built-up areas to towns and cities, they remained surprisingly unintegrated into their surroundings (Ravetz 2001, 177–178). A typical feature of council estates was their geographical isolation, not only on the forgotten periphery but also in central locations. So-called 'Island' estates were remote and depressing places encircled by main roads or cut off by a motorway. Those estates that had the 'deck access' design almost inevitably created estate 'fortresses' like the notorious Broadwater Farm in Tottenham, north London.

Most of those families who moved into these new estates had previously been part of vibrant, albeit poor, communities living in the Victorian and Edwardian terraces where the street itself played a role in building and maintaining community spirit (Chinn 1999, 111). Social surveys of tenants' attitudes to their new estates often reveal a longing for those old terraced streets, even though the physical amenities of their new homes may have been a significant improvement. Apart from their own intrinsic qualities, it is easy to account for the popularity of houses that were part of an ordinary street scene, or small infillings that blended into their surroundings. Social researchers often came to the conclusion that 'people liked living in an ordinary house on an ordinary street' (Ravetz 2001, 178).

By 1979 the nation's council housing programme was moribund (Harwood 1999, 158). The big local authority housing schemes conceived in the mid-1960s were finally completed, while the economic downturn ensured that little new building was begun thereafter. At its peak around 1975 council housing had supplied nearly one-third of the nation's housing stock. However, despite its visionary origins it was ultimately seen more as dystopia than utopia (Ravetz 2001, 2). The election of the Conservative Government in 1979 saw restrictions imposed on local government's capital expenditure which spelt the end of local authorities as the principal house builders. In 1981 the Greater London Council (the successor to the LCC) was made to pass all its housing stock to the London boroughs. Prime Minister Thatcher's popular 'Right to Buy' policy meant that many working class people could now purchase their council house or flat. Nevertheless, with the absence of any council house building this meant a steady decline in the availability of rented municipal housing for those who needed this. By now, the new buzzword in government circles was 'urban renewal' (or 'urban regeneration'), where a neighbourhood or district in a town or city was improved and rehabilitated rather than entirely demolished and rebuilt. The trend away from large scale demolition and redevelopment was signalled by the *Housing Act* 1969 (Chinn 1999, 130). In terms of housing provision it heralded the rehabilitation of existing properties that previously would have been declared unfit for living and demolished. It now seems that those rows of dilapidated Victorian terraced housing, previously regarded as an eyesore to be replaced by 'modern' council estates, were not so bad after all. In a remarkable reversal of fortune, some Victorian terraced housing in Cairns Street in Toxteth, Liverpool, was recently awarded the prestigious Turner Prize for modern art following an urban regeneration scheme (Allen and Jones 2015). The pollarded plane trees along the road were retained as part of the redevelopment and have now been supplemented by lots of planters with shrubs and herbs placed along the edge of the footway. If this trend continues across the country it should be good news for street trees.

CHAPTER EIGHT

Spa Towns and Seaside Resorts

During the eighteenth and nineteenth centuries spa towns and seaside resorts sprang up and flourished across Britain. As increasing numbers of visitors came to partake in and appreciate their specialist attractions, so these towns expanded in size and population and often became sophisticated centres for health activities, leisure and recreation, initially for the upper and middle class. Many of them included attractively landscaped suburban residential developments with their own distinct identity. With the passage of time the focus of the attractions in these spa towns and seaside resorts often broadened and changed as they began to attract large numbers of working class people. Many of these towns continue to be thriving centres for Britain's tourism industry. This chapter explores the rise of spa towns and seaside resorts and notes how greenspace, and especially tree-lined streets, played a significant role in encouraging visitors and building their reputation as attractive venues for health cures and holidays.

In both spa towns and seaside resorts there were efforts to extend the visitor season using trees, flowering shrubs, winter gardens and other means. Maximum advantage was taken of new and exotic trees, shrubs and flowers to create as much colour and variety as possible throughout the year. While this was achievable in parks and open spaces with some shelter or under glass in winter gardens, when street tree planting was becoming popular there was quite limited scope in tree selection. The demanding growing conditions in streets was much the same everywhere, with the potential for conflict with overhead and underground services, compacted soils and possible damage by pedestrians and road-users. On the positive side, the street trees in spa towns and seaside resorts did not usually have to cope with the levels of pollution that generally prevailed in the industrial towns and cities.

While the parks and open spaces of Victorian and Edwardian spa towns and seaside resorts are quite well documented in respect of their treecover (e.g. Johnston 2015, 224–226; Elliott 2016, 297–339), little is known about the nature and extent of their street tree planting. Consequently, a considerable amount of original research was undertaken using both primary and secondary sources. Photographic evidence in the form of picture postcards has been particularly useful, due to the countless numbers of postcards that were produced to meet the demand from tourists and residents. As well as assessing the nature and extent of early street tree planting in these towns, the research has attempted to gauge the degree to which this may have been influenced by the wider Victorian street tree movement. While the research undertook a preliminary examination of many different spa towns and seaside resorts, this chapter gives a more detailed account of several examples of each that were of special interest.

Spa towns

In Chapter 2 we looked at some early spa towns in relation to the influence of their walks and promenades on the initial development of systematic street tree planting in the Victorian era. In reintroducing the topic of spa towns here, it may be helpful in the first instance to give a brief recap on their origin and purpose.

A spa town is a specialist resort situated around a mineral spa which people visit to 'take the waters' for its supposed health benefits (Borsay, 1989, 31). Although some locations were used in Roman times, they came to the fore after the Restoration and particularly in the early 1700s. The city of Bath soon emerged as the leader in spa resorts, followed by other locations around England such as Buxton in Derbyshire, Leamington Spa in Warwickshire and Tunbridge Wells in Kent. Other examples outside England were Strathpeffer in Scotland and Builth Wells in Wales. Spa towns were not only venues where visitors came 'to take the waters'. One of the reasons these towns grew so rapidly was that they were also at the forefront of the development of a new culture of fashionable leisure and tourism for the upper class and those aspiring to this (Borsay 2012, 156).

When the Victorian street tree movement gathered pace during the latter part of the nineteenth century in major towns and cities such as London, Birmingham and Cardiff, to what extent was this reflected in the systematic planting of trees along the streets of the spa towns? In an effort to answer that question several spa towns were examined in detail.

Bath

By the beginning of the nineteenth century the city of Bath, in the county of Somerset, had established itself as a major urban centre with a population in the 1801 census of 40,020, making it one of the largest cities in Britain. While Bath was blessed with plenty of mature trees in its parks and open spaces, it seems that street tree planting was not an immediate priority for its civic leaders throughout much of the latter part of the nineteenth century. While other cities such as London, Birmingham, Coventry and Cardiff, were quite active in the early days of the Victorian street tree movement, Bath seems to have been a little slower to participate to any great extent. Nevertheless, a limited amount of street tree planting did take place from as early as the late 1870s. The OS Town Plan of Bath from 1880 shows a few of the main thoroughfares in the city centre planted with trees. These include Great Pulteney Street, Pulteney Road and the northern section of Bathwick Street.

Great Pulteney Street is a grand thoroughfare that connects Bathwick on the east of the River Avon with the centre of Bath, via the Robert Adam designed Pulteney Bridge. The history of trees in this street highlights a number of issues that would concern the modern urban tree manager. Images of this street from the 1830s show no trees along the street (Davis and Bonsall 2006, 168) and the original tree plantings, probably London plane, are likely to have been undertaken around the 1870s, or possibly earlier. By 1898, the trees were attracting adverse comment, which was typified by a report that appeared in the *Gardeners' Chronicle* in September of that year. In a short piece entitled 'Street trees of Bath' the anonymous author had some strong criticisms of the standards of tree selection and management of what was now a considerable mix of species:

> The residents of Bath are concerned about the trees in their [Great] Pulteney Street. Some of them are certainly in a parlous state. They are of varying sizes, the planes being by far the largest, and they appear at irregular intervals. The City Council has been discussing what is best to be done; some are in favour of filling up the gaps in the line on either side, others favour the more sensible plan of removing the trees entirely and planting young ones in the autumn. Pulteney Street is bounded by lines of houses of a pattern of one hundred years ago, severely formal in their primness, and needing such relief as trees afford. Along the sides of the street can be seen planes in clean and vigorous foliage; sycamores in deplorable condition through the ravages of insects and other causes; poplars and limes which have well-nigh shed their leaves; and mop-headed acacias. The planes have grown out of all proportions to the size of the others; and the robinias which are the youngest and smallest, do remarkably well and have dense heads of green leaves. It would be best to replant using either planes wholly or robinias wholly. Street planting appears to have been perfunctorily and injudiciously performed in some of the main thoroughfares of this delightful western city, and a good opportunity is now afforded to replant Pulteney Street, and establish a standard of selection and planting.
>
> *Gardeners' Chronicle* 1898, 238

There is no record of the reaction by the local authority staff to this criticism of their arboricultural competence. Appearing as it did in the leading horticultural magazine of the day it would have done little for morale. As well as criticising standards of selection and planting, the article raised an interesting issue regarding the relationship between street trees and the architecture of nearby buildings. It states that the Georgian terraced houses lining Great Pulteney Street are 'severely formal in their primness, and needing such relief as trees afford'. Their construction was commissioned by Sir William Pulteney, designed by the architect Thomas Baldwin and completed in 1789 (Elliott and Menneer 2004, 170). Great Pulteney Street is now regarded as one of the finest examples of Georgian architecture in Bath and the idea this needs the addition of trees to provide some 'relief' to its 'primness' would be dismissed by many today as laughable. However, there are no longer any trees in the main body of Great Pulteney Street, although there is a circle of birch trees around Laura Place at its western end. The question arises: when and why were the trees felled? An enquiry to the local authority failed to shed any light on this but the author's own investigation may offer some clues. Most of the trees were still there in the early 1930s, as indicated on the OS County Series Map of 1932, although there was a major gap in the treecover on the southern side. However, by the 1950s all the trees had gone and Great Pulteney Street remains treeless today. It is possible that the reason for felling the trees, or the reason they were not replaced if felling was necessary for arboricultural reasons, was related to the trees being perceived as obscuring the fine architecture. This has been an ongoing issue with five large plane trees in the Circus, one of the city's most famous examples of Georgian architecture (Manco 2004). This is located on the other side of the River Avon from Great Pulteney Street and was completed in 1768, designed by John Wood, the Elder. The story of this controversy gives an amusing twist to the expression 'Can't see the wood for the trees'. Soon after the first residents moved into the Circus they began complaining about the clouds of dust thrown up by horses and carriages trundling across the limestone pitching laid within its bare centre. Their solution was to lay down a central garden with railings. Many residents thought the garden would greatly improve their view. However, while guidebooks in the 1830s were referring to the Circus's 'charming shrubbery', by 1847, one guide was describing the trees there as already interfering with the light. By 1856 a letter in the local newspaper was complaining about the 'overpowering mass of dark foliage'. Calls for the removal of the trees have continued on a regular basis ever since. Dominating the Circus today are five majestic plane trees, thought to be about 190 years old (*ibid.*, 32). These are not strictly speaking street trees but grow together in a clump on the area of green space at the centre of the Circus. In 1961, the council's Planning Committee considered felling the trees but then backed away from the proposal when there were many objections from residents throughout the city, including a petition signed by 500 students at Bath Technical College (*ibid.*, 34). However, it was significant that the Chairman of the Circus Owners Association was in favour of removing the trees. The debate about the potential conflict between street trees and their obscuring of fine architecture continues to this day in Bath and other British cities.

Cheltenham and Pittville

Cheltenham's famous tree-lined walks surrounding its spas were first designed by Captain Henry Skillicorne, the spa town's 'founding father' (Hembry 1990, 179–181). He was assisted by a group of 'wealthy and travelled' friends who also understood the value of relaxing avenues of trees as the perfect complement to the beneficial water. The early influence of the famous Promenade at Cheltenham on the Victorian street tree movement has already been recorded in Chapter 2. These avenues of trees along the town's public walks and promenades were its particular distinction over rival spa resorts that could not offer quite so extensive arboreal delights (Hembry *et al.* 1997, 200). As we have seen, the trees that were initially planted along the Promenade in 1818 as part of a carriage drive then became formal street trees as built development of the area soon extended along both sides of this (see Figure 4).

However, the degree to which nineteenth century Cheltenham engaged in tree planting along its established or newly constructed streets is unclear. No doubt its civic leaders and prominent residents were aware of the interest generated by the Victorian street tree movement and the early achievements in planting by other towns and cities. There is evidence of a few excellent street tree planting schemes undertaken in Cheltenham in the late Victorian era. In 1860, planting began on each side of Landsdown Road, a major thoroughfare 1200 yards (1097 m) long and running west from the town. It was hoped that when these common lime trees matured this would be among the finest carriage drives in the country. This road still has some original trees which are now about 150 years old (Cheltenham BC 2016). Another fine planting scheme, also involving lime trees, was undertaken around 1880s along Christ Church Road, in an expensive middle class residential neighbourhood just west of the town centre. There are still a few original trees growing in the footway and grass verges along this broad and attractive road which continues to have extensive treecover. By contrast, the High Street in Cheltenham, a long road in the town centre, has never had any significant number of street trees.

While researching for evidence of early street tree planting in Cheltenham, an interesting discovery was made. An examination of sections of the Cheltenham Old Town Survey 1855–1857 indicated that many of the streets in the Pittville district of the town were planted with trees at that time (Figure 54). The extent of planting is quite noticeable in contrast to other streets outside this area that are devoid of trees. This prompted a detailed study of the history of Pittville and the origin of its street trees.

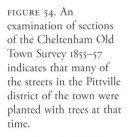

FIGURE 54. An examination of sections of the Cheltenham Old Town Survey 1855–57 indicates that many of the streets in the Pittville district of the town were planted with trees at that time.

EXTRACT OF MAP 38 USED WITH PERMISSION FROM THE CD ROM OF THE OLD TOWN SURVEY 1855–57, PUBLISHED BY THE CHELTENHAM LOCAL HISTORY SOCIETY © 2011 CHELTENHAM LOCAL HISTORY SOCIETY.

The exclusive residential estate of Pittville, located a short distance north-west of the Promenade, was developed from 1824 onwards by the banker Joseph Pitt as a suburb of Cheltenham (Stern *et al.* 2013, 28). Taking advantage of the town's booming economy, Pitt, who had previously developed Cheltenham's Royal Crescent, chose not to extend the spa town but instead build a separate suburban enclave of elegant houses intermixing terraced houses and villas. He envisaged Pittville as a new spa town which would rival Cheltenham. Although the land had been the subject of an *Enclosure Act* in 1801, it was not until 1806 that the final award was made when Pitt received 253 acres (102 ha) of land, including virtually the entire site of the future Pittville (Blake 1988, 8). Even if Pitt had the creation of Pittville in mind by 1806, it was not until the 1820s that he felt the time was right for its establishment. By then, there had been a significant growth in visitor numbers to Cheltenham and the national economic situation was more favourable. Pitt envisaged an estate of approximately 100 acres (40.5 ha), crossed by several miles of gravelled walks and rides, alongside which lots for between 500 and 600 houses were to be made available (*ibid.*, 9). The general layout of the estate was entrusted to a local architect, John Forbes. A plan of this was included in Griffith's (1826, 45) *New Historical Description of Cheltenham* and although this indicated trees in squares and gardens, it did not show any street trees. This plan is almost identical to the area as it is now, at least in terms of the street layout, although the density and arrangement of the houses is very different. In advance of the house building, which began in 1824, lines of wide roads and walks were constructed. Local nurseryman Richard Ware was engaged to lay out the walks and rides and the planting of the ornamental pleasure grounds (Campbell 1990–1991, 11). This included the planting of trees alongside the streets and the entire landscaping work was probably completed by 1827. The systematic planting of street trees in Pittville is a very early example of this and predates Margaretta Terrace in Chelsea (1851) (see Chapter 5).

The establishment of the estate layout and the building of the Pump Room were matched by preparations for the sale of building lots (Blake 1988, 13–14). Each lot was to be offered freehold, subject to an annual rent charge, payable to Joseph Pitt, which was intended as a contribution towards the general upkeep of the estate and provision of utility services. Each purchaser was required to abide by certain restrictive covenants, which included ensuring that no construction work could be undertaken forward of a 'building line' in the front of the property to prevent any encroachment onto the footways and the street. Building lots were first offered for sale in 1824 and a total of 216 houses were built between 1825 and 1860 (*ibid.*, 17–19). Almost all were built by property speculators and only 20 by their first occupiers and these were the most expensive villas for the very wealthy.

In an effort to maintain the exclusivity of the estate, the management imposed strict rules governing the use of the grounds of the estate. While the owners and occupiers had the right to use the landscaped walks and rides of the estate and its pleasure grounds, servants were not allowed unless they were in charge of children from the estate. Servants would have been allowed to walk unaccompanied along the tree-lined roads as long as they were attending some business on behalf of their employers or simply entering or leaving the estate. An impression of the street trees at Pittville some 20 years after planting can be gained from George Rowe's (1845) *Illustrated Cheltenham Guide*. An illustration of the Pittville Gates reproduced in the book shows as an impressive entrance to the estate viewed from Winchcombe Street (*ibid.*, 53). Behind the ornate iron gates the well-established trees can clearly be seen lining the side of the road in Pittville Lawn. In the section of the book where Rowe gives an account of Pittville Spa he describes his entry into the estate with the words:

> Passing the gates [of Pittville spa], our way lies through shady avenues of trees, just springing into maturity; a fine gravel walk, skirted on either hand by rows of handsome houses, leads us to the 'Little Spa', as it is called, and which serves as a sort of portico to this sylvan temple of the healthful goddess. ... Proceeding onwards from the Little Spa, we pass several roads running at right angles with our line of march, the whole laid out with shaded walks on either side, affording delightful vistas, while at every turn rise detached villas, conveying a very pleasing impression of the fashion and opulence of this part of the town.
>
> Rowe 1845, 56

The initial attraction of living at Pittville for its many wealthy nineteenth century residents was clear (Blake 1988, 25–26). The estate was within easy reach of both the Pump Room and the town, yet sufficiently removed from the busy centre to provide the spacious and socially exclusive combination of town and country so many sought. Nevertheless, while Pittville was effectively a very exclusive garden suburb, the estate was never the success that Pitt had hoped for. The popularity of the spa waters began to wane soon after the opening of the Pump Room and the fashionable life of Cheltenham remained focused to the south of the High Street, in the Promenade and Montpellier. Equally, the number of houses built fell short of Pitt's expectations, particularly in the estate's early years. Today, Pittville is still one of the most exclusive residential neighbourhoods in Cheltenham. Many of its streets remain tree-lined with majestic specimens of plane and lime, now interspersed with a range of other species, notably birch.

Leamington Spa

The town of Leamington Spa, in Warwickshire, became one of the most popular British spas. The American novelist Nathaniel Hawthorne, who stayed in the town in the 1850s, observed that from the spa waters 'have gushed streets, groves, gardens, mansions, shops and churches' (Watkins 2008, 7). The town's rapid expansion, from a population of only 543 in 1811 to 15,723 in 1851, was achieved largely through the efforts of a group of local landowners who were supported by a network of entrepreneurs drawn by the investment opportunities in the town. A further group vital to the establishment of Leamington as a health spa was the medical men specialising in 'water cures'.

Apart from the mineral waters themselves, Leamington's leafy parks, ornamental gardens and shady promenades were a major attraction (Cameron 2006; Watkins 2008). One of the first promenades was Linden Avenue in Pump Room Gardens that was planted in 1828, 'forming one of the finest promenades in the garden town'. In 1875, the Avenue was opened to the general public. Between the 1880s and the First World War, the borough engineer and surveyor William Louis de Normanville designed and planted a series of walks and green spaces along the river Leam (Elliott 2016, 311). A good description of Leamington's walks and gardens, as well as some of its tree-lined streets, can be gained from Abel Heywood's (1905) *Guide to Royal Leamington Spa*, first published in 1869. Heywood writes:

> The Regent Grove and Holly Walk, in the very centre of the town, is one of the finest avenues and promenades of this 'inland city of fashion'. This portion of Leamington, with Binswood and Beauchamp avenues and squares [north of Holly Walk], is most charming. The streets are of unusual width, and lined with linden and sycamore trees ... The Holly Walk, Regent Grove, New Warwick Road, Milverton Hill and Crescent, Clarendon Square, Avenue and Dale Streets, with those before mentioned, are the most fashionable streets, with their adjacent suburbs, in the New Town.
>
> Heywood 1905, 13

Heywood's mention of Binswood Avenue and Beauchamp Avenue highlights two of the finest tree-lined streets in late Victorian Leamington. Photographs of their mature lime trees taken *c.* 1905 indicate that they were probably planted in the 1860s (Figure 55). Heywood (1905, 5) indicates who was responsible for these plantings when he states, 'The efforts of the late Mr Hitchman should not be overlooked, for to him the idea of planting the roadsides with trees is due, and by his energy it was mainly carried out'. Dr John Hitchman was a surgeon who converted to homeopathy late in his medical career in 1865 and practiced in Leamington over many years until his death in 1867 (Anon 1867, 253). Perhaps his most recognised achievement began in 1851 when he bought 11 acres (4.5 ha) of land on the edge of the town and laid out The Arboretum, enriching it with thousands of flowers, shrubs and exotic trees and opening it free to the public. Before long he had extended it and then decided to build what could be described as a hospital in a park, bringing together landscape gardening and arboriculture with healing. The Arboretum Hydropathic Hospital opened in 1862, but only 5 years later Hitchman died suddenly at the age of 62. While his obituary in the *Monthly Homeopathic Review* gives an account of his medical career, it only hints at his efforts to promote street tree planting. The anonymous obituary states, 'Mr Hitchman was especially active in all matters bearing upon the sanitary improvement of towns' (*ibid.*, 254). As noted in Chapter 5, the Victorians used the term sanitary improvement or reform to embrace a wide range of

FIGURE 55. Binswood Avenue and Beauchamp Avenue were two of the finest tree-lined streets in late Victorian Leamington. This photograph of Beauchamp Avenue taken around 1905 suggests that the lime trees were probably planted in the 1860s.

urban initiatives with a health agenda, including street tree planting. There can be little doubt that John Hitchman was the driving force behind much of the early street tree planting in Leamington Spa.

During the nineteenth and much of the twentieth century, one of the most famous trees in England grew on the outskirts of Leamington Spa. The Midland Oak was claimed to mark the geographical centre of England and stood by the side of Lellington Road at its junction with Lillington Avenue (Watkins 2008, 60). This majestic remnant street tree was felled in 1967 because it had become a traffic hazard, with some claiming that its deteriorated condition was a result of its protective railings being removed for their scrap metal value in the Second World War. A new oak, grown from an acorn of the original, was planted at the same roadside location in 1988.

Some other spa towns

While the smaller spa towns could not hope to attract the visitor numbers of the larger and more famous locations, such as Bath and Harrogate, some endeavoured to build a reputation for offering special attractions which often involved gardens and trees. Buxton in Derbyshire has been known since Roman times for its warm mineral waters, although being located over 1000 ft (305 m) up in England's Peak District it only became readily accessible with the arrival of the railway in 1863 (Langham and Wells 1993). This prompted a dramatic increase in the town's trade and prosperity and its population which grew to over 6000 by 1881. Until the nineteenth century the town had been almost devoid of trees and gardens and the town elders believed that addressing this deficiency was a good way of attracting more visitors. Several walks and gardens were laid out and the famous Pavilion Gardens opened in 1871, designed by Joseph Paxton and Edward Milner. Despite all this provision of open space the town did not really embrace the planting of street trees until the 1880s and 1890s, as none are indicated on the detailed OS map of 1879 (High Peak 2007, 33). Early photographs show that when College Road was developed in 1892, this included the planting of an avenue of trees along its length. This remains a fine avenue of lime and sycamore with some of the largest street trees in Buxton (Gillespie pers. comm., 2016). Around 1900, there were a few mature street trees in the vicinity of the Opera House (Roberts 2012, 30) and some recent tree plantings with wrought-iron guards in front of small buildings along what became Eagle Parade (*ibid.*, 53). From 1910, street trees were planted elsewhere in the town, for example, along Fountain Street, Bath Road and London Road, with lime and sycamore a favourite choice. Nevertheless, an examination of many photographs of the town taken before the First World War suggest that Buxton's street tree population was not numerous at that time. It is only in relatively recent times that Buxton has acquired a significant number of street trees, which now make a major contribution to the landscape of this beautiful and popular spa town.

Ilkley is a spa town in West Yorkshire that initially flourished as a health resort, although in recent times it has become a general tourist destination. The town's growth as a health and leisure resort began with the creation of the Ben Rhydding Hydropathic Establishment in 1844 where a special scientific form of water-cure was practised (Davis 2012, 3). When the railway arrived in 1865, large numbers of people were able to travel to Ilkley in relative comfort and the town and its facilities expanded to accommodate them. It also became popular as a residential location for businessmen who could commute quickly to their work places in the booming nearby industrial towns. The town's expansion was largely facilitated by the sale of land from the Middleton family's estate over a 2-year period between 1867 and 1869 (Finlayson 2009, 83–89). The Middleton estate was responsible for the construction of roads, sewers and pavements, but when completed their upkeep was to be a charge on the public rates, so a Local Board was formed to oversee their management. By the late nineteenth century the popularity and belief in the healing powers of the hydros was in steady decline, but the town had little difficulty promoting itself as a fashionable inland resort for the tourist (Davis 2012, 4). As part of that effort, the Town Council resolved to have trees planted along some of the main streets. The planting was undertaken by the Middleton estate but once the trees were established they were managed by the Local Board. This introduction of street trees into the town was likely to have been a popular decision among the councillors since some of them were nurserymen, including Thomas Horsman, owner of the respected Rosemount Nurseries (Cockshott pers. comm., 2015).

One of the first streets to be planted in Ilkley was The Grove. Before the expansion of the town in the 1870s, this had been a country track called Green Lane with just a few buildings alongside (Cockshott and Shillitoe 2005, 62; Finlayson 2009, 109–111). Around 1890, when the Grove had become one of the town's main streets lined mainly with shops and some houses, it was planted with common lime trees along both sides (Figure 56). In the late 1890s, another major town thoroughfare called Brook Street, which ran north from the Grove, was planted with lime trees and this time the trees were protected with expensive wrought-iron guards (Davis 2012, 53). Both the Grove and Brook Street were specifically designed with wide footways to encourage visitors to promenade. In the late 1890s, Wells Road was also planted with trees, mostly common lime, along both sides of this road that had a picturesque view of the moors as a backdrop (*ibid.*, 28). Throughout the twentieth century the street tree population of Ilkley underwent some significant changes. There has been an increase in the number of street trees in the town, although the current population seems to be proportionally less than many other English spa towns. There has also been a noticeable trend towards smaller ornamental species as opposed to the forest-type species, mostly common lime, which featured in the early street plantings. A prominent example of that trend is the trees in

FIGURE 56. Around 1890, when The Grove had become one of Ilkley's main streets lined mainly with shops and some houses, it was planted with common lime trees along both sides. It was one of the first streets in the town to get street trees. This photograph was taken in 1909.

the Grove. Around 1960, many of the original limes were replaced with pink flowering cherries, with funding from the Ilkley Rotary Club (Dixon pers. comm., 2015). When many of these trees were looking rather dilapidated a few years ago, they in turn were replaced by a second set of flowering cherries. In terms of horticultural and landscape attractions, Ilkley was always overshadowed by the neighbouring and much larger spa town, Harrogate, in North Yorkshire. This was one of the most successful Victorian spa towns and it attracted huge numbers of visitors each year. Spurred on by its southern rival Bath's renewed municipal activity the civic leaders in Harrogate resolved to make the same level of urban improvements (Hembry *et al.* 1997, 161). From 1868 onwards, the commissioners and later the Corporation of Harrogate had the vision to create broad, tree-lined streets and increase its already extensive area of parks and gardens.

In Wales there are two sites just seven miles apart that became popular spa towns. These are Llandrindod Wells and Builth Wells, both located in what is now the county of Powys. Llandrindod Wells has always been the larger and more popular venue. In the mid-eighteenth century it enjoyed an economic boom and then, following the enclosure of common land in 1862, it underwent further expansion with the construction of new streets and elegant hotels, shops and houses. Although it has always had quite a lot of public open space and ornamental grounds, there is little evidence that the town responded to the Victorian street tree movement. In the Victorian and Edwardian era its main thoroughfares such as High Street, Spa Road, Temple Street and Middleton Street remained devoid of trees and in its quieter residential streets any trees were generally those in private front gardens. A notable exception was Ithon Road, one of the first residential streets built during the early stages of the town's development, where trees had been planted along both sides from around the 1890s (Wilson 1995, 19). Further planting in some other residential streets took place in the late 1920s, for example, in Broadway where there were grass verges specifically for the trees (Harries 1985, 24). While Llandrindod Wells today is an attractive and fairly leafy small town, it still does not have many street trees. Its close neighbour and rival spa town Builth Wells also missed out on the Victorian fashion for street trees, while at the same time missing out on its rival's attractive streetscapes. The narrow thoroughfares in its town centre, such as High Street and the rather misnamed Broad Street, have never had any significant number of street trees (Morrison 2010). In 1804, Benjamin Malkin, the writer and friend of William Blake, described Builth Wells in very unflattering terms, calling its streets as 'fashionless, miserable and dirty' and he was left wondering why a town which had 'favourable air and waters' and was surrounded by attractive scenery had been 'so little improved' (Malkin 1804, 256). It has been suggested that the lack of general improvements to its streetscape, not only at this time but also later, could have led to Llandrindod Wells becoming the more popular spa (Morrison 1989, 38).

Seaside resorts

Sea-bathing was practised in Kent and Lancashire as early the 1720s and by the mid-eighteenth century was becoming common in several early resorts (Brodie and Winter 2007, 11). Visitors were initially just a few wealthy people in search of cures for their ailments through the supposed beneficial effects of the fresh sea air and cold water bathing. As noted in Chapter 2, some of the early walks and promenades were associated with the first seaside resorts. A tree-lined promenade along the seafront where visitors could take in the bracing sea air was considered an important attraction for the resort and much in keeping with its image of health and vitality. Ladies Walk at Liverpool was a typical example (Borsay 2013, 56–57). In 1750, this was reported as being a very fine location, commanding views over the sea and divided into three parts by narrow strips of grass and two rows of trees. By the end of the eighteenth century, there was a network of resorts across Britain catering for a range of tastes and pockets (Brodie and Winter 2007, 11). These had often developed around small existing settlements but others were entirely new ventures. Many seaside resorts were founded by wealthy landowners and entrepreneurs but were later substantially expanded by the emerging local authorities. The coming of the railways also transformed many seaside towns, bringing them visitors in hitherto unimaginable numbers.

From the early nineteenth century, the motivation for people to visit the seaside evolved to become less about promoting their health and wellbeing and more about enjoying a range of leisure and entertainment opportunities. Commercial pleasure gardens were created, similar to those in other towns and cities, including seven which opened in and around Brighton before 1840 (Berry 2000, 225). Seafront parks and gardens were a crucial element in the design of the British seaside resort, adding natural ornamentation and seasonal colour (Gray 2006, 131–134). With the growth of local government, public finances were used to increase the visitor attractions of the resort, with the building of piers, the laying out of public parks and gardens and the planting of street trees (Brodie and Winter 2007, 32). A popular landscape feature was the seafront promenade running along the top of the sea wall providing visitors with a healthy, bracing place to walk and socialise, functioning in much the same way as the walks and promenades in the spa towns (*ibid.*, 36). These were often the location of formal gardens or mini-parks, usually in the form of long relatively narrow rectangular beds, whose shrubs and bedding plants were carefully chosen to be colourful yet robust enough to withstand storms and tolerate salt sea spray. Photographs of seafront promenades from Victorian and Edwardian times suggest that trees were not a common feature (Hannavy 2003). This may have been due to concerns that the trees would obscure the sea view for people in the hotels, guest houses and residences along the seafront, or perhaps the belief that the trees would grow poorly in the exposed position. The arrival of the motor car in the early decades of the twentieth century saw many of these promenades eventually transformed into busy seafront roads and their gardens converted to car parks (Brodie and Winter 2007, 61).

Horticultural and arboricultural books for most of the nineteenth century make little reference to the ornamental use of trees and shrubs in seaside locations, although it is occasionally mentioned in Victorian gardening magazines. While William Ablett's (1880, 404–413) book *English Trees and Tree-Planting* has a chapter on 'sea-side planting', this refers to forestry plantations and shelterbelts and not ornamental planting. With the enormous popularity of the seaside in Edwardian times, interest in the topic grew rapidly. To meet the demand for specialist knowledge about the cultivation of ornamental trees and shrubs in seaside locations, many books and articles on the subject were published (e.g. Gaut 1907; Webster 1918). These gave lists of suitable tree and shrub species for coastal areas, for both structural and ornamental planting, that could withstand the challenges of salt spray and fierce gales. It was common knowledge that it was usually easier to establish trees in the south of Britain than the north because of the milder conditions. Some authors (Gaut 1907, 5; Webster 1918, 14) writing about seaside planting also noted that it was generally easier to establish a much wider range of trees on the west rather than the east coast because of the milder conditions created by the Gulf Stream. In more recent years, palm-like trees and shrubs have become a popular choice, with species such as cabbage palm (*Cordyline australis*) and Chusan palm (*Trachycarpus fortunei*), to give the resort something of a subtropical or 'Riviera' look.

With regard to species selection for street tree planting in seaside resorts, the choice has always been more conservative than for their parks and gardens. This was undoubtedly a reflection of the more difficult growing conditions in streets. In the research undertaken for this chapter it was noticeable how often the usual Victorian and Edwardian choice of lime and plane continued to feature in the streets of seaside resorts. An account of several of those resorts is now given.

Eastbourne

Eastbourne was one of the first seaside towns in Britain to engage in the systematic planting of street trees. The town is located in East Sussex on the south coast of England, 19 miles (31 km) east of Brighton. Trees appear to have been a feature of Eastbourne from an early stage in its development and many of the old guide books refer to this. For example, one dated 1787 states, 'From Bourne-Place, go through a long street called South-Bourne, and Shadey-lane, with trees and hedges to the Sea-Houses' (Anon 1787). Later guides also refer to buildings screened with 'luxuriant trees'. It is likely that many of the trees alongside the older streets were part of the original field boundaries and incorporated when the roads were subsequently widened. An example is Meads Road where photographs from 1900 show large mature elm trees (probably *Ulmus glabra*), perhaps 60 years old, on either side of the road. Around 1890, when the area was developed from grazing land and cornfields, large houses were built and Meads became the 'smart end' of town (Surtees 2005). Its residents were the affluent middle class and included professionals, self-made men, retired officers and former members of the Colonial Civil Service.

While remnant trees formed an important element of Eastbourne's nineteenth century treescape, many of its street trees were planted as part of a planned policy. The main developers of the town were the Dukes of Devonshire and to a lesser extent the Gilbert Family (Cannadine 1980, 229–253). The Devonshires were determined to exclude heavy industry from the town and develop it as an attractive seaside resort with something of a rural atmosphere (*ibid.*, 255). All roads made in the town by their estate were not only wide but planted with trees before any building was allowed, so as to 'keep up the rural and ornamental aspects of the streets'. One guide book in 1886 noted that 'the streets are boulevards and the highways wooded avenues ... almost as green as the country lanes'. Brochure after brochure extolled the boulevard-like character of Eastbourne's streets and the prodigious use made of trees.

As early as 1873, the *Daily Telegraph* published an article singing the praises of Eastbourne's street tree planting efforts and its contribution to the town's attractions. This was reported in *The Garden* magazine which stated:

> We learn from the *Daily Telegraph* that during the present hot weather the street trees in our sea-side resorts, which form a special feature of Eastbourne, has been found a very agreeable shelter. This adds greatly to the beauty as well as to the comfort of that pleasant watering place.
>
> *The Garden* 1873, 127

In 1880, the *Gardeners' Chronicle* (1880, 18) declared in a rather mixed review that 'The pretty seaside town of Eastbourne in Sussex offers some instructive examples of both judicious and injudicious street planting'. After some debate, the town's street trees had become a municipal responsibility. Chambers (1880, 24) states, 'The trees in the street are now looked after by a Committee of the Local Board, but when this intelligent idea was first mooted, it was received with much ridicule; beyond doubt, however, common sense was on the side of the promoters of the movement. Trees are a real adornment to any town'.

Research for this book regarding Eastbourne discovered another very early example of systematic street tree planting in Britain, which could be the earliest example in a seaside resort. In Terminus Road around 1840 trees were planted alongside this prominent thoroughfare that leads to Grand Parade and the seafront (Figure 57). Although the species could not be determined precisely, it seems like they were elms, as were many other early street trees in the town. When the planting was undertaken Terminus Road was lined with expensive middle class houses. By the end of the nineteenth century, as the town's central entertainments area grew, this became the main shopping street as permission was given to convert many of the houses in this part

FIGURE 57. The tree planting in Terminus Road, Eastbourne, around 1840 is a very early example of systematic street tree planting in Britain, and could be the earliest example in a seaside resort. This print was made around 1860.

of the town into shops and hotels (Cannadine 1980, 264). By 1900 it was decided to plant more trees in the gaps between the existing trees in Terminus Road. These new trees were planes and it seems likely they were planned to replace the elm trees in due course. By the early 1950s, all that remained were ten plane trees which were now attracting negative comment. Their overhanging branches were considered a hazard to buses and their large leaves were reported by a local newspaper as 'being a menace [to pedestrians] when lying wet upon the pavement' (Anon 1951, 1). The trees were duly felled by the local authority. There are sections of Terminus Road that are now part of a pedestrianised precinct. The section of the road that still carries regular traffic and runs down to Grand Parade on the seafront is now planted with Swedish whitebeam (*Sorbus intermedia*).

Not all of Eastbourne's Edwardian residents were enamoured with the many trees that had been established in their streets. In 1913, one of the readers of the *Eastbourne Chronicle* declared in a letter to the editor,

> It seems obvious from the many letters which have appeared in your hospitable columns that there is a strong and practically unanimous feeling among those who reside in Eastbourne that our beautiful town is being spoilt by too many trees. Probably it is not enough to ventilate our grievances, so I would suggest that someone who has leisure, in each road affected – Carlisle Road, Darley Road, College Road, etc – gets up a petition from those who live in his own road, to our municipal authorities, asking to have every other tree cut down – and the rest lopped.
>
> Hodgson 1913, 10

Despite this regular controversy about 'too many trees', Eastbourne has managed to retain many of its street trees and regularly replace those that were lost. In 1954, the *Eastbourne Gazette* was proud to proclaim that 'Eastbourne before the last war was known as the "City of Trees" – a striking tribute to a town with no cathedral but great natural beauty. Many trees lining the roads have since been cut down owing to elm disease, but ... Eastbourne can still claim to mingle its buildings in a warm clothing of green leaves' (Anon 1954, 13).

Bournemouth

The town of Bournemouth, another seaside resort on England's south coast, is an interesting example of how substantial tracts of woodland from previously rural areas can be incorporated into expanding urban development as an attractive landscape setting for new roads and houses. In the early 1800s the area where Bournemouth now stands was largely remote and barren heathland (Lambert 2016). From 1810 onwards people began to move to the area and establish smallholdings which were the foundations of the settlement. Following recognition of its potential as a seaside resort it expanded rapidly and local government for the area was established in 1846. When the borough's heaths were enclosed following the passing of Enclosure Acts, vast numbers of pine trees were planted across this land (Bournemouth BC 2014, 3). As the town expanded throughout the nineteenth century with the building of new residential suburbs on this heathland many of the pine trees were retained. As early as the 1840s, the Bournemouth climate was being promoted by a local physician, Thomas Johnston Aiken, who composed a guide book extolling its equability, mildness and geniality (Elliott 2016, 327). By the 1890s, Bournemouth was an established seaside resort and had picked up the nickname of the 'Forest City' because of the vast number of pine trees now located within the town. As well as leaving these trees in private gardens, many were left to adorn the roads that had been constructed through the new residential districts. During the 1880s, Bournemouth Corporation embarked on a planned programme of planting and maintaining street trees, as evidenced by several references to this in its Roads Committee minutes (Cox pers. comm., 2016).

Alongside the sea air and bathing, the pine trees of Bournemouth were a key attraction for the town's early developers and visitors, together providing a semi-natural resort for families to escape from England's polluted towns and cities. The pine scent was considered to have health-giving properties; the presence of so many trees combined with sea breezes produced 'healthy clean air' which enabled the town to gain a reputation as a health spa and to grow rapidly. A pine tree can be found within the town's coat of arms. Elliott (2016, 326–337) has written an excellent account of the perceived health benefits of pine trees, with particular reference to Bournemouth.

As with Eastbourne, the large numbers of trees in Bournemouth's Edwardian streets did not meet with approval from all of its residents. As well as complaints there were 'too many trees', concerns were raised that when the trees blocked out light to nearby houses, this often prompted unauthorised and unsightly pruning. Mr Botting Hemsley of Bournemouth, writing in the *Gardeners' Chronicle* in 1909, stated:

> What is becoming more and more apparent is the fact that many gardens and streets are over-planted, with the result that mutilation follows to let in the light. Yet, generally speaking, trees are sacred in Bournemouth, especially the pines, whether dead or alive, and this is much better than indiscriminate felling. But this veneration for trees may be carried too far, especially if extended to poplars, and result in their survival to the detriment of the pines and other trees and shrubs, and also as a block to many pretty views.
>
> Botting Hemsley 1909, 132

Much to the credit of Bournemouth Borough Council, many years of careful tree management has ensured that pine trees continue to line some of the town's most attractive streets, especially in residential areas. Indeed, the town is unique in Britain for having so many mature pines as street trees and this essential aspect of its landscape character continues to be much admired by its many visitors.

Folkestone and Hove 'grand boulevards'

It was quite common for seaside resorts in late Victorian and Edwardian times to construct a 'grand boulevard', often leading down to the seafront, which was an attractive tree-lined avenue and often one of the main thoroughfares of the town. A good example of this is Castle Hill Avenue in Folkestone, Kent. This is a main road through the historic residential part of the town and is Folkestone's most famous thoroughfare (Figure 58). It extents for almost one mile (1.4 km), running down to the Leas on the seafront. In the nineteenth century the land in this part of the West End of Folkestone was owned by Lord Radnor who secured an Act of Parliament to enable building leases to be granted for his long-term plan for urban development (Bishop 1973, 98–99). He appointed London architect Sidney Smirke to develop the new estate which would be laid out with wide, tree-lined avenues. It has not been possible to establish a precise date when Castle Hill Avenue was laid out as a landscaped boulevard but a photograph from 1890 shows young trees that have only been planted in the past few years. There was a central reservation along most of the length of this road that included a promenade with seats. Trees were planted along the central reservation and those planted in the footways on either side of the road had sturdy wrought-iron guards. No record could be found of the species used. However, photographs taken *c.* 1905 suggest that there were mainly lime trees on the central reservation with some horse chestnuts in the footways. Nowadays, the landscape of Castle Hill Avenue has changed very little and it remains a fine tree-lined boulevard.

Another example of a 'grand boulevard' was Grand Avenue in Hove, a seaside resort in what is now the county of East Sussex and bordered to the east by

FIGURE 58. Castle Hill Avenue in Folkestone, Kent, is typical of the 'grand boulevard' that was quite common in late Victorian and Edwardian seaside resorts. These attractive tree-lined avenues often led down to the seafront and were one of the main thoroughfares of the town. This photograph was taken around 1905.

the larger resort of Brighton. The area of Hove between Cliftonville and the Brunswick and Adelaide estates was steadily developed from 1875 to around 1910 as the West Brighton Estate, a select residential development (Scott 1995, xii). At its heart are four numbered avenues (First, Second, Third and Fourth Avenues) either side of Grand Avenue, all of which exhibited an impressive variety of ornate Italianate and Victorian villas with carefully-planned artists' mews and artisan workshops. This was not housing for the working class but created specifically as a haven for the wealthy and artistic. These avenues, including Grand Avenue, were planted along both sides with Huntingdon or Chichester elm (*Ulmus x hollandica* 'Vegeta') as well as Wheatley elm (*Ulmus minor* 'Sarniensis') (Brothers pers. comm., 2016). Both these types of elms were also being planted extensively in the parks of Hove and Brighton and other south coast towns. The most significant reasons for the Victorian and Edwardian to select elm species is likely to have been their ability to survive coastal conditions and winds containing a high saline content together with their suitability for thriving in shallow chalk soils (Greenland pers. comm., 2016).

Grand Avenue in Hove was planted with its elm trees in the 1890s and while early photographs show its potential to become a 'grand boulevard', this never really happened as originally intended (Figure 59). As early as 1933 an aerial photograph shows that as much as 60% of the trees had already been lost. Today, most of the large Victorian houses on either side of Grand Avenue have been demolished and replaced with ugly blocks of flats. There are only a few trees remaining of the original elm avenue and little evidence of any recent replanting. There is a similar situation in the numbered avenues either side of Grand Avenue with just a scattering of trees left.

FIGURE 59. Grand Avenue in Hove, East Sussex, was planted with its elm trees in the 1890s and while early photographs show its potential to become a 'grand boulevard', this never really happened as originally intended. This photograph was taken around 1905.

Exmouth

The favourable climate of the West Country of England with its oceanic climate typified by cool winters with warmer summers has always been a favourite choice for those seeking a holiday by the sea. In 1841, Weston-super-Mare in Somerset became one of the first seaside towns to be connected by railway, which soon had a beneficial impact on visitor numbers. While this resort acquired some fine parks and gardens in the nineteenth century, street tree planting seems to have only gathered pace in the 1890s. In the case of another West Country seaside town, Exmouth in Devon, this could have started slightly earlier in the late 1880s. In 1895, the *Gardeners' Chronicle* (1895a, 650) reported that 'The first lime tree of the many which are to grace some of the principal streets in Exmouth was planted in most beautiful weather by Mr R. Lee, the Chairman of the District Council. Some outside pressure was brought to bear and a private committee offered to purchase several hundred of the trees if the Council would accept and plant them'. This prompted a quick response from one of its readers in the town who pointed out that street tree planting was not a new phenomenon for Exmouth. They also made some critical remarks about tree selection:

> The inference to be drawn from your note (p.650) respecting this is that the system has only but recently been introduced. Thanks to generosity of the Lord of the Manor, many of our principal roads were planted several years ago, others were planted last season, and at the present time we have nice avenues of trees, principally Limes. I regret, however, to say that this autumn the public have taken the matter up, and very few Limes, or perhaps what would be more suitable, Planes, are being planted, and our beautiful esplanade – perhaps one of the finest in the kingdom – has been disfigured by being planted with a mixed collection of Horse-Chestnuts,

Sycamores, Balsam, Lombardy, Black Italian, and other kinds of Poplars. The Chestnuts will certainly be a failure, for the situation is much exposed to the sea, and in gales they will get every leaf blackened. I may add, that since the trees have been planted many have been beheaded to bring them into shape. It is a matter of regret that the Council were so ill-advised as to consent to the planting of such varieties, for it only brings street-tree planting into disrepute.

Gardeners' Chronicle 1895b, 720

In a note from the editors at the end of this article they state that 'The kinds named are not, perhaps the best that could be chosen. Still, the only really unsuitable one is the Horse-Chestnut'. Whether it was poor tree selection or poor planting and maintenance, those trees on the Esplanade did not fare well. A photograph from 1906 of the section by the Jubilee Memorial Clock show the young trees in what appears to be relatively good health, considering their exposed position on the seafront. Another photo from 1910 shows the same trees looking less healthy, with some either dead or dying. By the 1930s the trees have gone from postcard images of this section of the Esplanade.

Skegness

Skegness is a seaside town in Lincolnshire on the east coast of England. It was primarily a fishing village and only after the arrival of the railway in 1876 did it begin to attract significant numbers of visitors (Kime 1994, 6–7). Recognising the tourist potential, Richard George Lumley, the ninth Earl of Scarborough and the largest local landowner, instructed his estate agent to devise a major plan for the development of an entirely new seaside resort (Kime and Wilkinson 2012, 6). The plan included comprehensive and generous provision of water and drainage, wide tree-lined streets, attractive pleasure gardens, cricket ground, pier, churches and schools (Gurnham 1972, 71–74). Work began in the late 1870s with the first phase of the development restricted to the area between Lumley Road and Scarbrough Avenue. The promenade (Grand Parade and South Parade) was constructed on the sea wall and opened in 1879. By 1882 Lumley Road was mostly built up along its entire length and that same year saw the construction of 'excellent houses' on Rutland Road, and 'villa residences' on Algitha Road and Wainfleet Road. The houses were built with private finance and the Earl wisely gave businessmen, builders and local farmers the opportunity for profitable investment by laying out the streets and drains in advance of them building houses. The construction of the streets included the planting of street trees, which were often located in grass verges. In the town's entertainment and commercial areas, where space was at a premium, trees were usually planted directly into the footway.

By the outbreak of the First World War in 1914, Skegness was a thriving and attractive seaside resort with many of its main thoroughfares and residential streets planted with trees. As much of this planting, especially in residential districts, had taken place some 20–30 years previously the trees were now quite large and making a significant contribution to the streetscape. Lumley Road, Lumley Avenue, Algitha

Road, Scarbrough Avenue and Roman Bank around the junction with Algitha Road were some of the most impressive tree-lined streets. When trees were first planted in the busy commercial parts of town, such as Lumley Road, they were generally protected with wrought-iron guards (Kime and Wilkinson 2012, 20). The species of tree commonly used in all these early plantings were lime and plane. Today, many of these streets continue to have good treecover, although there are often quite large gaps with the loss of original trees and there has been a trend towards small and medium sized ornamentals for replacement planting. Castleton Boulevard, a major thoroughfare in Skegness leading down to the seafront, was not constructed until 1934 (Kime and Wilkinson 2012, 6). An aerial view of this some 15 years after the trees on the central reservation were established shows its potential to develop into a very impressive boulevard. However, this has not been realised and there is no 'boulevard' effect. Many of the original trees have gone and there is a variety of species and ages, and at different spacings with some quite large gaps.

Llandudno

One of the most popular seaside resorts in Wales has always been Llandudno, located on the Creuddyn peninsula in what is now Conwy County Borough. In 1843, Edward Mostyn, Member of Parliament and later Lord Mostyn, guided an *Enclosure Act* through Parliament that gave him sole rights to develop the land in and around the little village of Llandudno (Thompson 2005, 7–8). Like many other enclosure initiatives at this time, this was quite a devious scheme that would be described today as a land-grab and a confidence trick (Jones 1975, 16). Untroubled by that, Mostyn had spotted the potential of the area as a seaside resort and tourist destination and was keen to capitalise on this. He commissioned a survey of the land from the Liverpool architect Owen Williams who then used this to create imaginative plans for the new town, shaped with a grid of spacious thoroughfares and a sweeping promenade along the seafront. In the town's formative years in the late Victorian era many new developments took place to provide accommodation, recreation and shopping for the growing numbers of visitors. With its temperate climate and fine setting Llandudno became an elegant resort unrivalled in Wales and was labelled 'Queen of the Welsh Resorts'.

The streets of Llandudno took shape between the 1850s and 1880s and the grid pattern layout was planned in parallel to the promenade, which was to become a feature of the resort (Thompson 2005, 11). At the time, many people considered Williams' decision to lay out a wide belt of seafront land as a promenade to be an extravagant waste of property (Jones 1975, 28). However, the wisdom of this became apparent over the years as the promenade developed into a hugely attractive feature for the town and the focus of much of its social and cultural activity.

Llandudno's promenade extends around almost 2 miles (3.2 km) of seafront and is widely regarded as one of the finest in Europe (Thompson 2005, 28). While seaside promenades were invariably not planted with many trees, the one at Llandudno was extensively planted from as early as the 1890s (Figure 60). The trees were mostly on the seaward side of the promenade and extended along much of its length from Neville Crescent to North Parade. By the early 1930s, most of the trees had gone. The reason for their removal or why they were not replaced is not entirely clear. However, it is likely to have been a combination of factors, including the exposed position leading to poor tree growth and concerns from residents and hoteliers about the blocking of the sea view. There were, however, some trees that survived through the 1940s and these were Camperdown elms (*Ulmus glabra* 'Camperdownii') (Lawson-Reay pers. comm., 2016). Today, a few of these elms can still be found along the promenade together with a scattering of cabbage palms. There are also a small number of 'mop-headed' ornamental trees on the seaward side of the promenade at its northern end on North Parade.

Mostyn Street was one of the first to be laid out and this took place in the 1850s (Thompson 2005, 62). This became Llandudno's main shopping street, its 'golden half-mile', with elegant and expensive shops and other buildings (Jones 1975, 51). The development of this main thoroughfare, in a gentle arc parallel with the promenade, began in Church Walks at its northern end. Early photographs suggest that both sides of Mostyn Street were not planted up at the same time, as images from the 1900s show the trees on the western side as quite mature, while most of those on the eastern side are perhaps 15 years old. Today, almost all of the original trees seem to have gone and the replacements have some large gaps between them. Nevertheless, there are two old street trees of special interest and these are Camperdown elms, the same species mentioned above on the promenade. This is a very unusual species for a street tree and it is also one of the elms more resistant to Dutch elm disease. This may have been why these trees survived while other elms in Llandudno succumbed, and also because they were given trunk injections in the

FIGURE 60. While seaside promenades were invariably not planted with many trees, the one at Llandudno in North Wales was extensively planted from as early as the 1890s. However, by the early 1930s, most of the trees had gone. This photograph was taken around 1910.

1980s to provide some resistance (Bardsley pers. comm., 2016). The history of these trees, located outside the Library, is fascinating. They were originally planted in a small garden in front of the original single-storey library, either side of the entrance, when this opened in 1877 (Draper and Lawson-Reay 2010, 80). When this facility proved too small it was demolished and a new two-storey library was built in 1910. The garden disappeared in this development but the two elm trees were retained and became located in the street. Considering the very close proximity of the new building, the developers did well to retain these trees without any significant damage to them. There were originally three Camperdown elms in this street until at least the 1970s. It is thought the third was planted in 1877 in grounds of Zion Chapel (Jones 1975, 71), which was erected in 1862 as a place of worship for English Baptists (Draper and Lawson-Reay 2010, 22). In 1967, when Mostyn Estates declined to renew the chapel's lease, it was decided to demolish the building and replace the classical grandeur of Zion Chapel with the brutal architecture of a branch of Boots the Chemists. Although this Camperdown elm was initially retained in the new development, it was subsequently felled. In 1992, the Boots building was replaced with the more tasteful architecture of the Victoria Centre.

Gloddaeth Street and its continuation Gloddaeth Avenue is a main thoroughfare that runs across the width of the peninsula at its narrowest point (Jones 1975, 61). Photographs of Gloddaeth Street in the 1900s show a tramline running down the centre and young trees about 5 years old, planted with a regular spacing of about 20 ft (6.1 m) on either side of the road. Now there are just a handful of trees left and the central section of the road is used for parking. Much of the rest of this thoroughfare is now dual carriageway and the central reservation on Gloddaeth Avenue was planted up in the mid-1990s, mainly with holm oaks (*Quercus ilex*) that have some incongruous-looking clipped shrubs around their base. There are hardly any trees in the footway on either side of the road. Although there is space along much of this thoroughfare for an architectural 'boulevard' style planting, the opportunity has not been taken.

From the evidence available it would appear that common lime was the most favoured species in the early days of street tree planting in Llandudno. These have now largely gone from the town centre. While many original or early planted street trees have also disappeared from the town's residential districts, there are some notable exceptions, such as Park Avenue which has managed to retain a high proportion of its early limes. Elsewhere, where a reasonable number of old trees remain, for example, in the western section of Roseberry Road, these have been severely pollarded. Nevertheless, in other cases where many street trees have been lost in residential neighbourhoods, the streets often still have a leafy and picturesque look due to the presence of garden hedges and trees and shrubs in front gardens.

Fleetwood

Lancashire in the north-west of England has long had a number of popular seaside resorts. Since the development of railway links workers and their families from the industrial towns of Lancashire have flocked to the north-west coast in holiday times to gain a much needed break from the toil of their everyday lives. From early Victorian times Blackpool has been the most popular resort but other venues have also been prominent, such as Southport, Lytham, Morecambe and Fleetwood. Fleetwood is of particular interest here. It was developed by landowner Peter Hesketh from a stretch of barren coastal land to become a fashionable seaside resort (Byrom 2013, 3). Work on building the future Fleetwood began in 1836 and was given a huge boost when the railway system from Preston was extended to the area. Hesketh employed the architect Decimus Burton to lay out the town and design a number of civic buildings. Using the last large sandhill along the coast as its central point and axis, which he called the Mount, the town's roads radiated out from this point like the spokes of a wheel. While a generous area of open space was included in the town layout, photographic evidence suggests that early street tree planting was limited.

One impressive planting scheme was undertaken around 1890 in Bold Street, a prominent thoroughfare running from the seafront and ending with a view of the Mount. The trees, probably limes, were planted at a close spacing and positioned in the road a few feet from the kerb (Figure 61). As the trees matured the planting developed into an attractive avenue and a notable landscape feature of the town centre. Now, there are only a few mature trees remaining but it is unlikely these are the original trees. Fortunately, there has been much replanting, especially in recent years, and in time the attractive avenue effect should be recreated, although this will involve a mix of species. The trees are now at a much wider spacing and no longer standing in the road but located in slightly raised planting areas next to the kerb that are about 3 ft (0.9 m) square with stone surrounds.

Helensburgh

In concluding this chapter some mention should be made of Scotland. This part of Britain never had many seaside resorts of the type that proliferated around the English coastline in Victorian and Edwardian times and which arose to a

FIGURE 61. One impressive planting scheme that was undertaken in Fleetwood, Lancashire, around 1890 was in Bold Street, a prominent thoroughfare running from the seafront and ending with a view of the Mount. The trees, probably limes, were planted at a close spacing and positioned in the road a few feet from the kerb. This photograph was taken around 1905.

lesser extent on the Welsh coast. Various factors were influential here, not least the climate that was not always conducive to relaxing on the beach or strolling along the promenade. A few of Scotland's limited number of seaside resorts were explored in this research. It seems that the lead taken in some Scottish cities in introducing trees into their streets in the late Victorian era was not followed to any extent by its seaside resorts. One exception is Helensburgh, a seaside town now located in the county of Bute and Argyll, which lies on the north shore of the Firth of Clyde on Scotland's west coast (Noble 2002). Helensburgh was founded in 1776 when Sir James Colquhoun built spa baths on the site of Ardencaple Castle. He then had the seaside resort town constructed to the east of the spa on a formal layout in the style of Edinburgh New Town, and named it after his wife Helen. In 1860, the Reverend John Bell of the Episcopal Church reported to the Town Council that a public meeting of local residents had called for trees to be planted in the streets (Crawford and Glen 2002, 30). It has not been possible to ascertain when planting actually began but there is a record from 1883 of 'broad and carefully trimmed ribands of turf betwixt the sidewalks and the carriageway, several [of which] are planted, boulevard fashion with small trees' (Dingwall 2002).

An examination of the photographic evidence shows that Sinclair Street, the town's main thoroughfare, was lined with fairly mature looking trees by 1907, possibly laburnums (Kerr pers. comm., 2016). Other tree-lined streets established before the First World War include the planting of cherry trees in Colquhoun Street and West Argyle Street and possibly the birch trees on West Montrose Street. These were part of a major phase of street tree planting was that initiated in 1910, the driving force behind this being town councillor, Dr J. Ewing Hunter (Argyll and Bute Council 2008, 36). In the inter-war years the extent of street tree planting in Helensburgh increased considerably and it gained a deserved reputation for its pleasant landscapes and attractive horticultural features. In the 1930s it was referred to as the Garden City of the Clyde (Sheen 2007).

In 2001, the Helensburgh Tree Conservation Trust was formed with the aim of promoting public awareness of the town's street trees and to stimulate action to conserve and enhance them. One of its first actions was to commission an arboricultural consultant to undertake a detailed tree survey which identified a total of 1829 street trees (Rodger 2003). The most common species was silver birch (*Betula pendula*) closely followed by the flowering cherry *Prunus* 'Hisakura', sometimes regarded as an early form of *Prunus* 'Kanzan'. Data from the survey was then used to produce a street tree management plan (Rodger 2005). This highlighted the variable condition of the tree population and the fact that it had not been actively managed for some years, due mainly to a lack of resources. In response to this the report contained a detailed tree planting and management strategy. The future now looks bright for the town's remarkable heritage of street trees, thanks to the commitment of the Helensburgh Tree Conservation Trust and the support of local people.

CHAPTER NINE

Visions of Garden Cities with Green Streets

During the course of British history there have always been some visionary individuals who have dreamt of the possibility of building ideal towns and cities in a future golden age. For them, the invariably depressing reality of urban life in their own time could be replaced by green and pleasant settlements of the future which would benefit all citizens. They often wrote about those visions in the hope that they might inspire others to work together to turn them into reality. In this chapter we explore some of these visionary ideas and the extent to which they were turned into reality. An account is given of various practical initiatives in Britain over the past few centuries to create new and attractive urban centres, such as the utopian settlements, the model and industrial villages, the Gardens Cities and the New Towns. In contrast to the garden suburbs (see Chapter 6), these visionary settlements were planned as self-sufficient and independent entities and not simply as suburbs of existing towns and cities. While some description of these new urban settlements is given, the emphasis is on the extent to which street trees played a role in delivering their aim of a greener, more attractive and sustainable urban environment.

Utopian communities and metropolitan visions

There have been a number of important early texts that inspired visions of the future with fictional descriptions of harmonious, beautiful and prosperous places, such as Sir Thomas More's book *Utopia* first published in Latin in 1516 (More 1895). However, it was not until the dawn of the Industrial Revolution that any significant attempts were made to create new planned settlements based on visionary ideas. One of the first was at Fairfield near Manchester, the capital of early industrialism (Creese 1966, 6–8). In 1784, the Moravian Church built the Moravian Fairfield Settlement, a group of homes, civic buildings and church facilities (Stern *et al.* 2013, 376). This was a pedestrian village and although contemporary pictures show plenty of open space, it was devoid of trees until hawthorn and ash were planted much later in 1848. In 1912, some middle class residents from Droylsden, about four miles from Manchester city centre, formed the Fairfield Tenants Association with the aim of building the Fairfield Housing Estate next to the original settlement. This involved semi-detached and terraced houses with 33 completed in 1914 and a further eight in 1920. The homes were placed on either side of a new

J-shaped street called Broadway that had wide verges planted with trees. Slightly earlier than this, trees were introduced into some of the streets of the old settlement, such as Brethren Street and Sisters' Street. Photos from *c.* 1920 show recently planted trees with wrought-iron guards positioned down the centre of the cobbled roads between the terraced houses (Figure 62). The scene nowadays is very similar and the only obvious difference is slightly fewer trees and cars are now parked on this central area next to the trees. In the nearby Broadway over the past few decades the verges have been replanted with small ornamental trees.

Perhaps the most socially innovative of the new settlements was New Lanark in Scotland, developed by Robert Owen (Davidson 1993; Morris 1997, 37). New Lanark was a cotton manufacturing village taken over by Owen in 1799 and subsequently governed as a community on paternalistic lines. The dwellings and gardens were grouped around a large open space and were separated by the roadway from the workshops and factories. While there was always plenty of greenspace around the houses and industrial buildings, street trees were never a feature of this settlement. Owen's work at New Lanark, and his later but less successful efforts at New Harmony in the United States, helped to inspire James

FIGURE 62. In 1784, the Moravian Church built the Moravian Fairfield Settlement, an early utopian community in Lancashire that was initially devoid of trees. In 1912, some middle class residents from Droylsden, about four miles from Manchester city centre, formed the Fairfield Tenants Association and built the Fairfield Housing Estate next to the original settlement. Slightly earlier than this, trees were finally introduced into some of the streets of the old settlement. This photograph from the 1920s shows the trees planted in Brethren Street.

Silk Buckingham in 1849 to propose his own plans for a visionary new town, although this was never realised. The town was called Victoria, in honour of the Queen, and was described in his book *National Evils and Practical Remedies* (Buckingham 1849). The centre of Victoria was to be dedicated to academic and civic buildings around which the town's concentric square bands would alternate between houses, streets, gardens, public buildings and glass-covered arcades housing shops and workshops. There was a strong emphasis on greenery with an expansive ornamental landscape throughout the town, a botanic garden and a public park located on its outskirts. Although there were four avenues leading into the Central Square, and Buckingham stressed the need for these and other streets in the town to be wide, there was no specific mention of any systematic planting of street trees (*ibid.*, 191–192).

As well as inspiring many beautiful landscapes and innovations in urban horticulture in the early nineteenth century, the great John Claudius Loudon also turned his attention to creating a vision for a greener London. In 1829, he set out his ideas in an article for *Gardener's Magazine* entitled *Hints on Breathing Places for the Metropolis* (Loudon 1829, 686–690). The essence of the plan was a series of concentric green belts or 'country zones', alternating with town zones, to surround London at 1 mile (1.6 km) intervals. In Loudon's vision for an ideal capital city he proposed a radial and concentric network of street and transport networks at surface level and a corresponding underground network of utility services. As might be expected from Loudon, this idyllic metropolis would also have a wealth of trees and public greenspace. However, he never specifically mentioned street trees, which was not altogether surprising since this was before the emergence of the Victorian street tree movement. For the plan to have been implemented it would have required a massive restructuring of governmental processes and this never happened (Simo 1981, 188).

Loudon's proposal for a Metropolitan Boulevard in London was more directly related to streets and trees (Loudon 1835, 1210–1211). Initially outlined in his first edition of the *Encyclopaedia of Gardening* in 1822, this was an urban improvement that would materially affect the entire metropolis and match some of the grandiose continental achievements such as the boulevards of Paris and Berlin's Unter den Linden. The route would encompass many existing roads and leave most private property intact, proceeding from Regent's Park to Kensington Gardens, through Hyde Park Corner and Piccadilly to Knightsbridge. From there it would cross Vauxhall Bridge to Kennington and eventually make its way to Greenwich. At this point it would cross the Thames again over a massive iron viaduct (tall enough for ships in full sail to pass) and then eventually circle back to Regents Park. As well as providing greatly improved communications and travel within the capital, the scheme had an underlying 'green' agenda. Loudon was thinking particularly of visitors to London who when travelling on the route would get great views of many fine gardens and see plenty of trees. While his proposal generated much interest, it was never realised.

Model or industrial villages

A range of new and visionary forms of urban settlement were developed during the nineteenth century and the first of these were the model or industrial villages. They were often far more spacious and greener than the earlier utopian settlements such as Fairfield and New Lanark and some of them had plenty of trees planted along their streets. They were clustered in the wool and worsted manufacturing centres of the West Riding of Yorkshire and were the initiative of a handful of wealthy industrialists (Creese 1966, 13–15). The first of the model villages to be built was Copley, developed from 1847–1853 by James Akroyd on 20 acres (8.1 ha) of land with 112 houses, organised in three long terraced rows (Stern *et al.* 2013, 702). While there were no street trees, there was sufficient garden space adjacent to the roads to grow small trees and shrubs.

Far more influential and ambitious than Copley was Saltaire, the second of the West Riding industrial villages, built near Bradford by Sir Titus Salt from 1848–1876 (Jackson *et al.* 2010). This took its name from its founder and from the River Aire that ran past the woollen mill. The built development eventually covered 25 acres (10.1 ha) and housed all Salt's extensive workforce in quite high-density but high-quality housing. The density of the development did not allow for much greenery to be introduced into the town fabric, and trees and shrubs were confined to wide setbacks in front of the school, institute and Alexandra Quadrangle, a group of 45 almshouses for the aged. There were no trees along its 22 streets even though there were now some early plantings in a few British towns and cities. To encourage self-sufficiency among his workers, Salt allowed an extensive area along the side of the mill to be used as allotments and this included many fruit trees. A public park of 14 acres (5.7 ha), known as Roberts Park, was opened in 1871 on land the other side of the river and railway. The building of Saltaire was a remarkable achievement that is now recognised in its designation as a World Heritage Site. While its public open spaces are maintained to a good standard, it still has no street trees (Firth 2002). Akroydon in Halifax was the third West Riding industrial village, developed by Edward Akroyd (Stern *et al.* 2013, 707). The settlement's central park, known as The Square, was located within a quadrangle of houses and was a step towards the single garden that was prophetic of some garden city developments (Creese 1966, 40). While this had trees around its periphery, there were no trees in the streets.

Two late nineteenth century industrial villages epitomised the social and economic benefits of attractive housing for workers in a landscaped setting. Port Sunlight was founded in 1888 by William Hesketh Lever, later Lord Leverhulme, for the factory workers of his adjacent palm oil soapworks in the Wirral (Hubbard and Shippobottom 2012, 1). The name of the new settlement was taken from his best-selling product, the world's first packaged soap for laundry and general household use. Port Sunlight is notable for being experimental in various aspects of town planning and urban design. It was one of the first industrial villages to depart from the grid pattern layout and emphasise the amenity setting of the homes (Rutherford 2014, 18). Many of the houses had space at the front which Lever was keen to keep unobstructed in a continuous frontage along the street, often referred to as the 'American open front' system. However, this system largely failed, as it did later in many other settlements in Britain, because the tenants enclosed their front yards with hedges to protect what they had planted from dogs, cats and children (Creese 1966, 117). Port Sunlight also experimented in the wider aspects of town planning and was very successful in this. When Lever engaged Thomas Mawson, the renowned planner and landscape architect, to assist the student Ernest Prestwick to prepare plans for the redevelopment and expansion of Port Sunlight this resulted in a bold and spectacular scheme for its central area (Mawson 1911, 278–287). Through his contacts and later visits to the United States, Mawson was influenced by the American Beaux-Arts style and City Beautiful movement and he used formal Beaux-Arts-style tree-lined boulevards to unite the overall design (Creese 1966, 133–135). The influences are particularly evident in the Diamond and the Causeway. In the core of the village the Causeway is a beautifully planned and wide tree-lined boulevard with Christ Church at one end. A second major boulevard known as the Diamond, which intersects with the Causeway, was laid out slightly later in 1910 as the central boulevard of the replanned village. This also has grand avenues of trees and terminates at its northern end with the Lady Lever Art Gallery, the final large building at the centre of Port Sunlight (Figure 63).

FIGURE 63. The town plan for Port Sunlight, founded in 1888 by William Hesketh Lever, shows the bold and spectacular vision for this new model village. It also reveals how Thomas Mawson used formal Beaux-Arts-style tree-lined boulevards to unite the overall design.

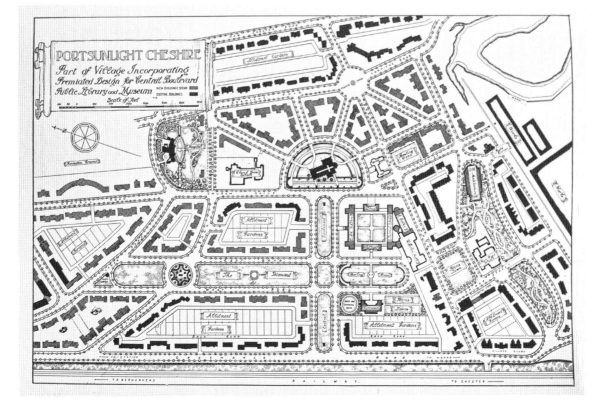

Apart from the grand boulevards, what stands out at Port Sunlight, in contrast to earlier industrial villages, is the commitment to extensive street tree planting across the whole development. Early photographs show many of the streets planted with trees at very close spacing, with a range of different trees used in different streets, although mainly forest-type trees with some smaller ornamental species (Beeson 1911; Davison 1916; Boumphrey and Hunter 2002; Tudsbery-Turner 2002). There is no doubt that the tree planting was assisted by aspects of the design of the streetscapes. The streets were wider than was typical for the time, with 24 ft (7.3 m) wide carriageways and 8–12 ft (2.4–3.7 m) wide footways. This made it easier to accommodate the larger forest-type trees. The 'open front' system for gardens, while it lasted, also helped facilitate tree planting in the footway because there were no concerns about trees overhanging front gardens as this was public open space maintained by estate workers. Today, Port Sunlight is a very attractive and desirable place to live and its wonderful and well-maintained street trees are the envy of many local authorities. There is just one small concern: with little evidence of recent planting it is hoped that these trees are being replaced when lost.

The model village of Bournville, founded by George Cadbury in 1895, was not meant to be an exclusively company settlement like Port Sunlight (Miller 2010, 10). The Cadbury family were devout Quakers and involved in the manufacture of chocolate. With their strong sense of social justice they were appalled by the miserable state of Birmingham's working class housing, despite all the 'improvements' which had been promised by Neville Chamberlain, and they were determined to ameliorate the situation. Up to half of the housing was available to non-Cadbury workers, which muted company paternalism and promoted social integration. By 1900, the estate included 313 cottages and houses set on 330 acres (133 ha) of land, and many more similar properties were built in the years leading up to the First World War. The estate tripled in size during the inter-war years and eventually grew to more than 1000 acres (405 ha) accommodating 7600 homes and 21,000 people (Stern *et al.* 2013, 225). The layout resembled a low-density suburb, with a central village green, shopping parade and nearby community buildings. Great attention was paid to house design, the provision of open space and environmental conditions as a whole. As part of this, there was an emphasis on large gardens and irregular street patterns which led Bournville to develop the cul-de-sac and the crescent, elements of planning arrangements that were later to become typical of garden suburbs (Morris 1997, 40). It has been said that Bournville's contribution to the garden city idea and its developing notions of suburban consciousness was not the invention of any fine architectural features but rather its innovation in street planning (Bayley 1975, 17–18). The 20 ft (6.1 m) wide setback added visual intent to the scene and gave room for the front gardens which Cadbury demanded. Indeed, one of the main differences with Port Sunlight was Bournville's emphasis on sizable private gardens, which were not commandeered as public open space. While Cadbury thought it was good for the workers to cultivate

FIGURE 64. The model village of Bournville, founded by George Cadbury in 1895, was not meant to be an exclusively company settlement like Port Sunlight. Up to half of the housing was available to nonCadbury workers, which muted company paternalism and promoted social integration. This photograph of Mary Vale Road from around 1910 shows the very close spacing of some of the early plantings.

their own gardens, this also gave scope for residents to plant their own trees and shrubs and therefore contributed to a green streetscape.

The specification for individual roads at Bournville varied, but was often around 42 ft (12.8 m) in width including the grass verges and footways. The developers considered the roads to be too wide for a residential area but they could not get approval from the District Council to vary the bye-laws (Bournville Village Trust 1956, 67). In the early days when these wide roads were first planted it was thought they looked quite bare but the situation improved once the trees started to mature. Indeed, in many of those planted roads, where plane and lime were the only trees used, every other tree was removed before it was fully grown because of complaints that these overshadowed the houses. This is not surprising given the very close spacing of some of the early planting. Photos taken *c.* 1910 show that in some streets, such as Linden Road, Mary Vale Road and Acacia Road, this was as little as 20 ft (6.1 m) (Figure 64). Although the selection of trees for street planting at Bournville had initially been similar to Bedford Park and much of Port Sunlight, which favoured forest-type species, in the inter-war years there was a preference for smaller ornamental trees, such as whitebeam, thorn, Japanese crab and cherries, almond, mountain ash, silver birch and laburnum (*ibid.*, 75; Creese 1966, 123). Where there was additional space on corner sites and wider setbacks, forest trees were still occasionally planted. A handbook on landscape planning and management produced by the estate in 1949 displays a clear dislike of plane and lime trees and the practice of pollarding (Bournville Village Trust 1949, 11). It also expresses a preference for the removal of many original street trees to break up the avenue appearance so that 'smaller trees in front gardens are revealed'. To emphasise the significance of the trees and reinforce their contribution to neighbourhood identity, streets were often named after the trees planted in them. In the 1950s the design, selection, planting and management of its street trees was promoted as a model for other urban areas (Salter 1953). Much of Bournville's reputation as a green and pleasant village has always been due to its roadside trees and these continue to be much admired today (Gumbley 1991; Booth *et al.* 2013).

Ebenezer Howard and the birth of the Garden City Movement

The model villages of Port Sunlight and Bournville had pointed a way forward to a brighter, greener, urban future – but not much else had happened. Life for the vast majority of people in the Victorian industrial city was a depressing, dull and monotonous existence. Repressive economic and political conditions ensured that efforts by the working class to organise and achieve genuine change were slow to make progress and often frustrated (Morton 1938, 432–439). Social and cultural progress was also drained by the devouring greed of industrial development. While growing numbers of the middle class were becoming concerned about the employment and living conditions of working people, there was very little action. What was urgently needed was a catalyst that could draw together some of these like-minded theories and people and harness this towards some real action on the ground.

Ebenezer Howard was born in London in 1850 to relatively comfortable middle class parents. He had left school by the age of 15, drifting between jobs and then moving to the United States and working on a farm in Nebraska (Clark 2003, 88). On his return to England in 1876, he was employed as a parliamentary reporter and this sharpened his awareness of the great social problems of the age. During that time he read widely and mingled with socialists, anarchists and other nonconformist freethinkers, and became friends with the socialists Sidney and Beatrice Webb and George Bernard Shaw (Beevers 1988, 13–18). Howard was very concerned about the steady migration of people from the countryside into the already overcrowded towns and cities. His philosophy was simple – he viewed town life as offering economic benefits and social opportunities, while country life offered all the human benefits. His idea was to create a community that offered the best of both town and country life, to be called the Garden City. This basic idea was encapsulated later in his now famous diagram of The Three Magnets, which skilfully summarised his concept of 'joyous union' between town and country (Howard 1898, 8).

Howard only wrote one major publication in his life but it transpired to be one of the most influential texts ever written on town planning and urban reform (Parsons and Schuyler 2002). Published in 1898 as *To-Morrow: A Peaceful Path to Real Reform*, it was significantly revised in 1902 as *Garden Cities of To-morrow*, the title by which it is now commonly known (Howard 1898). Many of the key ideas of his book were popular contemporary themes, which Howard duly acknowledged. He also generously gave credit for the inspiration he had gained from earlier pioneers, especially James Silk Buckingham, in a chapter entitled 'A Unique Combination of Proposals'. In Lewis Mumford's introduction to the 1976 edition of Howard's book, he identified the significant elements of his proposals as: (a) the permanent ownership of land by the municipality with leasing to private concerns; (b) the resultant recouping of unearned increment by the municipality rather than private landowners; (c) a sufficient diversity of activities, including social institutions; (d) industry; (e) agriculture to make the garden city fairly independent; (f) the use of a Green Belt for agriculture and to restrict the growth of the city; (g) a limit on the population to a planned size; and (h) further growth in new communities to be arranged as a 'Social City' (Howard 1976, 34).

Municipal control of the land was the key to Howard's scheme (Morris 1997, 49). Initially, this would be acquired by a private corporation that would hold it in trust for the future residents. The city's revenue was to be used for the benefit of the townspeople with the accrued money to be spent on the creation and maintenance of all public works. One of the reasons for the later success of the Garden City movement was Howard's description of this financial and administrative process in great detail. Arranging the municipal ownership of land in this way allowed the implementation of a comprehensive town plan. Within that plan, land-use zoning was a key feature.

The entire area covered by the Garden City plan would be 6000 acres (2428 ha) and the garden city itself, which would be built near the centre of this, would cover 1000 acres (405 ha). The plan of the ideal garden city would be laid out in circular form measuring nearly 0.75 miles (1.2 km) from centre to circumference. Howard gives the following description of the overall city:

> Six magnificent boulevards – each 120 ft [36.5 m] wide – traverse the city from centre to circumference, dividing it into six equal parts or wards. In the centre is a circular space of 185 yards [*c.* 170 m] in diameter, and containing about five and a half acres [2.2 ha], laid out as a beautiful and well-watered garden; and surrounding this garden, each standing in its own ample grounds, are the larger public buildings – town hall, principal concert and lecture hall, theatre, library, museum, picture-gallery, and hospital.
>
> Howard 1898, 14

Central to Howard's plan for the Garden City and providing much of the basic framework were a series of avenues and tree-line boulevards. Having stated that all the roads would be lined with trees, he then adds:

> Walking still towards the outskirts of the town, we come upon 'Grand Avenue'. This Avenue is fully entitled to bear its name, for it is 420 feet [128 m] wide, and forming a belt of green upwards of three miles [4.8 km] long, divides that part of the town that lies outside Central Park into two belts. It really constitutes an additional park of 115 acres [46.5 ha]– a park which is within 240 yards [219 m] of the furthest removed inhabitant. In this splendid avenue six sites, each of four acres [1.6 ha], are reserved for public schools and their surrounding play-grounds and gardens, while other sites are reserved for churches.
>
> Howard 1898, 15

Later in his book when Howard discusses the general nature of roads and streets in the Garden City, he states:

> Experts will also not forget that the cost of the road sites is elsewhere provided for. In considering the question of the actual sufficiency of the estimate they will also remember that of the boulevards one-half and of the streets and avenues one-third, may be regarded as in the nature of a park, and the cost of laying out and maintenance of these portions of the roads is dealt with under the head 'Parks'.
>
> Howard 1898, 53

Those short paragraphs on roads are especially revealing about Howard's radically new perspective on tree-lined boulevards that was to have a significant influence on the Garden City movement and subsequent town planning in general. Howard clearly regarded the planted sections of boulevards, avenues and streets as 'in the nature of a park', which says much about his perception of the role of these thoroughfares as both transport corridors and additional greenspace. These paragraphs also reveal that the inspiration for these avenues and boulevards was probably American (Hall and Ward 1998, 22). Likely examples in the United States were the Mall in Washington and especially Chicago's Medway, which now divides the Hyde Park district on the south side of the city. It is notable that Howard's Garden City had its Central Park and boulevards called Third Avenue, Fifth Avenue and so on. His appeal to the language and style of such symbolic urban metropolises as Chicago and New York shows he was never interested in building a pretty suburb. For Howard, the garden suburbs were highly dangerous manipulations of the Garden City principle (Hunt 2004, 330). They were simply more rarefied districts within the city suburbs. More damagingly, they served to accelerate rather than counter the suburban trend. It seemed that every ambitious family wanted to live in a suburb of large gardens, green lanes and generously proportioned houses. Writing during the First World War, Howard stated, 'They are rather dormitory districts with little or no provision for work, except, indeed, for work in the garden, and they tend to diffuse the corporate sense over so wide an area that in its diffusion that sense is apt to become largely lost' (Beevers 1988, 134).

While Ebenezer Howard had his dreams of a bright new urban future, he was not a professional architect or planner and it took two remarkable individuals from the next generation to help these dreams come true (Creese 1966, 158). They were Barry Parker and Raymond Unwin, both architects and town planners who came together in 1896 to form a partnership (Miller 2010, 13). Unwin's briefing paper on garden city housing, delivered at a conference in Bournville in 1901, led to a commission for a plan for New Earswick, near York, which was to become the testing ground for garden city design.

In 1901, Joseph Rowntree, another Quaker chocolate manufacturer, purchased the estate of New Earswick near his cocoa works, 3 miles (4.8 km) north-east of York (Creese 1966, 191). The site of 130 acres (53 ha) is bisected by the winding north–south Haxby Road. Establishing a Trust to lead the development, Rowntree did not intend his new settlement to be exclusively populated with his company's employees. His objective was less the creation of a town than the provision of good housing. The principal characteristic of the plan for New Earswick was its carefully considered informality (Parker 1937). The first phase of 28 houses, east of Haxby Road, was mapped out and built in 1902–1903 by Parker and Unwin, while the other half of the settlement, west of Haxby Road, was built later in 1919. The Rowntrees refrained from selling their houses to the tenants, because of the Cadbury's unfortunate experience at Bournville with rising values and speculative turnover (Creese 1966, 192). While many of the houses in New Earswick were quite plain, they had large gardens and there was plenty of land given up to recreation grounds and attractively landscaped open space (Stern *et al.* 2013, 229). The streets were planted extensively with trees, where the identifying trees for each street followed the earlier Bournville practice with names such as Chestnut Grove, Poplar Grove, Lime Tree Avenue and Sycamore Avenue (Trinder 1982, 252) (Figure 65). Most of the roads had generous grass verges, which was now becoming a typical feature of the garden suburbs. Photographs of New Earswick in its early years show quite extensive and attractive planting at reasonably close spacing in streets such as Lime Tree Avenue, Chestnut Grove and Station Avenue (Murphy 1987). The main Haxby Road itself was never planted with street trees but this has always been quite a 'green' road due to the trees on adjacent open space and in private gardens. Today, quite a number of the roads have large gaps between the trees as much of original planting has been lost with few replacements. Where replanting has occurred over the past 50 years there has been a preference for smaller

FIGURE 65. In 1901, Joseph Rowntree, another Quaker chocolate manufacturer, purchased the estate of New Earswick, three miles north-east of York. He then established a Trust to lead the development of his new model village, called New Earswick. The streets were planted extensively with trees, where the identifying trees for each street followed the earlier Bournville practice with names such as Chestnut Grove, Poplar Grove and Sycamore Avenue. This is Lime Tree Avenue photographed around 1930.

ornamental species. In those roads that were given tree names there is now little evidence of the designated species. Nevertheless, New Earswick remains quite a leafy and pleasant residential area with its trees and shrubs in private gardens contributing much of this.

The newer half of New Earswick contains some of the best examples of the cul-de-sac device which Parker and Unwin used to get around the awkwardness of irregular sites (Creese 1966, 195). This not only provided additional greenspace, often in the form of a distinct 'green' in the centre of the cul-de-sac, but the enclosed arrangement of the housing also acted as a buffer against the dust and noise of vehicles on the main roads. The cul-de-sac was to become a hallmark of Parker and Unwin work and a typical feature of the garden city, the garden suburbs and many of the more conventional residential suburbs. It is nevertheless interesting to note how little use was often made of the potential for tree planting on the 'green' of many culs-de sac, especially in suburbs and housing estates that were not designated as 'garden' developments.

Letchworth and Welwyn Garden Cities

Howard's book was respectfully received but it did not initially make huge waves. Undeterred by this he believed that what was needed was some form of organisation to take the ideas forward and realise them in a practical project. Fortunately, the book had helped to draw together a small group of influential supporters and in 1899, led by Howard, they formed the Garden City Association (later the Town and Country Planning Association) that mobilised like-minded people keen to finance and participate in this social experiment. The Association held its first conference in 1901 at Bournville, hosted by George Cadbury, and its second conference in 1902 at Port Sunlight, hosted by William Hesketh Lever (Miller 2010, 13).

The garden city idea finally became reality in 1903 with the establishment of the first settlement at Letchworth, 30 miles (48 km) from London (Purdom 1913; Anon 1935). This began with the formation of a company called First Garden City Ltd in 1903 which initially purchased 3,826 acres (1,548 ha) of agricultural land in the three adjacent villages of Letchworth, Willian and Norton. The site met the need for good communications being close to the old Great North Road (now the A1 motorway) and on the London Kings Cross to Cambridge rail route. A competition to determine the layout and character of the garden city was won by Parker and Unwin, whose plan was adopted in 1904 (Miller 1989, 42–58). Howard was closely involved in the implementation of the plan. In 1909, some of the work undertaken at Letchworth was included by Unwin in his definitive text, *Town Planning in Practice* (Unwin 1909). This set his ideas in a broad historical context and spelt out basic principles of site planning and density. The book was inspired by the introduction of a government bill that would become the *Housing and Town Planning Act* of 1909, empowering local authorities to prepare town plans.

The most characteristic feature of Letchworth was the very open layout of the roads and houses. Together with the extensive planting of trees, shrubs and hedges, this gave the whole town a park-like appearance befitting the term 'garden city' (Miller 2010, 22). Parker and Unwin designed the town and its housing around a Beaux-Arts-style formal axial road network focused on Broadway, a broad tree-lined spinal approach road, which opened into the formal Central Square (Rutherford 2014, 38). This was planted on either side with common lime that was soon made a double avenue. On the other side of Central Square leading to the station the Broadway had a space reserved for a tramway that was never realised. This was planted up at quite an early stage with trees and shrubs and converted into a landscaped pedestrian walk. When the trees and shrubs matured they gave the area a very green and informal look. However, all this was cut down recently and replaced with a formal landscape of birch trees and low clipped hedges on either side of the walk.

Much of the housing was low-density and developed around several 'village greens' (Creese 1966, 206–207). The precise density of housing per acre was a reflection of the cost of individual houses but never greater than 12 per acre for the cheapest houses. The dwellings were positioned on the plot to command the sunniest aspect and most pleasant prospect available, instead of merely aligning them with the street. Both Parker and Unwin were aware of the value of incorporating existing trees into built development. In giving advice to young planners, Parker urged them to do their best not to cut down a single tree. He was enormously proud of the fact that the building of Letchworth had only involved the destruction of one tree.

Many new trees were also planted along roads in narrow grass verges designed specifically for tree planting (Creese 1966, 229). In a scheme reminiscent of that at Bournville, each road had its own species of tree (45 in all) as part of a campaign to promote a sense of place and greater appreciation of the trees. Unwin observed:

> The Japanese have special holidays to celebrate the flowering times of certain trees; and even the English workman might be tempted to vary his route home, if in one street he would find the earliest blossoming trees, in another the first spring green, and in a third the last bright colours of autumn.
>
> Unwin 1904, 3

In the residential section of Broadway, the double avenue of lime trees gave this major street its identity and stature (Creese 1966, 208). This is now a very fine avenue leading into the centre of Letchworth. At the far end of Broadway at Sollershott Circus the first traffic roundabout to be built in Britain was completed in 1910, although never planted with trees. Norton Way South was another major thoroughfare near the centre of Letchworth that was planted with lime trees and which now forms an impressive avenue. A large part of Icknield Way, a major east–west road to the north of the civic centre, was planted up with small ornamental trees, especially flowering cherries (Pierce 2002, 53).

Elsewhere in the civic centre, Lombardy poplars were planted to define the building outlines in Central Square, although these were felled recently when the square was remodelled as Broadway Gardens in 2003 (Miller 2010, 22).

The trees, hedges and grass verges of the housing districts of Letchworth furnished a living and spatial screen for the homes and family life, which Parker and Unwin considered paramount (Creese 1966, 208–209). However, there has been some criticism made of the landscaping programme at Letchworth which believes that eventually nature swung out of balance and became something of a burden. The trees, shrubs and flowers were planted quickly, while the buildings lagged behind. This was especially noticeable around the Central Square of the town. By the 1950s, many older residents in the housing districts were complaining regularly that the trees were 'overgrown' and 'robbing' them of light and views.

Much could be written about the achievements and limitations of Letchworth as Britain's first Garden City but only a few brief points are mentioned here. The building of Letchworth made some significant contributions to policy. First, it established the concept of a planned, balanced and self-contained town, which influenced the development of town planning and eventually led to the series of state-funded New Towns after 1945 (Ravetz 2001, 67). Nevertheless, it should also be recognised that almost from the start it functioned as another commuter suburb serving London (Stern *et al.* 2013, 230). Secondly, its small house types provided a link between the model village and council housing from 1919. Lying somewhere between the two was the concept of the 'estate', which became an indispensable element of the new council housing (Ravetz 2001, 67). Thirdly, and most importantly for this book, it demonstrated what the 'garden' element of the Garden City was all about, with plenty of attractively landscaped open space, houses with adequate gardens and tree-lined streets (Figure 66). If this could be accomplished at Letchworth then it could, and should, be part of the plans for other new settlements. Visitors from all over the world still flock to Letchworth to admire and study this remarkable achievement in urban planning and design.

In 1919 when the First World War had ended, those promoting the garden city concept were concerned at the lack of action in creating another English initiative (Miller 2010, 31). There was disappointment with the government's neutral stance on garden cities compared to the generous grants and compulsion for local authority housing, despite this being encouraged to develop along 'garden city' lines. These developments had been prompted by the impact of the *Tudor Walters Report* on legislation and working class housing, published by the Local Government Board in 1918 (Rutherford 2014, 65). This had been much influenced by Unwin who by then had been appointed as a government official (Creese 1966, 256).

As a result of a personal initiative by Howard that was not part of any government plan, another garden city initiative was founded in 1920 in the form of Welwyn Garden City, located in Hertfordshire (Morris 1997, 52). This was closer to London than Letchworth, being only 19 miles (31 km) from Kings

FIGURE 66. This recent aerial photograph of Letchworth Garden City clearly shows what the 'garden' element was all about, with plenty of attractively landscaped open space, houses with adequate gardens and tree-lined streets. Parker and Unwin designed the town and its housing around a Beaux-Arts-style formal axial road network focused on Broadway, a broad tree-lined spinal approach road that can be clearly seen near the centre of the photo.

Cross station. It aimed to have a population of 50,000, although it grew rather slowly in the first 15 years. Welwyn eventually proved to be successful in many respects. Although close to London, it has retained its own identity and 85% of its residents still work in the town.

In 1920, Welwyn Garden City Limited was formed to plan and build the garden city. The layout of Welwyn was masterminded by Louis de Soissons, a French-Canadian architect, with Howard closely involved (Rutherford 2014, 42–43). The layout of the site was made difficult by being quartered by railways, with the main Great Northern Railway running north–south through the centre of the development. To meet this challenge de Soisson's proposed a grand focal Beaux-Arts layout that was planned around two formal axes. The main one was Parkway, a broad avenue on a north–south axis running parallel and to the west of the main railway. This was the impressive and equally scenic equivalent of Letchworth's Broadway, involving a great formal boulevard with a double avenue of trees. At the southern end this comprises Lombardy poplar in the inner rows and Swedish whitebeam (*Sorbus intermedia*) in the outer rows. At the northern end there is a double avenue of closely pruned limes. The Parkway terminates at its north end in the Campus, a semi-circular public space surrounded by civic buildings. A second and shorter landscaped boulevard, called Howardsgate, was located at right-angles to this and leading to the station (Miller 2010, 31). An aerial photograph from 1928, when the centre of Welwyn was still under development, shows the young trees along Howardsgate neatly planted in their rows before any other major landscaping or most of the nearby buildings had been constructed (Eserin 1995, 36). The planting is a double avenue of closely pruned limes with a few Lombardy poplars near the junction with Parkway. A number of other ornamental tree-lined boulevards eventually linked the different neo-Georgian buildings in the civic centre. Overall, landscaping was one of the highlights of Welwyn Garden City, especially the broad expanses and sweeping vistas of Parkway which surprised and impressed many visitors.

Despite the planners' avowed egalitarian aims and original intention to mix social classes, this did not happen. The company behind the development put the middle and upper class dwellings near the commercial and administrative centre on the west of the main railway (Rook 2001, 85). The working class housing was on the east, isolated by the railway and the industrial area, inevitably leading to a social divide and to people feeling they were literally 'on the wrong side of the tracks'. To save money the company was initially cautious about constructing many new roads, preferring to improve existing poorly-metalled ones wherever possible. These were called 'Lanes' on the town map. New roads, culs-de-sac and closes were constructed using gravel extracted on site. None of the roads was called a 'street' as it was thought the word was suggestive of smoky towns.

The extent of early street tree planting along roads in residential districts of Welwyn seems to have varied considerably, both between streets and also within the same street. The OS maps of the time only show trees in prominent locations such as the Parkway and Howardsgate but early photographs are revealing. While most roads were constructed with wide grass verges, substantial sections of many remained unplanted in the early years. This included large parts of Blakemere Road, Brookswood Lane, High Oaks Road and Longcroft Lane. In Valley Road it is curious that although trees were generally not planted in the main grass verge, a number were located in the much narrower strip of verge on the house side of the footway immediately in front of the garden hedges (Figure 67). Why the main verge was not used is unknown and many of those trees no longer survive. The extent to which all Welwyn's residential roads are now planted still varies significantly but in general they are well-treed, mostly with various small and medium-sized ornamental species, especially flowering cherries. From the age of the existing trees it seems that much of this planting took place after 1948 when Welwyn was designated one of the New Towns. The species of trees planted in the residential streets of Welwyn has always comprised quite a mix and during the early years this was undertaken partly to assess their suitability for street use (Sefton 1947). Very noticeable today is the substantial number of large mature trees, mainly native and indigenous species, that were incorporated into the streetscape as the roads and houses were being built. While the current street tree population of Welwyn often has some quite large gaps between the trees,

FIGURE 67. The street trees of Welwyn Garden City now make a fine arboreal feature that is befitting Britain's second Garden City. However, the extent of early plantings in its residential districts seems to have varied considerably, both between streets and also within the same street. This section of Valley Road, photographed in 1929, shows that trees were not planted in the main grass verge but in the much narrower strip of verge in front of the garden hedges.

the presence of many trees and shrubs in front gardens makes up for this. Overall, the street trees of Welwyn are a fine arboreal feature that is befitting Britain's second Garden City.

Rosyth and Wythenshawe

The only Scottish garden city was established during the First World War (Chalkley and Shiach 2005). Rosyth Garden City on the Firth of Forth was built to serve the workforce and their families in the Royal Navy Dockyard that had opened in 1915 (Rutherford 2014, 44). In 1913, the Admiralty had appointed Unwin to prepare a master plan that was then developed in detail by architect A.H. Mottram, a former employee of Parker and Unwin (Stern *et al.* 2013, 726). Building work began in 1915 and some 1600 houses were completed by 1918. Rosyth's layout and houses reflected the precedents set in England and adopted in the Glasgow Garden suburb. There were picturesque cottage-style houses arranged at low density, mostly in terraces of varying lengths but also some semi-detached pairs. Front gardens were hedged with privet, holly and beech, linked by broad, tree-lined streets that often had grass verges. Generous rear gardens were supplemented by plenty of communal greenspace, including a wide greenbelt around the town. A major thoroughfare called Kings Road ran north–south through the new settlement and served as a central spine. Queensferry Road, with a broad landscaped planting strip on either side, formed the principal residential axis from which culs-de-sac and short spurs branched off. In the 1930s more houses were built and after the Second World War Rosyth continued to expand through to the 1970s (Rogers 2009a, 3). Along many of the roads in these later developments there were no grass verges but often plenty of small plots of greenspace close to the houses.

Research on the nature and extent of Rosyth's early street tree plantings has been assisted greatly by the Rosyth Garden City Millennium Project's collection of early photographs of its streets (Chalkley and Shiach 2005). It has also sourced a number of aerial views showing substantial parts of the new garden city. From this evidence it can be seen that there was extensive tree planting along most of Rosyth's streets from an early stage. In those estates built in the 1960s and 1970s, where there were small plots of greenspace rather than conventional grass verges, these often contained plenty of trees. Over the decades Rosyth's street tree population has undergone considerable change. The Kings Road has been extensively redeveloped and the treecover on the most southerly section is now quite sparse. Queensferry Road has also undergone extensive redevelopment. At its northern end there is now a short stretch with a reasonable amount of treecover in the grass verge on one side but then a longer stretch on the same side without any trees. After the junction with Park Road on the southern section there is more treecover on both sides of the road, including large common limes that were early plantings. The extent of treecover on the minor roads in Rosyth is now very variable. In general, there has been an overall reduction and in many cases this has been quite dramatic. Along with many trees numerous sections of grass verge have also disappeared. In some cases the verges have been replaced with tree pits but in some cases these have not been planted or have been subsequently paved over. It seems likely that a major cause of the reduction in treecover and the loss of the grass verges, as in many residential districts in Britain in recent times, has been to facilitate car parking on hard-surfaced areas, either where the verges were once located or off-street in front gardens. A typical example of this is Parkside Street where all the original trees have gone and replacement planting is quite sparse. By contrast, the eastern part of Backmarch Street still has a leafy appearance with many of its original limes, although on the western section these trees now are quite widely spaced. A few years ago a large number of horse chestnut trees were felled in Middlebank Street in what had been a very leafy road (Anon 2014, 22) (Figure 68). Some residents had asked for them to be cut down because they feared they were a danger in windy conditions. As yet there is no replacement planting.

The recent loss of street trees and the lack of replacement planting may be linked to other concerns about the loss of Rosyth's heritage and character. In the mid-1980s, Dunfermline District Council designated the original Garden City part of Rosyth as a Conservation Area with the aim of preserving the character

FIGURE 68. Rosyth was originally established as the only Scottish garden city but has not developed in the same way as Letchworth or Welwyn. While there is evidence that there was extensive tree planting along most of Rosyth's streets from an early stage, many trees have subsequently been lost. This photograph shows a section of Middlebank Street where a few years ago a large number of horse chestnut trees were felled in what had been a very leafy road.

of the area (Rogers 2009b, 14). The Conservation Area designation soon came under criticism as the owners of properties found that they were unable to alter their properties in the way they wanted. In a referendum held among the residents in 1989, a significant majority of those voting favoured the withdrawal of the Conservation Area status and the District Council removed this in 1990. It has been stated that without this status to maintain consistency there has been a loss of coherence and character in the housing and other features of Rosyth (Denyer and Creswell 2015, 203).

At Wythenshawe near Manchester in the 1920s a major inter-war municipal housing project was started that was intended to be another garden city (Deakin 1989). It was planned by the Corporation of Manchester to provide new housing for families being moved out of the slums and squalor of industrial Manchester. In 1920, the Wythenshawe district was identified by Patrick Abercrombie, the eminent town planner, as the only undeveloped land suitable for building close to Manchester. He recommended building a satellite town, separated from the city by a green belt. The overall design of Wythenshawe was undertaken by Parker, this time without Unwin, and it was

to be his last and largest work (Creese 1966, 255). Although the project had the misfortune of being started at a time of national economic depression, it nevertheless had the political and financial weight of Manchester behind it. By 1935, it had already outgrown both Letchworth and Welwyn, testimony to the swift municipalisation of the garden city idea. Its proposed population was almost twice these, at around 90,000.

Wythenshawe has been described as one of the most complete municipal experiments in garden city design ever undertaken (Miller 2010, 80–82). Parker's plan certainly attracted much praise at the time with Lewis Mumford, the eminent American sociologist-planner, regarding his plan as a bold updating of Howard's garden city concept. It specified a hierarchy of streets and residential neighbourhoods with community facilities, a town centre, industrial zones, open spaces and a peripheral green belt. Most revolutionary were the main high-speed transport arteries, the parkways, which reflected Parker's enthusiasm for American innovations and advanced practice. He had visited the United States to attend conferences on urban planning and had been particularly inspired by the parkway system of Chicago (Creese 1966, 261).

The main parkway at Wythenshawe, called Princess Parkway, was the first of its kind in Britain and its bold scale and distinct environment ensured it stood out from the rest of the town's development (Creese 1966, 261–263). The essential purpose of a parkway is to provide a major corridor for free-flowing traffic that is segregated from nearby housing and minor roads by attractively landscaped greenspace. The first section of Princess Parkway to Altrincham Road was officially opened in 1932 and its high-quality landscaping and overall design was greatly admired by both professionals and locals (Deakin 1989, 49). The nearby houses were 150 ft (46 m) back from the parkway and limited vehicle access from side streets occurred approximately every quarter of a mile (0.4 km) (Creese 1966, 261–263). There were four lanes of traffic and on either side of this a broad verge planted with rows of trees and hedges. As well as the improvements in traffic flow through Wythenshawe, there were various supplementary benefits from the parkway. The belts of trees and dense shrubbery would not only act as a buffer against the dust, smell and noise of vehicles on the main road, but also be part of people's daily routines as 'pedestrian parkways', following the main streams of traffic but protected from them. The trees and shrubbery would also visually screen the houses from cars and boost residential values with green views.

Parker believed the parkway concept to be a refreshing alternative to the ubiquitous ribbon development (Creese 1966, 262). This had been an unwelcome and unsightly feature of much suburban expansion where built development, often poor quality and treeless, would closely follow the line of new roads extending out into previously rural areas (Williams-Ellis 1928, 162). Parker believed the parkway would eliminate the usual ribbons of 'shoddy houses, cheap shacks, petrol filling stations, garages, advertisement hordings, shabby tea-rooms and miserable shops' (Parker 1937, 19). In terms of traffic management, there would be free-flowing traffic, permanently open and clear of any parked cars. It is interesting to note that as a result of Parker's experience at Wythenshawe, the greenbelt in his philosophy was beginning to be elongated rather than circular because he felt that was more consonant with the velocity and direction of traffic (Creese 1966, 266). After the Second World War objections were raised that there was too much traffic passing through the area (*ibid.*, 263). Even more objections followed as Princess Parkway was extended out from Manchester beyond its first stopping point at Altrincham Road.

It was always intended to continue Princess Parkway south to Ringway, the new city airport (opened in 1938) and beyond (Miller 2010, 85). However, the *City of Manchester Plan 1945* recognised that the parkway would become a barrier, dividing rather than uniting Wythenshawe. Nevertheless, in 1969 work began on upgrading the parkway to motorway standard and the route was renamed the M56, part of a major motorway construction project eventually connecting Manchester and Cheshire. Some 50,000 trees and shrubs were sacrificed in the parkway upgrade, although this was compensated later by some additional planting (Deakin 1989, 152). For many people, what had been planned by Parker as a pioneering road renowned for its beautiful landscaping was now just another motorway.

Throughout the Wythenshawe development existing trees of amenity value were protected, often by adjusting the layout of the buildings and hard infrastructure. In the layout of the residential neighbourhoods Parker was influenced by the Canadian planner Noulan Cauchon who advocated the hexagon as opposed to the rectangle as the basis for residential street planning (Stern *et al.* 2013, 240). This made possible a 10% reduction in house length thereby saving on street length per house and creating safer and fewer road intersections. Parker extensively employed Cauchon hexagons in laying out the Roundwood estate in the Northenden section of Wythenshawe, widely agreed as the most confusing district in the suburb.

An assessment of early street tree planting across Wythenshawe was not undertaken for this research. Instead, two contrasting estates were explored in some detail. The Roundwood Estate is a district of private and mainly semi-detached housing located between the Parkway and the village. It has grass verges alongside of most of its roads that were planted soon after construction with mainly small ornamental trees such as flowering cherries and birch. While a number of original trees have now gone, evidenced by the empty sections of grass verge, there has also been some occasional replanting in recent years. Overall, the Roundwood Estate still looks leafy and attractive and its desirability is reflected in the current house prices.

The Benchill Estate in Wythenshawe is a vast area of council houses, with the typical inter-war arrangement of short terraces and semi-detached housing. Many of the roads originally had grass verges on either side. Photographs taken soon after the estate was completed show plenty of large mature trees of native

and indigenous species retained at the side of the new roads, usually in verges or small grass plots (Figure 69). There was also some new planting in the grass verges with common lime a popular choice. Roads without grass verges were generally devoid of trees. Nowadays, it is pleasing to see that many of the remnant trees remain as well as some of the early planting. However, there are also parts of Benchill with long stretches of grass verge or hard-surfaced footway without a tree in sight. Overall, the street treecover is now very patchy and there is little evidence of recent tree planting. While the Roundwood Estate has remained a relatively prosperous area, the fortunes of the Benchill Estate have declined dramatically. In 2000, Benchill was named in the Index of Multiple Deprivation as the most deprived ward out of 8414 in England. Following a visit in 2007 by David Cameron, then leader of the Opposition, the estate became notorious in the eyes of the popular media as a symbol of 'Broken Britain' (Hughes 2010).

Parker and his co-workers always regarded Wythenshawe as another garden city and in 1945 Unwin went as far as to praise it as the most perfect example of this (Rutherford 2014, 34). In reality it was always a garden suburb with an industrial zone. It is ironic that it has achieved fame as 'the world's largest council estate' rather than as the garden city that the planners intended. In many respects, the incorporation of American planning ideas, and the effort to balance

FIGURE 69. At Wythenshawe near Manchester in the 1920s a major inter-war municipal housing project was started that was intended to be another garden city. Its Benchill Estate had the typical inter-war arrangement of short terraces and semi-detached housing. Photographs taken soon after the estate was completed show plenty of large mature trees of native and indigenous species retained at the side of the new roads. This photo of Broadoak Road was taken around 1932.

the neighbourhood unit with the motor age, marks Wythenshawe as an end point to the long cycle of the garden city movement and not a new stage going forward (Stern *et al.* 2013, 240). The garden cities had promised so much and while they had failed to live up to all expectations, some beautifully landscapes suburbs with many miles of tree-lined roads had been created. However, in the words of historian Tristam Hunt:

> What they represent more than anything else is a slice of prosperous suburbia; beautiful, green and carefully designed with a remarkable collection of well-tended private gardens, but suburbia nonetheless ... This transition to suburbia was the historical tragedy of the Garden City movement.
>
> Hunt 2004, 328

Today's politicians, faced with a severe housing shortfall and rampant property prices in London and other 'hotspots', are again turning to the idea of the Garden City. How much any new initiative will reflect Howard's vision remains to be seen.

The New Towns programme

Launched after the Second World War, the New Towns Programme of 1946 to 1970 was a massive urban planning initiative that signalled a prolific period of urban development in Britain. In total, 32 new towns were designated following the *New Towns Act* of 1946 (Schaffer 1970; Alexander 2009). The New Towns programme owes a considerable debt to the Garden Cities movement and in many respects the ideas of Howard and his followers were vindicated by it (*ibid.*, 53–64). Although the idea was regularly debated between the wars, nothing was done. It was only after the Second World War that the devastation and urgent need for reconstruction promoted some action. The Labour government elected in 1945 was sympathetic to the planners' vision for the new towns and it also conformed to their socialist belief that the state should play a greater role in production and development. The *New Towns Act* of 1946 decreed that new town policy was to be implemented not by central government or the local authorities, but by individual and separate development agencies, the New Town Development Corporations, established specifically for the purpose of planning and building the new towns. These corporations were appointed and financed by government and given a degree of independence that the local authorities did not have.

Between 1946 and 1950, 14 new towns were designated, known as the 'first generation' (Morris 1997, 92). The first of these was Stevenage in Hertfordshire, designated in 1946. Eight were established in a ring around London and these were Bracknell, Crawley, Basildon, Hemel Hempstead, Stevenage, Harlow, Hatfield and Welwyn Garden City (first founded in 1920 as a garden city). These were intended to relieve congestion and pressure on housing in the capital. The other six provisional new towns were established to meet the special needs of regional decline in various parts of Britain. After Cumbernauld in 1956, the fifteenth new town, the government suspended the programme and embarked on what was known as the expanded towns programme (Alexander 2009, 41–51). This involved the substantial expansion of some existing towns to accommodate the overspill population from the cities. It was not regarded by government as particularly successful and was shelved in favour of more new towns, generally known as the 'second generation'. This comprised a second wave (1961–1964) of several new towns, followed by a third and final wave (1967–1970) involving several more.

Each first-generation new town had a population target of about 50,000 people (Morris 1997, 92). This gave an acceptable level of density and a convenient relationship of housing to industry, the town centre and the countryside. The industrial and residential districts were placed in separate zones, surrounding a geographically central town centre. The residential districts were based on the concept of the neighbourhood unit, usually of several thousand people, with a primary school, a few shops, a pub and a community centre. They were given a physical identity by main roads and mini-green belts separating each other. The vast majority of the housing was low-rise, which was actually cheaper to build at the time than high-rise blocks.

While the overall success of these pioneering urban settlements is still widely debated, there is no doubt the initiative involved the creation of many innovative green landscapes. The first-generation new towns, in particular, placed considerable emphasis on pleasant landscaping (Anon 1946; Schaffer 1970, 44; Morris 1997, 96). Hemel Hempstead, Crawley and Glenrothes were considered to be outstanding examples with good hard and soft landscaping in town centres and careful choice of trees and shrubs in housing areas. However, our purpose is to give an account of the street trees that were planted. While every new town was somewhat different in the nature and extent of its street tree planting, a few general points can be made.

While the new towns placed much emphasis on trees and landscaping, this did not necessarily translate into many miles of street trees. Trends in the design of the new towns were to result in a significant movement away from the use of conventional street trees. Some of these applied to the design of residential areas and were initially highlighted in the government's *Dudley Report on Housing* in 1944 (Alexander 2009, 74). New communities were to be built by using zoned separation of residential housing estates from industrial estates, the formation of housing into 'neighbourhood units', and the separation of these from each other by major roads and greenspace. The planner Frederick Gibberd's insertion of 'green wedges' throughout Harlow new town is an example of this. As a result, the use of trees shifted from traditional street or roadside planting to informal clumps of trees on public open space and on embankments along major roads. The tree planting alongside the grid system of roads at Milton Keynes exemplifies this where countless thousands of trees make a vital contribution to the new city's green infrastructure (Walker 1982, 30). Within the new town housing estates themselves, traditional street tree planting was also much reduced from the garden city or garden suburb models. The model for estate design called Radburn planning had been promoted by the government after the Second World War (see Chapter 7) (Ravetz 2001, 102–103). This was now a fundamental design principle applied, to a greater or lesser extent, across Britain's new towns (Alexander 2009, 76–78). As the houses were no longer arranged in rows along streets but in pedestrian-accessed blocks that cars could not penetrate, the whole idea of street trees was largely redundant. Roads that accessed these blocks tended to have informal clumps of trees on open space and not in neatly spaced lines alongside the road.

Another trend in new town planning that was to impact on conventional street tree planting was focused on the town centres. This was the creation of pedestrianised zones or precincts in town centres in which most or all vehicle traffic was prohibited. Pedestrianisation aims to provide better accessibility and mobility for pedestrians, to enhance the volume of shopping and business activity in the area and to improve the attractiveness of the local environment in terms of aesthetics, air pollution, noise and accidents involving pedestrians (Chiquetto 1997). The idea was resisted by some professionals involved with the new towns who preferred the traditional pattern of an all-purpose shopping street forming the spine of the town centre (Gibberd 1972, 100). Nevertheless, it became an increasingly common feature of the new towns, although resisted by Crawley and Hemel Hempstead. An obvious consequence of pedestrian zones is the absence of traditional street trees. Where trees are included in the landscape of these zones they are generally located in the hard-surfaced pedestrian walkways, in planters, or in patches of open space. Pedestrian zones have now become a feature in the redesign of many town and city centres in Britain. While it has meant the end of traditional street trees, the opportunity has often been taken to actually increase treecover in the urban core.

This account of the new towns concludes by looking at two quite different examples of street trees in the town centre. The first is Crawley where efforts were made to retain existing mature trees and the second is Milton Keynes and the creation of its boulevards.

Crawley

Crawley in West Sussex was designated as one of the first new towns in 1947 and since 1974 has come under the jurisdiction of Crawley Borough Council (Gwynne 1990, 155–157). The 5920 acres (2396 ha) of land set aside for the new town was predominantly open countryside in a part of the country that was still relatively well-wooded and with plenty of fine individual trees, especially in the hedgerows. From an early stage the planners and landscape architects were keen to retain as much as possible of the existing mature treescape. This would help to give a mature look to the otherwise 'raw' landscapes while the extensive tree planting became established (Green and Allen 1993, 35).

Many of the retained trees were native English oaks up to 200 years old that suddenly found themselves incorporated into new urban and suburban scenes.

While a substantial number were kept in the neighbourhood 'greens', many were also retained in the roadside verges of housing estates. Perhaps the most challenging task was to retain a handful of large mature oaks by the side of busy streets in the new town centre. When this was built, the old High Street, with its sixteenth century buildings and old coaching inn, was carefully preserved and linked to the new town centre by a pedestrian way (Schaffer 1970, 263). In advance of the development a tree survey was conducted and trees were marked for either felling or retention. A photograph from 1950 of the Northgate area to the north of High Street shows two old and dilapidated oak pollards in the footway, which were later removed (Bastable 1986, 138). Mature trees in good shape and health and in suitable locations were retained. This included a large oak in the High Street about 300 ft (91 m) from the coaching inn. Photos from *c.* 1900 show this as a semi-mature tree in a grassed area in front of the buildings on western side of the street. For protection it was retained in a small fenced-off open space where the tree continues to thrive today. A few more large oaks were retained in the Boulevard and with the addition of new planting this is now a very leafy road in the heart of Crawley (Figure 70).

FIGURE 70. Crawley is one of the new towns and considered to be a good example of hard and soft landscaping in its town centre and commended for the choice of trees and shrubs in its housing areas. It is also notable for its efforts to retain some large oaks in the town centre that were remnants from the previous landscape. This is the main thoroughfare called The Boulevard photographed in 1958.

For a number of years following the development of the town centre, some of the retained trees did not thrive and there were signs of significant dieback in the crown. In order to ensure the safety of the pedestrians and avoid damage to parked cars, deadwood had to be removed biannually. In recent years the trees have adjusted much better to their urban environment and now seem to be thriving. The mature trees retained in the neighbourhood 'greens' and alongside roads in the new housing estates had mixed fortunes. Those located in public open space and in the gardens of houses usually coped quite well with their new environment. While the oak trees located in the footway or verges by the roadside seemed initially to have coped well, by the late 1960s quite a few were showing signs of stress. After several years of progressive dieback the trees became 'stag-headed', a condition where large dead branches have the appearance of deer antlers sticking out of what is left of the foliage. The decline was said to be due to a build up of abiotic stress factors resulting from disruption to the rooting zone in the initial development process. Rather than fell the trees immediately, a programme of drastic pruning was instituted where the major branches were reduced leaving the trees resembling coat-stands. This was intended as a 'kill or cure' treatment that might 'shock' the tree into producing vigorous new growth that could then be trained into a new tree crown. Unfortunately, many of the trees died and had to be removed. While the efforts often ended in failure, Crawley should be congratulated for trying to incorporate these magnificent trees into its new town landscape. The survival of the large mature oak trees in the town centre is an indication of what can be achieved with careful planning and attention to detail. The overall landscape at Crawley is now regarded as one of the best examples in the new towns (Morris 1997, 96).

Milton Keynes

Milton Keynes in Buckinghamshire was designated in 1967 as the only green-field 'new city' and was planned for a population of 250,000 to anticipate the considerable growth in the south-east (Morris 1997, 117–119). It is widely considered the most successful of all the new towns and is unlike the others in a number of respects. The planners set out to create an attractively landscaped settlement with several linear parks that ran right through the urban area. The town-wide park system eventually occupied 20% of the land and was linked to the circulation system for pedestrians, cyclists and vehicles. While some new towns such as Runcorn were planned around their public transport system, Milton Keynes was planned for cars and other vehicles (Morris 1997, 118).

What is especially interesting about the landscape at Milton Keynes has been its emphasis on trees. The original design concept aimed to create the visual impression of 'a city in a forest' and the city's foresters and landscapers planted millions of trees from its own nursery in Newlands (Walker 1981). The extent of tree planting has been quite extraordinary and by 2006 the urban area had

20 million trees. There had been some challenges along the way, especially when the drought of 1976 laid waste to 200,000 newly-planted trees and shrubs (Bendixson and Platt, 1992, 181). Nevertheless, the rapid replacement of these losses ensured this was just a temporary setback.

A range of marketing strategies were employed to attract businesses and residents to Milton Keynes and many focused on promoting the city's 'green' image and especially its many trees (Bendixson and Platt 1992, 8). An early marketing strategy was developed around the name 'City of Trees', since trees were seen as a single unifying feature upon which to develop the character of Milton Keynes as a special place (Slater 2001). Advertisements appeared on television urging people to 'come and live and work in Milton Keynes – City of Trees'. Apart from the extraordinary extent of tree planting along the city's grid road system, the arboricultural feature that impresses most visitors is the boulevards of Central Milton Keynes (CMK), the city's business and civic centre.

In designing the road layout of CMK a strong influence on the planners was the work of Baron Hausmann and his famous boulevards of Paris (Walker 1982, 58). The London squares and roads such as the Mall and the Embankment were also an important influence. It was thought that a similar impact to these classic and formal urban treescapes could be created in CMK and this was reflected in the Milton Keynes Master Plan, which was then delivered on the ground (Hill 2007, 15). The CMK district has dual carriageway streets running broadly east-west called boulevards and north–south called gates. The three boulevards are called Silbury, Midsummer and Avebury, names which were chosen for their association with ancient sites to highlight the alignment of Midsummer Boulevard along the summer solstice axis (Figure 71). Each boulevard is nearly 250 ft (75 m) wide between building faces and has four rows of London plane trees at 20 ft (6 m) spacing, two rows located on a central reservation surfaced with gravel and the outer two rows in grass verges flanking the carriageways (*ibid.*, 90). The choice of the plane reflected the desire of the planners and landscape architects to have big and resilient forest trees lining the side of roads in the city centre to make an impact (Salter pers. comm., 2016). They would also be higher than the buildings and act as the skyline. It was thought that when the plane trees matured in about 90 years the scale of the boulevards and the stature of the trees would be fully appreciated. Although the planes did not initially thrive in their exposed locations and in the wet clay soil, once they had survived the first few years they began to flourish (Hill 2007, 99).

The gates in CMK have a less uniform design. Saxon Gate and Grafton Gate are dual carriageways and enjoy similar treatments to the boulevards but utilise horse chestnut instead of plane with grassed central reservations (Milton Keynes Council 2013, 11). Large car parking areas at block ends were also planted with planes. Outside the buildings on the walkways to the boulevards and side streets a wide range of secondary species were planted, including *Prunus, Sorbus, Acer, Robinia, Fraxinus ornus, Alnus cordata* and more recently *Carpinus betulus.*

FIGURE 71. If they are protected and nurtured then the trees that comprise the magnificent boulevards of Milton Keynes should eventually rank alongside the best examples of street tree planting in Europe. This is Silbury Boulevard in Central Milton Keynes photographed in 2016.

PHOTO: CAROLINE BROWN.

Today, the trees on the boulevards and side streets of CMK are generally in fine condition and there are firm guidelines to ensure they continue to be protected in any future development (Milton Keynes Council 2009). Nevertheless, there are concerns that plans to redevelop part of CMK will result in the loss of a significant number of forest-type trees on the boulevards and their replacement with smaller ornamentals (Urban Eden 2016). There was also concern that the plane trees would suffer from various diseases now active in Britain, not least in central London, but so far this has not materialised (Salter pers. comm., 2016). The focus is now on the horse chestnuts as various pathogens affecting this species spread across the country. Any threat to these magnificent boulevards must be taken very seriously. Of all the attractive treescapes created in the new towns, they are among the finest. When the trees of the boulevards of Milton Keynes eventually mature, they should rank alongside the best examples of street tree planting in Europe.

CHAPTER TEN

Threats and Conflicts in the Street Environment

The urban environment has always been a tough habitat for trees and those in streets often suffer the worst possible conditions. This chapter explores the history of some of the most potent threats and conflicts involving trees in the street environment. This not only includes those that are above ground and often more obvious but also those below ground that can be less apparent.

For several centuries, if there were any street trees at all in Britain, they were located in the roadway. There was no footway or kerb to provide protection and these trees were exposed to whatever came along. As noted in Chapter 4, most streets had no separation of pedestrian from vehicular traffic until at least the eighteenth century and often much later. For this reason street trees were regarded as an unnecessary obstruction and planting was discouraged. Then, with the start of the Victorian street tree movement in the mid-nineteenth century an increasing number of trees were planted in streets. The conditions were far from ideal. The busy, dirty, crowded and often cramped street environment of our Victorian cities and industrial towns were particularly hostile to successful tree establishment. While the situation has generally improved, our streets still remain one of the most challenging environments for trees. Lack of space and light, compacted and contaminated soil, suffocated roots and air pollution continue to take their toll. Then, either through lack of funding or just sheer neglect, there is often the absence of essential maintenance to ensure the trees, once planted, survive and flourish. Unlike trees in their natural habitat, street trees need plenty of care and attention, particularly when young, if they are to have much hope of growing to maturity. Without this, many of those harmful agencies in the urban environment begin to attack the already weakened tree. The first symptoms of ill-health are often shown by the leaves. These turn yellow and then brown and fall prematurely. Dead twigs become dead branches as the tree steadily dies back. When death eventually comes, or even before this, the tree has to be removed for safety reasons. Dead and dying street trees pose a major hazard to road users, pedestrians and property and cannot be left standing at the side of the road. Even where these trees manage to survive, the slow reduction in crown size through die-back and the pruning of deadwood can give the appearance that the trees are steadily shrinking (Figure 72). It is not surprising that the average life-span of a street tree is usually a lot less than the same species growing in an urban park.

Air pollution

Air pollution has been a significant threat to the health of our urban trees from as early as the seventeenth century (Johnston 2015, 74–76; Elliott 2016, 259–295). Thomas Fairchild (1722) was one of the first writers to delve into the subject in his influential book *The City Gardener* where he described the smoky and dirt conditions in London and made recommendation on tolerant plants. With the coming of the Industrial Revolution and stream power, cities became even dirtier (Trinder 1982). Those residents that could afford it ensured their homes were at a safe distance from the polluting factories. The wealthier suburbs were generally to the west of towns and cities, to avoid the air pollution that prevailing winds carried. As the problem of air pollution became more apparent, understanding of it also increased. The Victorians identified two types of air pollution, particulate and gaseous, and the different sources of each (Ravenscroft 1883, 6; Hartig 1894, 301). They also realised that very few conifers succeeded in or near industrial towns because when the dust and dirt clogged the stomata in the conifer needles, these remained on the tree for a few years, unlike deciduous trees that got fresh leaves every year. Fortunately, conifers with cypresses-like foliage did fare a little better.

In the late nineteenth century there was much discussion in the horticultural press about the difficulties of getting trees to grow in the polluted atmosphere of many big cities and northern towns (*Woods and Forests* 1885, 73–74). Indeed, as far as street trees were concerned it was a popular belief that these simply would not grow in the smoky cities (Walker 1890, 1). Although these pessimistic attitudes undoubtedly slowed the momentum of the Victorian street tree movement, where planting was undertaken successfully this was the best form of reassurance. The establishment of street trees on London's Embankment, despite some initial problems, was particularly influential in this respect (Webster 1893, 123).

Conflicts with motorised vehicles

Of all the agencies which have had a damaging impact on the extent of Britain's street trees, the most devastating has been the introduction onto our roads of motorised vehicles. Before that time, any direct damage inflicted on street trees by horse-powered transport was fairly limited. Occasionally, it was reported that a runaway horse and its cart had collided with a young street tree (Pettigrew 1901, 14). There were also incidences of horses gnawing the bark and leaves of young trees (Salter 1953, 7). However, this was nothing compared with what was to come.

In the 1890s and 1900s, electric trams were introduced into several major British cities and this rapidly became a popular mode of transport (Lay 1992, 134; Taylor and Green 2001, 48). When new tramways were constructed this often resulted in the damage or removal of large numbers of street trees that were in

FIGURE 72. Even when street trees survive, the slow reduction in crown size that often occurs through die-back and the pruning of deadwood can give the appearance that the trees are steadily shrinking. These two lime trees were planted at roughly the same time but the one on the right has really struggled over the years and will probably soon be felled.

the path of the proposed route. When tramlines were installed along the Victoria Embankment in 1906, there was a lack of protection to the young street trees. There is contemporary photographic evidence of soil and hardcore heaped up against the base of some trees to a depth of at least 4ft (1.2 m) (Harley 2005, 63). While there is no record of permanent damage to the trees, this is evidence of poor practice. In Glasgow in 1949, an avenue of 260 trees along the centre of Knightswood Boulevard (now the Great Western Road) that formed a fine tree-lined approach to the city was removed to make way for trams (GTLS 1949). The trees had been planted in 1932 with funding from public donations. Owing to the age of the trees only a few of the smaller ones could be transplanted to another site. When trees were retained or planted next to tramways, they were often subject to negative comments in autumn when the wet leaves lying on the line caused problems. This was usually a case of poor traction for the trams but could occasionally be far more serious. In Lancaster in 1920, the *Gardeners' Chronicle* (1920, 164) reported that wet leaves had 'caused a tramcar to get out of control, leaving the rails and dashing into some buildings, with the result that many passengers were injured and one died from the effect of injuries received'.

The introduction of tram services also had a negative impact on the extent of street tree planting. It greatly restricted the space for the crowns of street trees along these tram routes, particularly from the overhead cables that carried the electricity. After World War II when planners saw trams as old fashioned and a hindrance to the free flow of traffic, they began to disappear from British cities. The removal of the track was sometimes an opportunity for highway tree planting. In Birmingham, for example, the trams used to run along the central reservation of Bristol Road but when the tramway closed in 1952, the reservation was planted up with a long avenue of deciduous and coniferous trees (Johnston 2015, 187).

From the 1900s onwards, motor cars became an increasingly common sight on British roads. From being an expensive rarity enjoyed by the wealthy, their numbers soon multiplied as costs came down and demand soared (Lay 1992, 156–159). Cars were soon followed by numerous lorries for commercial and industrial use. The increases in vehicle numbers and speeds precipitated some fundamental changes in road construction and layout and led to a rapid expansion in Britain's road network. These new roads and road-widening schemes generally had a negative impact on existing street trees. This was especially damaging with the huge expansion in the road network following the dramatic growth in car ownership after the Second World War. From the early twentieth century many of the main arterial routes into towns and cities were tree-lined and when these were subject to improvement schemes the trees often disappeared with few replacements (O'Brien 1993, 2). A history of street trees in the second half of the twentieth century can seem like an ongoing battle between highway engineers and landscape professionals. Space for street trees was constantly being lost and claiming back new space was invariably an uphill struggle. One road improvement scheme that did attract praise was carried out along Park Lane, London, in 1958. This famous tree-lined thoroughfare that runs along the eastern boundary of Hyde Park was made a dual carriageway. To achieve this, a large section of Hyde Park bordering the road was lost. However, a line of majestic plane trees was retained on the central reservation ensuring that Park Lane's reputation as an arboreal landmark would continue (Johnston 2015, 173).

In the early days of road improvement schemes the treatment of the road surface often caused concern to tree and landscape professionals. The surface of many nineteenth century urban roads was comprised of little wooden blocks (Hammond 1994, 73). Later, when roads were resurfaced with tarmac or asphalt the blocks were sold for fuel. These new road surfaces were initially viewed with suspicion because it was thought that the roots of nearby street trees would be deprived of air owing to the supposed impermeability of these materials. One case that featured in the newspapers and gardening press at the time was the resurfacing of Sutton Court Road in London. As well as being regarded as one of London's prettiest thoroughfares with its robinia trees (*Robinia pseudoacacia*), it was adjoining the Royal Horticultural Gardens at Chiswick. It is worth repeating what one correspondent, who was not alone, thought of this road improvement scheme:

> The Local Board, however, have now got possession of the road, and their first proceeding has been to kerb and channel the sides with stone. Then they covered the paths with asphalte, thus excluding from the roots of the unfortunate Acacias [*Robinia*], henceforth and forever, all moisture and air; and finally, they are macadamising the road, so that every drop of rain which falls on it shall pass into the stone channels, and thence into the drains, to be carried where it is not wanted – into the Thames. About one foot square space has been left round the stems, but it need hardly be said that the end of these charming trees must be near. How true it is, that if God gave us the country, man – and too often very stupid man – makes the town.
>
> *Gardeners' Chronicle* 1883, 51

As well as destroying trees the construction of roads could also give rise to new opportunities to plant, although the extent of this varied considerably. It depended largely on the motivation of the highway authority to commit funding for this but also on the opportunities to plant trees offered by the road design. Roads with wide grass verges were often well planted, although sometimes the choice of small ornamental species did not make full use of the space available. Roundabouts were also becoming popular for both new and existing roads, although they were generally not planted with trees (Wells 1970, 301). The increasing volume and speed of motorised traffic on roads brought an end to one common arboricultural practice. Up until the 1910s it was not unusual to plant street trees in the road itself, close to the kerb (*Gardeners' Chronicle* 1898, 238) (see Chapter 11). However, the consequences of this were now painfully obvious.

When larger vehicles such as lorries and buses were introduced onto Britain's roads this necessitated some radical pruning or planting restrictions for many street trees. The advent of motorised double-decked buses in 1923, especially in densely built-up areas with large mature street trees, caused significant difficulties. Many existing trees had to be pruned drastically so that their crowns were lifted clear of the top deck and new plantings often had to be set back some distance from the kerb (Balfour, 1935, 167). However, the precise positioning of new tree planting in the footway was still a matter of debate. While some highway engineers preferred tree planting at the back line of the footway, partly to give greater clearance for vehicles, others still regarded the correct position to be within a foot of the kerb (Pettigrew, 1937, 183).

As the volume of road traffic increased it became clear that the presence of roadside trees could also have a negative impact on driving conditions, particularly in inclement weather. Roads shaded by nearby trees were slow to dry out when soaked by rain and the ice on frosty roads was slow to melt. Fallen leaves in autumn, combined with wet or frosty conditions could make the road surface especially treacherous for drivers. The truth of this was brought home in dramatic fashion to many arboriculturists in 1930 when Ernest Wilson, the great plant collector and authority on trees, was killed with his wife in Massachusetts, USA, by their car skidding from this cause (Balfour 1935, 167). Although street trees can be involved in serious or fatal accidents, they can also save the lives of pedestrians when cars leave the road. When the *Gardeners' Chronicle* (1931, 27) reported that many of Bermondsey's young street trees were being destroyed by cars, it also noted how mature street trees can act as a barrier to protect pedestrians.

Probably the greatest threat to street trees in Britain in recent times has arisen from the dramatic growth in car ownership. Mainly since the 1970s, this has led to increasingly intense competition for parking spaces in many residential streets. Continual parking underneath trees on grass verges has caused compaction in the rooting zone and many trees have suffered. Thousands of young street trees have also been fatally damaged when cars have reversed over them when parking on the verge or footway. Competition for parking has also prompted numerous homeowners to pave or concrete over their front gardens to provide personal car parking spaces (RHS 2006). This has led to countless garden trees being felled and the loss of these planting sites in the future, thus diminishing the contribution of privately owned trees to the streetscape. What has often received less attention are the many publicly owned street trees that have also been removed to facilitate access to these parking spaces via what are called dropped kerb vehicle crossings. The impact of this on Britain's suburbs was highlighted in Chapters 6 and 7. Not only have countless street trees been removed but the opportunities to plant more trees outside houses have been greatly reduced. From the high density inner city areas to the residential suburbs, many people now think that space for car parking by their home is more important than street trees.

Above ground conflicts

As Britain emerged from the Victorian era some of the earliest street tree planting was reaching maturity and it became obvious that the presence of large trees in many streets was fraught with potential problems. The typical urban street was steadily becoming a very crowded place. This did not just relate to the volume of traffic or pedestrians. The footways were also becoming crowded with the addition of street furniture such as traffic signs and lights, bollards and barriers, post boxes, street lighting, telephone boxes, bus and tram stops, taxi stands, benches, waste bins, public lavatories, fountains, watering troughs and memorials. Finding sufficient room for even a small number of street trees, particularly large-growing species, was becoming an increasingly difficult task.

Problems of light

Some of the first complaints about the presence of street trees related to the blocking out of daylight, particularly to the front rooms of residential properties. The obstruction of light to residential property caused by urban trees has a long history in English law, originating in 1663 with the 'doctrine of ancient lights' (Kerr 1865). This refers to the right of householder to the light received through his windows and the law stated that the windows used for light by an owner for 20 years or more could not be obstructed by the erection of an edifice or by any other act by an adjacent landowner. There are several caveats to this and there remains much public misunderstanding of the issue. Local authorities, the owners of most street trees, have always received many requests to prune large street trees to facilitate more light. However, individual requests are invariably declined as these trees are generally pruned systematically, every few years. Numerous references can be found in magazines and newspapers throughout the years to residents' complaints about overgrown street trees blocking out light. An early example was in Camberwell Grove, a street in south London, where the planting of horse chestnuts around 1880 had by 1907 'grown out of bounds' resulting in the dense foliage restricting daylight (*Gardeners' Chronicle* 1910a, 232) (Figure 73). In all these cases local authorities are requested either to prune the trees heavily or replace them with smaller ornamental species or those with less dense foliage. In 1915, a consultant's report to the Borough of Kensington recommended that planting should be focused on those streets which run north and south. It is stated that where lines of trees run east and west, they become a nuisance by blocking light to those living on the north side of the road (*Gardeners' Chronicle* 1915, 137). In a paper presented in 1934 to a meeting of the Institution of Municipal and County Engineers, the arboriculturist Frederick Balfour highlighted these light problems as a major liability of street trees. Consequently, he was not an advocate of

FIGURE 73. An early example of street trees blocking out light to residential properties was in Camberwell Grove, a street in south London, where horse chestnuts planted around 1880 had subsequently 'grown out of bounds' resulting in the dense foliage restricting daylight. This photograph was taken in 1907 just before extensive 'pruning' work was undertaken.

planting large forest-type trees in many streets, generally favouring small ornamentals. He declared:

> It is patent to anyone who drives along the Chelsea Embankment and on countless other planted London thoroughfares that it is little less than an outrage on the owners of house property that light and view should be denied them by the close proximity of rows of planes, the heavy foliage of which reached their windows. In such situations crabs, cherries, laburnums or other flowering trees of low stature are what the situation demands.

Balfour 1935, 165

Related to the problems of restricted daylight is the conflict between trees and street lighting. Just as residents have always complained about restricted daylight, many have also objected to trees interfering with street lighting at night. This began when the earliest street tree planting was maturing in an age when streets were lit by gaslight (*Gardeners' Chronicle* 1879, 693). In responding to these complaints with heavy pruning local authorities have often been accused of disfiguring trees. Alternatively, in the days before there were many motorised vehicles, rather than place trees and street lights in the same line along the footway, the lamp posts were sometimes placed down the centre of the road where the lights would not be overshadowed by the trees (Figure 74). Street lighting can have a disruptive effect on the tree's natural cycles where these are regulated by photoperiodism, the tree's physiological reaction to the length of day or night. One common effect is that the leaves emerge earlier than normal in the spring and stay on the tree longer in the autumn. In the long term this can have a debilitating effect on the trees. Some of the first studies on this were reported in the 1930s in the *Gardeners' Chronicle* (1933, 93) and

FIGURE 74. In the days before there were many motorised vehicles, rather than place trees and street lights in the same line along the footway where the trees could block out the light, the lamp posts were sometimes placed down the centre of the road where the lights would not be overshadowed by the trees. This is an example with plane trees in The Grove in Hammersmith, London, photographed in 1910.

the *American Journal of Botany* (Matzke 1936). These found that different tree species varied in their susceptibility and that the impact was more marked in the case of electric light than in that of gas or petroleum lighting.

A recent conflict between street trees and levels of light involves, ironically, the use of 'green' energy. The number of British households with solar panels increases every year and this has led to conflicts between solar access and the shade cast by trees in streets and residential gardens (Thayer 1983).

Overhead wires

Another source of conflict with street trees can occur with the many overhead wires and cables that criss-cross our city centre thoroughfares and residential streets. One of the first people to raise this issue was James McNab (1872, 1719), President of the Botanical Society of Edinburgh, in a paper to the Society in 1872. McNab highlighted the 'disfigurement annually going on to our roadside trees all over the country by the introduction of telegraph wires'. While in many instances he observed poor and careless pruning, in some districts the work was being undertaken with sensitivity and good practice. In his view the work needed much closer scrutiny and regulation. This invariable did not happen and the popular press and gardening magazines continued to report on the widespread mutilation and loss of trees. Nevertheless, there were some encouraging instances of cooperation between those responsible for street trees and the telegraph companies. In Bourneville before the First World War the early problems of severe pruning to street trees by telephone engineers and their manual workers were resolved through discussion with staff at Bourneville Village Trust (Salter 1953, 5). It was agreed that one engineer would be responsible for overseeing all the necessary tree pruning on the estate and this individual was given specific instructions on how the work should be undertaken to ensure that is was done in a sensitive manner without leaving unsightly trees.

There were similar problems with poor standards of pruning on street trees to facilitate the installation and maintenance of electricity cables. Again, trees were often severely disfigured and this could sometimes send them into terminal decline. In 1911, an interesting article appeared in the *Gardeners' Chronicle* that highlighted another problem with electricity cables and this was the harmful impact of the electric current itself:

> With the extending application of electricity to domestic and industrial uses we may expect more and more electric wires for our trees to contend against. Up to the present we have not had in this country any very serious trouble through escaping current, but in those neighbourhoods where electricity is much in use there have been many deaths amongst street trees. The subject is even more likely to cause trouble between the engineer and the town forester than the gas question, as it is not always so obvious what is the cause of the injury, especially as the damage may result from an instantaneous discharge. Of the two classes of current the direct is

much more injurious than the alternating. Fortunately, up to the present, we have few direct currents except those driving trams and railways.

Gardeners' Chronicle 1911a, 324

Other above ground conflicts

When street trees were first planted in the shopping and commercial districts of towns and cities it was not long before the authorities started to receive complaints about trees blocking the view of shop signs and advertising boards. In the 1850s the Austrian author Max Schlesinger (1853, 23–24) remarked on the proliferation of advertising boards on walls and temporary hoardings in London, which was in contrast to his experience of cities on the Continent. When the Victorian street tree movement was having a major impact in the 1880s and 1890s these signs and boards were a long established urban feature whereas the trees were something new. This often led to sharp differences of opinion about the benefits of planting trees in many streets between those who admired them and the shopkeepers who feared their businesses would be adversely affected (*The Garden* 1901, 118). The matter was usually resolved when the local authority promised to remove the lower branches of the trees as they matured to ensure the shop fronts and signage was visible (Figure 75). However, as late as the 1920s one landscape planner was saying that in shopping centres 'trees are almost always out of place' (Mattocks 1925, 255).

With the growth in television (TV) ownership since the 1950s, it was noted that trees could have a negative effect on TV reception, and street trees were often cited (AAIS 1998). Interference to signals tended to be worse when trees

FIGURE 75. As early street tree plantings began to mature in the 1880s and 1890s many shopkeepers feared their businesses would be adversely affected as the trees obscured their shops fronts and signs. The matter was usually resolved when the local authority promised to remove the lower branches of the trees as they matured to ensure greater visibility. This photograph from the late 1920s shows an example of such pruning in London Road, Thornton Heath.

were in full leaf and during bad weather conditions. Another more recent threat has resulted from the installation of thousands of CCTV cameras in urban areas. This has led to many street trees being removed or drastically pruned to facilitate improved surveillance (Body 2011).

This section concludes by mentioning some 'above ground' conflicts with street trees that have often been foremost in the public's mind. These are often considered as a 'nuisance' but can still have significant cost implications and result in costly insurance claims. The problems result from various types of tree debris dropping from trees, such as leaves blocking guttering, wet leaves and messy fruit creating slippery footways, and the sticky honey dew from lime and sycamore trees that tarnishes the paintwork of parked cars. Some species of street trees, such as cherry and robinia, are notorious for producing numerous suckers that emerge in the lawns of front gardens. Frequent references to most of these problems can be found in the popular press and gardening magazines going back to the Victorian era.

Below ground conflicts

While above-ground conflicts with street trees are often more apparent in the public eye, there are also many below-ground issues that have resulted in thousands of trees being removed or drastically pruned over the past 150 years. With regard to underground utility services the problems are essentially twofold. First, the increasing presence of pipes and cables, usually located under the footway, means less space to plant and successfully establish trees. Secondly, when street trees are already present and these services need to be installed or repaired, the excavation causes severe and often fatal disruption to the tree's rooting area. During Victorian times, the construction works associated with the installation of extensive underground sewerage systems in our major cities undoubtedly led to the removal of many trees in their vicinity. As other new underground services were installed in Victorian times, such as water and gas, the construction work had a detrimental impact on many street trees in their path. It is fortunate that our understanding of tree root biology in the built environment has improved enormously in recent years enabling many of the old conflicts to be resolved without some of the previous limitations on tree growth and function (Roberts *et al.* 2006).

Underground utility services

As early as 1829, John Claudius Loudon was aware of the problems ahead with different utility services competing for space underground and the difficulty of providing convenient access for maintenance and repair. He proposed that 'under every street we would have a sewer sufficiently large and so contrived as to serve at the same time as a subway for the mains of water and gas' (Loudon 1829, 689). While this obvious solution has never been widely adopted, efforts along these lines were attempted from the 1850s. In London, approval for the new Covent Garden Approach (Garrick Street) was granted by Act of Parliament in 1857 and before this was constructed the Metropolitan Board of Works decided to invite designs that would include 'some means of obviating the expense and inconvenience attending the breaking up of the pavement for the repair of pipes, mains, sewers and other underground works' (Edwards 1898, 27). Of the 39 designs submitted the one adopted was for an arched subway under the road that would accommodate all the services, which also had 12 arched side passages to deliver the services to the nearby houses. A similar and more large-scale approach to grouping services was used in 1865 in the construction of a new street connecting Commercial Road East with Whitechapel High Street (*ibid.*, 35). This street was 1200 ft (366 m) in length and 70 ft (21.3 m) in width and beneath it, along the centre of the street, was formed an arched subway of brickwork 12 ft (3.7 m) in width and 7.5 ft (2.3 m) in height. The stated purpose of this was to 'accommodate the gas, water and other pipes, to which access was thereby given for the purpose of laying, examination and repair, without breaking up the surface of the road'. Wide access points were provided close by and these openings were covered with perforated cast-iron plates, which served to ventilate and light the interior of the subway. These entrances were protected by granite kerbs and guard posts and served as a refuge for pedestrians at road crossings.

While the idea of grouping services in a subway under the street seemed sensible to the engineers, persuading the utility companies to cooperate was not easy. The London County Council (LCC) reported that 'a difficulty has recently arisen, however, because of the inability of the Council in some cases to compel companies to place their pipes inside the subway' (Edwards 1898, 177). The LCC believed that unless compulsory powers are obtained it was likely that the subways would remain empty and the companies would continue to lay their pipes under the street surface outside the subways. In 1893, the *London County Council (Subways) Act* was passed but this never provided a satisfactory resolution of the matter. The damage caused to street trees by frequent excavation to install and maintain different services continues to this day.

As the nineteenth century drew to a close, progressive highway engineers and tree experts were increasingly pessimistic at the prospects of successfully integrating trees into many of our urban streets, particularly in the crowded city centres. In 1902, an editorial in the *Gardeners' Chronicle* summed up the general despondency at the lack of effective action in resolving conflicts between street trees and the plethora of underground utility services when it declared:

> In the case of the older streets there is a bewildering labyrinth of sewers, railways, 'tubes', water-pipes, gas-pipes, pneumatic tubes, telegraph wires, telephone circuits, and we do not know what else, which render the introduction of trees always difficult and frequently impossible. In the broad new thoroughfares in course of construction, there is room for the formation either of a central belt or of rows of trees on either side, which may be so arranged as not to interfere with the network of pipes and wires. The unhappy trees would then not be poisoned by the escape of gas, or be

subjected to injury every time the road 'is up', which as Londoners know to their cost, is the case in the aggregate for at least six months out of the twelve.

Gardeners' Chronicle 1902, 306

Another article in the *Gardeners' Chronicle* in 1910 said much the same and reflected the same pessimistic view of the prospects for successfully incorporating trees into crowded city centre streets. This time the article was also accompanied by a diagram of a section of Kingsway, London, entitled 'Hindrances to Street Trees' that graphically illustrated the point:

A section of a London street [Figure 76] shows how different are the conditions from those that obtain in a park or garden. The entire surface of the road is paved, thus shutting out air and moisture from the soil. There can be no annual mulching or forking about the roots except beneath the small gratings where the trees are planted. The surface alone presents a tremendous problem to the town planter, but the works below ground are even more discouraging, for there may be drains, sewers, gas mains, water mains, electric mains, telegraph-ways, and a host of other things which make the ground a network of pipes and cement-cased channels.

Gardeners' Chronicle 1910b, 101

As the twentieth century progressed the conflict between street trees and underground utility services became more intense. As our urban society became increasingly 'high-tech' it required more and more services with their associated

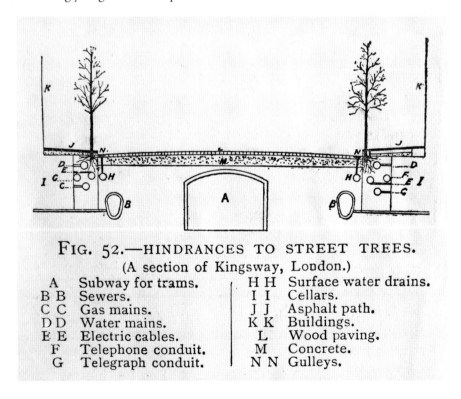

FIGURE 76. A diagram entitled 'Hindrances to Street Trees' from the *Gardeners' Chronicle* in 1910. This is actually a section of The Kingsway, a major thoroughfare in central London, and it shows the various services and infrastructure elements that can compete with the trees for space.

FIG. 52.—HINDRANCES TO STREET TREES.
(A section of Kingsway, London.)

A	Subway for trams.		H H	Surface water drains.
B B	Sewers.		I I	Cellars.
C C	Gas mains.		J J	Asphalt path.
D D	Water mains.		K K	Buildings.
E E	Electric cables.		L	Wood paving.
F	Telephone conduit.		M	Concrete.
G	Telegraph conduit.		N N	Gulleys.

cables and pipes for gas, electricity, water, telephone, cable television and broadband, located in the footways outside our houses and in streets throughout towns and cities.

As a way of avoiding any damage to street trees, it has long been suggested that a sensible way round the problem, quite literally, was to reroute the services away from the trees. Assuming that there was room to do this in a street situation, the cost of rerouting some types of services has always been very expensive. At the Arboricultural Association's national conference in 1981, a representative of the North East Electricity Board reported that the cost of the addition of two joints for an 11,000 volt cable was £1000 and for a 33,000 volt cable it was £10,000 (Deen 1981, 35). Another 'avoidance strategy' that has gained favour over the past few decades, perhaps more with landscape architects, has been the use of streetside 'planters'. These are usually very large freestanding containers, often made of concrete, that are placed on the footway or in other public spaces. Trees can be grown in these planters, although they have to be removed and replaced at some point when they outgrow them. One of the earliest references in Britain to the use of planters to avoid the problems of underground utilities was made in the 1920s (Mattocks 1925, 255). In 1974, Professor Gordon King of the University of Massachusetts promoted the idea at the Arboricultural Association's annual conference (Anon 1974, 19). King reported that local authorities in over 60 American cities now made extensive use of planters.

In the early 1990s, the introduction of cable television in Britain escalated the scale of the problem with underground services into an entirely new dimension (Tuffs 1995, 16). It required a vast programme of civil engineering that would involve excavating service trenches along the length of almost every street in the country. In the early stages of this work, little consideration was given to tree roots and this led to the loss of many mature street trees. The loss of roots resulted in trees becoming unstable and falling over in high winds or being felled as a safety precaution. Some trees just suffered a slow death as the loss of vital roots critically reduced their ability to take up water and nutrients. Local authorities became increasingly alarmed that unless adequate safeguards were established and implemented quickly, the work could result in the wholesale destruction of much of the nation's heritage of street trees. As the provision of public utilities had always been regarded by government as an essential service, any work undertaken in accordance with this did not need planning permission. In the absence of planning control many local authority tree officers wanted a rigorous code of practice for the utility industry that ensured the appropriate care and precautions were taken when excavating trenches near trees. In 1995, the National Joint Utilities Group published *NJUG 10: Guidelines for the Planning, Installation and Maintenance of Utility Services in Proximity to Trees*, prepared following several years of consultation with the arboricultural profession and the Department of the Environment (NJUG 1995). While this code of practice was widely regarded as providing adequate protection for street trees, compliance with it on the part of the utility companies was purely voluntary (Bassirian 1995, 5). As a result, the guidelines were frequently ignored and there were calls for local authorities to take a harder line and impose penalties on utility companies that damaged trees (Crane 1995, 20–23). There were many prominent tree and landscape professionals, environmental campaigners and others who predicted a 'chainsaw massacre' as a result of the damage done by the utilities. While no national survey was ever undertaken to establish how many street trees were lost, anecdotal evidence from local authority tree officers suggests this may have been many thousands.

Soil pollution

It was not just pollution from the air that was a threat to street trees; the harmful effects of various types of soil pollution were also being recognised in the late Victorian era (Hartig 1894, 281). Research in Germany had shown that the roots of trees were injured by coal gas when large quantities escaped from pipes into the soil. Coal gas was now used throughout Victorian towns and cities in Britain for street and domestic lighting. The escape of gas was a consequence of continuous interference with the supply pipes, caused mostly by roadworks and reconnections (Nead 2000, 90). There was also a problem with many competing gas companies and a lack of regulation. British highway engineers and urban landscape professionals were alerted to the problem as early as 1846 when the *Gardeners' Chronicle* reported on the mortality of trees on the boulevards of Paris that had occurred in 1842 and 1843. The trees had died as a result of escaping gas 'which had diffused itself throughout the soil to a distance of many yards from the pipes' (*Gardeners' Chronicle* 1846, 535). As with many controversial topics, scientific opinion was initially divided on this. Experiments by Dr Poselger in France had supposedly shown by repeated experiments 'that the growth of trees and shrubs is not interfered with by any quantity of coal gas that may escape in the soil and find its way to their roots' (*Gardeners' Chronicle* 1870, 1022). By contrast, experiments initially reported in *Scientific American* had shown that gas caused the death of cuttings of willow, however, 'not by direct action of the gas but in consequence of the poisoning of the soil' (*The Garden* 1874, 184). Eventually, after numerous reports on the death of street trees and the obvious smell of escaping gas prior to this, the evidence on the harmful effects of gas was overwhelming. Some quite high-profile trees had been affected, such as those along Lord Street in Southport (Anon 1901). Although there was now general agreement about the cause of the problem, there was some confusion about the best way to respond. This was largely a difference of opinion between highway engineers, who did not understand the requirements of street trees, and those responsible for the trees, mainly parks superintendents and city gardeners, who did not understand the limitation under which highway engineers had to work (*Gardeners' Chronicle* 1911b, 139).

The debate about the damage caused to street trees by gas leaks continued periodically at a low level in the professional press until it came briefly to the fore again with the introduction of natural gas. The conversion to this took ten years to complete and some leaks did occur until joint-sealing techniques improved. However, unlike coal gas this is not toxic to trees but some damage can still occur when the gas displaces air from the soil depriving the roots of the oxygen necessary for respiration (Deen 1981, 35).

A major cause of soil pollution affecting street trees in the twentieth century has been the application of salt on roads. Since the Second World War, rock salt (sodium chloride) has been used in ever greater quantities to minimise the danger to motorists and pedestrians from icy roads (Dobson 1991). The effect of salt damage on trees was first recognised in the USA in 1944 and soon became noticeable on roadside trees in Britain. Damage occurs through salt-contaminated water from melting snow and ice entering the soil and being taken up by tree roots, or by salt spray created by fast-moving traffic being deposited on leaves. There is no doubt that over the past 50 years many thousands of street trees in our towns and cities have either died or been severely debilitated as a result of salt application to roads. It is impossible to be precise because trees weakened in this way often subsequently die through other agencies. Fortunately, salt usage has been reduced in recent years and alternative de-icing materials used, such as urea and CMA (calcium magnesium acetate) (Rose and Webber 2011).

Trees roots and foundations

Another below-ground conflict that has led to the removal of many street trees, particularly in the latter part of the twentieth century, relates to trees roots and structural damage to building foundations. This can occur in shrinkable clay soils, particularly in periods of drought when tree roots remove significant amounts of soil moisture causing the soil to shrink and building foundations to subside. Some species of tree with a high water demand and extensive root systems, such as willows and poplars, are often involved when in close proximity to buildings.

Regardless of our more recent understanding of the nature of subsidence, there has always been some concern about the negative impact of tree roots on building foundations. In 1878, the *Gardeners' Chronicle* (1878, 726) reported on an incident in Ontario, Canada, where poplar trees had been identified as causing damage to the foundations of a building. The soil type was described as 'cold clay'. In more recent times, the problem first attracted significant attention in the very dry summer of 1947 (Biddle 1981, 17) and an indication of the importance given to this was the inclusion of an article on the subject in the first issue of *The Arboricultural Association Journal* (Webb 1965). It was particularly a problem with the extensive shrinkable clay soils in urban areas in the south east of England. The seasonal changes in moisture content that caused the soils to swell and shrink were exaggerated by the effects of tree roots resulting in subsidence and sometimes heave to the building foundations. In the very severe drought of 1976 extensive damage was caused leading to expensive insurance claims and the removal of large numbers of mature trees, particularly local authority street trees. This experience also had an impact on street tree policy in many at-risk areas with tree officers becoming reluctant to plant large-growing species to avoid any potential problems in the future (Britt and Johnston 2008, 214). Faced with expensive insurance claims, many local authorities have often been quick to remove street trees without an extensive site investigation. In many cases this might have revealed that defective foundations had played the most significant role (ISE 2000).

One long-standing problem concerning street trees roots that has become more prominent in recent times is where the growth of the roots lifts the surface or paving of the footway or displaces kerbstones (Roberts *et al.* 2006, 269–289). This then becomes uneven and a potential hazard to pedestrians who might trip over and injure themselves. In the past few decades many local authorities have paid out thousands of pounds in compensation for claims made against them on this basis. In extreme cases this has led to the removal of trees, often unnecessarily when other less drastic solutions are available.

Natural enemies of street trees

There is a wide range of what could be called 'natural enemies' of street trees – those natural occurrences such as extreme weather conditions and various pests and diseases. While these can be occasional events or an ongoing problem, the impact on street tree populations can be severe. Trees are damaged or destroyed and our ability to plant replacement trees can be quite limited. As much has already been written on these topics, including in an historical context, only an outline is given here.

Weather extremes

Extreme weather conditions, such as storm-force winds or drought, are a threat to any urban tree but can be especially damaging to those located in streets. In terms of storm-force winds, their regular wind speeds can be damaging enough, resulting in large branches splitting out and whole trees blown over. However, when the wind is funnelled between buildings its velocity and destructive power can increase dramatically. Street trees are also more vulnerable than trees in urban parks and open spaces because their roots systems are more restricted in the confines of the street environment.

The Great Storm of 1703 remains one of the most severe ever to hit Britain and was particularly damaging across much of England (Risk Management Solutions 2003). It uprooted countless thousands of trees as well as causing extensive structural damage to numerous buildings. Thousands of people also lost their lives, many of them seaman. It was not until recently that a storm of similar ferocity hit Britain and the southern part of England was also worse effected (Ogley 1988). This time, countless thousands of street trees were among those destroyed or severely damaged. In the early hours of the 16 October, 1987, hurricane-force winds swept across England resulting in some 15 million trees being blown down (*ibid.*, 17). The event is commonly known as the 'Hurricane', although some professionals call it the 'Great Storm', presumably unaware that this is the name of the 1703 event. The urban residents of towns and cities across the south of England were faced with scenes of major devastation – and particularly noticeable were the numerous street trees lying across roads, houses and parked cars. An enormous amount of damage was done to property of various kinds by falling trees and heavy branches. There were also many serious injuries and a small number of fatalities. A huge clear-up operation was undertaken by local authorities to remove the tree debris that lasted for months (Johnston 1991, 136). One beneficial outcome of this storm was the opportunity it provided scientists to study the rooting habits of a wide range of tree species (Cutler *et al.* 1990). Although the 1987 Hurricane was supposed to be a 'once in a lifetime' event, hurricane-force winds struck again in January 1990 (Anon 1990, 1). As well as covering similar ground, the damage extended into parts of Wales and the Midlands with four million trees lost, many of them urban. As our weather appears to become more unstable it seems likely that high winds will continue to wreak havoc with Britain's street trees.

Urban trees often suffer from a lack of water resulting in severe drought stress, especially in long, hot and very dry summers. The need for some urban trees to be irrigated frequently was recognised in early British works on urban horticulture (Fairchild 1722, 57). Trees in streets are especially vulnerable to drought stress and newly-planted trees are most at risk. They stand surrounded by the hard surfaces of the road and the footway. When rain falls on the tarmaced or paved surfaces it disappears quickly down drains and sewers before it has a chance to percolate into the tree's rooting area. When there is little rain, the problem is greatly exacerbated.

The most memorable drought in terms of its impact on urban trees occurred quite recently. The Great Drought of 1976 was the driest summer for 200 years and followed an unusually dry summer and winter the previous year (Cox 1978). Recently planted street trees were among the immediate casualties, particularly where they had received no watering by the local authorities in the springtime. As the summer became even hotter, the drought problem began to embrace other trees. In an effort to conserve water supplies, the authorities issued restrictions on the use of water for what were considered 'non-essential' purposes. Many local authorities issued a call to residents to help by watering young street trees with waste water from domestic baths and washing, provided this was not too contaminated. To the credit of the British public they responded magnificently. In a touching reminder of this, the author was called out to inspect a street tree outside a house in south London when working as a tree officer during the 1980s. The woman who lived in the house was upset because she thought the young tree might be dying. She explained that when the tree was just a sapling she had watered it regularly throughout the Great Drought of 1976 and it had survived. Fortunately, the inspection found there was nothing seriously wrong with the tree.

Pests and diseases

When many older people think of tree diseases, Dutch elm disease immediately comes to mind. The devastating outbreak of the virulent form of this disease from the late 1960s onwards remains a painful memory for those who witnessed its destructive transformation of the landscape in both rural and urban areas. By 1985, it was estimated that 30 million elms had died in Britain and trees continue to be lost as fresh outbreaks flare up periodically (Webber 2010). As well as being a dominant tree in many rural areas the elm was also a significant urban tree in northern England (Gibbs 1977, 110). Furthermore, in quite a number of towns and cities across Britain in the 1960s the elm was still an important street tree. While the epidemic rapidly took hold in lowland central and southern Britain, its progress has been much slower on the predominantly wych elm (*Ulmus glabra*) populations of Scotland and north-west England. The slower progress with this more resistant tree means that many mature elms can still be found in these areas today. This includes significant numbers of trees along some major roads in several Scottish towns and cities, such as Edinburgh and Dundee, where varieties of elm were a popular choice from the 1880s. The largest concentration of mature elms in Scotland remains in Edinburgh, where in 2009 an estimated 5000 still survived out of a population of 35,000 in 1976 (Coleman 2009). A strict policy of sanitary felling now keeps losses to a minimum each year.

The estimated 17,000 elms of Brighton and Hove constitute probably the most varied and important urban elm population in southern Britain, several of which are estimated to be over 400 years old (BHCC 2016). Quite a number of the remaining elms are located in streets and were planted by urban landscapers in late Victorian and Edwardian times (Greenland pers. comm., 2016). They created some magnificent avenues of elm, mainly using Huntingdon or Chichester elm (*Ulmus x hollandica* 'Vegeta') and Wheatley elm (*Ulmus minor* 'Sarniensis') (see Chapter 8). Sadly, many of the street tree elms have been lost. The survival of Brighton and Hove's remaining elms is due to the isolation of the area between the English Channel and the South Downs, and the stringent sanitation efforts of the local authority to identify and remove infected trees and branches.

Some other tree diseases in the second half of the twentieth century have been noticeable in urban areas and have had a major impact on street tree populations. Fireblight is caused by the bacterium *Erwinia amylovora* and is a serious disease of trees and shrubs in the family Rosaceae, sub-family Maloideae (pome fruits) (Strouts and Winter 2000, 124). This includes many ornamental tree species such as apple (*Malus*), hawthorn (*Crataegus*), pear (*Pyrus*), mountain ash and whitebeams (*Sorbus*), *Cotoneaster*, *Pyracantha* and *Amelanchier*. These have always formed a significant proportion of the nation's street tree population since the days of the garden suburbs but were then planted on a massive scale in the rapidly expanding suburbs from the 1930s and especially after the Second World War. The disease affects all the aerial part of the host plant, with withering and death of young shoots and flowers, and infected fruit turning brown or black. The first British finding of fireblight was in a pear orchard in Kent in 1957. It is now widespread in south and central England and also in Wales. The control is to fell and burn infected plants and not to plant susceptible species in affected areas.

Silver leaf disease also attacks many species of small ornamental trees in the Rosaceae family, particularly cherries (*Prunus*) and apples (*Malus*) and has also frequently been a problem for roadside trees in many suburban areas (Strouts and Winter 2000, 252). The disease is caused by a fungus (*Chrondrostereum purpureum*) whose airborne spores infect freshly exposed wood and live sapwood, especially pruning wounds, producing toxins that disrupt the tree's metabolism and water transport system. The leaves on infected branches assume a leaden or silvery colouration and then die and fall prematurely. Whole branches and parts of the crown may become dead and leafless. If pruning out and burning infected branches is not effective in halting the spread of the disease the whole tree will be lost. This disease was a particular problem for tree managers in Bourneville in the 1950s when a number of well-grown roadside ornamental trees were lost before the problem could be brought under control (Salter 1953, 7).

In the past few years, a major threat to the London plane tree (*Plantanus x acerifolia*) has emerged in our capital (LTOA 2013). London's most iconic tree that graces some of its finest tree-lined thoroughfares is threatened by a fungal menace known as massaria (*Splanchnonema platani*), previously unknown in Britain. The disease is particularly disturbing because London plane has been renowned for being tolerant to most pests and diseases and resilient to changes in environmental conditions. These factors have made it an ideal urban tree that has been widely used since Victorian times as a street tree in many British towns and cities (Milmo 2010). Although the disease is not known to kill trees, the Forestry Commission has warned that its ability to kill individual branches has created a risk to public safety requiring increased monitoring. A more deadly threat to Britain's plane trees could be with us soon. This is plane tree wilt, caused by a fungus (*Ceratocystis platini*) which originated in the eastern United States and is now working its way northwards through France at an alarming rate. If this disease reaches Britain it could decimate our plane trees and destroy some of our most famous arboreal landmarks (Bodkin 2016). Finally, ash dieback has now arrived in Britain and is threatening to decimate our ash trees (*Fraxinus excelsior*) (Derbyshire 2013). While concern has so far focused on rural areas, ash species and their cultivars also form a major proportion of our urban forests and are commonly used as street trees.

Not only do we have some new diseases threatening our urban trees, there are also deadly insect pests recently arrived in British towns and cities or likely to do so soon (O'Callaghan 2012). It appears that with this recent wave of new pests and diseases our urban trees, including thousands of miles of attractive tree-lined streets, now face an unprecedented threat. This only serves to emphasise the vital need to plant a wide range of species or genotypes to promote biodiversity in our urban tree populations that will improve their resilience against attack from deadly pathogens.

Vandalism and war

This section looks at vandalism and war, two topics in relation to street trees that have had very little coverage in an historical context. In both cases trees have been damaged or destroyed by aggressive human activity. With respect to acts of vandalism to trees, those located in streets have always been among the most vulnerable. That may have something to do with them being in prominent locations and noticed by the public, often in the evenings or at night when vandalism frequently occurs. This could be the 'casual' vandalism of the late-night drunken reveller who swings on the branches of a young tree in a moment of exuberance and is surprised when it breaks. However, it could be the 'deliberate' vandalism of the resident who is determined not to have a new street tree growing outside their house and sneaks out in the dead of night to do the damage.

Vandalism of urban trees may sometime be regarded as a feature of modern society but this has always occurred to some extent. In 1871, it was reported that several young trees on the Victoria Embankment, some of the first street trees to be planted in London, had been vandalised. This prompted the authorities to reconsider whether planting street trees in this location was a good idea. In an effort to deter this vandalism the Open Spaces Committee of the Metropolitan Board of Works recommended that a reward of £20 be offered for information that would lead to the conviction of any person damaging the trees (*The Garden* 1871, 271). Noel Humphreys, the well-known horticulturist, had some strong words to say about this incident:

> The 'rough' element of the lower stratum of our population still continues to exercise its propensity for the perpetration of wanton mischief. This fact has been disagreeably exemplified by the injuries inflicted for mere vicious amusement on the newly-planted trees on the Embankment, where this kind of depredation has been carried on to such an extent, and so daringly, that their official guardians, hopeless of affording them sufficient protection by the police or by any other means, have, in a fit of natural vexation, threatened to take them away altogether.
>
> Humphreys 1871, 380

In an early example of 'casual' vandalism, a correspondent in the *Gardeners' Chronicle* reported that trees lining a roadside through Hyde Park had been damaged (Dean 1872, 395–396). This had been caused by people climbing the trees along the route taken by the royal family in their procession on Thanksgiving Day. The correspondent did not blame the people involved as they were only trying to get a better view of the procession by climbing above the dense crowds that thronged the route. Instead, he blamed the authorities 'who must have known this was likely and took no steps to avoid it'. A substantial amount of damage was done to many of the trees that 'an adequate police presence could have avoided'.

As many towns and cities across Britain began to plant up their streets in the late Victorian era, reports of vandalism to the young trees were not uncommon in the local and regional newspapers. Those horticulturists, arboriculturists and civic leaders who were the driving force behind the Victorian street tree movement were alarmed at this threat to their well-meaning endeavours and sought to find ways to discourage this destructive behaviour. Some advocated even harsher penalties for those who were caught inflicting this damage. Others felt that the solution lay in better tree protection by providing sturdy wrought-iron tree guards that might act as a deterrent. This was often done in high-profile street tree planting schemes where the high cost of these guards was considered a price worth paying. However, not everyone agreed with that approach and there were some tree and landscape professionals that not only baulked at the cost but also believed that tree guards were unsightly and detracted from the natural beauty of the young trees. Munro Ferguson, a Member of Parliament and amateur arboriculturist, highlighted some of these issues in an article for the Royal Scottish Arboricultural Society. While having a very negative opinion of the character of the youth of his time, he also proposed the enlightened suggestion that the solution to the problem might be found in education:

> Our own youth are at present little better than a horde of Huns on the highway; for when a tree is planted at the cost of two or three pence, it takes two or three shillings to afford it a necessary protection, which, whatever its form, detracts from the beauty of all planting. In no respect do the suburbs of American towns more surpass our own than in the absence of railings and other similar monstrosities. A remedy for the destructive tendencies of the British barbarian is to teach botany in the schools, coupled with botanical excursions on the foreign system, and to extend gardens and pleasure-grounds, which teach people to care for and to safeguard plants and flowers.
>
> Munro Ferguson 1901, 389

While this early suggestion by Munro Ferguson that the education of children should have a role to play in reducing levels of tree vandalism, echoes of his view are hard to find in literature on urban tree management in the first half of the twentieth century. There is a notable contribution to this topic in R.G. Salter's (1953) booklet entitled *Roadside Tree Planting in Urban Areas*, which is based on his experience at Bournville. He acknowledges that vandalism to street trees in some districts is almost impossible to combat. These are areas 'where there is no well established tradition of growing bulbs, flowers and trees on spaces available to the public', which is in contrast to 'the older housing estates [where] these features are taken for granted and do not attract so much attention and damage'. He explains further:

> The only solution in these new areas is to build up a tradition over a number of years. Start in a small way with a few trees in suitable positions in front gardens, offering these flowering trees only to the occupiers who obviously take an interest in gardening. Then take a quiet road, such as a cul-de-sac, call on the occupiers and inform them of your intention to plant road trees, and try to get their interest. The experiment has been tried of getting children to join in the planting and making each child responsible for guarding one tree; it would certainly seem sound psychology to do this and to give a short talk at their school on trees in general and the proposals for the roads near their homes.
>
> Salter 1953, 3

The idea that local residents, let alone school children, should be allowed to help plant trees at the side of any sort of road would be looked upon today with some scepticism. In this risk-averse society all sorts of objections would be raised by many parents, teachers and local authority tree officers. Nevertheless, in some carefully controlled situations it should be possible.

Another approach to reducing the risk of tree vandalism has focused on the selection of certain types of trees. In 1901, William Wallace Pettigrew, the respected authority on park management, recommended that species with conspicuous flowers or fruits should not be planted in streets. His reasoning was that 'town youths seem to be under the impression that such things can only be intended as targets for their stone throwing, and then householders who suffer in consequence from broken windows begin to complain' (Pettigrew 1901, 14). He also stated that he would 'never pay more than 3s 6d or 4s for any kind of tree that is to be planted in the street' because the risk of failure, for a variety of reasons, is so great. Of these risks, he considered vandalism one of the common causes of death for young street trees. He reported that during the last two years in Cardiff 'more than 100 valuable young trees have been destroyed by boys, notwithstanding rewards offered for their detection'. While many arboriculturists, especially today, would never support Pettigrew's complete ban on species with conspicuous flowers or fruits, many would caution against planting some tree species in streets to reduce the risk of vandalism. Frequently mentioned in the literature down the years is the horse chestnut that is perennially damaged by children throwing branches into the tree to get the conkers (Arnold-Forster 1948, 51). Fortunately, there are sterile varieties of this tree that do not produce conkers.

One type of vandalism that is becoming common in residential neighbourhoods is the unauthorised heavy pruning of street trees by residents, usually to allow more light to reach their front rooms (Figure 77). It can sometimes be prompted when the normal pruning regime of forest-type trees is suspended by the local authority in an effort to save money. As no reputable tree care company would undertake unauthorised work on a street tree, the 'pruning' is often done by the resident themselves and results in the very unsightly 'hacking back' of the tree. Unfortunately, unless the resident is caught in the act, or a neighbour informs on them, the tree officer can often do little about this.

It has been said that warfare is a form of vandalism on a colossal and terrifying scale. When the horrors of war are inflicted on towns and cities, along with the death and suffering of ordinary residents, buildings and infrastructure are also destroyed or badly damaged. This infrastructure includes the green infrastructure of the urban tree population and those trees in streets are often especially vulnerable. Although Britain has experienced periodic wars and violent civil disturbances over the centuries and urban trees have suffered, it was in the twentieth century that the most damage was caused to street trees (Johnston 2015, 83–84). During the First World War, German forces targeted some British urban residential districts, mainly by Zeppelin airships, resulting in some collateral damage and destruction to a small number of street trees. It was the Second World War that had a huge impact on the street trees in some of our major cities (Le Sueur 1949, 96). This was a direct result of the intense aerial bombardment from German planes. Many mature street trees in cities such as London, Cardiff and Coventry had shrapnel from exploding bombs imbedded in their trunks and major branches (Figure 78). While this was not always a problem at the time it would present problems after the war. Large numbers of street trees were destroyed or seriously damaged by heat and fire when incendiary bombs struck nearby buildings. The revised edition of *The Care and Repair of Ornamental Trees* by Le Sueur (1949, 96) has a short chapter devoted to war and bomb damage. A very useful account of bomb damage to street trees in the London area is given by Hubert Taylor who managed the tree division of the London County Council (LCC), formed immediately after the Second World War (Johnston 2015, 55). One of Taylor's first tasks was to survey trees damaged by the London blitz and to decide which were to be retained and which were to be taken down (Stone and Brodie 1994, 50). Many were 'blast shaken' and it was necessary to bore into a tree to assess the internal damage as only then could it be decided whether it was safe enough to be left standing. According to Taylor, 'They may have looked perfect, but the inner trunk wood had lost structure and become rubbery. Many were pitted with shrapnel – if a chainsaw struck the piece of shrapnel embedded in a tree it could be very dangerous for the tree surgeon'. The danger resulted from the risk of 'kickback' from the chainsaw when it struck the metal, leading to serious injury when the chainsaw blade struck the operator.

Bomb damage could also have some quite unexpected effects on trees. In 1945, a correspondent reported in the *Gardeners' Chronicle* on the dropping of a V-bomb in June of the previous year that struck a large ash tree (Elkington 1945, 20). The impact of the blast defoliated a nearby horse chestnut and many varieties of *Pyrus* and *Crataegus*. Within a few weeks these trees burst into leaf

and flower again, having already done so at the normal time earlier in the year. The correspondent was interested to watch what effect it would have in the current year and was surprised to find it had caused little detriment to the trees. He remarked that 'The flowers were rather under normal size but were as numerous as usual and appeared in their proper season'.

One indirect consequence of the war that impacted on urban trees was the removal of railings around parks and open spaces so they could be melted down as a much needed raw material in the war effort (GTLS 1941). While some people welcomed the 'liberation' of these parks and open spaces, others remarked on the increase in damage and vandalism to trees and flowers when the railings had gone. Although a number of references have been found to the practice of removing railings during the war years, none could be found that specifically mentioned the removal of metal guards around individual street trees.

One wartime practice that was common with street trees was the painting of white lines around the lower trunk. This was to enable the trees to be more

FIGURE 77. One type of vandalism that is becoming common in residential neighbourhoods is the unauthorised heavy pruning of street trees by residents, usually to allow more light to reach their front rooms. The lime tree on the right was 'pruned' some years ago and has since gone into severe decline and will soon have to be felled.

CREDIT: EALING CENTRAL LIBRARY.

FIGURE 78. During the Second World War the aerial bombardment of some of our major cities caused extensive destruction, not only to people and property, but also to many street trees. This photograph from 1940 shows the aftermath of a bombing raid on Westfield Road in Ealing, London. While the trees still look in reasonable shape, they have probably suffered serious damage from the effects of the explosions and fires.

visible to drivers travelling at night during the 'blackout', thus reducing the risk of wandering off the road and colliding with the trees. Trees along some high-profile thoroughfares were painted in this manner, including those on the Embankment in London and Lord Street in Southport (Figure 79). An interesting mention of the practice occurred in 1942 when the Glasgow Tree Lovers Society made a request to Renfrewshire County Council on behalf of some residents to plant approximately 40 trees in Brooklee Drive (GTLS 1942). The request was refused by the local authority on the grounds that 'while black-out conditions exist, the time is not appropriate for planting trees in public streets'. However, in making the request the Society had pointed out that 'if birch trees were planted and the trunks of trees lime washed, they would be a guide to traffic in the dark'.

There were many other ways in which street trees suffered indirectly as a result of the Second World War. Almost no tree maintenance work was carried out on street trees by local authorities throughout the duration of the war unless it was urgently required for safety reasons or to remove fallen trees from buildings or roads. Any work undertaken was always the bare minimum necessary and paid scant attention to aesthetic appearance. Regular

tree maintenance or planting was hardly a priority in wartime and besides there was a shortage of skilled tree workers as most had joined the armed forces. As indicated above, new street tree planting virtually ceased during the war. After the war the neglect to Britain's street trees would take several years and considerable expense to put right. During its first few years the LCC's tree division were entirely preoccupied with rectifying the lopping and topping that had disfigured many of the capital's trees during the war (Leathart 1973, 104).

Risk-averse society

We conclude this chapter by highlighting a trend that has serious implications for the future of our street trees. In Britain over the past 50 years there has been a growing focus on urban trees as liabilities rather than assets. This has been fuelled in part by some sad incidents which have attracted much media attention where falling street trees or branches have caused death or serious injury (Figure 80). It has forced local authorities to increasingly focus resources on tree inspection regimes to identify potentially hazardous trees (Lonsdale 2000; NTSG 2011). Although tree-related fatalities are very rare, they have encouraged negative public attitudes towards urban trees. These concerns

FIGURE 79. One wartime practice that was common with street trees was the painting of white lines around the lower trunk. This was to enable the trees to be more visible to drivers travelling at night during the 'blackout', thus reducing the risk of wandering off the road and colliding with the trees. This example is Lord Street in Southport, photographed in 1940.

FIGURE 80. Although tree-related fatalities are very rare, they are often given extensive coverage in the regional and even the national media. This has helped to encourage negative public attitudes towards urban trees. These concerns about safety have also been reflected in an increasingly wary approach to tree selection for street planting by local authorities.

CREDIT: GLOUCESTER ECHO

about safety have also been reflected in an increasingly wary approach to tree selection for street planting by local authorities. Rather than use forest-type trees even where there is the space, the tendency is to favour small ornamental species. This has prompted fears that the trend will lead to a proliferation of 'lollipop landscapes' (Johnston 2010, 33). There are also major concerns that our increasingly risk-averse society will generate a growing tide of complaints and insurance claims resulting in the felling of ever greater numbers of mature street trees (Barkham 2007).

CHAPTER ELEVEN

Selection, Design and Planting

Any book on the history of street tree planting in Britain would not be complete without some account of the rationale and methods behind the selection and planting of those trees. It is often stated by modern arboriculturists that the trees selected for street tree planting in the past have not always been the most appropriate for the conditions. Also, when planting techniques from Victorian and Edwardian times are examined some surprise is often expressed at how these trees managed to survive. This chapter explores the selection, design and planting of street trees from the mid-nineteenth century to the present.

A search of the British horticultural and arboricultural literature of the past two hundred years has revealed many thousands of words written on the topics of tree selection and tree planting in towns and cities. There is also plenty of material on tree production. Much of the literature from the 1860s onwards is directly relevant to street tree planting. To give a detailed account of all this knowledge and comment would probably require an entire book. Unfortunately, limited space here only allows an outline of some salient points and it has not been possible to include material on nursery production. The chapter begins by looking at the topic of tree selection for street planting and then examines some of the factors that have influenced the use of these trees in the design of streetscapes. An account is then given of some Victorian and Edwardian techniques in the planting and establishment of street trees, including some that are often regarded as more recent innovations.

Selection of trees for street planting

Along with all the information about tree selection in magazines and books, various authors over the years have produced lists of trees that they regarded as suitable for street planting. One of the first to give an extensive list was Robert Walker (1890, 14–15), the eminent Scottish arboriculturist, who included separate categories for 'trees for smoky streets' and 'trees for streets and roads in the suburbs'. Nurserymen's catalogues of their trees for sale often included lists of those suitable for a range of sites, undoubtedly part of their marketing strategy, and lists of trees for street planting were increasingly common as this became an ever larger market. A quite recent exception to this occurred in possibly the most famous 'tree catalogue' of them all, the *Hillier's Manual of Trees and Shrubs* (Hillier 2014, 142). First published in 1971, this contained lists of trees for different landscape situations and ornamental features but did not have one on street trees. There was also no mention of trees suitable for streets in Harold Hiller's (1971) otherwise excellent booklet *A Tree for Every Site*, published by the Arboricultural Association.

From the late Victorian era onwards, some authors recommended that those responsible for urban or street planting should visit an urban arboretum or an extensively planted public park to get some idea of what trees would grow well under urban conditions. In terms of London, a visit to Kew Gardens was often mentioned, although other authors felt this was 'too far removed from the smoke' to be much help (*Gardeners' Chronicle* 1889a, 134). From the 1870s, in response to growing demand, some commercial nurseries began advertising in gardening magazines that they could offer trees specifically for 'street planting' (*Gardeners' Chronicle* 1879a, 483).

Comment and discussion in the historical literature on street tree selection has often focused on what qualities make a 'good street tree'. Opinions on this have always varied enormously and there are many quite opposite views. In reviewing this literature perhaps what is surprising to the modern arboriculturist is the lack of recognition of just how much soil and climatic conditions can vary in different streets across a town or city and how tree selection needs to reflect this. Very often the descriptions of a 'good street tree' were meant to apply to all situations regardless of the type of street or planting conditions. Another factor to emerge was that any discussion on the benefits of street trees focused almost exclusively on their aesthetic benefits and the pleasant shade they cast in hot summers (Mattocks 1925, 259). Even as late as 1968, when authorities on street tree management discussed their favourable attributes no mention was made of their wider environmental benefits (Boddy 1968, 3–4). Our modern focus on the many environmental, economic and social benefits of urban trees, including street trees, only began when the new research supporting this was brought together for the first time in the early 1970s by Gary Robinette (1972), an American landscape architect, in his groundbreaking book *People, Plants and Environmental Quality*. This outlined what we now regard as the very *raison d'être* for urban forest management. The body of research on the benefits of urban trees and what is often now referred to as 'green infrastructure' continues to grow (Forest Research 2010).

Plane, lime and horse chestnut

Three types of tree came to dominate the scene in the Victorian street tree movement and these were the plane, lime and horse chestnut, all large forest-type trees. The first two were by far the most widely planted and many of our urban streets dating from the late Victorian and Edwardian eras still have a legacy of these trees. The number of times these two trees have been mentioned in this book serves to underline their prominence. The horse chestnut, although initially a popular choice for street planting, later fell out of favour and by the early twentieth century seems to have been planted much less frequently than the other two. The overreliance on these three trees for street planting was often the subject of adverse comment and ridicule. For example, one correspondent in the *Gardeners' Chronicle* wrote:

> Every little town now begins to dream of its boulevards ... The decision to plant usually goes through unanimously, and then comes the question 'what shall we plant – Limes, Chestnuts, Planes?' It is almost certain to be one of these. London plants them; therefore we must, even with the pure air of the country.
>
> *Gardeners' Chronicle* 1907, 430

The type of plane tree most commonly planted in British streets is the London plane (*Platanus x acerifolia*), which is a hybrid of oriental plane (*P. orientalis*) and the American or western plane (*P. occidentalis*). It has long been regarded by many as the ideal street tree because of its ability to withstand air pollution, drought and compacted soil. However, in the Victorian and Edwardian eras it was often planted in quite narrow streets where it was allowed to outgrow its situation and cause a variety of problems. In the early nineteenth century the oriental plane was often the more popular choice (Sinclair 1832, 19). By contrast, Robert Walker (1890, 3), the Scottish arboriculturist, regarded the western plane (*P. occidentalis*) as the best urban tree for European cities.

It is interesting to speculate that if the tree chosen to adorn so many of our streets had been the oriental plane instead of its hybrid, how more attractive they might have looked (Mitchell 1996, 272). This plane from the eastern Mediterranean has as lighter foliage with a more attractive pale green colour. It lacks the hybrid vigour of the London plane, although this is not necessarily a disadvantage for street planting. While it has a reputation for growing large and spreading branches from near the base, this can be corrected with a little early training. When the London plane started to be planted in significant numbers in urban areas, it soon gained the ascendancy over the other forms for its ability to withstand the smoky air and for its rapid growth. Nevertheless, there was much early confusion in distinguishing between the three types of plane tree. For example, Walker (1890, 8) states, 'It has been said that the *oriental plane* is planted along the Thames Embankment in London, but the plane there planted is *Platanus occidentalis*, or western plane, and was imported from the Continent'. The confusion continued until Augustine Henry eventually sorted it out in 1911. From the late Victorian era onwards, the London plane became the preferred choice of local authorities for all types of urban planting. When researching the history of the plane tree in Scotland care needs to be taken as the common name 'plane' is often applied to sycamore.

As the Victorian street tree movement began to have a real impact, concerns about the overuse of the London plane became more vocal. In 1889, an editorial in the *Gardeners' Chronicle* (1889a, 134) declared, 'There is fear lest we may become slaves to routine, and go on planting Planes, and Planes only, as if there were no other trees equally suited to bear the dust and foul air of our great cities'. When plans for many new thoroughfares in central London were being considered, another editorial in the *Gardeners' Chronicle* expressed fears that only planes would be planted. The editors wrote:

> There are a number of trees, such as Maples of kinds, Poplars, Naples Alder, Oaks, Ailanthus, Robinias, Mountain Ash, deciduous Magnolias, species of Pyrus, and many others ..., which will thrive nearly, or quite as well as the monotonous Plane, and many of which, being of more modest dimensions, are more suitable for narrow thoroughfares than it.
>
> *Gardeners' Chronicle* 1902, 306

This plea for more variety seems to have fallen on deaf ears because Angus Webster (1918, 251), another eminent arboriculturist, reported some years later that 'Most of the new streets and roads in London of late years have been planted with the plane, and a nurseryman in the suburbs informs me that fully 75% of his London orders have been for this tree'. By the 1920s, there was quite widespread concern that the continuous use of plane had prevented the planting of other deserving subjects. In 1925, the council official responsible for street tree planting in Camberwell, London, declared that the plane 'has been banned here and no planting has taken place for several years' (King 1925, 467).

The common lime (*Tilia x europaea*) has had a similar early history to the London plane in its use as a street tree. Also, like the plane, it is a hybrid of two other species, the small-leaf lime (*T. cordata*) and the broadleaf lime (*T. platyphyllos*). Although both these trees have much merit, the great 'tree connoisseur' Alan Mitchell (1996, 334) believed that the common lime had only inherited the bad features from its parents. After listing all its failings, he states that the tree is the worst possible choice for planting in streets. While there were some nineteenth century horticulturists and arboriculturists who held a similar view of this tree, this did not stop it being extensively planted in Britain's streets on a similar scale to the plane. Also in common with the plane, the reaction against the overuse of the common lime was swift in coming. As early as 1879, a correspondent in the *Gardeners' Chronicle* (1879b, 536) warned against using this tree with the words, 'There is one tree, however, that should be avoided for town planting, and that is the Lime, the leaves of which often by the end of August look as if scorched, thus giving a most wretched appearance'. Much of the criticism centred on its poor shape, its habit of losing its leaves early and prolific suckering around its base. Nevertheless, the common lime continued to be widely planted in streets despite other types of lime being recommended in popular gardening magazines and books. In a letter to the *Gardeners' Chronicle* in 1890, no less an authority than George Nicholson (1890, 538), Curator of Kew Gardens, recommended two alternatives to the much-maligned common lime for street planting. These were the native small-leaf lime (*T. cordata*) and the Crimean or Caucasian lime (*T. x euchlora*). Both trees have a much better shape and far more attractive foliage and the latter has the additional advantage of not being attacked by insects and thus not secreting sticky 'honey dew'. It is unfortunate that local authorities at the time did not take the advice of this great horticulturist. If they had, tree officers today would not be faced with the enormous headache and expense of managing these trees when they have outgrown their situations or trying to implement replacement programmes (see Chapter 12).

The horse chestnut (*Aesculus hippocastanum*), the last of these three most commonly planted street trees, seems to have had an even shorter 'honeymoon period' than the other two. In 1872, when many towns and cities were only beginning to consider street tree planting, one contributor to *The Garden* (probably the editor William Robinson) warned local authorities and others against using this tree for 'boulevard planting'. They cited its poor performance on the boulevards of Paris where 'the leaves are scarce and withered, and many of the trees are quite leafless' (*The Garden* 1872a, 181). As well as losing its leaves early, the foliage of the horse chestnut is quite dense and this prompts many complaints about blocking out light. It is also a large tree and, like the plane and the lime, was frequently planted in quite narrow streets where unless it was regularly pruned it soon became a problem. As if all this was not enough of an incentive to omit it from street planting, its much admired flowers turn into conkers that young boys love to throw sticks at, causing nuisance and often damage.

While there is no data to support this, a review of the historical literature suggests that the popularity of horse chestnut for urban street tree planting started to decline significantly from the 1900s. However, it still remained fashionable as a highway tree on trunk roads. In the 1920s, its fall from grace as a street tree was probably accelerated by reports from Paris in the gardening press that the horse chestnuts on the boulevards were being replaced gradually with other species because of their 'persistent premature defoliation' (*Gardeners' Chronicle* 1925, 104).

Ever since the negative reaction towards planting forest-type trees in residential streets began in late Victorian times there have been calls to replace these trees with smaller and more ornamental species. Local authorities have often been keen to remove these larger-growing trees from their streets in an effort to reduce public complaints, maintenance costs and insurance claims. These replacement programmes are discussed in Chapter 12.

Poplar, robinia and ailanthus

Various types of poplar tree were commonly planted as street trees from the earliest days of the Victorian street tree movement, although the genus is less favoured for that purpose today. The fastigiate forms seemed an obvious choice with their upright habit, vigorous growth and acceptance of difficult urban conditions. One of the first to be used was the Lombardy poplar (*Populus nigra* 'Italica'), of Italian origin and originally introduced to Britain in 1758 (Mitchell 1996, 281). When street tree planting started to gather momentum from the 1860s, this soon became a common choice, noted for its tolerance of coal-smoke and chemical fumes (Webster 1910, 62). Another form recommended from the 1870s onwards was widely distributed as the 'new Canadian poplar' or *Poplus canadensis* 'Nova' (*Gardeners' Chronicle* 1876a, 748), although it seems likely that this was actually the cultivar now know as 'Regenerata' or the railway poplar (Bean 1976, 306). Yet another form that was promoted by Robert Walker (1890, 10) as an excellent street tree was the bolleana poplar (*Populus alba* 'Pyramidalis'), a fastigiate cultivar of the white poplar from Turkestan.

In the 1880s the problem of air pollution in some northern industrial cities had become so bad that even plane trees were suffering. One of the few trees to cope with the extensive pollution was the native black poplar (*Populus nigra* subsp *betulifolia*), which in its male form became known as the Manchester poplar as it was much planted in the city's parks, streets and industrial areas (Cooper 2006, 48–52). Although this later fell out of favour with many for street tree planting, Angus Webster (1910, 59) was still recommending it for this use in the Edwardian era based on a fine example in London's Gray's Inn Road. Also at this time, Webster believed the Lombardy poplar, next to the plane, was the most common London tree and noted that it was still being widely planted in London streets (*ibid.*, 62).

Since the Second World War most of the forms of poplar described above have not been generally regarded as suitable for street tree planting. What were once regarded as their favourable traits, especially their rapid growth and tolerance to air pollution, are no longer regarded as such important assets and their less attractive characteristics, such as their brittle branches and invasive root system, have come to be viewed as major liabilities. What might be surprising is how long it took for this overall assessment to be made. An article appeared as early in 1851 in the *Gardeners' Chronicle* (1851, 711), the leading British horticultural magazine of the day, which reported that the Germans were gradually replacing all the poplar trees along public roads. This was precisely because of problems of invasive roots and brittle branches, with the Lombardy poplar being the form chiefly proscribed.

In the 1870s, the robinia (*Robinia pseudoacacia*) from the south-eastern United States was starting to be recommended for street planting. This was often in preference to the lime as 'it retains its verdure for months after the common lime has become as rusty as an old carpet bag' (*The Garden* 1872b, 145). By the Edwardian era it had firmly established its reputation among some authorities as the most useful tree for street purposes (*Gardeners' Chronicle* 1909a, 204). This was mainly because it could adapt to the lack of soil and nutrients, which was often the case when engineers had dug down to subsoil when making new roads. It also has the advantage of nitrogen-fixing roots and a tolerance of hot, dry and paved-over soil. Nevertheless, there was also an awareness of its less desirable characteristics, particularly its vigorous habit and the brittleness of its branches when mature. Branches splitting out and falling across roads was a growing problem with this tree as road traffic increased in city centres. The potential danger to pedestrians of its sharp thorns could be overcome by using thornless varieties such as 'Bessoniana' and 'Inermis'. Robinia remained a popular street tree and was much planted in quieter suburban streets during the 1920s and 1930s

In the 1880s, the ailanthus or tree of heaven (*Ailanthus altissima*) from north-east and central China was being championed as a magnificent urban tree capable of tolerating the smokiest of atmospheres (*Gardeners' Chronicle* 1889a, 134). However, it was soon clear that its ultimate size and spread rendered it unsuitable as a street tree in most situations. Despite this, it was still widely planted in London streets in the late Victorian and Edwardian eras (Webster 1910, 57).

Small and medium-sized ornamental trees

There is evidence that some small and medium-sized ornamental trees were planted in streets from the earliest days of the Victorian street tree movement. However, when negative public reaction began to take hold against forest-type trees it was understandable that the demand grew for these smaller-growing species. As well as their compact size there was much emphasis given to their ornamental features, such as their flowers, fruit, bark, foliage and autumn colour. Even so, there were some notable horticulturists who were not in favour of many of these trees for street use. In 1873, an article in *The Garden* (1873, 500) reported that John Jay Smith of Philadelphia, the esteemed editor of *North American Sylva*, was 'not in favour of planting fruit or nut-bearing trees along our side-walks'. His reasons for this were occasionally repeated by others, including William Wallace Pettigrew (1901, 14), and focused on the fact that street trees, both large and small, with conspicuous flowers or fruits tended to act as a magnet for vandals. As a result, Wallace had removed various species of cherry and pear, as well as horse and sweet chestnut, from his list of trees for street planting. Other professionals disagreed, including those at Letchworth Garden City, who had used pear trees in their first street plantings and had experienced no problems (*Gardeners' Chronicle* 1909b, 157)

By the end of the nineteenth century many authorities on urban landscape believed that for narrow city streets or those in suburban districts it was generally more appropriate to consider planting small and medium-sized ornamental trees (*Gardeners' Chronicle* 1895, 99). However, this view was not always reflected by those actually responsible for planting and in some cases forest-type trees continued to be used whatever the street dimensions. Some of the genera of small ornamental trees frequently suggested for street planting in the early decades of the twentieth century included *Prunus, Sorbus, Malus, Pyrus, Crateagus, Amalanchier* and *Laburnum*. These sorts of trees were also considered by some experts to be very appropriate for embellishing the streets of seaside resorts, as long as they were relatively tolerant of coastal conditions (*The Garden* 1911, 486). As well as using quite colourful exotic species, there was also a trend towards some small native trees for planting in suburban roads, particularly those in some of the garden suburbs. Trees such as birch (*Betula pendula*) and the mountain ash or rowan (*Sorbus aucuparia*) were thought to be in keeping with the Arts and Craft character of some garden suburbs. In the early years of the twentieth century birch was used widely in several districts of Hampstead, north London, where it made a highly graceful and ornamental street tree (Webster 1920, 191). It is interesting that with the recent management policy for street trees in Brentham Garden Suburb, north London, small flowering trees were not considered appropriate for the architecture and character of the suburb (see Chapter 6).

While the preference for planting small ornamental street trees became increasingly common in the early decades of the twentieth century, after the Second World War it became very fashionable over vast areas of suburbia. Many of these suburban streets had grass verges that could easily accommodate a significant amount of tree planting. Mile after mile of ornamental cherries, thorns and similar trees adorned these suburban streets with a show of spectacular but often gaudy colour for a couple of weeks in the year (Figure 81). Even in streets with wide grass verges where larger-growing trees could be accommodated it was often fashionable to favour these small ornamentals. Eventually, the establishment of these types of trees on streets throughout suburbia became so extensive it provoked a negative reaction among many professionals and also members of the public. There was another factor which prompted a rethink of this planting policy. Many of these species were susceptible to a disease called fireblight that had been first recorded in Britain in 1957 (Strouts and Winter 2000, 124) (see Chapter 10). The extensive planting of susceptible species as street trees throughout suburbia had encouraged the rapid spread of the disease and during the 1960s, 1970s, and even later, the often scarce resources of many local authority tree sections had to be diverted into extensive programmes of sanitation felling.

Unusual species, tailored trees and native species

As public parks and arboreta became popular in the Victorian era they were planted with an increasingly wide range of exotic trees collected and introduced by the plant explorers. Although it was generally recognised that the growing conditions for trees in streets were far more demanding than those in parks, professionals were often suggesting various exotic species for trial as possible street trees.

It was widely recognised from Victorian times that conifers, which fared badly in cities because of the air pollution, would not make suitable street trees. Nevertheless, it was noticed that the ginkgo (*Ginkgo biloba*), a deciduous conifer from China, was an exception to this and was found to thrive in some of the smokiest conditions (*Gardeners' Chronicle* 1889a, 134). In 1910, Angus Webster (1910, 77) noted that despite its tolerance of pollution and always fresh foliage, it was still rarely planted in streets, although he had noticed a large tree in London's Commercial Road.

From the 1970s, partly encouraged by North American practice, some tree officers began to experiment with planting a much wider range of species as street trees. This included ginkgo and other generally untried species such as dawn redwood (*Metasequoia glyptostroboides*), Italian alder (*Alnus cordata*) and various species of *Acer*, *Betula* and *Sorbus* (Mitchell 1989). Some tree officers had undoubtedly been encouraged to try these unusual species by college tutors during their arboricultural education. To meet this growing demand for more unusual street trees British commercial tree nurseries started to stock a much wider range of species. Also prompted by North American practice, they began to offer a range of trees specially bred for street conditions. Following tree breeding programmes, which began in the United States in the 1970s, nurseries could now offer a selection of 'tailor-made' street trees (Santamour *et al.* 1976). These had been specially developed with qualities that made them ideally suited as street trees and they soon became popular in local authority planting schemes. Many were medium-sized species which offered a welcome change from the proliferation of small ornamental trees that had come to dominate many post-war planting schemes, particularly in suburban streets.

FIGURE 81. Mile after mile of ornamental cherries, thorns and similar trees adorn many of our suburban streets with a show of spectacular but often gaudy colour for a couple of weeks in the year. Even in streets with wide grass verges where larger-growing trees could be accommodated it has often been fashionable to favour these small ornamentals. The trees here are *Malus* 'Profusion' and are on the Speke Estate in Liverpool.

As the public in Britain became more environmentally conscious in the 1970s and 1980s, there was a growing lobby of conservationists and others wanting to promote the planting of 'native' rather than 'exotic' tree species in our towns and cities. This was in the belief that it would encourage wildlife and the approach embraced all areas of urban green space, including street tree planting. However, as landscape professionals should know, many of our 'native' trees are either too large or spreading for most streets or do not thrive in the polluted air or poor soil conditions of urban environments (Johnston *et al.* 2011). In the 1990s, many local Biodiversity Action Plans stated that native trees should be preferred to non-native in the mistaken believe that even in urban areas these generally had greater biodiversity value. It is ironic that attempts to accommodate this policy in street planting often involved the use of trees such as the 'native' fastigiate oak (*Quercus robur* 'Fastigiata'). All specimens of this tree are genetically identical clones and do nothing to increase the biodiversity of an urban tree population.

Landscape design with street trees

It would be difficult to over-emphasise the importance of good urban planning as the basis for creating opportunities for good urban design with trees. The layout of streets, including their width, direction, length and orientation has always had a crucial bearing on how these can accommodate trees and what type of trees are most suitable. However, the reality in Britain is that many of our towns and cities have developed in an organic manner over several centuries and for the most part are not the product of any major urban planning initiative. The classic example is the City of London that still has a street pattern that largely reflects the original medieval layout of narrow, winding streets. In situations like this there has never been much scope for bold and imaginative boulevard-type planting schemes. This is in contrast to continental cities such as Paris, Brussels, Vienna and Berlin, and some American cities such as Washington and Chicago. Up to the 1920s, British literature on the planting and management of street trees, with the notable exception of Thomas Mawson (1911), seems to have given little consideration to the crucial role of urban planning and design. In 1911, when the pioneering American planner Charles Mulford Robinson (1911) published his book entitled *The Width and Arrangement of Streets*, there was nothing similar published in Britain and his work seems to have gained little recognition here among those promoting street trees.

Accommodating trees in narrow streets

From the early days of the Victorian street tree movement there was a commonly held view frequently expressed in the popular press that British streets were generally too narrow to accommodate any trees. Those trying to promote street tree planting were constantly having to battle against this misconception. Robert Walker, the Scottish arboriculturist, was always keen to point out that from his own travels around Britain he had seen many city centre streets that were at least 100 ft (30.5 m) wide. In his view these streets was often significantly wider than many continental boulevards yet they had not been planted with trees (Walker 1890, 1–2). Conscious of the impact of street width on limiting the opportunities for tree planting, some professionals suggested adopting a recognised standard width above which some planting should be possible. While views varied on this standard width, it was generally in the region of 40–45 ft (12.2–13.7 m) including carriageway and footways (*Gardeners' Chronicle* 1892, 530). Sometimes a minimum width for the footway was also stipulated. However, it is clear from the author's research that planting was often undertaken in streets below these recommended minimum widths.

While many professionals in the late Victorian and Edwardian eras were focused on trying to accommodate at least some tree planting in Britain's narrow streets, others were advocating a bolder approach that involved urban planning solutions. In the early 1900s, Thomas Mawson, the eminent landscape architect and town planner, was a vociferous advocate of the creation of wide and impressive boulevards in the style of Paris. An example of his bold and imaginative approach was his proposed scheme for the Grand Boulevard in Dunfermline, Scotland, that would terminate at the town's Guildhall (Mawson 1911, 250). This would comprise three roadways and two avenues, giving a total width of 150 ft (45.7 m). If the scheme had been undertaken as Mawson intended, he believed this would have created the finest boulevard in Britain. The scale of Mawson's vision for impressive urban boulevards is typified by the range of tree species he recommended for street planting in his classic work *Civic Art* (*ibid.*, 355). Of over 30 trees listed, the majority are large forest-type trees that would make a major impact on the urban landscape when planted as extensive avenues.

The design of street or boulevard planting has invariably followed that which has traditionally been prescribed for avenue planting in other landscape settings. This has included the double or single avenue and the square or quincunx design (Pradines 2009, 23). Double avenues were often used for prestige plantings on main thoroughfares in the heart of the city, for example, at the Mall in London in the 1900s (see Figure 28). This has also been used as a landscape feature on less prestigious routes where there was sufficient space. An example is De Pary's Avenue, Bedford, where an impressive double avenue of limes was planted in the 1890s (Figure 82).

'A jungle of variety'

Ever since street tree planting became fashionable in Britain in the 1870s and 1880s there has been much debate about whether to mix different species of trees in the same street. One of the earliest comments on this topic was in an

FIGURE 82. Double avenues were often used for prestige plantings on main thoroughfares in the heart of major cities. However, they have also been used as a landscape feature on less prestigious routes where there was sufficient space. This example is De Pary's Avenue, Bedford, where an impressive double avenue of limes was planted in the 1890s. The photograph dates from around 1915.

article in *Gardeners' Chronicle* from 1870 by an English correspondent who cited an American example of mixing species:

> I may here remark that whatever tree is used for street or avenue planting only one kind should be employed in each particular street, as two or three sorts in the same street produce a patchy appearance, and destroy that unity of expression which street planting should aim at securing. In proof of this, Norfolk in Virginia affords good examples. There is to be found there the most varied collection of ornamental trees that I have ever met with in one city; nevertheless, owing to their being planted without order as to kind, the grand effect which they would otherwise have produced is lost.
>
> Newton 1870, 1088

This view was supported by leading figures in the world of horticulture, such as the landscape gardener Alexander McKenzie (1875, 7475) who stated that 'for the sake of uniformity the same class of trees should be planted'. Similar comments are repeated regularly in the horticultural and landscaping literature through to the present day. Only very occasionally has the opposite view been expressed. Charles Mulford Robinson (1901, 120) proposed the use of two different species in some streets by the alternate planting of trees of rapid growth with those that mature more slowly. As the latter increase in size and demand more room, the temporary trees, which had then served their purpose, could be cut down. Nevertheless, he still favoured the aim of achieving eventual uniformity of planting in the same street. Frank Kingdon-Ward (1943, 146), the famous plant collector, made a contribution to the debate in one of his rare comments on street trees. He suggested that both single species and varieties can be appropriate, depending on the situation, but for short roads and streets where formality is required, uniformity is better than a 'jungle of variety'. Alan Mitchell, the 'tree connoisseur' and always a bit of a maverick, was one of the few who saw a positive side of this 'jungle of variety' when he remarked:

> A walk through some suburban roads, especially some fairly recent ones in residential areas, is as good as a visit to an arboretum.
>
> Mitchell 1974, 9

Despite the balance of opinion having always been heavily in favour of uniformity in the selection of species for the same street, it is remarkable how often this is not reflected in the composition of street trees in Britain today. One of the most common reasons for this is where losses from single species avenues of forest-type trees have been replaced with smaller ornamental species, often with different species on different occasions thus adding considerably to the resulting mixture. Some arboriculturists have recently been actively promoting a significant mix of species in the same street on the grounds of increasing the biodiversity of the urban tree population. However, this can still be achieved by varying the species used in different streets rather than ignoring urban design principles and streetscape aesthetics.

Spacing and siting of street trees

Another street tree design topic that has always been widely discussed is how far apart trees should be spaced. Naturally, the answer to that question has always depended to some extent on the species being planted and the presence of any obstructions above or below ground. With regard to planting distances from obstructions such as public utilities and street furniture, there has always been much debate about this. Different distances have been proposed in respect of a wide range of situations by many different authorities, although it was generally recognised that the distance between trees should be as uniform as the circumstances allowed (Mattocks 1925, 27). With the general lack of agreement on this topic it was proposed in the 1960s that aspects of this, such as the minimum planting distances from the carriageway or the building line for different types of trees, should be stipulated by some industry body and enforced if necessary by legislation (Youens 1963, 83). In 1963, it was suggested that the Institute of Park Administration's Special Committee on Trees in Urban Areas, which was currently considering a range of related issues, should produce this type of information when their recommendations were published. However, a response from the Chairman of the committee indicated that this was not a straightforward matter because of problems with definitions and enforcement and it was unlikely that the matter would be resolved quickly (Marshall 1963, 83). In 1968, the respected arboriculturist Fred Boddy (1968, 5–9) tried to set out some 'golden rules' on this topic in his booklet *Highway Trees* and although many of his recommendations were widely adopted, they were not universally agreed. Boddy (1964, 53) was also one of the few arboriculturists that did not like regular spacings for street trees, even where this was possible, declaring that it was 'often wise to avoid the stereotyped planting of regimented rows, which only constitute true avenues when they are reasonable straight and have some sort of vista at one or both ends'. While there is now some recognised guidance on some of these planting distances, it is still largely at the discretion of the local authority.

There were also basic design considerations determining planting distances, such as whether the crowns of street trees should touch each other (Mattocks 1925, 23). In addition there were management considerations such as whether trees should be planted at a spacing that would suffice when they were fully grown, or whether double the amount should be planted for immediate effect and then alternate trees removed as the planting matured (Butterworth 1923, 353). An examination of hundreds of photographs of early street tree plantings from the Victorian and Edwardian eras has revealed that the spacing of street trees was extremely close by modern standards (see Figures 64 and 83). Furthermore, from an exploration of the history of many individual sites it appears that trees were invariably planted at what was considered their final spacing without any intention to remove alternate trees at a later date. However, with forest-type trees planted in narrow streets, the removal of alternate trees was later considered as a management option when they began to mature (see

FIGURE 83. An examination of hundreds of photographs of early street tree plantings from the Victorian and Edwardian eras has revealed that the spacing of street trees was extremely close by modern standards. These young plane trees are in Ranelagh Avenue in Fulham, London, and were photographed around 1910. Many of the original trees are still there although the spacing is now much wider.

Chapter 12). As the twentieth century progressed planting distances between trees increased, no doubt in response to the growing number of constraints on closer distances. It is also likely that the experience of managing trees at very close spacings, particularly when pruning regimes were not rigorously applied, prompted a change of policy in response to many complaints from the public about 'overgrown' trees. In an effort to give individual trees more room, it was sometimes recommended that in narrow streets the trees on either side of the road should be planted alternately instead of opposite (Mattocks 1925, 23). This method of alternate planting could also be applied to double avenues where the space available between the rows is not sufficient to prevent the trees growing together and an arched effect across the road was not desirable.

Research for this book shows that many formerly homogeneous street plantings of plane, lime and other species, established in late Victorian and Edwardian times, have now changed dramatically. As these trees have been removed, for whatever reason, they have frequently not been replaced or have been replaced by different species, often smaller ornamental trees. This has generally had a negative impact on the overall aesthetic appearance of the streetscape, resulting in an assortment of trees that has no overall design or coherence. Nowadays, there are no longer the spaces available on many streets for regular avenue-type planting, since many planting sites have been lost for various reasons, not least to facilitate parking and vehicle access and to accommodate new street furniture. Furthermore, when trees are removed because they are dead or dangerous they are often not replaced, either because the local authority decides this is not a priority or the nearby residents do not want a replacement. This has left many streets, especially those in the former Victorian and Edwardian suburbs, with trees at irregular spacing and often very long gaps between them. Then, with the frequent mix of species and ages the treescape appears very fragmented. While this clearly is not what the original planners and planters envisaged, for many professionals today this is an unfortunate 'fact of life' in most of these residential streets. However, these professionals would probably also agree on the need to maintain at all costs the coherence and uniformity of high profile avenues such as the Mall in London, the Promenade in Cheltenham or the Broadway in Letchworth. The contribution of these majestic avenues to urban design is readily acknowledged but perhaps too often forgotten in less famous locations (Shepheard 1955, 1981).

Shaping street trees

Ever since trees were first planted in the streets of European cities they have often been trained and pruned to give a very formal appearance, especially with round or square shapes. This close clipping is similar to topiary which has long been a feature of traditional garden design. In 1864, Count Des Cars (1881, 25–27) published his classic book *Tree Pruning: A Treatise on Pruning Forest and Ornamental Trees* and this included an account of how the dendroscope, a small handheld device, could be used to guide the shaping of trees into a uniform appearance. When William Robinson (1869, 259) stayed in Paris in 1867 he was struck by some of the unusually shaped trees that he saw, in both streets and parks, although could not see 'any real necessity for this clipping'. Charles Mumford Robinson was another authority who did not approve of the Parisian's love of street tree shaping, although he thought this was not as extreme as the Italians. He remarked:

> The principal criticism one can make of the trees in the Paris streets, is that their arrangement is very formal, and that the trees themselves are too small. As to the first condition, formalism as opposed to naturalism in landscape architecture is of course a matter of taste. Paris does not, at least, go as far as some of the Italian cities in cutting and training trees into grotesque artificial forms. The second, and more serious condition, appears to be due to crowding and pruning; it should therefore be easy to avoid.
>
> Robinson 1901, 119

Throughout the history of street trees in Britain there has never been much enthusiasm for the shaping of these trees in the manner often undertaken in continental Europe. This is despite the occasional efforts by some writers to highlight the aesthetic possibilities of pleaching and close pruning in an attempt to encourage its application to street trees (Mattocks 1925, 30) (Figure 84). There are probably a number of factors behind the British reluctance to embrace this practice. One reason might be the same public attitudes about the 'unnatural' appearance of trees that condemns pollarding as a 'mutilation' of the natural form of the trees. Nevertheless, the British public has always had a general acceptance of topiary work in gardens even though the same fundamental pruning principles apply. A major factor in recent years has probably been the cost of the work, which is both expensive and time-consuming, and the requirement for specially trained tree pruners. Furthermore, with the introduction of new cultivars with neat and compact crowns, such as *Carpinus betulus* 'Fastigiata', which became increasingly popular as street trees in the latter part of the twentieth century, this 'shaped' appearance could be achieved to a certain extent in a line of street trees without the need for any expensive clipping.

Trees in urban design

As already noted, the aesthetic benefits of street trees has traditionally focused on their individual characteristics, such as crown form, flowers, fruit, bark and autumn colour. This approach dominated the literature in the Victorian and Edwardian eras. In the early twentieth century there were some British authors who described how trees could be arranged in streets in various formations with an eye to urban design (e.g. Mawson 1911; Purdom 1913, 258; Mattocks 1925, 256). However, for much of the twentieth century it seems that the idea of using

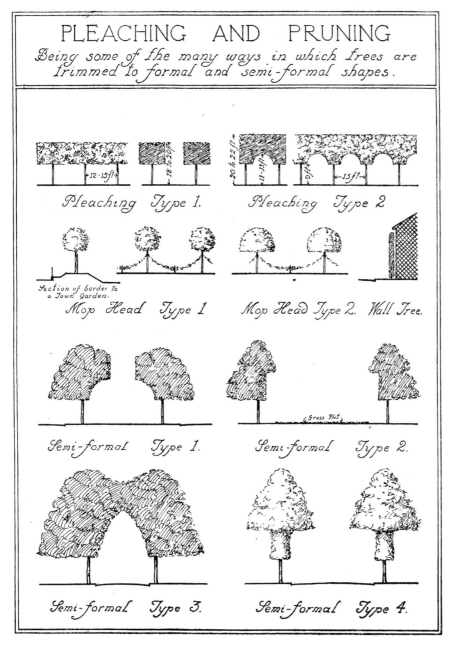

FIGURE 84. Throughout the history of street trees in Britain there has never been much enthusiasm for the shaping of these trees in the manner often undertaken in continental Europe. This is despite the occasional efforts by some writers to highlight the aesthetic possibilities of pleaching and close pruning in an attempt to encourage its application to street trees.

MATTOCKS 1925.

trees collectively as a major element of urban design was not explored to any great extent in Britain or elsewhere, and not much beyond anything more than recognition of the concept of avenue or boulevard planting. It was not until the 1980s with the publication of *Trees in Urban Design*, the groundbreaking book by American landscape architect Henry Arnold (1980), that the subject entered a new and more imaginative dimension. Arnold stressed the need for order, coherence and appropriate scale in urban treescapes and highlighted how the relationship of trees to buildings and streets can be used to define and reinforce urban spaces. The book has had a significant impact on many British arboriculturists, although with their limited responsibilities in terms of urban design they have not usually been in a position to put these ideas into practice.

The introduction of new road layouts and features has sometimes heralded new opportunities for street tree planting. From 1910, as many major thoroughfares in British cities became increasingly busy with traffic they were often redesigned as dual carriageways with a central reservation (median strip). This provided opportunities for tree planting, although this was often not taken or small ornamental trees were planted that did not optimise the space available. Another feature in road design that became popular from the 1920s was a new form of traffic junction known as the roundabout. The first roundabout in Britain was in Letchworth Garden City in 1909 and this innovation became popular for new and existing roads. Unfortunately, they were generally not much planted or the planting design was poor (Wells 1970, 301). Often they were used for expensive and temporary displays of bedding plants rather than as a site for permanent tree planting, even when there was space for this (*Gardeners' Chronicle* 1951, 118). In recent years, traffic calming measures that involve the use of kerb extensions, short protections from the footway into the road, have provided some new sites for tree planting, usually with small ornamental species. There has also been some exciting new work in the field of urban design that has reinforced the importance of tree-lined boulevards in the modern city. This has emphasised how they relate to many issues that are central to urban life, including liveability, mobility, safety, economic opportunity, mass transit, and open space (Jacobs *et al.* 2002).

Planting and establishment

There has always been much debate among professionals regarding what might be considered 'best practice' in planting and establishing these trees. Although there was often a consensus among the recognised 'experts' on some of the fundamental principles, it is remarkable how often incidents of 'poor and ignorant practice' were reported down the years in the pages of the horticultural and landscape press. While street tree planting in Britain was largely inspired by the boulevards of some continental European cities, it is noticeable how European planting techniques often got mixed reviews from the British press. In spite of this, there were those who understood that to establish those great boulevards, their standards of practice could not be too bad. Loudon was one of the first and most receptive of the British authorities and as early as 1827, long before the emergence of the Victorian street tree movement, he was contrasting British practice in urban planting with that on the Continent, stating that 'Planting and pruning practice is much more advanced for the trees on the Boulevards of Brussels' (Loudon 1827, 461). However, when street tree planting in Britain did get underway in earnest, disparaging and dismissive attitudes towards continental and French practices in particular were not slow to emerge. These were summed up in 1861 by one correspondent in the *Gardeners' Chronicle* (1861, 943) who declared that in the selection, planting and aftercare of their urban trees 'the French appear to be still so far behind ourselves that it is useless to enter into particulars'. Other writers were quick to point out some of the many examples of poor practice in early British street tree planting. Typical of the comments made was the criticism voiced by another correspondent in the *Gardeners' Chronicle* (1873, 1215) who stated, 'If anyone desired a superb example of "how not to do it", they would find it illustrated in a plantation of limes opposite the railway station in the town of Weston-super-Mare'. Quite often, failures in street tree planting were laid at the door of incompetent officials and operatives. Angus Webster (1910, 15) believed that far too often 'the important operations of preparing the ground and planting the trees are left in the hands of the surveyor or builder, who has little or no knowledge to fit him for the work, the operation being carried out by labourers who are also perfectly ignorant of what is required or the conditions necessary for successful tree or shrub culture'. Some writers expressed concern that the high failure rate in many plantings and the consequent waste of money was turning much of the public against the whole idea of street trees (*Woods and Forests* 1884a, 498). Being much in the public eye the early street tree planting on the Victoria Embankment in London came in for very close scrutiny. Some criticism focused on the lack of open soil around the base of the trees, believing this would restrict available moisture and limit root growth (*Gardeners' Chronicle* 1871, 711). By contrast, some other high-profile early plantings attracted much praise. In 1876, the *Gardeners' Chronicle* announced:

> Of the 99 trees planted in Broad Street [Birmingham] this spring, only two are dead. All the others, with two or three exceptions, are in good health and foliage, and have made fair growth, and this is really a matter for surprise [because of air pollution and gas leaks in the soil]. Mr R.H. Vertegans, of the Chad Valley Nurseries, Birmingham, supplied the trees and undertook the planting. In every case the paving-stones were lifted, and large holes 6 to 7 ft [1.8–2.1 m] across were excavated about 3 ft [0.9 m] deep and filled in with new soil, and the trees very carefully planted, men being ready to fix circular tree-guards at once, iron gratings 3 ft [0.9 m] square to fix into the pavements around each tree, and to firmly secure the trees to the guards. Of course, clean, young, robust, healthy, well-rooted specimen trees were selected, each being from 14 to 15 ft [4.3–4.6 m] in height.
>
> *Gardeners' Chronicle* 1876b, 355

In terms of the size of nursery stock that should be used for street planting, it has been widely recognised that this needs to be quite large so as to be sufficiently robust in this demanding environment. While little forest transplants and whips may be suitable for planting at the side of rural roads, these would not last long if located in the footway. The risk of vandalism was often mentioned to justify the use of larger stock, although it significantly increased the cost of planting. In recent years, there has been a tendency to use even larger-sized nursery stock for street planting, such as heavy standards and semi-mature trees (*Gardeners' Chronicle* 1981, 18–19), although not everyone has supported that trend (Labey 1991, 17). In 1965, the publication of a British Standard on *Specifications for Nursery Stock* did much to clarify what had been an often confusing situation regarding the various categories and terminology related to tree planting material (BSI 1965).

It has generally been accepted that urban trees should be planted in the dormant season to ensure better survival rates. However, there has always been an ongoing debate about the best time to do this during that dormant season. Many Victorian writers such as Ravencroft (1883, 35) favoured planting these trees in the spring 'just when the trees are starting into growth; for the winter is such a fearful ordeal to all vegetation [and] by planting in the spring the shock is not so great'. The Edwardian authority Angus Webster (1909, 262) also agreed with the view that early spring was 'in most cases preferable'. The trend in recent years towards the use of containerised nursery stock for street tree planting rather than using more delicate bare-rooted trees has allowed greater flexibility in the timing of planting operations.

Soil amendments and innovations in planting practice

In contrast to many garden soils, urban soils are notoriously lacking in many of the qualities required for successful tree establishment (Urban 2008, 103–116). Those soils found under the roads and footways of our older towns and cities are often particularly poor environments for tree growth. Some of these problems were mentioned in Chapter 10 and include contaminants, compaction, lack of nutrients and extremes of moisture content.

Acknowledged experts on street tree planting and those responsible for the actual work have usually agreed that the best course of action to overcome the limitations of urban soils is to replace the soil in the planting hole with good quality top soil. In his book *Town Planting* the Victorian expert Ravenscroft (1883, 36) states, 'By far the best plan is to bring some nice fresh loam from the country; just enough to each tree to start it will do, say a cart-load or a "yard" to each, but if you can give more, do so'. Many Victorian and Edwardian experts were keen to stress the importance of having a large planting pit with an adequate volume of soil for the size of trees planted. This factor was emphasised in an early article on good practice in street tree planting, which appeared in 1884 in the magazine *Woods and Forests* (1884b, 356–357). The question of whether to add any amendments to the existing soil in order to improve the prospects of successful street tree establishment has been much debated in the history of British horticultural and arboricultural literature and it continues to divide opinion. From the earliest days of the Victorian street tree movement various organic and inorganic substances were suggested as additives to improve the quality of the soil. Ravenscroft (1983, 36) was quite sceptical about adding anything. He specifically did not recommend mixing manure into the loam, frequently suggested by his contemporaries, because 'it causes a soft and rank growth which does more harm than good'. However, he believed using a little leaf mould could be useful to give the soil 'richness'. Nowadays, it is quite common to add various organic and inorganic amendments to the soil in the planting hole (Urban 2008, 176–186). Nevertheless, some professionals continue to be sceptical about many of these, suggesting their promotion often has more to do with product marketing than with aiding successful tree establishment. It is pointed out that the Victorians managed to establish millions of street trees quite successfully without using these 'essential' amendments. While this is true, it should also be recognised that soil conditions under many urban streets are significantly worse today than they were in Victorian times, due to another 100 years or more of urban abuse.

One problem that has undoubtedly increased over the past century is that of soil compaction. The rapid growth of vehicle and pedestrian traffic, the enormous weight of many modern vehicles and the vast density and weight of an endless sprawl of built structures, have all been factors in this. Highly compacted soils have a negative impact on tree growth and survival by altering soil structure, impeding root growth, and inhibiting the movement of soil water and gases (Watson and Himelick 2013, 10). Some modern solutions to this include the use of structural soils, a specially designed medium that has a high load-bearing capacity while remaining root penetrable and supportive of tree growth (*ibid.*, 29). These invariably involve carefully controlled mixes using coarse sand or crushed stone, organic matter, and clay or clay loam. Another solution commonly found today is the use of suspended pavements or footways (sometimes called cantilevered sidewalks in North America). This is where the surface of the footway is engineered to be suspended above the soil creating a subsurface void space that is filled with soil for root growth. This ensures that the soil does not have to be compacted to support the footway. Drainage and irrigation systems are usually installed as well. Suspended pavements range from elaborate designs constructed on site to simple precast concrete structures or specially designed plastic cells. While these techniques for alleviating the problems of soil compaction in street tree planting are regarded as very modern developments, research for this book suggests otherwise. Writing in the *Gardener's Magazine* John Claudius Loudon records his observations on the early boulevards of Paris, before the days of Haussmann, during a European tour in 1828. His description of techniques for the mitigation of 'superincumbent pressure' include what may be the earliest references to the use of both suspended pavements and a form of structural soil in association with street tree planting:

> The success of the trees planted in such a situation as that of the Boulevards, the species being properly chosen, depends almost entirely on the quality of the soil, its quantity, distribution as to depth and to the supply of moisture, and more especially on guarding against the evils of superincumbent pressure. The last point is by far the most difficult to manage. The pressure under the carriage pavement we shall not attempt to get rid of; because, if the pressure on the footway be properly

provided against, a stratum under it of proper soil, 3 or 4 ft. [0.9–1.2 m] in depth, will insure the vigorous growth of the trees till they attain a mature size, and strength sufficient to force their roots into the surrounding strata. The modes of lessening the superincumbent pressure on the soil under the footway are three: First, by vaulting; filling the vaults with the proper soil, preserving vertical and lateral communications for the introduction of water from the gutter between the pathway and the roadway, and forming a footpath of gravel, or other suitable material, over the vaults. Secondly, by building up piers from the bottom of the stratum of prepared soil to the surface, and on these piers resting flag-stones to form the footpath; provision for the entrance of water being made as before, along the side next to the roadway. Thirdly, by mixing the prepared soil with chips of wood and fragments of compressed manure, which will decay and leave interstices for the roots; and with the gravel and rubbish of old buildings, in vertical or oblique strata, which will keep the soil open for the free reception of water, and thus assist the roots in penetrating the soil, in this case unavoidable more compressed than in the other two. Over this last preparation the footway may be formed of flag-stones, causewayed, or laid with gravel or any other suitable material. When the roots of trees must unavoidable depend for their nourishment on a prepared stratum, laid under a Macadamised or causewayed street, the last mode of preparation is the most suitable for general adoption; and, indeed, it is that which will answer perfectly well for footways unless in extraordinary cases.

Loudon 1830, 645–646

Another early reference to the use of suspended pavements, this time in Britain, can be found in *History of London Street Improvements, 1855–1897* by Percy Edwards (1898). Edwards was Clerk of the Improvements Committee for the London County Council and he describes the tremendous care taken to ensure the survival of trees on Northumberland Avenue:

To secure the well-being of the trees, pits were formed and filled with proper soil, and a footway surrounding the trees was covered with an open grating to admit the rain and air to the soil, and to enable it to be stirred and kept loose on the surface. The grating and footway were supported independently by girders over the tree pits, so as to prevent the settlement of the paving and the hardening of the ground around the roots of the trees. Plane trees were selected as most suitable for the atmosphere and the metropolis.

Edwards 1898, 59

While this standard of work was already being employed in some street tree planting schemes in Paris and some other continental cities, it was all rather new in Britain. It was not until the latter part of the twentieth century that the use of suspended pavements became common practice here.

Tree stakes and ties

Newly-planted street trees need some method of mechanical support to keep them in an upright position (Watson and Himelick 2013, 137). The stake and the ties attaching it to the tree should remain in place until the tree is established successfully and the roots system grown sufficiently to support the tree in normal circumstance without assistance. In Victorian and Edwardian times the stake was normally made of wood, such as oak, ash or sweet chestnut. Metal stakes were sometime used, either specially purchased or by the improvised use of freely available gas piping cut to the required length, as these did not rot quickly or break like some wooden stakes (*Gardeners' Chronicle* 1889b, 502). Evidence from numerous photographs has shown that staking practices throughout the history of street tree planting in Britain have varied enormously. While a tripod of three stakes was often used for tree planting in public parks, this was only occasionally used in streets where planting was at the edge of the roadway itself in the days before many motor vehicles (Figure 85). Tripods were generally not used in the footway because the space taken up by the stakes was considered to form an obstruction for pedestrians. For this reason single stakes were invariable used and this is the practice today, although two stakes are still common with large-sized planting stock. One factor that has varied enormously has been the diameter and height of the stakes and some past practices were quite extreme by today's standards. An examination of photos of street tree

FIGURE 85. While a tripod of three stakes was often used for tree planting in public parks, this was only occasionally used in streets where planting was at the edge of the roadway itself in the days before many motor vehicles. This example was in Gaywood Road, Kings Lynn, and was photographed around 1905.

FIGURE 86. An examination of photographs of street tree planting in Chiswick, London, in the 1880s and 1890s showed single tree stakes that were up to 5 inches (12.7 cm) square and as much as 20 ft (6.1 m) in height above the ground. At the time *The Garden* magazine described this as 'ludicrous'. This example is Sutton Lane South, Chiswick, photographed around 1900. The men with the cart are selling flowers.

planting in Chiswick, London, in the 1880s and 1890s showed single tree stakes that up to 5 inches (13 cm) square and as much as 20 ft (6.1 m) in height above the ground (Figure 86). A similarly bizarre method of staking was found in photos from Handsworth, Birmingham, in the 1900s (Figure 87). Some contemporary horticulturists were quick to ridicule this method of staking and one commented:

> The paragraph in *The Garden* of 28 December, 1889, (p611) might have been written of other districts than Chiswick, but the way the trees are planted and staked in this suburb is sufficiently ludicrous. ...Though each tree is surrounded by an iron cage to prevent thoughtless youths and boys from cutting the bark and destroying the branches, a long pole of the same height as the sapling itself and twice its thickness has been placed to each tree for the purpose apparently of giving support. The poles are neither planed nor trimmed, but stand forth in their bold ugliness to disfigure the road and trees and chafe the stem. ...The roots, through which the thick poles must have been thrust, must have received permanent injury. The poles were not even tarred at the bottom to prevent speedy decay.
>
> *The Garden* 1890, 65

There are a few examples of early street planting where tree stakes are not used. Instead, the tree was secured to a tree guard which acted as a means of support. This was seen in a photograph from 1910 of planting in Hendy Street in Cardiff. It is interesting that this is mentioned as a method of support for young trees and an alternative to the conventional wooden tree stake by William Pettigrew (1901, 14), who was responsible for parks and tree planting in Cardiff around that time.

In the 1980s, there was much debate in the horticultural and arboricultural press about whether the use of short or tall stakes was best for planting with standard-sized trees (Patch 1982, 20–21). Recent research had demonstrated that the use of a short stake, about one-third the height of the tree, was generally more beneficial (Patch 1984). This was sufficient to provide good anchorage for the root system while at the same time allowing some movement of the stem above the tie which encouraged stem diameter growth and crown development. Those arguing for tall stakes often stressed that these gave greater protection against vandalism. However, mathematical modelling showed that when a short stake was used the force was distributed along the longer length of the stem and the tree was more likely to just bend. With a tall stake the tree was more likely to break, and at the point just above where the top tie was attached. In Victorian and Edwardian literature on planting with standard-sized trees the use of tall stakes is invariably recommended. A few writers did recommend using short stakes and sometimes the benefits assigned to this were quite similar to those identified in the modern research (Webster 1888, 544). Nevertheless, photographic evidence indicates that tall staking, and often very tall, was common practice for all street tree planting until this was challenged in the 1980s. Even today, many local authorities still use tall stakes for planting in streets and often justify this as protection against vandalism.

Before the production of specially designed tree ties various materials were used to tie newly-planted trees to their stakes. Most commonly used were rope or wire. The likelihood of the wire cutting into the delicate bark of the young tree, especially when this was attached quite tightly, does not seem to have attracted much concern. Where rope was used some experts recommended that this should be specially prepared tar rope as this was more durable (Webster 1909, 262). In accordance with modern practice, it was often suggested that some kind of spacer should be used between the stake and the tree so that damage to the bark by chaffing did not occur. From the 1900s, it was increasingly common to see commercially produced tree ties offered for sale in the gardening magazines (*Gardeners' Chronicle* 1903, 327).

Tree guards and grilles

Tree guards to protect the newly-planted street tree from physical damage appeared from the earliest days of the Victorian street tree movement. Indeed, some fairly expensive but very durable iron tree guards were being produced by the late 1820s which would have been useful for street tree planting had this been happening at that time (Loudon 1929, 674). When street planting got underway in earnest in Britain, in locations where tree guards were used, two basic types were common: metal or wood. From the photographic evidence is appears that where metal types were used, wrought-iron tree guards were most popular and generally more favoured by the experts. In the words of Angus Webster (1909, 262), 'The iron tree guard has many advantages over those of wood or expanded metal and being made in two sections it can be readily placed in position after the tree has been planted'. These guards were available in different shapes; some widest at the top, others at the bottom, and others with their narrowest point in the middle. Sometime, the individual trees were surrounded by a small metal fence, as in the planting along Princes Avenue, Liverpool (see Figure 31). However, all these metal guards had one major disadvantage – their cost. In order to reduce the expense of using tree guards, wooden ones were often employed. In a survey of nine London districts in 1892, it was found that eight districts used wooden guards and the remaining one used expanded metal guards (*Gardeners' Chronicle* 1892, 530). The design of wooden guards was also quite varied. Sometimes these looked rather odd, as with those used by the Local Board at Barking in Essex in the late 1880s, which were a box-like construction made of four thick planks about 6 ft (1.8 m) long (*Gardeners' Chronicle* 1889c, 180). Another more conventional design comprised about half-a-dozen poles or uprights, about 7 ft (2.1 m) long, joined together around the tree trunk by means of wire (Webster 1909, 262).

When young trees had become well-established, usually about 5 or 6 years after planting, it was common practice to remove the tree guards. These were then often replaced with wire netting, put around the stems to protect them from injury and periodically adjusted every few years as the trees grew (Pettigrew 1901, 14). Where wrought-iron guards were removed these were often repaired if damaged and used again in new plantings, thus significantly reducing the cost of one of the most expensive items in street planting. Because of this initial cost, even with the less expensive wooden guards, in most street plantings during the Victorian and Edwardian era tree guards were not used.

The only protection for these trees was the tree stake. From the photographic evidence is seems that tree guards, and especially the more expensive wrought-iron guards, were generally only used in high-profile locations or in the more salubrious neighbourhoods.

Some street tree planting involved the use of tree grilles, which was another expensive addition to planting costs. These grilles normally consisted of an arrangement of iron latticework plates forming a grating around the base of the tree. The most common designs in Victorian and Edwardian times were square and involved two plates that could be placed around the tree and joined together once it had been planted. There was a hole in the centre of the grill to accommodate the tree, which was large enough to allow for future growth over a number of years. The grill enabled the tree to receive natural rainwater and some protection again soil compaction from pedestrian traffic. The tree grilles used in Victorian and Edwardian street plantings were often no more than 3 ft (0.9 m) square (Figure 88). The use of these grilles seems to have been less common than that of wrought-iron tree guards, although again they were generally only used in high-profile locations or the more expensive neighbourhoods.

Having mentioned the expense of using tree guards and tree grilles, this is a convenient point to mention a general observation about street tree planting costs. From the earliest days of the street planting movement there had been frequent comments in the horticultural and arboricultural literature about the false economy of local authorities and other public bodies using poor quality planting stock and materials. An early comparison was often made between the cost of most trees planted and that of the guards used to protect them, which was often several times more (*Woods and Forests* 1884a, 498; *The Garden* 1886, 86). Another false economy that was often highlighted was the lack of adequate

FIGURE 88. The tree grilles used in Victorian and Edwardian street plantings were often no more than 3 ft (0.9 m) square. The use of these grilles seems to have been less common than that of wrought-iron tree guards, although again they were generally only used in high-profile locations or the more expensive neighbourhoods. These newly planted trees with grilles are in Windermere Road in the exclusive north London suburb of Muswell Hill, photographed in 1911.

preparation work in tree pits and the use of existing poor quality soil rather than purchasing good top soil.

In 1872, some of the gardening magazines published a report on the costs associated with tree planting on the boulevards of Paris (*Gardeners' Chronicle* 1872, 73). This undoubtedly raised quite a few eyebrows among the British horticultural establishment and concentrated minds on how the costs for British street planting could be reduced. The average total cost at that time for planting a street tree in Paris was FRF 202. Of that, the cost of the tree was FRF 5, the cast-iron grill was FRF 47 and the iron guard was FRF 9. Most of the remaining cost was incurred with the excavation and preparation of the tree pit.

Planting location

The precise location for tree planting in the street is another topic that has been much debated. In the residential streets of the new suburbs, garden cities and new towns, where there were often grass verges specifically designed to accommodate trees, this was not so much an issue. However, in the streets of town and city centres and in the older residential and commercial districts, where there was just a hard-surfaced footway and no verge, this required some thought. Before we discuss the factors involved in making these decisions, one very interesting historical fact needs to be highlighted. While looking through early photographs of street tree plantings in the Victorian era it became clear that many of the trees were actually planted in the road and not on the footway. Research into this matter revealed that until the 1910s it was not unusual to plant street trees a few feet out into the road (see Figures 61 and 85). This was to ensure that the trees were nearer the channels by the roadside, which allowed more rainwater to reach the roots than when they were planted in the footway (*Gardeners' Chronicle* 1898, 238). Naturally, this practice was discontinued once motor vehicles began to travel along our roads in ever greater numbers and at faster speeds.

From the early years of the twentieth century when all street trees were planted in the footway, the debate about the best location focused on whether this should be at the front nearest the kerb or at the back and furthest away from the road. The factors that determined this were generally not matters relating to urban design but had more to do with ensuring that the trees did not cause an obstruction. In the 1920s, one leading expert proposed a general rule that it was better to plant near the roadway on wide roads, and better to plant near the property line on narrow roads with deep building lines (Mattocks 1925, 257). This would help to ensure there was less conflict between the trees and various utilities and street furniture. In the 1930s, some highway engineers preferred tree planting at the back line of the footway, partly to give greater clearance for vehicles, while others still regarded the correct position to be within a foot or so of the kerb (Pettigrew 1937, 183). Nowadays, the presence of underground utility services has a significant influence on the precise location for street tree planting.

Post-planting maintenance

This chapter concludes with a brief mention of post-planting maintenance. This involves those activities that are often crucial to the future health and vitality of the young tree, such as watering, weeding around the base and adjusting and removing tree stakes and ties. While there are references to these activities throughout the historical literature, what is surprising to the modern reader is how little is made of this vital part of the tree planting process. Today, much attention is given to the need for a programme of systematic post-planting maintenance to help reduce the high mortality rates in street tree plantings, which in England average around 23% (Britt and Johnston 2008, 218–222). The scale of these losses and the consequent waste of public money may come as a shock to many readers, especially when the task of engineering trees into concrete landscapes could not be described as 'rocket science'. However, it does seem that the situation has improved since Victorian and Edwardian times. Although there were no national surveys then, reports in contemporary gardening magazines suggests that tree losses in many street tree planting schemes were frequently very high and substantial numbers of replacements were often required. It also seems that there was a greater acceptance of high mortality rates among newly planted street trees and much less emphasis on the need for post-planting maintenance.

CHAPTER TWELVE

Maintenance and Management

Once trees have been established successfully in a street environment this is just the beginning of an ongoing programme of maintenance and management. This is essential to ensure they contribute a wide range of benefits to urban communities. Periodic maintenance work is also necessary to make sure street trees avoid conflict with traffic, pedestrians, built development and urban infrastructure. Nevertheless, some people still believe that street trees simply grow by themselves, as they do in their natural habitat, and just need to be removed at the end of their useful lifespan.

As with the previous chapter, there is a considerable volume of published and unpublished historical material relating to the maintenance and management of urban trees in Britain. Although we focus here on street trees, limited space only allows for an outline of some of the more significant points. The chapter begins by looking at standards in arboricultural work and the availability of relevant expertise. Tree maintenance operations are then examined, with an emphasis on types of pruning. The equipment and machinery used to maintain street trees has evolved over the years and some of the most important developments are outlined. The chapter then addresses the topic of municipal arboriculture, the governance of street trees and relevant management plans and strategies. This includes an appraisal of management and maintenance regimes, such as regular pollarding and replacement programmes for forest-type trees. Finally, a brief account is given of the influence since the 1950s of ideas and practice from modern arboriculture and urban forestry.

Arboricultural standards and education

The care of large mature trees in the built environment is a job that requires specialist skills that extend far beyond those normally possessed by the horticulturist or landscape gardener. The ability to climb trees with ropes and a safety harness, the pruning and removal of large and heavy branches, and the use of chainsaws at height, all demand expertise in a range of exacting skills. Furthermore, these skills need to be possessed by an individual with a high level of physical fitness, considerable agility and a head for heights. In a parkland setting this work would be dangerous enough but then add the risks involved when working in a busy street, with traffic and pedestrians, buildings and utility services such as overhead electric power lines. While street conditions in late Victorian times were generally not as intense as they are today, many of those factors still applied.

The growth of street tree planting in the second half of the nineteenth century established vast numbers of new trees lining the roads of our towns and cities. It had also signalled a far more urban focus in British arboriculture, although the term 'arboriculture' was only just beginning to be used in that context (Johnston 2015, 18–21). Although planting and caring for trees in many urban parks and gardens was not radically different from similar locations in rural areas, the street was a purely urban realm. By the beginning of the twentieth century, many of the new street trees had matured and required routine maintenance, such as pruning, felling and remedial work. The specialist skills required to work on mature trees have been recognised since Roman times when the term 'arborator' was used to describe an expert tree worker. In more recent times, following the development of arboriculture in the late nineteenth century as a specialist profession focusing on amenity trees, names such as 'tree surgeon' or 'arborist' have come to be used for manual workers engaged in maintaining mature trees (*ibid.*, 20–32).

Ever since the early days of the Victorian street tree movement there were difficulties in getting suitably trained and experienced personnel to undertake tree maintenance. It seems that this maintenance work, as with the initial planting, was too often left to unskilled and inexperienced labourers. Various efforts were made to highlight the situation and affect some remedy. As early as 1863 the Royal Horticultural Society had formed an Arboricultural Committee to focus on all matters relating to amenity trees. No sooner had this announcement been made than the gardening magazines were expressing the hope that this would lead to the raising of standards in the planting and maintenance of urban trees, particularly with regard to those trees in London (*Gardeners' Chronicle* 1863, 699–700). It seems that this was a forlorn hope because in 1874 the popular *Pall Mall Magazine* launched a strident attack on the standards of local authority tree pruning done by unskilled workers and its views were repeated in some leading gardening magazines (*The Garden* 1874, 551). Some local authorities considered street tree pruning as little more than an opportunity for 'poor relief' and saw no problem in engaging unemployed men for this work (*Gardeners' Chronicle* 1910, 232). Throughout the late Victorian and Edwardian eras the poor standards of tree work in Britain was often contrasted with those in France, Germany and the United States where many experts considered arboricultural knowledge to be more advanced (*Gardeners' Chronicle* 1909, 90). When it came to the type of professional background that was most appropriate for those responsible for supervising tree work, the early debate in Britain revolved around the disciples of horticulture and forestry. James McNab, superintendent of the Royal Botanic Gardens, Edinburgh, had firm views on this:

> All trees, both old and young, under municipal control, ought to be put under the management of a properly certificated forester, instead of committing them to the mercy of anyone whom the municipal owners for the time being chose to call in to attend them, and this often after mischief has been done, not unfrequently by parties who posses but a very indifferent knowledge of pruning operations. Unless an experienced inspector is often amongst such trees, and observing from time to

time the requirements necessary for their preservation, it will be difficult to get them kept in the condition in which they ought to be ... The manipulation requisite for the management of forest or ornamental trees in towns is frequently entrusted to gardeners, but they often do not possess that scientific arboricultural knowledge which has from long practice been acquired by a thorough-bred forester; the latter knows the time and method of pruning, both of old and young trees, so as to prevent that internal injury that often befalls them; and, for securing the proper development of the trees in after-years, he is the proper person to employ for such work.

McNab 1874, 401

This preference for forestry expertise at a supervisory or management level was evident again with the Cockburn Association (1899, 9–10) in Edinburgh which rather unfairly contrasted the achievements of the city's Superintendent of Parks and Gardens, a horticulturist, with the outstanding success of Aberdeen where the forester Robert Walker was employed (see Chapter 5). Nevertheless, whether it was foresters or horticulturists in charge of looking after street trees this was always better than having somebody with no appropriate expertise or experience. Just before the First World War, the front page of *The Garden* magazine gave a bleak overall assessment of arboricultural standards with street trees but also made some distinction between standards in the larger cities and those in smaller towns:

This is the season when municipal and urban authorities usually turn their attention to the so-called pruning of the street trees in their respective districts, and, judging by past experience, a word of warning is very necessary. All too often we see these trees so hacked and mutilated as to render them cripples for life, and mere caricatures of what Nature intended them to be. In larger cities, where the street trees are usually under the control of a practical and experienced man, the evil is not often perpetrated; it is in the smaller towns, where the work is supervised by the town clerk or sanitary inspector, that the mutilation is rife.

The Garden 1914, 113

By the 1930s there continued to be concern at the lack of arboricultural expertise among local authorities. While the planting and maintenance of street trees was usually the responsibility of the highways department, the work involved was often carried out by parks department workers where such a department existed (Pettigrew 1937, 182). Whilst highways workers had no formal training in practical arboriculture, the parks workers' arboricultural skills also tended to be limited, particularly in terms of maintaining mature trees. When the pruning of street trees became necessary to reduce conflicts with built development or ensure public safety, the standard of routine maintenance was often very poor. Frederick Balfour highlighted some of these problems in his usual unequivocal fashion:

The pruning of street and roadside trees is all too often left by councils to a committee who may be eminently able to deal with engineering problems but who have not an iota of knowledge of how trees should be treated or, indeed, any clear idea of what they should ultimately look like. In some of the larger cities and London boroughs men are employed to take charge of street trees well qualified and expert in their art. There are, however, many glaring exceptions, and too often the care of trees is regarded by those responsible for roads as a side issue of little or no importance.

Balfour 1935, 173

Many of those responsible for street trees in the inter-war years seemed unaware of some of the advances now being made by professionals in the USA. In 1929, an American text was published entitled *Roadside Development* that focused on the planting, maintenance and management of roadside trees in both urban and rural situations (Bennett 1929). The author, Jesse Merle Bennett, had gained much experience as Superintendent of Parks and Forestry at Wayne County in Michigan. As the title of the book was 'roadside development' and it was not published in Britain, this probably ensured it was not read by local authority staff engaged in tree work. Although arboricultural standards within British local authorities were often poor during the 1920s and 30s, this was a time when the Royal Botanic Gardens at Kew became established as a 'centre of excellence' for arboriculture and significant advances were made at the 'leading edge' of the profession (Johnston 2015, 22). Some of the staff at Kew, such as William Dallimore and Arthur Osborn, were establishing their reputations as authorities on the subject of tree care. Not to be left out, Edinburgh Botanic Gardens had its own early twentieth century expert in Professor Isaac Bayley Balfour, described by Frederick Balfour (no relation) as the best pruning authority of his time (Balfour 1935, 173). Unfortunately, these advances in arboricultural principles and practice at Kew and Edinburgh were to have little impact on the nation's standards of street tree maintenance and management. The students who qualified from these establishments at that time usually went into employment in private gardens or estates or in other botanical gardens and arboreta. They rarely got jobs looking after trees for local authority parks departments and almost never ended up with any responsibility for street trees.

One individual who was not a product of either Kew or Edinburgh RBG stands out as the pre-eminent British arboriculturist of this era: Denis Le Sueur (Boulton 1969; Johnston 2015, 22–23). After studying arboriculture and forestry Le Sueur worked as a forestry consultant in London, often engaged by the City of London where a significant portion of his work was with amenity trees, including street trees. His book *The Care and Repair of Ornamental Trees* was the most important work on practical tree surgery to be published in Britain in the first half of the twentieth century and contains much that is relevant to street trees (Le Sueur, 1934).

After the Second World War many of the nation's street trees were in a poor state having been neglected for several years. As local authorities tried to get to grips with the situation the response was very patchy and standards of arboricultural work extremely variable. The arboriculturist Fred Boddy (1947, 72) repeated the old complaint that street trees often came within the jurisdiction of those responsible for roads maintenance, who in most cases had little arboricultural knowledge. A revealing insight into street tree management by one local authority just after the Second World War has been gained from an oral history interview with a former employee of Brighton Council, Henry Wilmshurst (1996). His job title is given as 'street tree forester' and the interview reveals how little training was given to some local authority workers engaged on street tree maintenance in the late 1940s and 1950s. Among many local authorities there was also a lack of adequate equipment for work that was potentially very dangerous to both the workers and the public. Anecdotal evidence indicates that the situation with tree work operations in the major cities was sometimes a little better.

In the late 1960s a major development occurred that was to have a lasting impact on raising standards in tree maintenance and this was the establishment of full-time educational courses in arboriculture. At last arboriculture had been recognised as a subject in its own right rather than being included as an aspect of horticulture or forestry. The history of arboricultural education has been covered elsewhere (Johnston 2015, 27–31). What is important to stress here is the impact this had on finally providing a steady stream of suitably qualified personnel who had the practical skills to look after the nation's street trees. This major advance in British arboriculture was reinforced in 1966 with the publication of the British Standard 3998 entitled *Recommendations for Tree Work* (BSI 1966). This was the first attempt to encourage everyone in the arboricultural industry to aspire to the same standards in many aspects of practical tree work.

Tree maintenance operations, especially pruning

Having looked at overall standards of arboricultural work on street trees from an historical perspective, we now consider some aspects of tree maintenance with a particular focus on pruning. Trees are 'living history' in ways that are more than just part of a heritage landscape. It is often said that an experienced arboriculturist can learn much about the life history of an urban tree from its current form and overall appearance. Interpreting the evidence of its branch structure, old pruning wounds and previous remedial tree surgery can reveal much about past maintenance work and why this might have been undertaken. This was especially relevant in the research for this book when examining old photographs of street trees.

As the first street trees planted in the Victorian era began to mature it was not long before conflicts arose between the growth of the trees and surrounding buildings and urban infrastructure. Some sort of pruning was necessary to control the overall size and development of the tree's crown, especially when forest-type trees had been planted in quite narrow streets.

Some of the first trees to come under close scrutiny for the way they were pruned were the London planes (*Platanus x acerifolia*) on the Thames Embankment, just as they had attracted much attention when initially planted. Pruning operations started in 1874 just 5 years after the first trees had been planted when the trees had their side branches removed in what was described by one observer as a 'merciless and barbarous way' (*Gardeners' Chronicle* 1874, 672). It was suggested at the time that the pruning was undertaken because the lower branches were deemed an obstruction to pedestrians and a temptation to vandals. While some correspondents in the gardening magazines complained about 'unnecessary' early pruning on the Embankment planes, a few years later others were urging quite drastic measures. William Baxter Smith (1884, 399) felt that the trees had been planted too close together and as a result 'the branches must soon intermingle, their graceful sweep will be prevented, and the individuality of the trees destroyed unless some are removed'. In 1895, the *Gardeners' Chronicle* was so dismayed at some of the inappropriate pruning being undertaken on London's street trees that it was moved to publish an editorial on this. It declared, 'The advantage of possessing a few trees in our streets is sadly marred when these are improperly pruned'. It highlighted some recent work on Oriental planes in streets in Fulham and West Kensington and it had strong words to say about the standard of pruning:

> Those persons who were employed by the Vestry to carry out the work could have possessed but a scintilla of the principles on which tree pruning is based, for the whole of the branches have been most severely cut back, and the trees will long remain in evidence of the incompetence of the workmen or their employer, we do not know which.
>
> *Gardeners' Chronicle* 1895, 99

What is interesting about this article is that the editors not only felt obliged to criticise the standard of pruning but they also went on to describe what they believed was the correct pruning practice. While it was recognised that street tree pruning was not a difficult job if the worker is given proper training and some supervised practice, bad pruning could have serious consequences. In no time at all the inexpert pruner could quickly waste considerable sums of public money and permanently ruin growth that had been carefully tended for years.

Pollarding is a common pruning technique that generated much heated debate in Victorian and Edwardian times, and still does. Pollarding was originally developed as a variation on an ancient form of woodland management called coppicing where the branches, instead of being cut at ground level, were cut several feet above ground to avoid damage from browsing animals (Petit and Watkins 2003; Rackham 2003, 173). It was subsequently adapted as a method of pruning forest-type street trees, primarily to maintain them at a predetermined height and spread. The process involved removing most of the crown but leaving some shortened framework branches (Figure 89). At the point where the branches were cut a number of new shoots then sprouted the following season. In order to maintain this regrowth within certain dimensions the shoots are regularly pruned back to the original pollard point, which subsequently became a swollen 'knuckle' of wood after several cycles of pruning (BSI 2010). This section of the chapter focuses on pollarding as a pruning technique and later in the chapter we focus on this as a tree management regime.

FIGURE 89. Pollarding is a common pruning technique that generated much heated debate in Victorian and Edwardian times, and still does. It was originally developed as a variation on an ancient form of woodland management called coppicing and was subsequently adapted as a method of pruning forest-type street trees, primarily to maintain them at a predetermined height and spread. The process involved removing most of the crown but leaving some shortened framework branches. These pollarded limes were photographed in the 1920s in Leighton Road in Old Trafford, Manchester.

The pollarding of urban trees has always divided opinion among those that regard this as an acceptable pruning technique to maintain a small crown and those who consider it a form of tree 'mutilation'. Before it had been applied to street trees Loudon (1835, 1143) had stated, 'Pollarded trees may be considered in most cases as injurious deformities'. Pollarding could only be carried out on certain species of tree that were tolerant of this very heavy and systematic pruning. Planes and limes, the common choice for many street tree plantings, were tolerant and pollarding therefore seemed an ideal pruning technique to ensure these trees were 'kept within certain bounds' (Dallimore 1926, 45–46). Pollarding was usually undertaken on an annual or biannual basis, although sometimes the cycle was a little longer. When first undertaken or immediately after regular pruning, the trees do look far from natural (Figure 90). The sight of many of the nation's street trees being subjected to this regular 'mutilation' was too much for some experts (Webster 1909, 400). William Wallace Pettigrew, when he was responsible for street trees in Cardiff, tried to add some balance to the debate in an article on this topic in *The Garden*. He observed:

> The pruning of street trees is a much debated subject and the responsible authorities have often been severely criticised by the gardening press for the manner in which the London street trees are annually mutilated. I remember one editor asserting in connection with this matter, that if a tree could not be allowed to develop its natural character he would rather not see it grown in a street. This sentiment is all very well in its way, but it must be remembered that trees are not grown in streets as they are in parks, to develop into specimens, but simply as a means of ornamenting the town. In many instances it would be out of the question to allow trees to develop to

FIGURE 90. When pollarding is first undertaken or immediately after regular pruning, the trees look far from natural. In late Victorian and Edwardian times the sight of many of the nation's street trees being subjected to this regular 'mutilation' was too much for some experts. This photograph from 1912 shows pollarded trees in King Charles Road, Surbiton, and demonstrates how the appearance can be quite startling.

their natural size, and under such circumstances it is much better to adopt a sensible style of pruning, to doing away with them altogether.

Pettigrew 1901, 14

While Pettigrew made a reasoned case for pollarding forest-type trees in confined streets, for some professionals it was simply a standard treatment whenever planes and limes were used as street trees. Photographic evidence from the early 1900s indicates that some local authorities chose to pollard these trees even when there was sufficient room for them to develop a relatively natural crown. While there has been much opposition to pollarding street trees in Britain, this has always been a perfectly acceptable form of management in many other European cities. This opposition in Britain may help to explain why there is little mention of the techniques of pollarding street trees in our arboricultural literature of the twentieth century even though this was widely practised.

A number of variations on the basic technique of pollarding were developed in Victorian and Edwardian times. Sometimes the tree would be allowed to grow fairly naturally before its central leader (uppermost vertical shoot) was cut back at about 30 ft (9.1 m) and other pollard points established evenly throughout the branch framework. As the young tree developed the side branches would be pruned off to create a clear stem for about 15 ft (4.6 m) (Figure 91). An alternative approach involved not having a central leader but a framework of several separate vertical branches emanating from about 15 ft up the stem. Most of the pollard points were towards the top of the branch framework and there would also be a clear stem for about 15 ft (Figure 92). These two examples of pollarding are sometimes referred to as 'high pollards' and in both cases the subsequent regrowth was often pruned back biannually. In what can be referred to as 'low pollarding', the main stem of the tree was

cut back at about 10 ft (3 m) in height. The subsequent regrowth was then pruned back on an annual or biannual cycle to ensure a small mop-headed crown on a very short branch framework (Figure 93). An examination of early photographs suggests that where low pollarding was applied this was usually in the narrowest streets.

While pollarding kept the entire tree crown within certain dimensions, other forms of pruning were undertaken to give clearance from a range of more specific obstructions. Where tall buildings were located at the edge of the

FIGURE 93. A form of 'low pollarding' on London planes in Galton Street near Kensal Green, north-west London, photographed around 1910. The children playing in the street is a sign of those times when motor vehicles were a rarity. Some of the trees that remain in the street today may be original plantings.

footway and forest-type trees were planted, complaints were soon made about trees blocking daylight to the front rooms and also branches scratching against the windows. Those side branches nearest the buildings were removed, which alleviated the problem but gave the trees a lopsided appearance (see Figure 33). When electric trams were introduced into many British towns and cities from the 1890s, this was a major source of conflict with street trees (see Chapter 10). Where existing trees were retained or new trees planted this invariably involved severe pruning to keep the branches clear of the electricity cables and moving trams (Figure 94). A pruning technique called 'elbowing in' was often employed that involved the shortening back of side branches to a vertical shoot that was then encouraged to develop upwards leaving a right-angled junction in the branch that resembled a bent elbow (Webster 1909, 400). Another form of pruning was the removal of all the lower branches to a considerable height, an exaggerated crown lifting, to allow more light to ground floor front rooms or greater visibility for shop fronts (see Figure 83). Some species of lime, especially the common lime (*Tilia x europaea*), produce substantial amounts of shoots (epicormic growth) that sprout from the base. By the end of the summer this growth can be sufficient to cause an obstruction for pedestrians and needs to be pruned back to the trunk annually to prevent this. While this disadvantage of the common lime was noticed from the earliest days of street tree planting it did not discourage countless thousands of the trees being planted.

In order to ensure effective clearance from various obstacles and regulate pruning practices there have been various attempts made over the years to

FIGURE 94. When electric trams were introduced into many British towns and cities from the 1890s, where existing trees were retained or new trees planted this invariably involved severe pruning to keep the branches clear of the electricity cables and moving trams. This photograph was taken around 1905 and shows plane trees and a tram in Norwich Road, Ipswich.

establish recognised standards that stipulated minimum distances between trees and potential obstructions (Boddy 1986, 17–18). Some have had added weight after incorporation into Highways legislation or in industry recommended standards or codes of practice.

Deadwooding is another pruning operation regularly undertaken on many street trees. Trees generate dead branches as part of their natural development, particularly as they approach maturity, although this varies between species. Trees under stress, such as those in streets, usually produce more deadwood. If dead branches of any size are left to fall this can be a hazard for pedestrians and road users and therefore regular deadwooding, the pruning out of deadwood, is necessary to prevent this. When street trees were first planted in British streets this was not initially considered an issue. However, as many of the early plantings were reaching maturity and generated quantities of deadwood, this also coincided with a greater risk as urban streets were becoming much busier places as motorised vehicles became increasingly common. In order to reduce the hazard of deadwood, local authorities from the early twentieth century began to include deadwooding as a routine tree maintenance operation, particularly with large street trees that were not regularly pollarded.

It may be difficult for us to understand today but in Victorian and Edwardian times concerns about tree pruning could stir up intense debates. One particularly high-profile case that occurred just before the First World War gives some indication of the power of this topic to arouse national interest. In 1911, adverse criticism was appearing in the popular press and gardening magazines regarding the pruning of the recently planted plane trees along the Mall in London (*Gardeners' Chronicle* 1911, 144). The government responded by requesting Professor Balfour of the Royal Botanic Garden, Edinburgh, to produce a report about the treatment the trees had received. As this broad avenue formed the main approach to the nation's monument to Queen Victoria, public interest was enormous. In his report Balfour not only approved of the pruning and exonerated those responsible but he also described the trees as 'patterns of what street trees should be'. His report was presented to both Houses of Parliament by command of King George V and reprinted in full in the *Gardeners' Chronicle* (Balfour 1911, 144–146). His report makes fascinating reading for the modern arboriculturist.

For many centuries the techniques of tree pruning and some other tree care practices were based largely on an anthropomorphic approach where treatments were administered to 'the patient' in much the same ways as a doctor or dentist would work. Limbs were amputated, wounds were dressed and cavities were filled. Indeed, the popular name of 'tree surgery' for this work seems to encapsulate this approach. That was all to change in the late 1970s as a result of new research in the USA which had a profound impact on practical arboriculture, including the care of street trees. Dr Alex Shigo of the USDA Forest Service developed a new model for tree decay that has become known by its acronym CODIT (Compartmentalization of Decay in Trees). According to the CODIT model, when a tree is wounded its cells undergo changes to form 'walls' around the wound, slowing or preventing the spread of disease and decay to the rest of the tree (Shigo 1977). The implications for accepted tree care practice at the time were enormous. Flush cutting in pruning, traditional wound sealants, cavity draining and filling, along with other traditional practices were all questioned and no longer regarded as good practice. However, not all of this was entirely new. For example, in Le Sueur's (1934, 18) classic work published in 1934 he urges against flush cutting and advocates pruning to the furthest extent of the 'branch ring' (now called the branch collar in Shigo's work). Furthermore, while the use of wound sealants was always considered a hallmark of good pruning (Webster 1910, 29), and was still being recommended in the 1966 British Standard for Tree Work (BSI 1966), their effectiveness had been questioned periodically before Shigo's groundbreaking work.

In examining the various pruning techniques for street trees in Victorian and Edwardian times it is clear there are some similarities to modern techniques, certainly in terms of the objectives of tree pruning such as crown lifting, crown thinning and deadwooding. However, there are also some radical differences in the overall approach which often bears little resemblance to modern methods, for example, to the principles and practice of structural pruning (Gilman 2012, 221–268).

Innovations in street tree maintenance equipment

The equipment and machinery used in the maintenance of street trees in Britain has improved steadily since Victorian times. Some of the first significant advances were in the equipment used to climb trees. The traditional combination of ladders and ropes was beginning to be superseded in the early twentieth century with the introduction of specialist tree climbing equipment involving safety-belts or harnesses used in conjunction with climbing ropes. In the late nineteenth century the French had developed the 'City of Paris' safety-belt, used initially for tree pruning on the Parisian boulevards. This specially designed tree climbing aid, one of the first of its type, later became adopted by some tree pruning crews in other countries, including Britain (Le Sueur 1934, 30). While safety-belts like this were available in Britain from the 1920s, anecdotal evidence suggests that many local authorities avoided using them until as late as the 1960s when arboricultural training schemes became established in local government training centres. The introduction of chainsaws was another major innovation in tree work operations. Some of the earliest types were used on urban trees in Britain from Victorian times. In 1878, the *Gardeners' Chronicle* (1878, 171) reported that Mr Gladstone, the famous Liberal politician, had been in Tulse Hill observing experiments with a patent steam tree-feller. From the late 1930s and 1940s more manageable models of petrol driven chainsaws were sometimes used for felling and cutting up street trees. However, it was only in the 1970s with the development of smaller and more lightweight models that a dramatic advance was made. These models could now be taken into the tree and used by the tree surgeon to replace handsaws for large branch removal (Bridgeman 1976, 46).

The 1970s and 1980s witnessed the introduction into Britain of a wide range of new arboricultural machinery and equipment with some of it especially applicable to street tree maintenance. Peter Bridgeman's book *Tree Surgery*, published in 1976, gives a good account of the relevant technological developments at that time (Bridgeman 1976). Some of the heavy machinery that was useful for street tree work had initially been developed in the United States, although as it became popular here some British companies began to manufacture their own versions. Hydraulic or aerial platforms enabled tree workers to access the crown of the tree without having to use a rope and harness. These platforms had initially been used by the London County Council's (LCC) new tree section in the early 1960s and only later became more widely used by other local authorities (Stone and Brodie 1994, 50). When working systematically along an avenue of street trees and undertaking tasks such as reducing overhanging branches, the use of a platform could dramatically increase the speed and efficiency of this work. Another LCC innovation from the early 1960s was its specially adapted open-top London Transport bus that was used for street tree pruning. The bus would travel along some of the main London thoroughfares, usually when traffic levels were reduced, and the tree crew on the top of the bus would prune back overhanging branches to ensure sufficient clearance for commuter buses and other high-sided vehicles (Figure 95).

Two further developments in heavy machinery relevant to street tree work were the brushwood chipper and the stump grinder. Again, these became

FIGURE 95. From the 1960s the London County Council used a specially adapted open-top London Transport bus for some of its street tree pruning. The bus would travel along some of the main London thoroughfares, usually when traffic levels were reduced, and the tree crew on the top of the bus would prune back overhanging branches to ensure sufficient clearance for commuter buses and other high-sided vehicles.

PHOTO: GRAHAM COSTER.

increasingly common in tree maintenance work from the 1970s. When branches had been removed in pruning operations, they could be feed into a brushwood chipper that would reduce them to wood chips. These would take up less than one-tenth of the space of the original branches and thus reduce transport costs as well as being a recycled product with a number of uses. When street trees were felled, the stumps had to be removed so they did not cause an obstruction on the footway. Machines called stump grinders would be positioned over the stump and literally grind or chip away at this until its height was reduced to below the level of the footway. The shallow hole was then backfilled and the footway surface reinstated.

In 1973, a commercial company called Cricklewood Tree Surgeons, based in north London, introduced into Britain the latest word in heavy machinery for street tree work (*Gardeners' Chronicle* 1973, 17). The company specialised in street pruning for local authorities and one of its contracts covered 300 trees for Ealing Council. This new machine was effectively a lorry known as a combination unit that incorporated a hydraulically controlled aerial platform and a brushwood chipper. The platform could take its insulated basket, essential for working close to electricity cables, to a height of 50 ft (15.2 m) and with its hydraulic saw a further 8 ft (2.4 m) could be reached. The company owner, Alan Smith, had purchased the unit from the Asplundh Corporation in the United States at the cost of £21,000, then a substantial investment in equipment for a British tree surgery company. As well as using the unit on its own street tree contracts it was also being offered for hire at £15 per hour. At that time it was not unusual for local authority tree sections to initially hire in expensive specialist equipment such as brushwood chippers and stump grinders until they were certain they had sufficient work for these machines to justify their own purchase (*Gardeners' Chronicle* 1982, 31).

Municipal arboriculture and governance of street trees

With the growth of local government in Britain in the Victorian era, urban tree management became essentially a local authority function. The overall development of municipal arboriculture within this context has been covered elsewhere (Johnston 2015, 50–58). The focus here is on highlighting aspects that impacted directly on the management of street trees.

In the early days of the Victorian street tree movement a wide range of public bodies and institutions were responsible for the planting and management of these trees. These included various Local Boards, Corporations, Vestries, Improvement Commissions and Surveyors of Highways and the precise responsibilities of each in respect of street trees were not always clearly defined (see Chapter 5). With respect to the planting of street trees, particularly in new suburban districts, this was often undertaken and paid for by the private developers themselves (see Chapters 5 and 6). The trees and the streets where they were located were later adopted by the local authority which took over the responsibility for planting and management. In some instances the cost of the initial tree planting was paid for by the new residents themselves. In other cases new street tree planting would be paid for and sometimes also carried out by voluntary organisations with a focus on civic amenities. For example, in London from the 1880s the Metropolitan Public Gardens Association played a prominent role in planting new street trees in various areas (see Chapter 5). These plantings by voluntary organisations were often focused on main thoroughfares or commercial districts where many people would get the benefit rather than in the quieter backstreets of residential neighbourhoods. In the twentieth century other major voluntary organisations played a national or regional role in the planting and protection of street trees, such as the Roads Beautifying Association and the Council for the Preservation of Rural England (Johnston 2015, 190–195).

As local government evolved and responsibility for streets and street trees changed hands between various public bodies this often signalled an improvement in arboricultural standards – but not always. As we have noted, the popular gardening magazines of Victorian and Edwardian times are full of examples of both good and bad practice with local authority street trees. One contentious issue that was raised periodically was the situation in the large cities where different public bodies were concerned with street trees in different districts across the city. This led to considerable variation in the numbers of street trees planted in those districts and in general standards of tree maintenance and management. Some commentators wished that the governance of British cities was similar to Paris where the benefits of more centralised and autocratic control had enabled Baron Haussmann to establish new thoroughfares and magnificent boulevards in the face of quite determined opposition (*Gardeners' Chronicle* 1868, 717). It was also suggested that having some sort of central commission of relevant experts would promote high standards of planting and maintenance across the cities rather than having a patchwork of local control where there was often little or no expertise. These views in relation to the governance of street trees and the example of Paris were also voiced by the great American urban planner, Charles Mulford Robinson (1901, 115–120).

Within different local authorities (LAs) and other public bodies the overall responsibility for street trees varied between different professionals and even some individuals with no professional background. As noted above, municipal engineers were often entrusted with street trees along with many other responsibilities (Buchanan 1985). By the early twentieth century, municipal engineering had become a very broad discipline embracing many aspects of local government, such as town planning, roads, parks and public housing. Many of these areas were subsequently embraced by specialist individuals with their own professional bodies but nevertheless still came under the overall responsibility of an individual whose job title was 'Borough Engineer' or similar. Another group of professionals that often had managerial responsibility for street trees in the late nineteenth and early twentieth century was the Borough Surveyors, who were qualified and experienced property professionals. Unfortunately, these LA officers with engineering or surveying backgrounds invariably had no specialist training or experience in the planting and management of street trees and often learnt about the topic 'on the job'. However, that did not preclude these professionals from making a valuable contribution to the greening of the streets in their district.

The situation where Borough Engineers, Borough Surveyors or Parks Superintendents had managerial responsibility for LA street trees continued through the first half of the twentieth century. That situation only changed from the 1950s onwards with the development of arboricultural education and the appointment of the first tree officers in mainly urban local authorities (Johnston 2015, 55–58). This flowering of municipal arboriculture in Britain began in London in 1946 when the LCC Parks Department created a new division to look after all its trees (Leathart 1973, 103). Outside of London other LAs such as Sheffield City Council began to recognise the importance of having a specialist tree officer and teams of skilled manual workers (Jorgensen 1991, 20). These tree officers and their tree sections were directed to undertake the planting and management of street trees along with all trees in parks, open spaces, housing estates and other council properties.

Rather than employ their own manual workers for street tree maintenance and other arboricultural work, LAs have always had the option of engaging contractors to do this work. As early as the 1870s, invitations from local authorities for contactors to tender for the supply and planting of street trees began appearing in the gardening and trade press. Later, this expanded into routine maintenance work on mature street trees. The advantages and disadvantages of using direct labour or contractors for the provision of LA services has always been the subject of much debate since the first direct labour organisations were developed under the Progressive Party in the LCC in the 1890s (Ravetz 2001, 87). The debate reached heated levels with the election of a Conservative government in 1979, led by Prime Minister Margaret Thatcher (Travers 2013). In 1980, the *Local Government, Planning and Land Act* introduced compulsory competitive tendering (CCT) that required public sector organisations to allow private sector firms to bid for the delivery of public services (Painter 1991). While the introduction of CCT had a detrimental impact on the arboricultural services of many LAs (Ball 1995), it also had some positive impact. Because arboricultural work now had to be put out to tender, this prompted LAs to undertake extensive surveys of their trees, often for the first time. Street tree maintenance work was often the first arboricultural work to be subjected to tender.

Another measure introduced by the Conservative government in the 1980s that had a major impact on many LA's arboricultural services was 'rate-capping'. This imposed a legally enforceable ceiling on the rating power of LAs with the aim of penalising high-spending authorities (Travers 2013). This led to many LAs making substantial cuts in their services in order to reduce their rates. Tree planting and tree maintenance was an obvious target for cuts in many LAs, being a relatively low priority in comparison to some other services. Some LAs suspended or seriously limited their tree planting programmes, perhaps hoping this would not be noticed by the public. In other LAs the frequency of street tree pruning regimes was extended to save money, although after a few years this led to many complaints from residents about trees blocking light to residential properties (Anon 1980). In a few LAs dead or dangerous street trees that had to be felled were left with their stumps at waist-height to save money on not having to remove these immediately and reinstate the pavement (Figure 96). The stump was then perceived to be like a bollard and not a hazard to pedestrians. In some city streets these stumps remained for a number of years until the financial climate improved. In the past five years, government economic policy has again seen some massive reductions in local authority services with reports that many LA tree officers have been made redundant and arboricultural services severely cut back.

Management plans and strategies

Urban trees need long-term plans and strategies for good sustainable management but the problem for LA tree managers has always been that because of financial constraints and uncertainties they cannot usually plan for more than a year or two ahead. In the research for this book evidence was sought in the historical literature for the existence of management plans and strategies in relation to street trees. It is understandable that in the early days

FIGURE 96. In the 1980s following the introduction of 'rate-capping' from central government, many local authorities had to make substantial cuts in their services in order to reduce their rates. Tree planting and tree maintenance was an obvious target for cuts, being a relatively low priority in comparison to some other services. In a few local authorities dead or dangerous street trees that had to be felled were left with their stumps at waist-height to save money on not having to remove these immediately and reinstate the pavement. This tree stump was photographed in a south London borough in 1980.

of the Victorian street tree movement there is no real evidence of this since the focus was on getting trees planted and established rather than concern for their long-term management. One of the earliest mentions of some sort of management plan for street trees dates from the 1880s and relates to the trees on the Thames Embankment in London. In a letter to the *Gardeners' Chronicle* the Superintendent of Finsbury Park, J. Edward Cochrane (1889, 222), reported that in 1886 he had submitted a report to the Parks Committee of the late Metropolitan Board of Works that set out the long-term management of the trees. Part of this involved the removal of alternate trees within the

FIGURE 97. One of the earliest mentions of some sort of management plan for street trees dates from the 1880s and relates to the trees on the Thames Embankment in London. In 1886, the Superintendent of Finsbury Park, J. Edward Cochrane, submitted a report to the Parks Committee of the Metropolitan Board of Works that set out the long-term management of the trees. This image is dated *c.* 1882 and is from a magic lantern slide.

next eight to ten years, the replacement of a few unhealthy trees with vigorous specimens from Finsbury and Southwark Parks, and an appropriate pruning regime for the remaining trees (Figure 97). In 1895, an editorial in *Gardeners' Chronicle* (1895, 99–100) recommended that where large forest-type trees have been planted at less than 30 ft (9.1 m) apart, which was often the case, then alternate trees should be removed after a few years as the trees became established. This was considered a more appropriate management plan than the intensive pruning regime that was normally used, which was both costly and time-consuming.

In 1910, another editorial in the *Gardeners' Chronicle* focused on the 'proper management of street trees'. This was prompted by the 'considerable criticism [that] has been offered with respect to the way Camberwell Council has dealt with the trees in Camberwell Grove and Grove Park'. The editorial continued:

It appears that, in the opinion of this [Camberwell] Council, the trees in certain districts of the borough have grown out of bounds, and, in some instances, have become a danger to the public. As a result, a wholesale pruning, lopping and cutting

down of the trees has been in progress for some time, and this work has apparently been confided mainly to the 'unemployed'.

Gardeners' Chronicle 1910, 232

While this editorial echoes the criticism of poor standards of pruning frequently made in Victorian and Edwardian times that were highlighted earlier in this chapter, the editors go on to stress the need for an appropriate long-term management plan. They also express sympathy with those LA officers charged with managing streets and the often thankless nature of their task:

> What with the protesting householder and the people who object to a single branch of a tree being pruned, the lot of those charged with the management of public trees is not an enviable one. At the same time, if the branches of street trees growing in such places as Camberwell Grove were systematically thinned out and the more obstructive branches shortened, there would never arise the need to prune and lop in the manner recently adopted by the Camberwell Council. Where lopping is really necessary it is desirable to treat a few trees each season rather than lop all the trees of an avenue at one time. The system of thus pruning by instalments is practiced with marked success in some provincial towns.

Gardeners' Chronicle 1910, 233

By the 1920s, most LAs with large forest-type trees in their small or medium width streets were engaged in some form of systematic pruning to keep the crown of these trees within certain dimensions. The form of pruning employed was invariably some type of high or low pollarding, usually carried out on a one, two or three year cycle. Occasionally, where the width of the streets was considerable, plane and lime trees were allowed to continue to grow fairly naturally with just minor pruning and without any resort to pollarding.

The wrong trees or wrong management?

The planting of countless thousands of forest-type trees in numerous urban streets across Britain in Victorian and Edwardian times has often been characterised as an arboricultural blunder of historic proportions. The conventional view is that those responsible for these plantings got it badly wrong when it came to selecting suitable trees for most of these streets. It has often been said that although the London plane and the common lime are very tolerant of urban conditions, they would inevitably outgrow those narrow streets where many of them were planted and the problems this would create would eventually be a major management 'headache'. Criticism of what was regarded as poor tree selection began early in the Victorian street tree planting movement and became quite common by the 1890s. The blame for this was usually laid at the door of the Borough Surveyor or Engineer who had little or no arboricultural knowledge. The following is typical of this view:

> The vestries of London, having practically no knowledge of the subject, have left the very important matter of street planting to the parochial surveyor, and he, through

lack of knowledge on his part, has not always selected the right species of trees. Barclay Road is a capital example of the evil of planting a forest tree of large natural dimensions in a narrow thoroughfare.

Gardeners' Chronicle 1895, 100

When the historical evidence from the literature and photographs is considered, this view of an 'historic blunder' seems like an oversimplification of what was a more complex issue. When the Victorian street tree movement started in Britain, trees such as the London plane, common lime and horse chestnut had been growing here for many decades and large mature specimens could readily be viewed in parks and gardens across the country. It seems hard to imagine that even the untrained eye of the engineer or surveyor would fail to notice that rows of these trees as fully grown specimens in even moderately narrow streets might just cause a bit of a problem. Furthermore, if there was any doubt about the ultimate dimensions of these trees there were plenty of tree experts willing to give advice. It seems that a more rational explanation involves a mixture of poor tree selection and lack of expected management. While there were undoubtedly mistakes made in selecting these forest-type trees for very narrow streets, there was also the understanding that where they were planted in moderately narrow or medium width streets they would be subject to regular pollarding that would keep the crown 'within bounds'. In many cases, problems occurred when the pollarding regime lapsed or never actually started, the regular cycle was extended or the work was not done properly. It should also be remembered that in late Victorian times many of the modern conflicts associated with forest-type trees and the built environment were not present or not recognised. The parameters of street tree selection then were in many respects significantly less complex than those that exist now.

While pollarding continued as an acceptable form of street tree management through the 1920s and 1930, attitudes towards this began to shift in the years immediately after the Second World War. The war had left many street trees in a very neglected and overgrown condition as maintenance and management had largely ceased over that period. Where forest-type trees had been planted at a close spacing the problems were particularly acute. In London, the LCC's new tree section under the leadership of Hubert Taylor instituted a change in management away from regular heavy pollarding to what he considered a 'more sympathetic regime which considered the natural form of species and individual specimen trees' (Stone and Brodie 1994, 50). Some LAs followed Taylor's example, although many of those without arboricultural expertise just continued with the previous pollarding regime.

From the early 1960s, with the development of full-time arboricultural education and the appointment of a specially qualified tree officer in many LAs, pollarding came under severe scrutiny as a management practice for street trees. The old arguments about 'tree mutilation' were aired again as a new generation of qualified arboriculturists sought to find more imaginative and 'aesthetically pleasing' solutions to this traditional method of management. In the early

1970s, many urban LAs tried to regrow the crowns of their pollarded street trees, mostly planes and limes, in an attempt to give them a more attractive and natural appearance (Brown 1972, 36). This change in pruning policy was often prompted by lobbying from local amenity societies, residents associations and conservation groups that viewed pollarding as an unsightly practice and much the same as 'lopping'. Once the tree crowns had been allowed to regrow to a limited extent, they were then kept from getting any larger by regular crown reductions. Unfortunately, the resulting crowns were often unstable due to extensive decay in the pollard points. When high winds occurred many trees would suffer from branches splitting out, causing a danger to people, property and vehicles.

Although alternatives to traditional pollarding continue to be sought by many LA tree officers, in recent years there has been more acceptance of the value of these trees as part of heritage streetscapes. LAs continue to manage large numbers of pollarded street trees and ensure they make a significant and sustainable contribution to the urban landscape and the environment (Figure 98). Some forwarding-thinking LAs have even produced written policies for the management of these trees (Torbay Council 2011). There has also been

FIGURE 98. Although alternatives to traditional pollarding continue to be sought by many tree officers, in recent years there has been more acceptance of the value of these trees as part of heritage streetscapes. Local authorities continue to manage large numbers of pollarded street trees and ensure they make a significant and sustainable contribution to the urban landscape and the environment. These pollarded planes in Fountayne Road, Tottenham, are managed by the London Borough of Hackney.

PHOTO: RUPERT BENTLEY WALLS

some useful research on the appropriate management of neglected pollards (Lonsdale 2000, 23). Nevertheless, for many professionals and members of the public, a gradual programme of tree replacement is often considered the best solution to the 'problems' of pollarded forest-type street trees.

Replacement programmes for forest-type trees

Over the past ten years there has been much coverage in the popular media about some LA programmes to undertake the wholesale replacement of many of their forest-type street trees. As these trees are removed, they are usually replaced with smaller-growing and short-lived ornamental species such as cherry, whitebeam and hawthorn. However, the felling of many mature street trees has frequently led to protests by residents who saw their leafy treescape being replaced by newly-planted trees that had little landscape impact. Some residents were also conscious of the reduction in the value of their properties resulting from the felling of the mature trees. Trying to implement a long-term replacement programme for these forest-type street trees continues to pose a management headache for many tree officers (Condron 2005). Recently, Sheffield City Council has been the focus of much media interest in this topic (Winson 2016). The LA's announcement that it was assessing 36,000 of its street trees to decide which needed to be felled as part of a major road improvement scheme provoked a bitter row with many residents (Kirby 2015). By the end of 2015 some 2000 'problem' trees had already been felled as part of its Streets Ahead scheme, although it was planned to replace these with 'more suitable species'.

With all the publicity that tree replacement programmes are currently attracting, it might be assumed that this is a recent phenomenon. However, examples go back at least to Edwardian times. In 1905, Aberdeen Corporation changed its mind about the suitability of one of its more common species of street tree (Anon 1905). Various forms of poplar, which had initially been highly regarded for use in streets, were now maturing and causing a range of problems. As a result, the Corporation announced that 'wherever opportunity occurs, poplars are being rooted out and their place taken by other and more suitable trees'.

Immediately after the Second World War when many forest-type street trees were neglected and overgrown, calls for the replacement of these trees became increasingly widespread. This was prompted not only by the problems these trees were causing but also by changing public tastes with small flowering trees becoming increasingly popular (see Chapter 11). Fashionable Hampstead in London was keen to be part of this trend. In 1947, the *Gardeners' Chronicle* reported:

> The large trees now lining the streets of Hampstead, London N.W., are to be replaced by smaller, flowering trees. The Trees and Open Spaces Committee have the list prepared and hope soon to get the new trees established. Hampstead residents are always touchy about the removal of trees and there will probably be some opposition to the changeover. But the large trees require a great deal of lopping and attention,

without which they are apt to become a danger. A severe gale, such as that of the night of 16 March, may easily bring casualties from falling trees or boughs; and it is difficult in these days to secure sufficient skilled labour to keep the trees in a safe condition.

Gardeners' Chronicle 1947, 174

In order to limit any opposition to this policy, some LAs undertook the replacement in two phases; alternate trees would be removed first and when the replacements for these had become well-established, the remainder of the large trees were removed (*Gardeners' Chronicle* 1949, 162). By the 1950s, it was being reported that the planting of forest-type street trees had declined dramatically in many LA districts in favour of using small ornamental trees (Hornsey 1953, 170). As well as being popular with many members of the public, this policy of replacing these 'Victorian relics' had the support of some prominent tree experts such as Fred Boddy (1947, 72) and Wilfred Fox (1953, 204) of the Roads Beautifying Association. Nevertheless, there were also some dissenting voices among the ranks of professionals responsible for urban landscapes and street trees. One leading critic of this policy was Peter Shepheard (1956, 386), the eminent architect and landscape architect. In an article on urban trees written for the *Architectural Review* he declared:

Above all, we need *large forest trees*. Small trees, however decorative they may be in certain places, are no substitute for big ones. It is specially sad that so much reliance is placed on the pink varieties of the Japanese cherry, garish in flower, gawky and dull-leaved when not, and short-lived as well.

Shepheard 1956, 386

Criticism of these tree replacement policies today has echoes some of the points made up to 50 years ago. Recent research has confirmed that it is the large-growing species of urban trees that generally deliver far more environmental, economic and social benefits to urban dwellers than small-growing species (Armour *et al.* 2012). These replacement programmes are also viewed by many as a way for LAs to save money by reducing tree maintenance and management costs without taking into account a comprehensive cost-benefit analysis. The accusation that these replacement programmes are really driven by a basic cost-cutting agenda was cited in the past and could be particularly relevant again in the current climate of local authority expenditure. Whatever the merits of the arguments on both sides of this debate, the removal of these large forest-type trees should normally be undertaken only as a last resort. In many cases solutions can be found to the problems they may be causing and all alternatives should be explored before taking the drastic action of felling trees that have sometimes graced our streets for over a century. There are real fears that the loss of these trees and their replacement by small-growing and short-lived species will lead to a proliferation of 'lollipop landscapes' in our towns and cities

(Johnston 2010, 33). These fears are supported by data from the government-commissioned *Trees in Towns II* survey of urban trees and their management in England, published in 2008 (Britt and Johnston 2008).

The influence of modern arboriculture and urban forestry

Since the 1950s, a wide range of remarkable advances in the theory and practice of urban tree management have revolutionised how we plant and care for our urban trees (Johnston and Hirons 2014). This chapter concludes with a brief outline of the impact of these developments on how LAs manage their street trees.

The influx of specialist arboricultural expertise from the 1950s undoubtedly transformed many LA's tree management services, which had often changed little over the previous 50 years. An equally significant impact was felt with the development of urban forestry ideas and practice, a concept originating in North America in the 1960s (Johnston 1997a; 1997b). This emphasised the need for a planned, systematic and integrated approach to ensure the sustainable management of the 'urban forest', all the trees and woodland in and around an urban area. The emergence of urban forestry and the development of modern arboriculture brought with it new technologies and radical new approaches that were especially relevant to street tree management.

The introduction of computerised technology into tree management in Britain in the early 1980s enabled an increase in the efficiency and effectiveness of many LA's tree programmes (Hope 1982; Bickmore and Hall 1983; Thurman 1983). In particular, it encouraged LAs to keep up-to-date, accurate and easily accessible records of their trees and use these to formulate maintenance programmes and management plans. Street trees were usually the first category of trees to be included in computerised management programmes. Over the past few decades, LA urban tree management has also become more environmentally conscious. For example, there is much greater awareness of the need to recycle urban tree debris generated by pruning and felling operations (Britt and Johnston 2008, 208–210). Previously, all this branchwood and timber would be dumped in landfills sites or burnt outside the smokeless zones. This change was greatly assisted by the introduction of brushwood cutters and other machinery that could process this debris into useful products. LAs have also become more aware of the need to involve local communities in what happens to the urban forest in their district. This means developing and operating a range of programmes embracing education, consultation and practical participation (*ibid.*, 515–530). With regard to street trees this could include giving talks and producing publications that inform residents of the many benefits of their trees. LAs are also now encouraged to give residents advanced notification of any maintenance work in their street rather than creating alarm by just turning up without any warning and starting up the chainsaws (*ibid.*, 294–296). In terms of residents' participation in any practical work, this is understandably far more limited due to safety considerations and the specialist skills required. Even when residents can assist with tree planting this is usually best left to parks and open spaces and avoided in streets when there are the dangers of traffic and underground services.

One major development in LA tree management that should encompass many of these radical changes has been the production of tree strategy documents (DoE 1994; Britt and Johnston 2008, 531–544). These strategies set out the necessary policies and plans to protect and enhance the urban forest, usually over a five-year period. While there are now some excellent examples, many LAs still do not have a comprehensive tree strategy that is based on recent survey data, either as a separate document or as a distinct part of a wider strategy. Tree strategies should also include information on the history of the urban forest in their district, highlight those street trees and other treescapes that have historical significance and set out management plans to protect and enhance their heritage value. It would also be good to see tree strategies with management targets to increase planting in those residential districts where traditionally there have been very few street trees, which are usually the deprived neighbourhoods where the poorer residents live. It is possible that many LAs are perpetuating this historical imbalance in street treecover by simply responding in areas where demand for new street trees is greatest. Anecdotal evidence from tree officers indicates that requests for more street trees and replacement planting often tends to come more from middle class neighbourhoods and those that already have a reasonable level of street treecover. Tree strategies with specific planting targets for different residential districts are one way of addressing that imbalance.

References

Chapter 1. Introduction and Research Methods

Dawe, G.F. (2011). Street trees and the urban environment. In: Douglas, I., Goode, D., Houch, M. and Wang, R. (eds) *The Routledge Handbook of Urban Ecology*. Routledge: London.

DCLG (2015) *English Indices of Depravation 2015*. Department for Communities and Local Government: London https://www.gov.uk/government/statistics/english-indices-of-deprivation-2015

Forest Research (2010) *Benefits of Green Infrastructure*. Report to Defra and CLG. Forest Research: Farnham. Accessed 20 November, 2016: http://www.forestry.gov.uk/pdf/urgp_benefits_of_green_infrastructure_main_report.pdf/$FILE/urgp_benefits_of_green_infrastructure_main_report.pdf

Fry, A.W. (2003) *Road and Way: An Analysis of these Expressions in the Highways and Related Acts of Parliament c. 1500 to 1929*. Published privately: Alresford.

Gunn, S. and Faire, L. (eds) (2016) *Research Methods for History*. Second edition. Edinburgh University Press: Edinburgh.

Johnston, M. (2015) *Trees in Towns and Cities: A History of British Urban Arboriculture*. Windgather Press: Oxford.

LSE (2016) Charles Booth's London: Poverty Maps and Police Notebooks. Website of the London School of Economics. Accessed 10 January 2016: http://booth.lse.ac.uk/map/14/-0.1174/51.5064/100/1

Mattheck, C. (1994) *The Body Language of Trees: A Handbook for Failure Analysis*. Research for Amenity Trees 4. The Stationary Office: London.

Oliver, R. (1993) *Ordnance Survey Maps: A concise guide for historians*. Charles Close Society for the Study of Ordnance Survey Maps: London.

Schroeder, H.W. (2012) Does beauty still matter? Experiential and utilitarian values of urban trees. In: Johnston, M. and Percival, G. (eds) *Trees, People and the Built Environment*. Forestry Commission Research Report. Forestry Commission: Edinburgh. Accessed 24 September, 2016: http://www.forestry.gov.uk/pdf/FCRP017.pdf/$FILE/FCRP017.pdf

Smith, C.H.J. (1852) *Parks and Pleasure Grounds; or Practical Notes on Country Residences, Villas, Public Parks, and Gardens*. Reeve and Sons: London.

Thompson Reuters (2016) Practical Law: Highway Classification. Text from the webpages of 'Practical Law: A Thompson Reuters Legal Solution. Accessed 20 November, 2016: http://uk.practicallaw.com/2-516-8168#a197978

Wegner, J.D., Branson, S., Hall, D., Schindler, K. and Perona, P. (2016) Cataloging Public Objects Using Aerial and Street-Level Images – Urban Trees. In: *Proceedings of IEEE Conference on Computer Vision and Pattern Recognition (CVPR)*, Las Vegas, June, 2016. Institute of Electrical and Electronic Engineers: New York, NY.

Wilson, P. (2013) *A–Z of Tree Terms: A Companion to British Arboriculture*. Ethelburga House: Lyminge. http://www.treeterms.co.uk/

Chapter 2. Walks, Allées, Promenades and Cours

Ackerman, R. (1810) Carriage or promenade dress. In: *The Repository of Arts, Literature, Commerce, Manufactures, Fashions and Politics*. Vol. 3 and January issue, 45–46. Printed for and published by R. Ackerman: The Strand, London.

Amherst, A. (1907) London Parks and Gardens. Writing as the Hon. Mrs Evelyn Cecil. A. Constable and Co: London.

Amsinck, P. (1810) *Tunbridge Wells and its Neighbourhood, Illustrated by a Series of Etchings and Historical Descriptions*. William Miller and Edmund Lloyd: London.

Biddle, P.G. (1977) *Survey of the Trees in the Promenade, Cheltenham*. A Report to the Borough of Cheltenham. Tree Conservation Ltd: Wantage.

Blake, S. (1988) *Pittville 1824–1860: A Scene of Gorgeous Magnificence*. Cheltenham Art Gallery and Museums: Cheltenham.

Borsay, P. (1986) The rise of the promenade: the social and cultural use of space in the English provincial town *c. 1660–1800*. *Journal for Eighteenth-Century Studies* 9(2), 125–140.

Borsay, P. (1989) *The English Urban Renaissance: Culture and Society in The Provincial Town 1660–1770*. Oxford University Press: Oxford.

Borsay, P. (2012) Town or country? British spas and the urban–rural interface. *Journal of Tourism History* 4(2), 155–169.

Borsay, P. (2013) Pleasure gardens and urban culture in the long eighteenth century. In: Conlin, J. (ed.) *The Pleasure Garden, from Vauxhall to Coney Island*. University of Pennsylvania Press: Philadelphia.

Bouchenot-Dechin, P. and Farhat, G. (2013) *André Le Nôtre in Perspective*. Yale University Press: New Haven, CT.

Boynton, H.E. (2002) *The History of New Walk, Leicester*. Published by the author: Leicester.

Chambers, W. (1773) *A Dissertation on Oriental Gardening*. Second edition with additions. W. Griffin, T. Davies and J. Dodsley: London.

Conlin, J. (ed.) (2012) *The Pleasure Garden, from Vauxhall to Coney Island*. University of Pennsylvania Press: Philadelphia.

Cook, M. (1676) *The Manner of Raising, Ordering, and Improving Forest-Trees: Also, How to Plant, Make and Keep Woods, Walks, Avenues, Lawns, Hedges, etc*. Peter Parker at the Leg and Star: London.

Couch, S.M. (1992) The practice of avenue planting in the seventeenth and eighteenth centuries. *Garden History* 20(2), 173–200.

Defoe, D. (1724) *A Tour Through the Whole Island of Great Britain*. Vol. 1. Introductions by Cole, G. and Browning, D. and republished in 1962 in Everyman's Library by J.M. Dent: London.

De la Bédoyère, G. (1992) *Roman Towns in Britain*. English Heritage series. Batsford: London.

Dickmann, D.I. and Kuzovkina, J. (2014) Poplars and willows of the world with emphasis on silviculturally important species In: Isebrands, J.G. and Richardson, J. (eds) *Poplars and Willows: Trees for Society and the Environment*. CABI: Wallingford.

Downing, S.J. (2009) *The English Pleasure Garden 1660–1860*. Shire: Oxford.

Evelyn, J. (1664) *Sylva or a Discourse of Forest-Trees, and the Propagation of Timber in His Majesties Dominions*. J. Martyn and J. Allestry: London.

Everett, N. (1994) *The Tory View of Landscape*. Yale University Press: New Haven, CT and London.

Fiennes, C. (1888) *Through England on a Side Saddle in the Time of William and Mary, being the Diary of Celia Fiennes, with an Introduction by the Hon Mrs Griffiths*. Field and Tuer: London.

Friends of the Walks (2016) *History of the Walks*. Website of the Friends of the Walks, Kings Lynn. Accessed 3 February, 2016: http://www.thewalks.uk/history-of-the-walks/

Girouard, M. (1990) *The English Town*. Yale University Press: New Haven, CT and London.

Harding, V. (1990) Gardens and open space in Tudor and Early Stuart London. In: Galinou, M. (ed.) *London's Pride: The Glorious History of the Capital's Gardens*: Anaya: London.

Harris, J. (1979) *The Artist and the Country House*. Sotheby Parke Burnet: London.

Hart, G. (1981) *A History of Cheltenham*. Second edition. Alan Sutton: Stroud.

Hembry, P. (1990) *The English Spa 1560–1815: A Social History*. Athlone Press: London.

Hodson, J. (ed.) (1997) *An Historical Gazetteer of Cheltenham*. Bristol and Gloucestershire Archaeological Society: Cheltenham. http://www.bgas.org.uk/publications/cheltgazintro.html

Jellicoe, G., Jellicoe, S., Goode, P. And Lancaster, M. (1986) *The Oxford Companion to Gardens*. Oxford University Press: Oxford and New York.

Johnson, R. (1607) *The Pleasant Walkes of Moore-fields, etc*. Henry Goffon: London.

Johnston, M. (2015) *Trees in Towns and Cities: A History of British Urban Arboriculture*. Windgather Press: Oxford.

Keene, D. (2000) The medieval urban landscape AD 900–1540. In: Waller, P. (ed.) *The English Urban Landscape*. Oxford University Press: Oxford.

Knyff, L. and Kip, J. (1984) *Britannia illustrata*. Harris J. and Jackson-Stops G. (eds). Published privately for the members of The National Trust by Paradigm Press: Bungay.

Langley, B. (1728) *A Sure Method of Improving Estates by the Plantation of Oak, Elm, Ash, Beech and Other Timber-trees, Coppice-woods, etc*. Francis Clay at the Bible, and Daniel Browne, at the Black Swan, without Temple-Bar: London.

Larwood, J. (1880) *The Story of London Parks*. Chatto and Windus: London.

Lawrence, H.W. (1988) Origins of the tree-lined boulevard. *Geographical Review* 78(4), 355–378.

Lawrence, H.W. (1993). The neoclassical origins of modern urban forests. *Forest & Conservation History* 37(1), 26–36.

Lawrence, H.W. (2006) *City Trees: A Historical Geography from the Renaissance through the Nineteenth Century*. University of Virginia Press: Charlottesville, VA and London.

Longstaff-Gowan, T. (2001) *The London Town Gardens 1740–1840*. Yale University Press: New Haven, CT and London.

Loudon, J.C. (1835) *Encyclopaedia of Gardening, Comprising the Theory and Practice of Horticulture, Floriculture, Arboriculture and Landscape-gardening*. A new edition. Longman, Rees, Orme, Brown, Green and Longmans: London.

MacLeod, D. (1972) *The Gardener's London*. Gerald Duckworth: London.

Mattocks, R.H. (1925) *The Planting of Trees in Streets and Woodlands*. Reprinted from *The Town Planning Review*, Vols X and XI. University Press of Liverpool: Liverpool.

Morris, A.E.J. (1994) *History of Urban Form before the Industrial Revolution*. Third edition. Longman Scientific and Technical: Harlow.

Nead, L. (2000) *Victorian Babylon: People, Streets and Images in Nineteenth-Century London*. Yale University Press: New Haven, CT and London.

Nuttgens, P. (ed) (2001) *The History of York: From Earliest Times to the Year 2000*. Blackthorn: Pickering.

Pattacini, L. (1998) André Mollet, Royal Gardener in St James's Park, London. *Garden History* 26(1), 3–18.

Pepys, S. (1661) *The Diary of Samuel Pepys, Vol. 2, 1661*. A new and complete transcription published in 2000 by the University of California Press: Berkeley and Los Angeles, CA.

Pradines, C. (2009) *Road Infrastructures: Tree Avenues in the Landscape*. Fifth Council of Europe Conference on the European Landscape Convention CEP-CPDATEP. Cultural Heritage, Landscape and Spatial Planning Division, Council of Europe: Strasbourg.

Procter, R.W. (1874) *Memorials of Manchester Streets*. Thomas Sutcliffe: Manchester.

Smith, C.H.J. (1852) *Parks and Pleasure Grounds; or Practical Notes on Country Residences, Villas, Public Parks, and Gardens*. Reeve and Sons: London.

Strutt, J. (1810) *Sports and Pastimes of the People of England*. Second edition. T. Bensley: London.

Walford, E. (1878) *Old and New London: a Narrative of its History, its People, and its Places*. Vol. 4, Chapter 30. Cassell, Petter and Galpin: London.

Whately, T. (1771) *Observations on Modern Gardening*. Third edition. T. Payne: London.

Williamson, T. (1995) *Polite Landscapes: Gardens and Society in Eighteenth Century England*. John Hopkins University Press: Baltimore, MD.

Wroth, W. (1896) *The London Pleasure Gardens of the Eighteenth Century*. Macmillan: London and New York.

Chapter 3. Remnants from Past Landscapes

Anderson, B. (2015) Rusholme and Victoria Park Archive webpages. Author: Bruce Anderson. Accessed 21 December, 2015: http://rusholmearchive.org/

Anon (1894) A rising watering-place: Bexhill-on-Sea. *The Sketch*, 11 July, 1894, 601.

Anon (1921) The last of the Old Walnut Tree. *Bexhill-on-Sea Observer*, 30 July, 1921, 4.

Anon (1985) Putting the oak in Selly Oak. *Birmingham Evening Mail*, 29 March 1985, 5.

Brentwood Council (2015) *Brentwood Town Centre Heritage Trail*. Leaflet researched and devised by Brentwood Museum. Brentwood Borough Council: Brentwood.

Conway, H. (1991) *People's Parks: The Design and Development of Victorian Parks in Britain*. Cambridge University Press: Cambridge.

Croucher, B. (1995) *Ramsbury – Then and Now*. Published privately by the author: Ramsbury.

Davies, L. (2012) *History of the Old Oak*. Leaflet with text sourced from the *Carmarthen Journal*. Carmarthen Town Council: Carmarthen.

Davies, N. (1993) The Death of Trust. *The Guardian*, 1 September, 1993. Accessed 26 February, 2016: http://www.nickdavies.net/1993/09/01/the-death-of-trust/

Dowling, G., Giles, B. and Hayfield, C. (1987) *Selly Oak Past and Present: a Photographic Survey of a Birmingham Suburb*. Department of Geography, University of Birmingham: Birmingham.

Elvin, H. (1950) *The Story at Canons*. Peter Garnett: London.

Greaves, W. (1983) Stumped by a great elm. *Daily Mail*, 1 March, 1983, 7.

Guldi, J. (2012) *Roads to Power: Britain Invents the Infrastructure State*. Harvard University Press: Cambridge, MA.

Hyland, J. (no date) A Brief History of Selly Oak. Text on the webpages of William Dargue entitled *A History of Birmingham Places and Names ...from A–Y*. Accessed 7 June, 2015: http://billdargue.jimdo.com/placenames-gazetteer-a-to-y/places-s/a-brief-history-of-selly-oak-by-james-hyland/

Jenkins, S. (2015) St Giles in 1779. *Oxford History* webpages. Author: Stephanie Jenkins. Accessed 10 September, 2015: http://www.oxfordhistory.org.uk/stgiles/old_pictures/1779.html

Leicester City Council (2014) *Pine Tree Avenue, Tree Consultation*. Issued in April 2014. Leicester City Council: Leicester.

Leonard, F.W. (1933) *The Story of Selly Oak, Birmingham.* Published privately on behalf of St Mary's Parochial Church Council: Selly Oak.

MacKinnon, J. (1825) *Account of Messingham – 1824, In the County of Lincoln.* Edited by Edward Peacock in 1880. Reproduced in 2007 by the Messingham History Group: Messingham.

McKenna, J. (1990) *Acocks Green.* Text on the website of the Acocks Green Historical Society, edited by Michael Byrne. Accessed 14 February, 2016: http://aghs.jimdo.com/mckenna-history/

Messingham History Group (2006) *A Brief History of Messingham.* Messingham History Group: Messingham.

Mitchell, A. (1996) *Alan Mitchell's Trees of Britain.* Harper Collins: London.

Pyke, C. (2014) Welsh History Month: Many Welsh towns face problems of how to preserve their past but also accommodate the needs of their inhabitants. Wales Online, the online presence of the *Western Mail.* Accessed 3 October, 2014: http://www.walesonline.co.uk/lifestyle/nostalgia/welsh-history-month-many-welsh-7875720

Randall, A.B. (1980) Carmarthen and Merlin the Magician. *Carmarthenshire Historian,* 17, 5–24.

Richardson, J. (1999) *A History of Camden: Hampstead, Holborn and St Pancras.* Historical Publications: Whitstable.

Shaw-Lefevre, G. (1894) *English Commons and Forests.* Cassell and Company: London.

Stevenson, C. (2009) Residents fear for future of ancient pines in Leicester road. *Leicester Mercury,* posted 5 October, 2009. Accessed 12 December, 2015: http://www.leicestermercury.co.uk/Residents-fear-future-ancient-pines-Leicester-road/story-12069203-detail/story.html

The Garden (1874) The Dying Elms on Cheyne Walk. *The Garden* 5, 524.

Thompson, S.C. (ed.) (1979) *Southampton Common: Its Place in the Life of Southampton Over the Centuries.* City of Southampton Society: Southampton.

Walford, E. (1878) Chelsea. In: *Old and New London,* Vol. 5, 50–70. Cassell, Petter and Galpin: London. Accessed: 8 March, 2016: http://www.british-history.ac.uk/old-new-london/vol5/pp50-70

Weston Wright, H. (1922) The Trees in Platt Lane. Letter from the Rev. H. Weston Wright, Platt Rectory, Rusholme. *Manchester Guardian,* 27 March, 9.

Wilks, J.H. (1972) *Trees of the British Isles in History and Legend.* Frederick Muller: London.

Williams, G. (1978) *The Royal Parks of London.* Constable: London.

Wood, L. (1974) *St Giles' Oxford, Yesterday and Today: The Story of the Parish of St Giles.* Published privately by Leslie Wood in June, 1974. Abbreviated version accessed 11 December, 2015: http://www.st-giles-church.org/stgiles/find-us/history-of-area/

Wreyford, P. (2013) *The A–Z of Curious Essex: Strange Stories of Mysteries, Crimes and Eccentrics.* History Press: Stroud.

Chapter 4. Early Influences from Overseas

Alphand, A. (1867) *Les Promenades de Paris, histoire, description des embellissements, dépenses de création et d'entretien des bois de Boulogne et de Vincennes, Champs-Elysées, parcs, squares, boulevards, places plantées. Etudes sur l'art des jardins et Arboretum.* J. Rothschild: Paris.

Anon (1901) Lord Street Trees: How they were once destroyed but are now preserved. *Southport Visiter,* 22 January, 1901, no page number.

Bisgrove, R. (2008) *William Robinson: The Wild Gardener.* Frances Lincoln: London.

Bland, E. (1903) *Annals of Southport and District. A Chronological History of North Meols from Alfred the Great to Edward VII.* J.J. Riley: Southport.

Boulton, E.H.B. (1969) A.D.C. Le Sueur, OBE: an appreciation. *Arboricultural Association Journal* 1(9), 247–248.

Campbell-Culver, M. (2006) *A Passion for Trees: The Legacy of John Evelyn.* Eden Project: London.

Chargueraud, A. (1896) *Les arbres de la ville de Paris: Traité des plantations d'alignement et ornement dans les villes et sur les routes départementales; installations, culture, taille, élagage, entretien, remplacement, rendement, dépenses, législation.* J. Rothschild: Paris.

Clarke, C.B. (1883) Letter to the editor on Street Planting in Calcutta. *Gardeners' Chronicle,* new ser. 20, 107.

Cook, M. (1676) *The Manner of Raising, Ordering, and Improving Forest-Trees: Also, How to Plant, Make and Keep Woods, Walks, Avenues, Lawns, Hedges, etc.* Peter Parker at the Leg and Star: London.

Du Breuil, A. (1865) *Manuel D'arboriculture Des Ingénieurs. Plantations D'alignement, Forestières Et D'ornement Boisement Des Dunes, Des Talus Haies Vives Des Parcelles Excédantes Des Ohemins De Fer.* Victor Masson et Fils: Paris.

Edwards, P.J. (1898) *History of London Street Improvements, 1855–1897.* London County Council: London.

Elmes, J. (1828) *Metropolitan Improvements; or London in the Nineteenth Century*. Jones and Company: London.

Evelyn, J. (1664) *Sylva or a Discourse of Forest-Trees, and the propagation of timber in His Majesties Dominions*. J. Martyn and J. Allestry: London.

Evelyn, J. (1901) *The Diary of John Evelyn*. Edited in 1901 from the original manuscript by William Bray in two volumes. Vol. 1. M. Walter Dunne: New York and London.

Evelyn, J. (1938) *London Revived, Consideration for its Rebuilding in 1666*. De Beer, E.S. (ed). Clarendon Press: Oxford.

Fairchild, T. (1722) *The City Gardener – Containing the Most Experienced Method of Cultivating and Ordering such Evergreens, Fruit-trees, Flowering Shrubs, Exotick Plants, etc, as will be Ornamental, and Thrive Best in London Gardens*. Printed for T. Woodward: London.

Gardeners' Chronicle (1878) Tree planting in Washington. *Gardeners' Chronicle* new ser. 9, 501.

Gardeners' Chronicle (1896) Street planting. *Gardeners' Chronicle* 3rd ser 20, 400.

Gardeners' Chronicle (1897) Street planting. *Gardeners' Chronicle* 3rd ser. 21, 165.

Gardener's Magazine (1827) Boulevards of Brussels. *Gardener's Magazine* 2, 87.

Girouard, M. (1985) *Cities and People: A Social and Architectural History*. Yale University Press: New Haven, CT and London.

Hardy, C. (2000) *Francis Frith's Around Southport*. Frith Book Company: Salisbury.

Hart, W.O. (1959) Local government in London. *Journal of the Society of Public Teachers of Law*, new ser. 5(2) (December), 62–76.

Hibbert, C. (1987) *The Grand Tour*. Thames Methuen: London

Hobsbawm, E. (1987) *The Age of Empire 1875–1914*. Pantheon: New York.

Hou, S. (2013) *The City Natural: Garden and Forest Magazine and the Rise of American Environmentalism*. University of Pittsburgh Press: Pittsburgh.

Humphreys, N. (1873) Trees wanted in the broad thoroughfares of Western London. *The Garden* 3, 130.

Hunt, T. (2004) *Building Jerusalem: The Rise and Fall of the Victorian City*. Weidenfeld and Nicolson London.

Jacobs, A.B., Macdonald, E. and Rofé, Y. (2003) *The Boulevard Book: History, Evolution, Design of Multiway Boulevards*. MIT Press: Cambridge, MA.

Jenkins, R. (2000) How Southport was right up Napoleon's street. *The Times*, 25 April, 5.

Johnston, M. (2015) *Trees in Towns and Cities: A History of British Urban Arboriculture*. Windgather Press: Oxford.

Kirkland, S. (2013) *Paris Reborn: Napoleon III, Baron Haussmann, and the Quest to Build a Modern City*. St Martin's Press: New York.

Lawrence, H.W. (1988) Origins of the tree-lined boulevard. *Geographical Review* 78(4), 355–378.

Lawrence, H.W. (2006) *City Trees: A Historical Geography from the Renaissance through the Nineteenth Century*. University of Virginia Press: Charlottesville, VA and London.

Le Sueur, A.D.C. (1934) *The Care and Repair of Ornamental Trees*. Country Life: London.

Longstaffe-Gowan, T. (2001) *The London Town Garden 1740–1840*. Paul Mellon Centre for Studies in British Art: London.

Loudon, J.C. (1827) Trees in Public Walks. *Gardener's Magazine* 2, 461.

Loudon, J.C. (1830) Notes and reflections made during a tour through part of France and Germany in the autumn of the Year 1828. *Gardener's Magazine* 5, 641–649.

Loudon, J.C. (1831a) General results of a gardening tour, during July in the present year, by a circuitous route from Manchester, by Chester and Liverpool, to Dumfries. *Gardener's Magazine* 7, 513–557.

Loudon, J.C. (1831b) Notes and reflections made during a tour through part of France and Germany in the autumn of the Year 1828. *Gardener's Magazine* 7, 1–20.

M'Nab, J. (1874) Tree management in or near towns. *The Garden* 6, 401.

Mollie, C. (2007) *Des Arbres dans la Ville: L'urbanisme végétal*. Actes Sud/Cité Verte: Paris.

Nevin, C. (2004) Oh la Lancashire. *The Guardian*, Article by Charles Nevin in the Weekend feature. Saturday 21 August, 2004. http://www.theguardian.com/books/2004/aug/21/features.weekend

Nierhaus, A. (2014) An urban revolution. In: Faber, M., Martz, J., Mattl, S., Nierhaus, A., Orosz, E. and Morton, F. (eds) *Vienna's Ringstrasse – The Book*, 18–39. Hatje Cantz: Ostfildern.

Pradines, C. (2009) *Road Infrastructures: Tree Avenues in the Landscape*. Fifth Council of Europe Conference on the European Landscape Convention CEP-CPDATEP. Cultural Heritage, Landscape and Spatial Planning Division, Council of Europe: Strasbourg.

Robinson, F. (1848) *A Descriptive History of the Popular Watering Place of Southport in the Parish of North Meols, on the Western Coast of Lancashire.* Arthur Hall and Co: London

Robinson, W. (1869) *The Parks, Promenades and Gardens of Paris Described and Considered in Relation to the Wants of our own Cities and of Public and Private Gardens.* John Murray: London.

Rudé, G. (1971) *Hanoverian London 1714–1808.* Martin Secker and Warburg: London.

Rutger, T. (1835) Some remarks on the suburban gardens of the metropolis, and on the mode of laying out and planting the public squares. *Gardener's Magazine* 11, 513–515.

Sala, G.A. (1864) The streets of the World. Paris: the passage des panoramas. *Temple Bar* 10 (February 1864), 335–341.

Simo, M.L. (1988) *Loudon and the Landscape: From Country Seat to Metropolis.* Yale University Press: New Haven, CT and London.

Sitte, C. (1889) *City Planning According to Artistic Principles.* Translated in 1965 by George R. Collins and C.C. Collins. Columbia University Studies in Art History and Archaeology 2. Phaidon: London.

Solotaroff, W. (1910) *Shade-Trees in Towns and Cities.* Wiley: New York and London.

Stewart, J. (1771) *Critical Observations on the Buildings and Improvements of London.* J. Dodsley: London.

Stübben, J. (1885) *Practical and Aesthetic Principles for the Laying Out of Cities.* English translation by W.H. Searles and published in 1893. Transactions of the American Society of Civil Engineers. Accessed 2 June, 2014: http://www.library.cornell.edu/Reps/DOCS/stubb_85.htm

Stübben, J. (1890) *Der Städtebau (Handbuch der Architektur).* 1980 reprint of first edition. Vieweg Verlagsgesellschaft: Braunschweig, Wiesbaden.

The Garden (1873) Lectures in arboriculture by Professor Du Breuil. *The Garden* 3, 330.

The Garden (1874a) The cost of planting the Paris boulevards. *The Garden* 5, 205.

The Garden (1874b) The boulevards of Vienna. *The Garden* 6, 402.

Tillery, W. (1861) The Trees of Paris. *Gardeners' Chronicle and Agricultural Gazette* 42, 928.

Willebrand, J.P. (1775) *Grundriß einer schönen Stadt* (Plan for a beautiful city). Published by the author: Hamburg and Leipzig. Accessed 2 March, 2016: http://www.cloud-cuckoo.net/openarchive/Autoren/Willebrandt/Willebrandt1775.htm

Woods and Forests (1884) The trees of Paris. *Woods and Forests* 1, 35, 499.

Chapter 5. The Victorian Street Tree Movement

Anon (1862) London as it strikes a stranger. *Temple Bar*, 5 June, 1862, 382.

Anon (1879a) Ornamental trees for the esplanade. *Evening Telegraph* (Dundee), 28 April, 1879, no page number.

Anon (1879b) The trees on the esplanade. *Evening Telegraph* (Dundee), 6 May, 1879, no page number.

Anon (1882) The trees on the esplanade. *Evening Telegraph* (Dundee), 30 September, 1882, no page number.

Anon (1905a) Tree-planting in Aberdeen: I. *Aberdeen Daily Journal*, 29 June, 1905, 4.

Anon (1905b) Tree-planting in Aberdeen: II. *Aberdeen Daily Journal*, 30 June, 1905, 4.

Anon (1914) Street trees – sylvan decoration in Aberdeen. *Aberdeen Daily Journal*, 2 May, 1914, 5.

Anon (1930) Beautified open spaces – death of former parks superintendent. *Press and Journal* (Aberdeen), 21 April, 1930, 6.

Barker, F. and Hyde, R. (1982) *London as it Might have Been.* John Murray: London.

Briggs, A. (1968) *Victorian Cities.* Penguin: London.

Burnett, J. (1986) *A Social History of Housing 1815–1985.* Second edition. Routledge: London and New York.

Carley, M., Dalziel, R., Dargan, P. and Laird, S. (2015) *Edinburgh New Town: A Model City.* Amberley: Stroud.

Chadwick, G.F. (1966) *The Park and the Town: Public Landscape in the 19th and 20th Centuries.* Frederick A. Praeger: New York and Washington, DC.

Chinn, C. (1999) *Homes for People: Council Housing and Urban Renewal in Birmingham, 1849–1999.* Brewin: Studley.

Cockburn Association (1879) *Report by the Council to the Fourth Annual Meeting of the Association, Edinburgh, July 1879.* Cockburn Association: Edinburgh.

Cockburn Association (1882) *Report by the Council to the Seventh Annual Meeting of the Association, Edinburgh, July 1882.* Cockburn Association: Edinburgh.

Cockburn Association (1884) *Report by the Council to the Ninth Annual Meeting of the Association, Edinburgh, July 1884.* Cockburn Association: Edinburgh.

Cockburn Association (1888) *Report by the Council to the Thirteenth Annual Meeting of the Association, Edinburgh, July 1888.* Cockburn Association: Edinburgh.

Cockburn Association (1889) *Report by the Council to the Fourteenth Annual Meeting of the Association, Edinburgh, July 1889*. Cockburn Association: Edinburgh.

Cockburn Association (1897) *The Cockburn Association: A Short Account of its Objects and its Work – 1875–1897*. Cockburn Association: Edinburgh.

Cockburn Association (1899) *Report by the Council to the Twenty-third Annual Meeting of the Association, Edinburgh, May 1899*. Cockburn Association: Edinburgh.

Cockburn Association (1902) *Report by the Council to the Twenty-sixth Annual Meeting of the Association, Edinburgh, May 1902*. Cockburn Association: Edinburgh.

Cockburn Association (1935) *Report by the Council to the Fifty-seventh Annual Meeting of the Association, Edinburgh, January 1935*. Cockburn Association: Edinburgh.

Conway, H. (1991) *People's Parks: The Design and Development of Victorian Parks in Britain*. Cambridge University Press: Cambridge.

Edwards, B. (1993) Glasgow Improvements, 1866–1901. In: Reed, P. (ed) *Glasgow: The Forming of the City*. University of Edinburgh Press: Edinburgh.

Edwards, P.J. (1898) *History of London Street Improvements, 1855–1897*. London County Council: London.

Elliott, P.A. (2016) *British Urban Trees: A Social and Cultural History, c. 1800–1914*. White Horse Press: Winwick.

Engels, F. (1892) *The Condition of the Working Class in England in 1844*. Swan Sonnenschein and Company: London. Transcribed from the January 1943 George Allen and Unwin reprint of the March 1892 edition by David Price. Accessed 2 April 2016: http://www.latin-american.cam.ac.uk/sites/default/files/engels-_the_condition_of_the_working_class.pdf

Gardeners' Chronicle (1863) Street planting. *Gardeners' Chronicle and Agricultural Gazette* 10, 219.

Gardeners' Chronicle (1876) The planting of trees in large towns. *Gardeners' Chronicle* new ser. 6, 354–355.

Gardeners' Chronicle (1878a) Tree planting in London. *Gardeners' Chronicle* new ser. 10, 50.

Gardeners' Chronicle (1878b) Trees in suburban thoroughfares. *Gardeners' Chronicle* new ser. 10, 534.

Gardeners' Chronicle (1878c) The planting of trees in towns. *Gardeners' Chronicle* new ser. 10, 560.

Gardeners' Chronicle (1879a) Trees at the west-end. *Gardeners' Chronicle* new ser. 11, 375.

Gardeners' Chronicle (1879b) Trees planting in the north of London. *Gardeners' Chronicle* new ser. 12, 656.

Gardeners' Chronicle (1880) Trees in the streets of London. *Gardeners' Chronicle* new ser. 14, 18.

Gardeners' Chronicle (1881) Town trees. *Gardeners' Chronicle* new ser. 16, 374.

Gardeners' Chronicle (1882) Tree planting in towns. *Gardeners' Chronicle* new ser. 18, 306.

Gardeners' Chronicle (1887) Trees of London. *Gardeners' Chronicle* 3rd ser. 2, 462.

Gardeners' Chronicle (1890) Tree planting. *Gardeners' Chronicle* 3rd ser. 8, 597.

Gardeners' Chronicle (1892) Look on this and picture that. *Gardeners' Chronicle* 3rd ser. 12, 530.

Gardeners' Chronicle (1897) Street trees. *Gardeners' Chronicle* 3rd ser. 21, 165.

Gardeners' Chronicle (1905) Trees in Kingsway. *Gardeners' Chronicle* 3rd ser. 38, 313.

Gardeners' Chronicle (1910) Planting of trees in Glasgow streets. *Gardeners' Chronicle* 3rd ser. 48, 490.

Gauldie, E. (1974) *Cruel Habitations: History of Working Class Housing, 1780–1918*. Allen and Unwin: London.

Gosport, J.G. (1886) Planting street trees. *The Garden*, 30, 121.

Harley, R.J. (2005) *London's Victoria Embankment*. Capital History: Harrow.

Hobsbawm, E. (1975) *The Age of Capital 1848–1875*. Weidenfeld and Nicolson: London.

Hogg, A. (1973) *Scotland, the Rise of Cities, 1694–1905*. Evans Brothers: London.

Humphreys, N. (1871) Thames Embankment by Noel Humphreys. *The Garden* 1, 47–48.

Humphreys, N. (1873) Trees wanted in the broad thoroughfares of Western London. *The Garden* 3, 130.

Humphreys, N. (1874) Grand avenues for London. *The Garden* 6, 277.

Hunt, T. (2004) *Building Jerusalem: The Rise and Fall of the Victorian City*. Weidenfeld and Nicolson: London.

Johnston, M. (2015) *Trees in Towns and Cities: A History of British Urban Arboriculture*. Windgather Press: Oxford.

Lasdun, S. (1991) *The English Park: Royal, Private and Public*. Andre Deutsch: London.

Lawrence, H.W. (1988) Origins of the tree-lined boulevard. *Geographical Review* 78 (4), 355–378.

Malchow, H.L. (1985) Public gardens and social action in late Victorian London. *Victorian Studies* 29(1), 97–124.

Masson, R. (1926) *Scotia's Darling Seat 1875–1925*. Published for the Cockburn Association by Robert Grant and Son: Edinburgh.

Maver, R. (1998) Glasgow's public parks and the community, 1850–1914: a case study in Scottish civic interventionism. *Urban History* 25(3), 323–347.

McLellan, D. (1894) *Glasgow Public Parks*. John Smith and Son: Glasgow.

Morton, A.L. (1938) *A People's History of England*. Victor Gollancz: London.

MPGA (1898) *Fifteenth Annual Report of the Metropolitan Public Gardens Association (in connection with the National Health Society) for the year 1897*. Metropolitan Public Gardens Association: London.

Munro Ferguson, R.C. (1901) The Arboricultural adornment of towns. *Transactions of the Royal Scottish Arboricultural Society* 16 (1899–1901), 388–398.

Mynors, C. (2002) *The Law of Trees, Forests and Hedgerows*. Sweet and Maxwell: London.

Newton, J. (1870) Street planting. *Gardeners' Chronicle and Agricultural Gazette* 33, 1087–1088.

Pettigrew, A.A. (1926) *The Public Parks and Recreation Grounds of Cardiff*. Vol. 2. Chapter on Street Trees. Unpublished study in Cardiff Central Library.

Pettigrew, W.W. (1937) *Municipal Parks: Layout, Management and Administration. Journal of Park Administration*: London.

Phené, J.S. (1880) On the sanitary results of planting trees in towns. *Transactions of the National Association for the Promotion of Social Science, Edinburgh, 1880*, 615–616.

Porter, D.H. (1998) *The Thames Embankment. Environment, Technology and Society in Victorian London*. University of Akron Press: Akron, OH

Robinson, C.M. (1901) *The Improvement of Towns and Cities or the Practical Basics of Civic Aesthetics*. G.P. Putnam's Sons: New York and London.

Robinson, W. (1869) *The Parks, Promenades and Gardens of Paris Described and Considered in Relation to the Wants of our own Cities and of Public and Private Gardens*. John Murray: London.

Roger, R. (2000) Slums and suburbs: the persistence of residential apartheid. In: Waller, P. (ed.) *The English Urban Landscape*. Oxford University Press: Oxford.

Rudé, G. (1971) *Hanoverian London 1714–1808*. Martin Secker and Warburg: London.

The Garden (1872) Trees in Coventry. *The Garden* 2, 76.

The Garden (1878a) Street trees. *The Garden* 14, 500.

The Garden (1878b) Planting trees in roads. *The Garden* 13, 239.

The Garden (1882) Planting trees on the road-sides. *The Garden* 22, 74.

The Garden (1890) Tree planting in Manchester. *The Garden* 38, 570.

The Garden (1891) Tree growing in towns: Manchester. *The Garden* 39, 18.

The Garden (1904) Trees for George Street, Edinburgh. *The Garden* 65, 70.

Thompson, E.P. (1963) *The Making of the English Working Class*. Victor Gollancz: London.

Trevelyan, G.M. (1952) *Illustrated English Social History. Volume Four: The Nineteenth Century*. Longmans, Green and Co: London.

Walker, R. (1890) *On the Planting of Trees in Towns: Being the Paper read before the North of Scotland Horticultural Association by Robert Walker, Keeper of the Victoria Park*. University Press: Aberdeen.

Woods and Forests (1885) Tree planting in London. *Woods and Forests* 2, 70.

Chapter 6. Victorian and Edwardian Suburbs

Atkins. P.J. (1993) How the West End was won: the struggle to remove street barriers in Victorian London. *Journal of Historical Geography* 19(3), 265–277.

Barratt, N. (2012) *Greater London: The Story of the Suburbs*. Random House: London.

Barson, S. (1999) Infinite variety in brick and stucco: 1840-1914. In: Honer, J. (ed.) *London Suburbs*. Merrell Holberton in Association with English Heritage: London.

Bick, J (2012) *Old Bordesley Green*. Stenlake: Catrine.

Birmingham CC (2006) *Trees in the Public Highway*. A Report to the City Council on a Review of Trees in Public Highway, dated 7 February 2006. Birmingham City Council.

Birmingham CC (2012) *Moor Pool Conservation Area – Character Appraisal and Management Plan*. Birmingham City Council.

Brand, K. (1990) *The Park Estate, Nottingham*. Nottingham Civic Society: Nottingham.

Briggs, A. (1968) *Victorian Cities*. Penguin: London.

Burnett, J. (1986) *A Social History of Housing 1815–1985*. Second edition. Routledge: London and New York.

Cannadine, D. (1980) *Lords and Landlords: The Aristocracy and the Towns 1774–1967*. Leicester University Press: Leicester.

Chinn, C. (1999) *Homes for People: Council Housing and Urban Renewal in Birmingham, 1849-1999*. Brewin Books: Studley.

Cooper, G. (2002) *The Illustrated History of Manchester's Suburbs*. Breedon Books: Derby.

Covins, F. (1989) *The Arboretum Story: A Social and Historical Record of the Arboretum Area of Central Worcester*. Arboretum Residents' Association: Worcester.

Creese, W. (1966) *The Search for Environment: The Garden City Before and After*. Yale University Press: New Haven, CT.

Cronin, J. and Rhodes, F. (2010) *Longsight*. Britain in Old Photographs. History Press: Stroud.

Dargue, W. (2016a) *A History of Birmingham Places and Placenames ... From A–Z. Bordesley Green* webpages. Author: William Dargue. Accessed 4 July 2016: http://billdargue.jimdo.com/placenames-gazetteer-a-to-y/places-b/bordesley-green/

Dargue, W. (2016b) *A History of Birmingham Places and Placenames ... From A–Z. Edgbaston* webpages. Author: William Dargue. Accessed 6 July 2016: http://billdargue.jimdo.com/placenames-gazetteer-a-to-y/places-e/edgbaston/

Dargue, W. (2016c) *A History of Birmingham Places and Placenames ... From A–Z. Handsworth* webpages. Author: William Dargue. Accessed 8 July 2016: http://billdargue.jimdo.com/placenames-gazetteer-a-to-y/places-h/handsworth/

Dargue, W. (2016d) *A History of Birmingham Places and Placenames ... From A–Z. Sparkbrook* webpages. Author: William Dargue. Accessed 9 July 2016: http://billdargue.jimdo.com/placenames-gazetteer-a-to-y/places-s/sparkbrook/

Dargue, W. (2016e) *A History of Birmingham Places and Placenames ... From A–Z. Sparkhill* webpages. Author: William Dargue. Accessed 9 July 2016: http://billdargue.jimdo.com/placenames-gazetteer-a-to-y/places-s/sparkhill/

Drake, P. (1998) *Handsworth, Hockley and Handsworth Wood*. Images of England. Tempus: Stroud.

Durie, B. (2001) *Glasgow Past and Present*. Sutton and W.H. Smith: Swindon

Dyos, H.J. (1961) *Victorian Suburb: A Study of the Growth of Camberwell*. Leicester University Press: Leicester.

Elliott, P.A. (2016) *British Urban Trees: A Social and Cultural History, c. 1800–1914*. White Horse Press: Winwick.

Fishman, R. (1987) *Bourgeois Utopias: The Rise and Fall of Suburbia*. Basic Books: New York.

Galinou, M. (2010) *Cottages and Villas: The Birth of the Garden Suburb*. Yale University Press: New Haven, CT and London.

Gardeners' Chronicle (1876) The planting of trees in large towns. *Gardeners' Chronicle*, new ser. 6, 354–355.

Gardeners' Chronicle (1890) Town trees. *Gardeners' Chronicle* 3rd ser. 8, 700.

Gay, K. (1999) *A History of Muswell Hill*. Hornsey Historical Society: London

Girouard, Mark (1985) *Cities and People: A Social and Architectural History*. Yale University Press: New Haven, CT and London.

Graham, K. and Taverner, J. (2004) *Rhiwbina*. Images of Wales. Tempus: Stroud.

Greeves, T.A. (1975) *Bedford Park: the First Garden Suburb*. Anne Bingley: London.

Hall, P. and Ward, C. (1998) *Sociable Cities: the Legacy of Ebenezer Howard*. Wiley: Chichester

Hammond, C. and Hammond, P. (1994) *Chiswick*. The Old Photographs Series. Chalford Publishing: Stroud.

Harrison, M. (1976) Burnage Garden Village: an ideal for life in Manchester. *Town Planning Review* 47(3), 256.

HGS Residents Association (2016) *The Hampstead Garden Suburb Act 1906*. Text on the webpages of the Hampstead Garden Suburb Residents Association. Accessed 20 July, 2016: http://www.hgs.org.uk/history/h00012000.html

Hull CC (1998) Character Statement for the Avenues. Avenues/Pearson Park Conservation Area. Urban Conservation and Design, Hull City Council. Accessed 14 July, 2016: http://www.hullcc.gov.uk/pls/portal/docs/PAGE/HOME/PLANNING/CONSERVATION/CONSERVATION%20AREAS/AVENUES%20APPRAISAL.PDF

Hunt, T. (2004) *Building Jerusalem: The Rise and Fall of the Victorian City*. Weidenfeld and Nicolson: London.

James, D.C. (1984) Disease, debility and death in a Welsh town: Cardiff 1845–1865. *Public Health* 98(3), 157–162.

Jones, C. (1902) *Ealing From Village to Corporate Town, Or Forty Years of Municipal Life*. S.B. Spaull: London.

Ketchell, C. (ed.) (1989) *An Illustrated History of The Avenues and Pearson Park, Hull: From Victorian Suburb to Conservation Area*. Avenues and Pearson Park Residents Association: Hull.

LB Barnet (1999) *Hampstead Garden Suburb Street Tree Strategy: Maintenance Proposals for Trees on Highways Land*. October, 1999. London Borough of Barnet.

Loobey, P. (1994) *Wandsworth*. Archive Photographs Series. Chalford Publishing: Stroud.

Loobey, P. (2000) *Battersea and Clapham: The Second Series*. Images of England. History Press: Stroud.

Mackenzie, J.M. (1999) 'The second city of the Empire':
Glasgow – imperial municipality. In: Drive, F. and
Gilbert, D. (eds) *Imperial Cities: Landscape, Display
and Identity*. Manchester University Press: Manchester

Marks, J.T. (1913) Road trees in the suburb. *The Record
– Hampstead Garden Suburb*, August 1913, 11.

Mellors, R. (1926) *The Gardens, Parks and Walks of
Nottingham*. J. and H. Bell: Nottingham.

Miller, M. (1995) *Hampstead Garden Suburb: Past
and Present*. Archive Photographs Series. Chalford
Publishing: Stroud.

Miller, M. (2010) *English Garden Cities: An Introduction*.
English Heritage: Swindon.

Morgan, D. (2003) *The Illustrated History of Cardiff's
Suburbs*. Breedon Books: Derby.

Nettlefold, J.S. (1906) *Slum Reform and Town Planning:
The Garden City Idea applied to existing Cities and
their Suburbs*. Published privately: Birmingham.

Nettlefold, J.S. (1908) *Practical Housing*. Garden City
Press: Letchworth.

Oates, J. and Hounsell, P. (2014) *Ealing: A Concise
History*. Amberley: Stroud.

Pryor, F. (2010) *The Making of the British Landscape*.
Allen Lane: London.

Purkis, H. (1989) Trees in the Avenues. In: Ketchell,
C. (ed.) *An Illustrated History of The Avenues
and Pearson Park, Hull: From Victorian Suburb
to Conservation Area*. Avenues and Pearson Park
Residents Association: Hull.

Ravetz, A. (2001) *Council Housing and Culture: The
History of a Social Experiment*. Routledge: London.

Reed, P. (1993) The Victorian suburb. In: Reed, P.
(ed.) *Glasgow: The Forming of the City*. Edinburgh
University Press: Edinburgh.

Reid, A. (2000) *Brentham: A History of the Pioneer
Garden Suburb 1901–2001*. Brentham Heritage
Society: Ealing, London.

Rogers, H.B. (1962) The suburban growth of Victorian
Manchester. *Journal of the Manchester Geographical
Society*. 58, 1–12.

Rutherford, S. (2014) *Garden Cities*. Shire: Oxford.

Schwitzer, J. and Gay, K. (1995) *Highgate and Muswell
Hill*. Images of England. Tempus: Stroud.

Slater, T. (2012) *Edgbaston – A History*. Phillimore:
Chichester.

Stern, R., Fishman, D. and Tilove, J. (2013) *Paradise
Planned: The Garden Suburb and the Modern City*.
Monacelli: New York.

Stilwell, M. (2015) *Early London County Council Housing*.
Part 3 – The Schemes in Detail, 24 – Totterdown

Fields Estate. Paper published by the author:
London.

Sussex, G., Helm, P. and Brown, A. (1987) *Looking Back
at Levenshulme and Burnage*. Willow: Timperley.

Tilney, C. (1985) *Cardiff in Old Picture Postcards*.
European Library: Zaltbommel.

Twist, M. (2004) *Handsworth Volume II*. Images of
England. Tempus: Stroud.

Unwin, R. (1909) *Town Planning and Modern
Architecture at the Hampstead Garden Suburb*. T.
Fisher Unwin: London.

Vision of Britain (2016) GB Historical GIS/University of
Portsmouth, Chiswick St Nicholas CP/AP through
time. Population Statistics, Total Population. *A
Vision of Britain through Time*. Accessed 2 July, 2016:
http://www.visionofbritain.org.uk/unit/10021364/
cube/TOT_POP

Wandsworth Council (2009) *Shaftesbury Park Estate
Conservation Area Appraisal and Management
Strategy*. Wandsworth Conservation and Design
Group, Wandsworth Council: London.

Wandsworth Council (2010) *Totterdown Fields
Conservation Area Appraisal and Management
Strategy*. Wandsworth Conservation and Design
Group, Wandsworth Council: London.

Whitelaw, M. (1992) *A Garden Suburb for Glasgow: The
Story of Westerton*. Published by the author: Glasgow.

Whitton Associates (2007) *The Park Estate, Nottingham:
Street Tree Planting Strategy*. Whitton Associates:
Cirencester.

Williams, G.R. (1975) *London in the Country: The
Growth of Suburbia*. Hamish Hamilton: London.

Wylie, W.H. (1855) *Old and New Nottingham*. Longman,
Brown, Green and Longmans: London.

Chapter 7. Suburbia in the Twentieth Century
AGHS (2016) *Housing Between the Wars*. Text on the
Acocks Green History Society webpages. Accessed
22 July 2016: http://aghs.jimdo.com/foxholwalker/
housing-between-the-wars/

Allen, G. and Jones, C. (2015) This Liverpool housing
estate just won the Turner Prize for modern art.
Daily Mirror, 8 December. Accessed 23 July 2016:
http://www.mirror.co.uk/news/weird-news/turner-
prize-2015-winner-liverpool-6971488

Anon (1923) The development of South Manchester: a
new housing estate at Burnage. *Manchester Guardian*,
14 August, 1923, 14.

Anon (1926) Compulsory acquisition of Withington
estates. *Manchester Guardian*, 18 May, 1926, 9.

Anon (1969) Failure of a high-rise system. *Concrete Construction*. 1 March, 1969. Reprinted from *Architectural Record*, November 1968. MacGraw-Hill: New York.

Barratt, N. (2012) *Greater London: The Story of the Suburbs*. Random House: London.

Barson, S. (1999) Infinite variety in brick and stucco: 1840–1914. In: Honer, J. (ed) *London Suburbs*. Merrell Holberton in Association with English Heritage: London.

Bermondsey Council (1927a) *Minutes of the Beautification and Public Amenities Committee*, 1 November, 1927, 258–260.

Bermondsey Council (1927b) *Minutes of the Beautification and Public Amenities Committee*, 18 October, 1927, 230.

Birmingham CC (2016) History of Hall Green. Text on the webpages of Birmingham City Council, Libraries Department, Archives and Heritage. Accessed 22 July 2016: http://www.birmingham.gov.uk/cs/Satellite?c=Page&childpagename=Lib-Hall-Green%2FPageLayout&cid=1223092585306&pagename=BCC%2FCommon%2FWrapper%2FWrapper

Briam, E. (1982) Doncaster's parks and public open spaces, No. 2 – The Town Field. *Doncaster Civic Trust Newsletter*, No. 37, July 1982.

Brockway, F. (1949) *Bermondsey Story: The Life of Alfred Salter*. George Allen and Unwin: London.

Burnett, J. (1986) *A Social History of Housing 1815–1985*. Second edition. Routledge: London and New York.

Byrne, M. (1996) *Hall Green*. Images of England. Tempus: Stroud.

Byrne, M. (1997) *Acocks Green*. The Archive Photographs Series. Chalford Publishing: Stroud.

Chinn, C. (1999) *Homes for People: Council Housing and Urban Renewal in Birmingham, 1849–1999*. Brewin Books: Studley.

Cooper, G. (2002) *The Illustrated History of Manchester's Suburbs*. Breedon Books: Derby.

Davey, R. (1984) *Reminiscing Around Rivelin*. Neil Richardson: Sheffield.

Gardeners' Chronicle (1931) Street trees and traffic. *Gardeners' Chronicle* 3rd ser. 89, 27.

Green, O. (1987) *Metro-land 1932 Edition*. Facsimile edition with an introduction by Oliver Green. Oldcastle Books: Harpenden.

Harwood, E. (1999) The Road to Subtopia: 1940 to the present. In: Honer, J. (ed) *London Suburbs*. Merrell Holberton in Association with English Heritage: London.

Harwood, E. (2000) Post-War landscape and public housing. *Garden History* 28(1), 102–116.

Hollow, M. (2011) Suburban ideals on England's interwar Council estates. *Garden History* 39(2), 203–217.

Home, R. (1997) *'A Township Complete in Itself' – A Planning History of the Becontree/Dagenham Estate*. Libraries Department, London Borough of Barking and Dagenham and School of Surveying, University of East London: London.

Lebas, E. (1999) The making of a Socialist Arcadia: arboriculture and horticulture in the London Borough of Bermondsey after the Great War. *Garden History* 27(2), 219–237.

Lewis, D. (2003) *The Illustrated History of Liverpool's Suburbs*. Breedon Books: Derby.

Ministry of Health (1948) *The Appearance of Housing Estates*. Central Housing Advisory Committee, report of the sub-committee on the means of improving the appearance of local authority housing estates. HMSO: London.

Morgan, D. (2003) *The Illustrated History of Cardiff's Suburbs*. Breedon Books: Derby.

MPGA (1914) Minutes of the Metropolitan Public Gardens Association, Vol. 2 (4 November 1914), 24. Metropolitan Public Gardens Association: London.

Olechnowicz, A. (1997) *Working-class Housing in England Between the Wars: The Becontree Estate*. Oxford Historical Monographs. Clarendon Press: Oxford.

Parrott, K. (1996) *West Derby and Norris Green*. The Archive Photographs Series. Chalford Publishing: Stroud.

Ravetz, A. (2001) *Council Housing and Culture: The History of a Social Experiment*. Routledge: London.

Stern, R., Fishman, D. and Tilove, J. (2013) *Paradise Planned: The Garden Suburb and the Modern City*. Monacelli: New York.

Swenerton, M. (1981) *Homes Fit For Heroes: The Politics and Architecture of Early State Housing in Britain*. Heinemann: London.

Winson, A. (2015) The Lime Trees of Rivelin. Posting on the AWA Tree Blog, dated 20 November, 2015. Author: Adam Winson. Accessed 14 July, 2016: http://awatrees.blogspot.co.uk/

Young, T. (1934) *Becontree and Dagenham*. Pilgrim Trust: London.

Chapter 8. Spa Towns and Seaside Resorts

Ablett, W.H. (1880) *English Trees and Tree-planting*. Smith, Elder: London.

Anon (1787) *East-bourne; Being a Descriptive Account of that Village, in the County of Sussex, and its Environs*. Hooper: London.

Anon (1867) Obituary: John Hitchman, Esq. *Monthly Homeopathic Review*, 1 April, 1867, 253.

Anon (1951) Removal of dangerous trees. *Eastbourne Gazette*, October 31, 1951, 1.

Anon (1954) Eastbourne still a 'City of Trees'. *Eastbourne Gazette*, September 22, 1954, 13.

Argyll and Bute Council (2008) *An appraisal of the Conservation Areas in Helensburgh*. Helensburgh Conservation Areas Group. Argyll and Bute Council: Lochgilphead.

Berry, S. (2000) Pleasure gardens in Georgian and Regency seaside resorts: Brighton, 1750–1840. *Garden History* 28(2), 222–230.

Bishop, C.H. (1973) *Folkestone: The Story of a Town*. Headley Brothers: Ashford.

Blake, S. (1988) *Pittville 1824–1860: a Scene of Gorgeous Magnificence*. Cheltenham Art Gallery and Museums: Cheltenham.

Borsay, P. (1989) *The English Urban Renaissance: Culture and Society in The Provincial Town 1660–1770*. Oxford University Press: Oxford.

Borsay, P. (2012) Town or country? British spas and the urban–rural interface. *Journal of Tourism History* 4(2), 155–169.

Borsay, Peter (2013) Pleasure gardens and urban culture in the long eighteenth century. In: Conlin, J. (ed.) *The Pleasure Garden, from Vauxhall to Coney Island*. University of Pennsylvania Press: Philadelphia, PA.

Botting Hemsley, W. (1909) Street trees. *Gardeners' Chronicle* 3rd ser. 46, 132.

Bournemouth BC (2014) *Bournemouth Tree Strategy: A Strategy for the Sustainable Management and Development of Bournemouth's Trees*. Bournemouth Borough Council.

Brodie, A. and Winter, G. (2007) *England's Seaside Resorts*. English Heritage: Swindon.

Byrom, P. (2013) *Fleetwood and Thornton Cleveleys Through Time*. Amberley: Stroud.

Cameron, J. (2006) *Royal Leamington Spa*. Images of England. Pocket Images. Nonsuch: Stroud.

Campbell, A.J. (1990–1991) Pittville Nursery Garden and the Ware mortgage: a cautionary tale. *Cheltenham Local History Society Journal* 8, 11–18.

Cannadine, D. (1980) *Lords and Landlords: The Aristocracy and the Towns 1774–1967*. Leicester University Press: Leicester.

Chambers, G.F. (1880) *Handbook and Directory for East-Bourne*. Twelfth edition. Farncombe: Eastbourne.

Cheltenham BC (2016) The importance of trees in Cheltenham. Text from the webpages of Cheltenham Borough Council, Environment and Communities. Accessed 4 March, 2016: http://www.cheltenham.gov.uk/info/505/tree_management/511/the_importance_of_trees_in_cheltenham

Cockshott, A. and Shillitoe, D. (2005) *Ilkley Past and Present*. Britain in Old Photographs. History Press: Stroud.

Crawford, K. and Glen, N. (2002) Chapter 4: Public Administration. In: Noble, S.N. (ed.) *200 Years of Helensburgh 1802–1902*. Argyll: Glendaruel.

Davis, G. and Bonsall, P. (2006) *A History of Bath: Image and Reality*. Carnegie: Lancaster.

Davis, M. (2012) *Ilkley Through Time*. Amberley: Stroud.

Dingwall, C. (2002) *Preliminary Notes on the Hermitage Park and other Public Open Spaces in Helensburgh*. Unpublished manuscript in Helensburgh Public Library, Reference Section.

Draper, C. and Lawson-Reay, J. (2010) *Llandudno Through Time*. Amberley: Stroud.

Elliott, K and Menneer, N. (2004) *Bath*. Frances Lincoln: London.

Elliott, P.A. (2016) *British Urban Trees: A Social and Cultural History, c. 1800–1914*. White Horse Press: Winwick.

Finlayson, R. (2009) *Ilkley: The History of the Wharfedale Town*. Phillimore: Chichester.

Gardeners' Chronicle (1880) Trees in the streets of London. *Gardeners' Chronicle* new sr. 14, 18.

Gardeners' Chronicle (1895a) Tree planting at Exmouth. *Gardeners' Chronicle* 3rd ser. 18, 650–651.

Gardeners' Chronicle (1895b) Tree planting at Exmouth. *Gardeners' Chronicle* 3rd ser. 18, 720.

Gardeners' Chronicle (1898) Street trees in Bath. *Gardeners' Chronicle* 3rd ser. 24, 238.

Gaut, A. (1907) *Seaside Planting of Trees and Shrubs*. Country Life: London.

Gray, F. (2006) *Designing the Seaside: Architecture, Society and Nature*. Reaktion: London.

Griffith, S.Y. (1826) *Griffith's New Historical Description of Cheltenham and its Vicinity*. Vol. 2, second edition. Longman, Rees, Orme, Brown and Green: London.

Gurnham, R. (1972) The creation of Skegness as a resort town by the 9th Earl of Scarborough. *Lincolnshire History and Archaeology* 7, 63–76.

Hannavy, J. (2003) *The English Seaside in Victorian and Edwardian Times*. Shire History in Camera. Shire: Princes Risborough.

Harries, O. (1985) *Llandrindod Wells in Old Postcards*. Christopher Davies: Llandybie.

Hembry, P. (1990) *The English Spa 1560–1815: A Social History*. Athlone Press: London.

Hembry, P.M., Cowie, L.W. and Cowie, E.E. (1997) *British Spas from 1815 to the Present: A Social History*. Fairleigh Dickinson University Press: Madison, NJ.

Heywood, A. (1905) *Abel Heywood and Son: A Guide to Royal Leamington Spa*. Abel Heywood and Son: Manchester.

High Peak (2007) *Buxton Conservation Areas Character Appraisal*. Mel Morris Conservation for High Peak Borough Council: Buxton.

Hodgson, F.R. (1913) Too many trees. Letter to the editor. *Eastbourne Chronicle*, 15 November 1913, 10.

Johnston, M. (2015) *Trees in Towns and Cities: A History of British Urban Arboriculture*. Windgather Press: Oxford.

Jones, I.W. (1975) *Llandudno: Queen of the Welsh Resorts*. John Jones Cardiff: Cardiff.

Kime, W. (1994) *Around Skegness in Old Photographs*. Alan Sutton: Stroud.

Kime, W. and Wilkinson, K. (2012) *Skegness Past and Present*. History Press: Stroud.

Lambert, T. (2016) *A Brief History of Bournemouth*. Text from webpages. Author: Tim Lambert. Accessed 4 March, 2015: http://www.localhistories.org/bournemouth.html

Langham, M. and Wells, C. (1993) *Buxton: A Pictorial History*. Phillimore: Chichester.

Malkin, B. (1804) *The Scenery, Antiquities, and Biography, of South Wales, from Material Collected during two Excursions in the Year 1803*. Longman and Rees: London.

Manco, J. (2004) *The Hub of the Circus: A History of the Streetscape of the Circus, Bath*. Planning Services, Bath and North East Somerset Council: Bath.

Morrison, M. (1989) *A Pictorial History of Builth Wells*. Published privately by the author: Builth Wells.

Morrison, M. (2010) *Builth Wells Through Time*. Amberley: Stroud.

Noble, S.N. (ed) (2002) *200 Years of Helensburgh 1802–1902*. Argyll: Glendaruel.

Roberts, A. (2012) *Buxton Through Time*. Amberley: Stroud.

Rodger, D. (2003) *Helensburgh Street Tree Survey*. Survey report for Helensburgh Tree Conservation Trust. Donald Roger Tree and Woodland Consultant: Gullane.

Rodger, D. (2005) *Helensburgh Street Trees Management Plan*. Report for Helensburgh Tree Conservation Trust. Donald Roger Associates, Arboricultural Consultants: Gullane.

Rowe, G. (1845) *Rowe's Illustrated Cheltenham Guide*. George Rowe: Cheltenham.

Scott, E. (1995) *Hove: A Pictorial History*. Phillimore: Chichester.

Sheen, M.R. (2007) *Helensburgh: The 'Garden City of the Clyde'*. Helensburgh Study Group: Helensburgh

Stern, R., Fishman, D. and Tilove, J. (2013) *Paradise Planned: The Garden Suburb and the Modern City*. Monacelli: New York.

Surtees, J. (2005) *Eastbourne's Story*. SB Publications: Eastbourne.

The Garden (1873) Street Trees. *The Garden* 4, 127.

Thompson, D. (2005) *Llandudno*. Images of Wales. Tempus: Stroud.

Watkins, J. (2008) *Royal Leamington Spa Revisited*. Images of England. Tempus: Stroud.

Webster, A.D. (1918) *Seaside Planting: For Shelter, Ornament and Profit*. T. Fisher Unwin: London.

Wilson, C. (1995) *Around Llandrindod Wells*. Archive Photographs Series. Chalford Publishing: Stroud.

Chapter 9. Visions of Garden Cities with Green Streets

Alexander, A. (2009) *Britain's New Towns: Garden Cities to Sustainable Communities*. Routledge: London.

Anon (1935) *Letchworth: The Well-Planned Beautiful Town*. Silver Jubilee Souvenir, 1910–1935. First Garden City: Letchworth.

Anon (1946) *Landscape Treatment of New Towns*. Institute of Landscape Architects: London.

Anon (2014) Trees felled in Rosyth after 25-year battle. *Dunfermline Press*, 1 May 2014, 22.

Bastable, R. (1986) Crawley: *The Making of a New Town*. Phillimore: Chichester.

Bayley, S. (1975) *The Garden City (Course A305)*. Open University Press: Maidenhead.

Beeson, E.W. (1911) *Port Sunlight; the Model Village of England: A Collection of Photographs*. Architectural Book Publishing: New York.

Beevers, R. (1988) *The Garden City Utopia: A Critical Biography of Ebenezer Howard*. Macmillan: Basingstoke and London.

Bendixson, T., and Platt, J. (1992) *Milton Keynes: Image and Reality*. Granta: Cambridge.

Booth, R., Shutt, R., Harris, K. Williams, D. and Woodhouse, R. (2013) *Bournville Through Time*. Bournville Society and Amberley Publishing: Stroud.

Boumphrey, I. and Hunter, G. (2002) *Port Sunlight: A Pictorial History 1888–1953*. Ian and Marilyn Boumphrey: Prenton.

Bournville Village Trust (1949) *Landscape and Housing Development*. Batsford: London.

Bournville Village Trust (1956) *The Bournville Village Trust, 1900–1955*. Bournville Village Trust: Bournville.

Buckingham, J.S. (1849) *National Evils and Practical Remedies, with the plan for a model town*. Peter Jackson, late Fisher, Son, and Co: London.

Chalkley, L. and Shiach, M. (eds) (2005) *Rosyth: Garden City and Royal Dockyard*. Rosyth Garden City Millennium Project: Rosyth.

Chiquetto, S. (1997) The environmental impacts from the implementation of a pedestrianization scheme. *Transportation Research Part D: Transport and Environment* 2(2), 133–146.

Clark, B. (2003) Ebenezer Howard and the marriage of town and country: an introduction to Howard's garden cities of to-morrow (selections). *Organization and Environment* 16(1), 87–97.

Creese, W. (1966) *The Search for Environment: The Garden City Before and After*. Yale University Press: New Haven, CT.

Davidson, L. (ed.) (1993) *The Story of New Lanark*. New Lanark Conservation Trust: New Lanark.

Davison, T. Raffles (1916) *Port Sunlight: A Record of Its Artistic and Pictorial Aspect*. Batsford: London.

Deakin, D. (1989) *Wythenshawe: The Story of a Garden City*. Phillimore: Chichester.

Denyer, S. and Cresswell, E. (2015) United Kingdom: 20th-century heritage at risk. *Heritage at Risk*, 202–206. Historic England: London.

Eserin, A. (1995) *Welwyn Garden City*. Images of England Series. Tempus: Stroud

Firth, G. (2002) *Salt and Saltaire*. Images of England Series. Tempus: Stroud

Gibberd, F. (1972) The master design; landscape; housing; the town centres. In: Evans, H. (ed) *New Towns: The British Experience*. Charles Knight: London.

Green, J. and Allen, P. (1993) *Crawley New Town in Old Photographs*. Alan Sutton: Stroud.

Gumbley, E. (1991) *Bournville: A Portrait of Cadbury's Garden Village in Old Picture Postcards*. S.B. Publications: Seaford.

Gwynne, P. (1990) *A History of Crawley*. Phillimore: Chichester.

Hill, M. (2007) *The Story of the original CMK*. Living Archive, Milton Keynes: Milton Keynes.

Hall, P. and Ward, C. (1998) *Sociable Cities: the legacy of Ebenezer Howard*. Wiley: Chichester.

Howard, E. (1898) *To-Morrow: A Peaceful Path to Real Reform*. Swan Sonnenschein: London.

Howard, E. (1976) *Garden Cities of Tomorrow*. Edited by Frederick Osborn with an Introduction by Lewis Mumford. Faber and Faber: London.

Hubbard, E. and Shippobottom, M. (2012) *A Guide to Port Sunlight Village*. Second edition. University of Liverpool Press: Liverpool.

Hughes, M. (2010) Whatever happened to the hoodie Cameron told us to hug? *The Independent*, Tuesday 13 April. Accessed 9 July 2016: http://www.independent.co.uk/news/uk/politics/whatever-happened-to-the-hoodie-cameron-told-us-to-hug-1944065.html

Hunt, T. (2004) *Building Jerusalem: The Rise and Fall of the Victorian City*. Weidenfeld and Nicolson London.

Jackson, N., Lintonbon, J. and Staples, B. (2010) *Saltaire: The Making of a Model Town*. Spire: Reading.

Loudon. J.C. (1829) Hints for breathing places for the metropolis, and for country towns and villages, on fixed principles. *Gardener's Magazine* 5, 686–690.

Loudon, J.C. (1835) *Encyclopaedia of Gardening, Comprising the Theory and Practice of Horticulture, Floriculture, Arboriculture and Landscape-gardening*. A new edition. Longman, Rees, Orme, Brown, Green and Longmans: London.

Mawson, T.H. (1911) *Civic Art: Studies in Town Planning, Parks, Boulevards and Open Spaces*. Batsford: London.

Miller, M. (1989) *Letchworth: The First Garden City*. Phillimore: Chichester.

Miller, M. (2010) *English Garden Cities: An Introduction*. English Heritage: Swindon.

Milton Keynes Council (2009) *Street Trees in Central Milton Keynes: Guidance on the Development Process*. Urban Design and Landscape Architecture, Milton Keynes Council, Development Control in association with Milton Keynes Partnership: Milton Keynes.

Milton Keynes Council (2013) *CMK Development Framework, Supplementary Planting Guidance*. Urban Design and Landscape Architecture, Milton Keynes Council: Milton Keynes.

More, Thomas (1895) *The Utopia of Sir Thomas More*. In Latin from the edition of March 1518 and in English from the first edition of Ralph Robyson's Translation in 1551. Clarendon Press: Oxford.

Morris, E.S. (1997) *British Town Planning and Urban Design: Principles and Policies.* Addison Wesley Longmans: Harlow.

Morton, A.L. (1938) *A People's History of England.* Victor Gollancz: London.

Murphy, J. (1987) *New Earswick: A Pictorial History.* William Sessions, Ebor Press: York.

Parker, B. (1937) Site planning. As exemplified at New Earswick: illustrated. *Town Planning Review* 17(2), 79.

Parsons, K.C. and Schuyler, D. (eds) (2002) *From Garden City to Green City: the legacy of Ebenezer Howard.* John Hopkins University Press; Baltimore, MD.

Pierce, M. (2002) *Letchworth Garden City 1903–2003: A Centenary Celebration of the World's first Garden City in Picture Postcards.* Yesterdays World Publications: Letchworth Garden City.

Purdom, C.B. (1913) *The Garden City: A Study in the Development of the Modern Town.* Dent: London.

Ravetz, A. (2001) *Council Housing and Culture: The History of a Social Experiment.* Routledge: London.

Rogers, M. (2009a) *Rosyth Through Time.* Amberley: Stroud.

Rogers, M. (2009b) Rosyth Garden City. *Scottish Local History* 76, 11–14.

Rook, T. (2001) *Welwyn Garden City Past.* Phillimore: Chichester

Rutherford, S. (2014) *Garden Cities.* Shire: Princes Risborough.

Salter, B. (2001) Transcript of a tape recorded interview with Brian Salter, formerly Chief Executive of the Milton Keynes Parks Trust, dated 22 October, 2001. Milton Keynes Museum, Living Archive, Accession reference: PMK/T/200.

Salter, R.G. (1953) *Roadside Tree Planting in Urban Areas.* Bournville Village Trust, Bournville: Birmingham.

Schaffer, F. (1970) *The New Town Story.* MacGibbon and Kee: London

Sefton, M. (1947) Street Trees at Welwyn. *Gardeners' Chronicle* 3rd ser. 122, 700.

Simo, M.L. (1981) John Claudius Loudon: on planning and design for the garden metropolis. *Garden History* 9(2), 184–201.

Stern, R., Fishman, D. and Tilove, J. (2013) *Paradise Planned: The Garden Suburb and the Modern City.* Monacelli: New York.

Trinder, Barrie (1982) *The Making of the Industrial Landscape.* Dent: London.

Tudsbery-Turner, S. (2002) *Port Sunlight in Old Picture Postcards.* European Library: Zaltbommel.

Unwin, R. (1904) The Improvement of Towns. Paper read at the Conference of the National Union of Women Workers of Great Britain and Ireland. November 8, 1904, 3. *Craftsman* 7, 809–816.

Unwin, R. (1909) *Town Planning in Practice; an Introduction to the Art of Designing Cities and Suburbs.* T. Fisher Unwin: London.

Urban Eden (2016) Text entitled 'CMK Boulevards' on the homepage of the website of Urban Green, Milton Keynes. Accessed 20 August, 2016: http://urbaneden.org/

Walker, D. (1982) *The Architecture and Planning of Milton Keynes.* Architectural Press: London.

Williams-Ellis, C. (1928) *England and the Octopus.* Geoffrey Bles: London.

Chapter 10. Threats and Conflicts in the Street Environment

AAIS (1998) *The Effect of Trees on Television Reception.* Arboriculture Research Note, ref 146/98/TV. Arboricultural Advisory and Information Service. Tree Advice Trust: Farnham.

Anon (1901) Lord Street Trees: How they were once destroyed but are now preserved. *Southport Visiter* 22 January, 1901, no page number.

Anon (1974) Trees in Towns. *Gardeners' Chronicle & Horticultural Trades Journal* 176, 18–20.

Anon (1990) Severe storms strike again. *Urban Forests.* Spring 1990, Issue 3, 1. A Seed in Time: Hoddesdon.

Arnold-Forster, W. (1948) *Shrubs for the Milder Counties.* Country Life: London.

Balfour, F.R.S. (1935) The planting and after care of roadside trees. *Quarterly Journal of Forestry* 29, 163–188.

Barkham, P. (2007) Chainsaw massacre. *The Guardian.* Thursday 3 May, 2007. Accessed 2 October 2016: http://www.theguardian.com/lifeandstyle/2007/may/03/climatechange.gardens

Bassirian, H. (1995) Call for penalties on cable layers who damage trees. *Horticulture Week*, 19 October, 5.

BHCC (2016) National Elm Collection. Brighton and Hove City Council website. Accessed 1 October 2016: http://www.brighton-hove.gov.uk/content/leisure-and-libraries/parks-and-green-spaces/national-elm-collection

Biddle, G. (1981) Physical problems caused by trees to buildings and services. In: Clouston, B. and Stansfield, K. (eds) *Trees in Towns: Maintenance and Management.* Architectural Press: London.

Bodkin. H. (2016) Tree disease could wipe out London's most historic vistas. *Daily Telegraph*, 31 July 2016.

Accessed 1 October 2016: http://www.telegraph. co.uk/news/2016/07/30/tree-disease-could-wipe-out-londons-most-historic-vistas/

Body, S. (2011) Investigation into the interactions between closed circuit television and urban forest vegetation in Wales. In: Johnston, M. and Percival, G. (eds) *Trees, People and the Built Environment.* Forestry Commission Research Report. Forestry Commission: Edinburgh.

Britt, C. and Johnston, M. (2008) *Trees in Towns II: A New Survey of Urban Trees in England and their Condition and Management.* Department for Communities and Local Government: London.

Coleman, M. (2009) *Wych Elm.* Royal Botanic Gardens Edinburgh: Edinburgh.

Cox, Evelyn (1978) *The Great Drought of 1976.* Hutchinson: London.

Crane, B. (1995) Trench warfare. *Horticulture Week*, 6 April, 20–23.

Cutler, D.F., Gasson, P.E. and Farmer, M.C. (1990) The wind blow tree survey: analysis of results. *Arboricultural Journal* 14(3), 265–286.

Dean, A. (1872) The trees in the parks. *Gardeners' Chronicle & Agricultural Gazette* 12, 395–396.

Deen, J. (1981) A hole lot of trouble. *Gardeners' Chronicle & Horticultural Trades Journal* 190, 35–37.

Derbyshire, D. (2013) Thought the threat to our noble ash trees was over? They could ALL be lost in ten years. *Daily Mail*, 14 May 2013. Accessed 1 October 2016: http://www.dailymail.co.uk/news/article-2324089/Ash-dieback-Thought-threat-noble-ash-trees-They-ALL-lost-10-years.html

Dobson, M.C. (1991) *De-icing Salt Damage to Trees and Shrubs.* Forestry Commission Bulletin 101. HMSO: London.

Edwards, P.J. (1898) *History of London Street Improvements, 1855–1897.* London County Council: London.

Elkington. A. (1945) Effect of bomb blast on trees. *Gardeners' Chronicle* 118, 20.

Elliott, P.A. (2016) *British Urban Trees: A Social and Cultural History, c. 1800–1914.* White Horse Press: Winwick.

Fairchild, T. (1722) *The City Gardener.* T. Woodward and J. Peele: London.

Gardeners' Chronicle (1846) On the death of trees caused by the leakage of gaspipes in the soil. *Gardeners' Chronicle & Agricultural Gazette* 32, 535.

Gardeners' Chronicle (1870) Gas. *Gardeners' Chronicle & Agricultural Gazette* 31, 1022.

Gardeners' Chronicle (1878) Trees and foundations. *Gardeners' Chronicle* new ser. 10, 726.

Gardeners' Chronicle (1879) Town planting. *Gardeners' Chronicle* new ser. 12, 693.

Gardeners' Chronicle (1883) Street trees. *Gardeners' Chronicle* new ser. 20, 51.

Gardeners' Chronicle (1898) Street trees in Bath. *Gardeners' Chronicle* 3rd ser. 24, 238.

Gardeners' Chronicle (1902) Street planting. *Gardeners' Chronicle* 3rd ser. 32, 306.

Gardeners' Chronicle (1910a) The management of common and street trees. *Gardeners' Chronicle* 3rd ser. 47, 232–233.

Gardeners' Chronicle (1910b) Street trees. *Gardeners' Chronicle* 3rd ser. 47, 101.

Gardeners' Chronicle (1911a) The electric current and trees. *Gardeners' Chronicle* 3rd ser. 49, 324.

Gardeners' Chronicle (1911b) Street trees and gas effects. *Gardeners' Chronicle* 3rd ser. 49, 139.

Gardeners' Chronicle (1915) London street trees. *Gardeners' Chronicle* 3rd ser. 57, 137.

Gardeners' Chronicle (1920) Tram accident caused by wet leaves. *Gardeners' Chronicle* 3rd ser. 68, 164.

Gardeners' Chronicle (1931) Street trees and traffic. *Gardeners' Chronicle* 3rd ser. 89, 27.

Gardeners' Chronicle (1933) Street trees and artificial lighting. *Gardeners' Chronicle* 3rd ser. 93, 33.

Gibbs, J.N. (1977) A review of Dutch elm disease control programmes in England, Wales and the Channel Islands – Autumn 1976. *Arboricultural Journal* 3(2), 110–114.

GTLS (1941) *Glasgow Tree Lovers Society Annual Report for 1940–1941.* GTLS: Glasgow.

GTLS (1942) *Glasgow Tree Lovers Society Annual Report for 1941–1942.* GTLS: Glasgow.

GTLS (1949) *Glasgow Tree Lovers Society Annual Report for 1948–1949.* GTLS: Glasgow.

Hammond, C. and P. (1994) *Chiswick.* The Old Photographs Series. Chalford Publishing: Stroud.

Harley, R.J. (2005) *London's Victoria Embankment: A History of the Embankment and its Bridges.* Capital History: Harrow.

Hartig, R. (1894) *Textbook of the Diseases of Trees.* Translated by William Somerville and revised and edited, with a preface, by H. Marshall Ward. Country Life: London.

Humphreys, N. (1871) Trees on the Thames Embankment. *The Garden* 1, 380.

ISE (2000) *Subsidence of Low Rise Buildings.* Second edition. Institution of Structural Engineers: London.

Johnston, M. (1991) The Forest of London: I – planting an idea. *Arboricultural Journal* 15, 127–143.

Johnston, M. (2010) Trees in Towns II and the contribution of arboriculture. *Arboricultural Journal* 33, 27–41.

Johnston, M. (2015) *Trees in Towns and Cities: A History of British Urban Arboriculture.* Windgather Press: Oxford.

Kerr, R. (1865) *On Ancient Lights, and the Evidence of Surveyors Thereon.* John Murray: London.

Lay, M.G. (1992) *Ways of the World: A History of the World's Roads and the Vehicles that Used Them.* Rutgers University Press: New Brunswick, NJ.

Leathart, P.S. (1973) Profile: Hubert Taylor. *Arboricultural Association Journal* 2(4), 101–105.

Le Sueur, A.D.C. (1949) *The Care and Repair of Ornamental Trees.* Second edition. Country Life: London.

Lonsdale, D. (2000) *Hazards from Trees: A General Guide.* Forestry Commission Practical Guide. Forestry Commission: Edinburgh.

Loudon, J.C. (1829) Hints for breathing places for the metropolis, and for country towns and villages, on fixed principles. *Gardener's Magazine* 5, 686–690.

LTOA (2013) *Massaria Disease of Plane: Practical Management Guide.* London Tree Officers Association: London.

Mattocks, R.H. (1925) *The Planting of Trees in Streets and Woodlands.* Reprinted from *The Town Planning Review* 10 and 11. University Press of Liverpool: Liverpool.

Matzke, E.B. (1936) The effect of street lights in delaying leaf-fall in certain trees. *American Journal of Botany*, 446–452.

McNab, J. (1872) On the disfigurement of trees along roadsides to suit telegraph wires. *Gardeners' Chronicle & Agricultural Gazette* 52, 1719.

Milmo, C. (2010) Fast-spreading new disease threatens plane trees. *The Independent*, Sunday, 10 October 2010. Accessed 1 October 2016: http://www.independent.co.uk/environment/nature/fastspreading-new-disease-threatens-plane-trees-2103182.html

Munro Ferguson, R.C. (1901) The arboricultural adornment of towns. *Transactions of the Royal Scottish Arboricultural Society* 1899–1901, Vols 16, 28, 388–398.

Nead, L. (2000) *Victorian Babylon: People, Streets and Images in Nineteenth-Century London.* Yale University Press: New Haven, CT and London.

NJUG (1995) *NJUG 10: Guidelines for the Planning, Installation and Maintenance of Utility Services in Proximity to Trees.* Publication 10. National Joint Utilities Group: London.

NTSG (2011) *Common Sense Risk Management of Trees.* National Tree Safety Group. Forestry Commission: Edinburgh.

O'Brien, D. (1993) *Street Trees for Cities and Towns.* Imago: Bondi Junction.

O'Callaghan, D.P. (2012) Tree pest and diseases – wake up and smell the coffee. *Arb Magazine* 159, 28–30.

Ogley, B. (1988) *In the Wake of the Hurricane.* National Edition. Froglets Publications: Westerham.

Pittigrew, W.W. (1901) Town gardening, street planting. *The Garden* 59, 13–14.

Pettigrew, W.W. (1937) *Municipal Parks: Layout, Management and Administration.* Journal of Park Administration: London.

Ravenscroft, B.C. (1883) *Town Gardening.* Routledge: London.

RHS (2006) *Front Gardens.* Gardening Matters Urban Series. Royal Horticultural Society: London.

Risk Management Solutions (2003) *December 1703 Windstorm – 300-year retrospective.* Risk Management Solutions: London.

Roberts, J., Jackson, N. and Smith, M. (2006) *Tree Roots in the Built Environment.* Research for Amenity Trees 8, Department for Communities and Local Government. Stationery Office: London.

Rose, D. and Webber, J. (2011) *De-icing Salt Damage to Trees.* Pathology Advisory Note 11. Forest Research. Forestry Commission: Edinburgh.

Salter, R.G. (1953) *Roadside Tree Planting in Urban Areas.* Bournville Village Trust: Birmingham.

Schlesinger, M. (1853) *Sauntering In and About London.* English Edition by Otto Wenckstern. Nathaniel Cook: London.

Stone, J. and Brodie, L. (1994) *Tales of the Old Gardeners.* David and Charles: Newton Abbot.

Strouts, R.G. and Winter, T.G. (2000) *Diagnosis of Ill-health in Trees.* Research for Amenity Trees 2. Second edition. Department of the Environment, Transport and the Regions. Stationary Office: London.

Taylor, S. and Green, O. (2001) *The Moving Metropolis: The History of London's Transport Since 1800.* Laurence King: London.

Thayer, R.L. (1983) Solar access and the urban forest. *Arboricultural Journal* 7, 179–190.

The Garden (1871) Damaging trees on the Thames Embankment. *The Garden* 1, 271.

The Garden (1874) Gas pipes fatal to trees. *The Garden* 6, 184.

The Garden (1901) Street trees. *The Garden* 59, 118–119.

Trinder, B. (1982) *The Making of the Industrial Landscape.* Dent: London.

Tuffs, L. (1995) Trees are casualties of trench warfare. *Horticulture Week*, 26 October, 16.

Walker, R. (1890) *On the Planting of Trees in Towns: Being the paper read before the North of Scotland Horticultural Association by Robert Walker, Keeper of the Victoria Park.* University Press: Aberdeen.

Webb, J. (1965) How tree roots affect buildings. *Arboricultural Association Journal* 1(1), 15–17.

Webber, J. (2010) *Dutch Elm Disease – Q&A.* Pathology Advisory Note 10, Forest Research: Wrecclesham.

Webster, A.D. (1893) Trees and shrubs for planting in towns. *Transactions of the Royal Scottish Arboricultural Society* 1891–1893, Vol. 13, 123–144.

Wells, D.V. (1970) History of the Roads Beautifying Association. *Arboricultural Association Journal* 1(11), 295–306.

Woods and Forests (1885) Trees in smoky towns. *Woods and Forests* 2, 73–74.

Chapter 11. Selection, Design and Planting

Arnold, H.F. (1980) *Trees in Urban Design.* Van Nostrand Reinhold: New York.

Bean, W.J. (1976) *Trees and Shrubs Hardy in the British Isles.* Vol. 3. Eighth edition revised. John Murray: London.

Boddy, F.A. (1964) Highway Trees – the problem of siting and planting. *Gardeners' Chronicle* 155, 18 January, 53.

Boddy, F.A. (1968) *Highway Trees.* Clarke and Hunter: London.

Britt, C. and Johnston, M. (2008) *Trees in Towns II: A New Survey of Urban Trees in England and their Condition and Management.* Department for Communities and Local Government: London.

BSI (1965) *Specification for Nursery Stock. Part 1. Trees and Shrubs.* British Standard 3936: Part 1: 1965. British Standards Institution: London

Butterworth, J. (1923) Trees for street planting. *Gardeners' Chronicle* 3rd ser. 73, 352–353.

Cooper, F. (2006) *The Black Poplar: History, Ecology and Conservation.* Windgather Press: Macclesfield.

Des Cars, A. (1881) *Tree Pruning: A Treatise on Pruning Forest and Ornamental Trees.* Translated from the seventh French edition by Charles S. Sargent. A. Williams and Company: Boston.

Edwards, P.J. (1898) *History of London Street Improvements, 1855–1897.* London County Council: London.

Forest Research (2010) *Benefits of Green Infrastructure.* Report to Defra and CLG. Forest Research: Farnham.

Gardeners' Chronicle (1851) Road-side trees. *Gardeners' Chronicle & Agricultural Gazette* 45, 711.

Gardeners' Chronicle (1861) Response to 'W.T.'. *Gardeners' Chronicle & Agricultural Gazette* 43, 943.

Gardeners' Chronicle (1871) Trees on the Thames Embankment. *Gardeners' Chronicle & Agricultural Gazette* 22, 711.

Gardeners' Chronicle (1872) Cost of trees planted in Paris boulevards. *Gardeners' Chronicle & Agricultural Gazette* 3, 72.

Gardeners' Chronicle (1873) Careless planting. *Gardeners' Chronicle & Agricultural Gazette* 36, 1215.

Gardeners' Chronicle (1876a) Trees for planting in towns. *Gardeners' Chronicle* new ser. 6, 748.

Gardeners' Chronicle (1876b) The planting of trees in large towns. *Gardeners' Chronicle* new ser. 6, 354–355.

Gardeners' Chronicle (1879a) Trees for Avenue, Park or Street Planting (Advertisement). *Gardeners' Chronicle* new ser. 12, 483.

Gardeners' Chronicle (1879b) Town trees and shrubs. *Gardeners' Chronicle* new ser. 11, 536.

Gardeners' Chronicle (1889a) Town trees. *Gardeners' Chronicle* 3rd ser. 6, 134.

Gardeners' Chronicle (1889b) Iron tree-stakes. *Gardeners' Chronicle* 3rd ser. 5, 502.

Gardeners' Chronicle (1889c) A rude tree guard. *Gardeners' Chronicle* 3rd ser. 5, 180.

Gardeners' Chronicle (1892) Look on this picture and on that. *Gardeners' Chronicle* 3rd ser. 12, 530.

Gardeners' Chronicle (1895) London trees and their treatment. *Gardeners' Chronicle* 3rd ser. 17, 99–100.

Gardeners' Chronicle (1898) Street trees in Bath. *Gardeners' Chronicle* 3rd ser. 24, 238.

Gardeners' Chronicle (1902) Street planting. *Gardeners' Chronicle* 3rd ser. 32, 306.

Gardeners' Chronicle (1903) Beckett's tree-ties. *Gardeners' Chronicle* 3rd ser. 34, 327.

Gardeners' Chronicle (1907) Street trees. *Gardeners' Chronicle* 3rd ser. 42, 430–431.

Gardeners' Chronicle (1909a) Robinia pseudoacacia as a street tree. *Gardeners' Chronicle* 3rd ser. 46, 204.

Gardeners' Chronicle (1909b) Fruit trees in streets. *Gardeners' Chronicle*, 3rd ser. 46, 157.

Gardeners' Chronicle (1925) Street trees of Paris. *Gardeners' Chronicle* 3rd ser. 77, 104–105.

Gardeners' Chronicle (1951) Traffic islands. *Gardeners' Chronicle* 3rd ser. 130, 118.

Gardeners' Chronicle (1981) Big trees in Bristol. *Gardeners' Chronicle & Horticultural Trade Journal* 189, 18–19.

Hillier, J. (2014) *Hillier: The Plants, the People, the Passion.* Outhouse Publishing: Winchester.

Hillier, H.G. (1971) *A Tree for Every Site.* Arboricultural Association: Surrey.

Jacobs, A.B., Macdonald, E. and Rofé, Y. (2003) *The Boulevard Book: History, Evolution, Design of Multiway Boulevards.* MIT Press: Cambridge, MA.

Johnston, M., Nail, S. and James, S. (2011) 'Natives versus Aliens': the relevance of the debate to urban forest management in Britain. In: Johnston, M. and Percival, G. (eds) *Trees, People and the Built Environment.* Forestry Commission Research Report. Forestry Commission: Edinburgh.

King, H.G. (1925) Roadside trees. *Gardeners' Chronicle* 3rd ser. 78, 466–468.

Kingdon-Ward, F. (1943) Roadside trees. *Gardeners' Chronicle* 3rd ser. 113, 146.

Labey, B. (1981) Comparing costs of urban trees. *Gardeners' Chronicle & Horticultural Trade Journal* 209, 17.

Loudon, J.C. (1827) Trees in public walks (and boulevards in Flanders). By the conductor. *Gardener's Magazine* 2, 461.

Loudon, J.C. (1829) Garden memorandums – illustration of tree guard Fig. 149. *Gardener's Magazine* 5, 674.

Loudon, J.C. (1830) Notes and reflections made during a tour through parts of France and Germany, in the Autumn of the year 1828. By the conductor. *Gardener's Magazine* 6, 641–649.

Marshall, D. (1963) The problem of roadside trees. *Gardeners' Chronicle & Gardening Illustrated* 153, 20 April, 280.

Mattocks, R.H. (1925) *The Planting of Trees in Streets and Woodlands.* Reprinted from *The Town Planning Review*, 10 and 11. University Press of Liverpool: Liverpool.

Mawson, T.H. (1911) *Civic Art: Studies in Town Planning, Parks, Boulevards and Open Spaces.* Batsford: London.

McKenzie, A. (1875) Promenade trees In: Hibberd, S., *The Floral World and Garden Guide – A Complete Manual.* Vol. 18, 74–76. Groombridge and Sons: London.

Mitchell, A. (1974) *A Field Guide to the Trees of Britain and Northern Europe.* Collins: London.

Mitchell, A. (1989) The plant hunters and their effect on the introduction of exotic species to the urban environment. In: Chaplin, J. (ed.) *Celebration of Trees: Silver Jubilee Conference Proceedings,* 155–170. Arboricultural Association: Ampfield.

Mitchell, A. (1996) *Alan Mitchell's Trees of Britain.* HarperCollins: London.

Newton, J. (1870) Street planting. *Gardeners' Chronicle & Agricultural Gazette* 33, 1087–1088.

Nicholson, G. (1890) Tree and shrub planting in towns. *Gardeners' Chronicle* 3rd ser. 8, 538.

Patch, D. (1982) In support of trees. *Gardeners' Chronicle & Horticultural Trade Journal* 191, 20–21.

Patch, D. (1984) *Tree Staking.* Arboricultural Research Note 40/84. Department of the Environment, Arboricultural Advisory and Information Service: Farnham.

Pittigrew, W.W. (1901) Town gardening, street planting. *The Garden* 59, 13–14.

Pettigrew, W.W. (1937) *Municipal Parks: Layout, management and administration.* Journal of Park Administration: London.

Pradines, C. (2009) *Road Infrastructures: Tree Avenues in the Landscape.* Fifth Council of Europe Conference on the European Landscape Convention CEP-CPDATEP. Cultural Heritage, Landscape and Spatial Planning Division, Council of Europe: Strasbourg.

Purdom, C.B. (1913) *The Garden City: A Study in the Development of the Modern Town.* Dent: London.

Ravenscroft, B.C. (1883) *Town Gardening.* Routledge: London.

Robinette, G.O. (1972) *People, Plants and Environmental Quality.* United States Department of the Interior in collaboration with the American Society of Landscape Architects Foundation: Washington D.C.

Robinson, C.M. (1911) *The Width and Arrangement of Streets.* McGraw-Hill: New York.

Robinson, C.M. (1901) *The Improvement of Towns and Cities or the Practical Basics of Civic Aesthetics.* G.P. Putnam's Sons: New York and London.

Robinson, W. (1869) *The Parks, Promenades and Gardens of Paris Described and Considered in Relation to the Wants of our Own Cities and of Public and Private Gardens.* John Murray: London.

Santamour, F.S., Gerhold, H.D. and Little, S. (1976) *Better Trees for Metropolitan Landscapes.* Symposium Proceedings. USDA Forest Service General Technical Report E-22: Upper Darby, PA.

Shepheard, P. (1955) Landscape of the town. *Municipal Journal,* July 22, 1955, 1981–1983.

Sinclair, G. (1832) *Useful and Ornamental Planting.* Baldwin and Cradock: London.

Strouts, R.G. and Winter, T.G. (2000) *Diagnosis of Ill-health in Trees*. Research for Amenity Trees 2. Second edition. Department of the Environment, Transport and the Regions. The Stationary Office: London.

The Garden (1872a) Notes of the week. *The Garden* 2, 181.

The Garden (1872b) Robinia as a street tree. *The Garden* 2, 145.

The Garden (1873) Street trees. *The Garden* 4, 500.

The Garden (1886) In street planting. *The Garden* 29, 86.

The Garden (1890) Street trees. *The Garden* 37, 65.

The Garden (1911) Ornamental flowering trees for street planting. *The Garden* 75, 486–487.

Urban, J. (2008) *Up By Roots: Healthy Soils and Trees in the Built Environment*. International Society of Arboriculture: Champaign, IL.

Walker, R. (1890) *On the Planting of Trees in Towns: Being the Paper Read before the North of Scotland Horticultural Association by Robert Walker, Keeper of the Victoria Park*. University Press: Aberdeen.

Watson, G. and Himelick E.B. (2013) *The Practical Science of Planting Trees*. International Society of Arboriculture: Champaign, IL.

Webster, A.D. (1888) Staking newly-planted trees. *The Garden* 33, 544.

Webster, A.D. (1909) Town planting. *Gardeners' Chronicle* 3rd ser. 45, 262.

Webster, A.D. (1910) *Town Planting: And the Trees, Shrubs, Herbaceous and Other Plants that are Best Adapted for Resisting Smoke*. Routledge: London.

Webster, A.D. (1918) London trees. *Gardeners' Chronicle* 3rd ser. 63, 251.

Webster, A.D. (1920) *London Trees*. Swarthmore Press: London.

Webster, J.B. (1888) Staking newly-planted trees. *The Garden* 33, 544.

Wells, D.V. (1970) History of the Roads Beautifying Association. *Arboricultural Association Journal* 1(11), 295–306.

Woods and Forests (1884a) Street tree planting. *Woods and Forests* 1, 498.

Woods and Forests (1884b) Street trees. *Woods and Forests* 1, 356–357.

Youens, F. (1963) The problem of roadside trees. *Gardeners' Chronicle & Gardening Illustrated* 153, 2 February, 83.

Chapter 12. Maintenance and Management

Anon (1905) Tree-planting in Aberdeen: II. *Aberdeen Daily Journal*, 30 June, 1905, 4.

Anon (1980) They can't see the wood for the trees. *Balham and Tooting News*, Friday 27 June, 1.

Armour, T., Job, M. and Canavan, R. (2012) *The Benefits of Large Species Trees in Urban Landscapes: A Costing, Design and Management Guide*. Construction Industry Research and Information Association (CIRIA): London.

Balfour, F.R.S. (1935) The planting and after care of roadside trees. *Quarterly Journal of Forestry* 29, 163–188.

Balfour, I.B. (1911) Tree pruning in the Mall. *Gardeners' Chronicle* 3rd ser. 50, 144–146.

Ball, R. (1995) White collar Compulsory Competitive Tendering (CCT): the death knell for arboricultural officers and the end of professional street tree management. *Arboricultural Journal* 19(3), 285–293.

Baxter Smith, W. (1884) Trees for towns. *Woods and Forests* 1, 399.

Bennett, J.M. (1929) *Roadside Development*. Macmillan: New York.

Bickmore, C.J. and Hall, T.H.R. (1983) *Computerisation of Tree Inventories*. A.B. Academic: Berkhamsted.

Boddy, F.A. (1947) The use and misuse of street trees. *Gardeners' Chronicle*, 3rd ser. 122, 72.

Boddy, F.A. (1986) Street Life. *Horticulture Week* 200, 11 July, 17–18.

Boulton, E.H.B. (1969) A.D.C. Le Sueur, OBE: an appreciation. *Arboricultural Association Journal* 1(9), 247–248.

Bridgeman, P.H. (1976) *Tree Surgery: A Complete Guide*. David and Charles: Newton Abbot.

Britt, C. and Johnston, M. (2008) *Trees in Towns II: A New Survey of Urban Trees in England and their Condition and Management*. Department for Communities and Local Government: London.

Brown, G.E. (1972) *The Pruning of Trees, Shrubs and Conifers*. Faber and Faber: London.

BSI (1966) *Recommendations for Tree Work*. British Standard 3998: 1966. British Standards Institution: London

BSI (2010) *Tree Work – Recommendations*. British Standard 3998: 2010. British Standards Institution: London

Buchanan, R.A. (1985) Institutional proliferation in the British engineering profession, 1847–1914. *Economic History Review* 38(1), 42–60.

Cochrane, J.E. (1889) The trees on the Thames Embankment. *Gardeners' Chronicle* 3rd ser. 6, 222.

Cockburn Association (1899) *Report by the Council to the Twenty-third Annual Meeting of the Association Edinburgh, May 1899*. Cockburn Association: Edinburgh.

Condron, S. (2005) They have stood proudly for 130 years. Now the compensation culture could fell 4,500 lime trees. *Daily Mail*, Thursday 24 March, 39.

Dallimore, W. (1926) *The Pruning of Trees and Shrubs: Being a Description of the Methods Practised in the Royal Botanic Gardens, Kew*. Dulau: Oxford

DoE (1994) *Urban Tree Strategies*. Research for Amenity Trees 3. Prepared for the Department of the Environment by Land Use Consultants. HMSO: London.

Fox, W. (1953) Street trees. *Gardeners' Chronicle* 3rd ser. 134, 204.

Gardeners' Chronicle (1863) Trees in London – RHS Arboricultural Committee. *Gardeners' Chronicle & Agricultural Gazette*, 25 July, 699–700.

Gardeners' Chronicle (1868) Trees in the city. *Gardeners' Chronicle & Agricultural Gazette*, 3 July, 717.

Gardeners' Chronicle (1874) The trees on the Thames Embankments. *Gardeners' Chronicle* new ser. 1, 672–673.

Gardeners' Chronicle (1878) Mr Gladstone and tree felling. *Gardeners' Chronicle* new ser. 8, 171.

Gardeners' Chronicle (1895) London trees and their treatment. *Gardeners' Chronicle* 3rd ser. 17, 99–100.

Gardeners' Chronicle (1909) The care and preservation of street trees. *Gardeners' Chronicle* 3rd ser. 45, 90.

Gardeners' Chronicle (1910) The management of common and street trees. *Gardeners' Chronicle* 3rd ser. 47, 232–233.

Gardeners' Chronicle (1911) Tree pruning in the Mall. *Gardeners' Chronicle* 3rd ser. 50, 144.

Gardeners' Chronicle (1947) Flowering trees for Hampstead streets. *Gardeners' Chronicle* 3rd ser. 121, 174.

Gardeners' Chronicle (1949) Flowering trees for Hampstead road. *Gardeners' Chronicle* 3rd ser. 126, 162.

Gardeners' Chronicle (1973) Space-age tree surgery. *Gardeners' Chronicle: The Horticultural Trade Journal* 173, 17.

Gardeners' Chronicle (1982) Hire and fire away. *Gardeners' Chronicle & Horticultural Trade Journal* 192, 31.

Gilman, E.F. (2012) *An Illustrated Guide to Pruning*. Third edition. Delmar Cengage Learning: Clifton Park, NY.

Hope, F. (1982) Well filed trees. *The Gardeners' Chronicle & Horticultural Trade Journal* 191, 18–19.

Hornsey, W.M. (1953) Street trees. *Gardeners' Chronicle* 3rd ser. 134, 170–171.

Johnston, M. (1997a) The early development of urban forestry in Britain: Part I. *Arboricultural Journal* 21, 107–126.

Johnston, M. (1997b) The early development of urban forestry in Britain: Part II. *Arboricultural Journal* 21, 317–330.

Johnston, M. (2010) Trees in Towns II and the contribution of arboriculture. *Arboricultural Journal* 33, 27–41.

Johnston, M. (2015) *Trees in Towns and Cities: A History of British Urban Arboriculture*. Windgather Press: Oxford.

Johnston, M. and Hirons, A. (2014) Urban trees. In: Dixon, G. and Aldous, D. (eds) *Horticulture: Plants for People and Places, Volume 2: Environmental Horticulture*. Springer: New York.

Jorgensen, C.W. (1991) Silver Jubilee Commemorative Event 25 Years of Arboriculture. In: Hall, T.H.R. (ed.) *The First Twenty-five Years*. Arboricultural Association: Ampfield.

Kirby, D. (2015) Sheffield residents in bitter row with council over tree-felling proposals. *The Independent*, Saturday 17 October. Accessed 7 December 2016: http://www.independent.co.uk/environment/sheffield-residents-in-bitter-row-with-council-over-tree-felling-proposals-a6698471.html

Leathart, P.S. (1973) Profile: Hubert Taylor. *Arboricultural Association Journal* 2(4), 101–105.

Le Sueur, A.D.C. (1934) *The Care and Repair of Ornamental Trees*. Country Life: London.

Lonsdale, D. (2000) *Hazards from Trees: A General Guide*. Forestry Commission Practical Guide. Forestry Commission: Edinburgh.

Loudon, J.C. (1835) *Encyclopaedia of Gardening, Comprising the Theory and Practice of Horticulture, Floriculture, Arboriculture and Landscape-gardening*. Longman, Rees, Orme, Brown, Green and Longmans: London.

McNab, J. (1874) Tree management in and near towns. *The Garden* 6, 401.

Painter, J. (1991) Compulsory competitive tendering in local government: the first round. *Public Administration* 69(2), 191–210.

Petit, S. and Watkins, C. (2003) Pollarding trees: changing attitudes to a traditional land management practice in Britain 1600–1900. *Rural History* 14(2), 157–176.

Pittigrew, W.W. (1901) Town gardening, street planting. *The Garden* 59, 13–14.

Pettigrew, W.W. (1937) *Municipal Parks: Layout, Management and Administration*. Journal of Park Administration: London.

Rackham, O. (2003) *Ancient Woodland: Its History, Vegetation and Uses in England*. New edition. Castlepoint Press: Dalbeattie.

Ravetz, A. (2001) *Council Housing and Culture: The History of a Social Experiment*. Routledge: London.

Robinson, C.M. (1901) *The Improvement of Towns and Cities or the Practical Basics of Civic Aesthetics*. G.P. Putnam's Sons: New York and London.

Shepheard, P. (1956) Trees. *Architectural Review*, December issue, 381–386.

Shigo, A.L. (1977) *Compartmentalization of Decay in Trees*. Agriculture Information Bulletin 405. United States Department of Agriculture, Forest Service: Washington, DC.

Stone, J. and Brodie, L. (1994) *Tales of the Old Gardeners*. David and Charles: Newton Abbot.

The Garden (1874) The 'Pall Mall' on London tree-pruning. *The Garden* 5, 551.

The Garden (1914) Pruning street trees. *The Garden* 78, Mar 7, 113.

Thurman, P. W. (1983) The management of urban street trees using computerised inventory systems. *Arboricultural Journal* 7, 101–117.

Torbay Council (2011) *Pollarding Policy*. Natural Environment Service, Torbay Council: Torbay.

Travers, T. (2013) Local Government: Margaret Thatcher's 11-year war. *The Guardian – Professional*, Tuesday 9 April. Accessed 2 December 2016: http://www.guardian.co.uk/local-government-network/2013/apr/09/local-government-margaret-thatcher-war-politics

Webster, A.D. (1909) Town planting – pruning of trees and shrubs. *Gardeners' Chronicle* 3rd ser. 45, 400.

Webster, A.D. (1910) *Town Planting: And the Trees, Shrubs, Herbaceous and Other Plants that are Best Adapted for Resisting Smoke*. Routledge: London.

Wilmshurst, H. (1996) Transcript of interview with Harry Wilmshurst (born 1917), street tree forester for Brighton Borough Council Parks and Gardens Department. ESRO reference: amsll/6729/10. East Sussex Record Office: Brighton. http://www.thekeep.info/collections/getrecord/GB179_AMS6729_10

Winson, A. (2016) How can Sheffield heal divisions over the tree-felling controversy? *Sheffield Telegraph*, 15 December, 2016, 6.

Index

....

Numbers in italics denote pages with illustrations